Physical-Layer Security, Quantum Key Distribution and Post-quantum Cryptography

Physical-Layer Security, Quantum Key Distribution and Post-quantum Cryptography

Editor

Ivan B. Djordjevic

MDPI • Basel • Beijing • Wuhan • Barcelona • Belgrade • Manchester • Tokyo • Cluj • Tianjin

Editor
Ivan B. Djordjevic
University of Arizona
USA

Editorial Office
MDPI
St. Alban-Anlage 66
4052 Basel, Switzerland

This is a reprint of articles from the Special Issue published online in the open access journal *Entropy* (ISSN 1099-4300) (available at: http://www.mdpi.com).

For citation purposes, cite each article independently as indicated on the article page online and as indicated below:

LastName, A.A.; LastName, B.B.; LastName, C.C. Article Title. *Journal Name* **Year**, *Volume Number*, Page Range.

ISBN 978-3-0365-5003-9 (Hbk)
ISBN 978-3-0365-5004-6 (PDF)

© 2022 by the authors. Articles in this book are Open Access and distributed under the Creative Commons Attribution (CC BY) license, which allows users to download, copy and build upon published articles, as long as the author and publisher are properly credited, which ensures maximum dissemination and a wider impact of our publications.

The book as a whole is distributed by MDPI under the terms and conditions of the Creative Commons license CC BY-NC-ND.

Contents

About the Editor vii

Ivan B. Djordjevic
Physical-Layer Security, Quantum Key Distribution, and Post-Quantum Cryptography
Reprinted from: *Entropy* **2022**, *24*, 935, doi:10.3390/e24070935 1

Ziwen Pan and Ivan B. Djordjevic
Geometrical Optics Restricted Eavesdropping Analysis of Satellite-to-Satellite Secret Key Distillation
Reprinted from: *Entropy* **2021**, *23*, 950, doi:10.3390/e23080950 5

Ivan B. Djordjevic
On Global Quantum Communication Networking
Reprinted from: *Entropy* **2020**, *22*, 831, doi:10.3390/e22080831 13

Yuang Wang, Shanhua Zou, Yun Mao and Ying Guo
Improving Underwater Continuous-Variable Measurement-Device-Independent Quantum Key Distribution via Zero-Photon Catalysis
Reprinted from: *Entropy* **2020**, *22*, 571, doi:10.3390/e22050571 23

Ivan B. Djordjevic
Surface-Codes-Based Quantum Communication Networks
Reprinted from: *Entropy* **2020**, *22*, 1059, doi:10.3390/e22091059 39

Wen-Fei Cao, Yi-Zheng Zhen, Yu-Lin Zheng, Shuai Zhao, Feihu Xu, Li Li, Zeng-Bing Chen, Nai-Le Liu and Kai Chen
Open-Destination Measurement-Device-Independent Quantum Key Distribution Network
Reprinted from: *Entropy* **2020**, *22*, 1083, doi:10.3390/e22101083 49

Masakazu Yoshida, Ayumu Nakayama and Jun Cheng
Distinguishability and Disturbance in the Quantum Key Distribution Protocol Using the Mean Multi-Kings' Problem
Reprinted from: *Entropy* **2020**, *22*, 1275, doi:10.3390/e22111275 67

Luis Adrián Lizama-Pérez, J. Mauricio López R. and Emmanuel H. Samperio
Beyond the Limits of Shannon's Information in Quantum Key Distribution
Reprinted from: *Entropy* **2021**, *23*, 229, doi:10.3390/e23020229 83

Carlos E. González-Guillén, María Isabel González Vasco, Floyd Johnson and Ángel L. Pérez del Pozo
An Attack on Zawadzki's Quantum Authentication Scheme
Reprinted from: *Entropy* **2021**, *23*, 389, doi:10.3390/e23040389 107

Xiaoxu Zhang, Yang Wang, Musheng Jiang, Yifei Lu, Hongwei Li, Chun Zhou and Wansu Bao
Phase-Matching Quantum Key Distribution with Discrete Phase Randomization
Reprinted from: *Entropy* **2021**, *23*, 508, doi:10.3390/e23050508 117

Anton Pljonkin, Dmitry Petrov, Lilia Sabantina and Kamila Dakhkilgova
Nonclassical Attack on a Quantum Key Distribution System
Reprinted from: *Entropy* **2021**, *23*, 509, doi:10.3390/e23050509 129

Michael Ampatzis and Theodore Andronikos
QKD Based on Symmetric Entangled Bernstein-Vazirani
Reprinted from: *Entropy* **2021**, *23*, 870, doi:10.3390/e23070870 . . . . **143**

Miroslav Mitev, Arsenia Chorti, E. Veronica Belmega and H. Vincent Poor
Protecting Physical Layer Secret Key Generation from Active Attacks
Reprinted from: *Entropy* **2021**, *23*, 960, doi:10.3390/e23080960 . . . . **161**

Roderick D. Cochran and Daniel J. Gauthier
Qubit-Based Clock Synchronization for QKD Systems Using a Bayesian Approach
Reprinted from: *Entropy* **2021**, *23*, 988, doi:10.3390/e23080988 . . . . **173**

Bruno Costa, Pedro Branco, Manuel Goulão, Mariano Lemus and Paulo Mateus
Randomized Oblivious Transfer for Secure Multiparty Computation in the Quantum Setting
Reprinted from: *Entropy* **2021**, *23*, 1001, doi:10.3390/e23081001 . . . . **185**

About the Editor

Ivan B. Djordjevic

IVAN B. DJORDJEVIC is a professor of electrical and computer engineering and optical sciences at the University of Arizona, director of the Optical Communications Systems Laboratory (OCSL) and Quantum Communications (QuCom) Lab, and co-director of the Signal Processing and Coding Lab. He is both IEEE Fellow and Optica (formerly OSA) Fellow. He received his PhD degree from the University of Nis, Yugoslavia in 1999. Professor Djordjevic has authored or co-authored 10 books, more than 570 journal and conference publications, and he holds 54 US patents. Dr. Djordjevic serves as an Editor/Member of the Editorial Board for the following journals: IEEE TRANSACTIONS ON COMMUNICATIONS, OPTICAL AND QUANTUM ELECTRONICS, and FREQUENZ. He served as an associate editor for OSA (OPTICA)/IEEE JOURNAL OF OPTICAL COMMUNICATIONS AND NETWORKING from 2019 to 2022. He served as editor/senior editor/area editor of IEEE COMMUNICATIONS LETTERS from 2012 to 2021. He served as editorial board member/associate editor for IOP JOURNAL OF OPTICS and ELSEVIER PHYSICAL COMMUNICATION JOURNAL from to 2016 to 2021. Prior to joining the University of Arizona, Dr. Djordjevic held appointments at the University of Bristol and University of the West of England in UK, Tyco Telecommunications in USA, National Technical University of Athens in Greece, and State Telecommunication Company in Yugoslavia.

Editorial

Physical-Layer Security, Quantum Key Distribution, and Post-Quantum Cryptography

Ivan B. Djordjevic

Department of Electrical and Computer Engineering, University of Arizona, 1230 E. Speedway Blvd., Tucson, AZ 85721, USA; ivan@email.arizona.edu; Tel.: +1-520-626-5119

Citation: Djordjevic, I.B. Physical-Layer Security, Quantum Key Distribution, and Post-Quantum Cryptography. *Entropy* **2022**, *24*, 935. https://doi.org/10.3390/e24070935

Received: 27 June 2022
Accepted: 4 July 2022
Published: 6 July 2022

Publisher's Note: MDPI stays neutral with regard to jurisdictional claims in published maps and institutional affiliations.

Copyright: © 2022 by the author. Licensee MDPI, Basel, Switzerland. This article is an open access article distributed under the terms and conditions of the Creative Commons Attribution (CC BY) license (https://creativecommons.org/licenses/by/4.0/).

The growth of data-driven technologies, 5G, and the Internet pose enormous pressure on underlying information infrastructure. There are numerous proposals on how to deal with the possible capacity crunch [1]. However, the security of both optical and wireless networks lags behind reliable and spectrally efficient transmission [2]. Significant achievements have been recently made in the arenas of quantum computing [3] and quantum communication [4,5]. Because most conventional cryptography systems rely on computational security, which guarantees security against an efficient eavesdropper for a limited time, with advancements in quantum computing, this security can be compromised. To solve for these problems, various schemes providing the perfect/unconditional security have been proposed, including physical-layer security (PLS), quantum key distribution (QKD), and post-quantum cryptography. Unfortunately, it is still unclear how to integrate those different proposals with higher-level cryptography schemes. Thus, the purpose of this Special Issue was to integrate these various approaches and enable the next generation of cryptography systems whose security cannot be broken by quantum computers.

The topics addressed in this Special Issue include physical-layer security [2], quantum key distribution (QKD) [2], post-quantum cryptography [6], quantum-enhanced cryptography [7], stealth communication [2], and covert communication [8]. There are 14 papers published in this Special Issue, distributed as follows: 1 review paper, 1 perspective paper, and 12 articles.

In the review paper [9], authors apply the restricted Eve's concept to the satellite-to-satellite secret key distillation. In conventional QKD, it is assumed that Eve is the omnipotent, limited only by the laws of physics. This represents an unreasonable assumption for certain applications, where the presence of Eve is easy to detect, such as free-space optical communications, particularly satellite-to-satellite communications. By introducing geometrical optics within a restricted model, authors have shown that the secret key rate (SKR) can be significantly improved compared to the conventional QKD. Authors analyze SKRs from Bob's perspective through the exclusion zone approach and from Eve's perspective through dynamic positioning of the receiver aperture.

In the perspective paper [10], the author discusses how to build a global quantum communication network (QCN) by interconnecting the disconnected terrestrial QCNs through LEO satellite QCN, based on the cluster state concept. This heterogenous global QCN will provide unprecedented security for future 5G+/6G wireless networks, Internet of Things (IoT), optical networks, and autonomous vehicles.

In the first article paper [11], authors discuss the underwater QKD. Authors apply measurement-device-independent (MDI) QKD with the zero-photon catalysis (ZPC) performed at the emitter of one side to improve the SKR and extend the transmission distance. Numerical results indicate that the proposed ZPC-based scheme outperforms the corresponding single photon subtraction-based scheme in the extreme asymmetric case.

In the second article paper [12], the author describes how to build the multipartite QCN based on the surface code (SC) concept. The key idea is to simultaneously entangle multiple nodes in an arbitrary topology based on the SC approach. The author also describes how to extend the transmission distance between nodes to beyond 1000 km using SCs.

In the third article paper [13], authors introduce an open-destination MDI QKD network that provides security against untrusted relays and all detector side-channel attacks, in which all user users are capable of distributing keys with the help of other users.

In the fourth article paper [14], authors introduce a QKD protocol which employs the mean multi-king problem in which a sender shares a bit sequence with receivers as a secret key. Authors study the relation between eavesdropper's information gain and disturbance introduced into legitimate users' information, known as the information disturbance theorem, used for the BB84 protocol. Authors show that Eve's extracting information disturbs the quantum states and increases the error probability, as expected.

In the fifth article paper [15], authors introduce a QKD post-processing method, cubically raising the SKR in the number of double matching detection events. In the proposed protocol, contrary to the conventional QKD protocols, the secret bits rely on Bob's measurement basis selection rather than Alice's transmitted bits. Furthermore, the proposed protocol combines the sifting, reconciliation, and amplification into a unique process, thus requiring a single-round iteration without sending redundancy bits.

In the sixth article [16], authors study a recent proposal for quantum identity authentication from Zawadzki [17] and formally prove that the corresponding protocol is insecure.

In the seventh article [18], authors study the phase-matching QKD (PM-QKD) protocol, employing discrete-phase randomization and the post-compensation phase to quadratically improve the SKR. Unfortunately, according to the authors, the discrete-phase randomization opens a security loophole. Authors introduce the unambiguous state discrimination measurement and the photon-number-splitting attack against PM-QKD with imperfect phase randomization, demonstrating the rigorous security of decoy state PM-QKD with a discrete-phase randomization protocol.

In the eight article [19], authors introduce a nonclassical attack on the QKD system and propose a corresponding countermeasure method. The proposed attack is based on the sync pulses attenuated to a photon level to determine the signaling interval. To solve this attack, authors propose using variable power synchronizing pulses at varying lengths, combined with the controlled signal attenuation.

In the nineth article paper [20], an entanglement-based QKD protocol is proposed that employs a modified symmetric version of the Bernstein–Vazirani algorithm to achieve secure and efficient key distribution, with two variants presented (fully symmetric and semi-symmetric).

In the 10th article paper [21], related to the physical-layer security, authors study the impact of injection and jamming attacks during the advantage distillation in a MIMO wireless system and show that the man-in-the-middle attack can be mounted as long as the attacker has one extra antenna with respect to the legitimate users. To solve for this problem, authors propose reducing the injection attack by using a particularly designed pilot randomization technique. Then, by employing a game-theoretic approach, authors evaluate the optimal strategies available to the legitimate users in the presence of reactive jammers.

In the 11th article [22], authors introduce a Bayesian probabilistic algorithm that incorporates all published information in a qubit-based synchronization protocol to efficiently determine the clock offset without sacrificing any secure key. Given that the output of the algorithm is a probability, it can be used to quantify the synchronization confidence.

In the final article paper [23], related to the secure computation, authors present randomized versions of two known oblivious transfer protocols—one being quantum and the other being post-quantum with ring learning and an error assumption, thus demonstrating their security in the quantum universal composability framework with the use of a common reference string model.

Funding: This research received no external funding.

Conflicts of Interest: The author declares no conflict of interest.

References

1. Djordjevic, I.B. *Advanced Optical and Wireless Communications Systems*, 2nd ed.; Springer Nature Switzerland AG: Cham, Switzerland, 2022.
2. Djordjevic, I.B. *Physical-Layer Security and Quantum Key Distribution*; Springer International Publishing AG: Cham, Switzerland; Heidelberg, Germany, 2019.
3. Djordjevic, I.B. *Quantum Information Processing, Quantum Computing, and Quantum Error Correction: An Engineering Approach*, 2nd ed.; Elsevier/Academic Press: London, UK; San Diego, CA, USA, 2021.
4. Cariolaro, G. *Quantum Communications*; Springer International Publishing AG: Cham, Switzerland; Heidelberg, Germany, 2015.
5. Djordjevic, I.B. *Quantum Communication, Quantum Networks, and Quantum Sensing*; Elsevier/Academic Press: London, UK, 2022.
6. Bernstein, D.J.; Buchmann, J.; Dahmen, E. *Post-Quantum Cryptography*; Springer: Berlin, Germany, 2009.
7. Djordjevic, I.B. QKD-enhanced Cybersecurity Protocols. *IEEE Photonics J.* **2021**, *13*, 7600208. [CrossRef]
8. Bash, B.A.; Goeckel, D.; Towsley, D. Limits of reliable communication with low probability of detection on AWGN channels. *IEEE J. Sel. Areas Commun.* **2013**, *31*, 1921–1930. [CrossRef]
9. Pan, Z.; Djordjevic, I.B. Geometrical Optics Restricted Eavesdropping Analysis of Satellite-to-Satellite Secret Key Distillation. *Entropy* **2021**, *23*, 950. [CrossRef] [PubMed]
10. Djordjevic, I.B. On Global Quantum Communication Networking. *Entropy* **2020**, *22*, 831. [CrossRef] [PubMed]
11. Wang, Y.; Zou, S.; Mao, Y.; Guo, Y. Improving Underwater Continuous-Variable Measurement-Device-Independent Quantum Key Distribution via Zero-Photon Catalysis. *Entropy* **2020**, *22*, 571. [CrossRef] [PubMed]
12. Djordjevic, I.B. Surface-Codes-Based Quantum Communication Networks. *Entropy* **2020**, *22*, 1059. [CrossRef] [PubMed]
13. Cao, W.-F.; Zhen, Y.-Z.; Zheng, Y.-L.; Zhao, S.; Xu, F.; Li, L.; Chen, Z.-B.; Liu, N.-L.; Chen, K. Open-Destination Measurement-Device-Independent Quantum Key Distribution Network. *Entropy* **2020**, *22*, 1083. [CrossRef] [PubMed]
14. Yoshida, M.; Nakayama, A.; Cheng, J. Distinguishability and Disturbance in the Quantum Key Distribution Protocol Using the Mean Multi-Kings' Problem. *Entropy* **2020**, *22*, 1275. [CrossRef] [PubMed]
15. Lizama-Pérez, L.A.; López, R.J.M.; Samperio, E.H. Beyond the Limits of Shannon's Information in Quantum Key Distribution. *Entropy* **2021**, *23*, 229. [CrossRef] [PubMed]
16. González-Guillén, C.E.; González Vasco, M.I.; Johnson, F.; Pérez del Pozo, Á.L. An Attack on Zawadzki's Quantum Authentication Scheme. *Entropy* **2021**, *23*, 389. [CrossRef] [PubMed]
17. Zawadzki, P. Quantum identity authentication without entanglement. *Quantum Inf. Process.* **2019**, *18*, 7. [CrossRef]
18. Zhang, X.; Wang, Y.; Jiang, M.; Lu, Y.; Li, H.; Zhou, C.; Bao, W. Phase-Matching Quantum Key Distribution with Discrete Phase Randomization. *Entropy* **2021**, *23*, 508. [CrossRef] [PubMed]
19. Pljonkin, A.; Petrov, D.; Sabantina, L.; Dakhkilgova, K. Nonclassical Attack on a Quantum Key Distribution System. *Entropy* **2021**, *23*, 509. [CrossRef] [PubMed]
20. Ampatzis, M.; Andronikos, T. QKD Based on Symmetric Entangled Bernstein-Vazirani. *Entropy* **2021**, *23*, 870. [CrossRef] [PubMed]
21. Mitev, M.; Chorti, A.; Belmega, E.V.; Poor, H.V. Protecting Physical Layer Secret Key Generation from Active Attacks. *Entropy* **2021**, *23*, 960. [CrossRef] [PubMed]
22. Cochran, R.D.; Gauthier, D.J. Qubit-Based Clock Synchronization for QKD Systems Using a Bayesian Approach. *Entropy* **2021**, *23*, 988. [CrossRef] [PubMed]
23. Costa, B.; Branco, P.; Goulão, M.; Lemus, M.; Mateus, P. Randomized Oblivious Transfer for Secure Multiparty Computation in the Quantum Setting. *Entropy* **2021**, *23*, 1001. [CrossRef] [PubMed]

Review
Geometrical Optics Restricted Eavesdropping Analysis of Satellite-to-Satellite Secret Key Distillation

Ziwen Pan * and Ivan B. Djordjevic

Department of Electrical & Computer Engineering, College of Engineering, The University of Arizona, 1230 E Speedway Blvd, Tucson, AZ 85721, USA; ivan@arizona.edu
* Correspondence: ziwenpan@email.arizona.edu

Abstract: Traditionally, the study of quantum key distribution (QKD) assumes an omnipotent eavesdropper that is only limited by the laws of physics. However, this is not the case for specific application scenarios such as the QKD over a free-space link. In this invited paper, we introduce the geometrical optics restricted eavesdropping model for secret key distillation security analysis and apply to a few scenarios common in satellite-to-satellite applications.

Keywords: geometrical optics restricted eavesdropping; secret key distillation; satellite-to-satellite

1. Introduction

Quantum key distribution is known to guarantee unconditional security. The first QKD protocol, BB84, was developed in 1984 [1], which uses the polarization states of single photons to safely distribute keys. This was also known as the first discrete variable (DV)-QKD. Different protocols have since been studied, such as device-independent protocols that study the security with compromised apparatus [2–5], high dimensional protocols that exploit high dimensional degrees of freedom to increase the key rate [6–10] and decoy state protocols [11–13] that use decoy states against the photon-number-splitting attack [14]. Another major category in the study of QKD protocols, the continuous variable (CV) protocols [15,16] that encode keys into CV observables of carrier fields [17], are known to be more easily implementable for their compatibility with current communication devices instead of relying on single-photon generation and detection like most DV protocols.

Generally, in this paper, we assume that Alice uses a multi-photon source governed by the mean photon number without photon-number-resolving detectors so that she is limited in knowing whether she is transmitting a multi-photon wave packet, for example, if she only has a Geiger mode detector that clicks when one or more photons are detected. For security analysis of the quantum key distribution under these assumptions, conventionally, an omnipotent eavesdropper (Eve) that can gather information from the multi-photon wave packets transmitted from Alice to Bob by collecting every photon that does not arrive at Bob's receiver is assumed [18–25]. However, this is not the case for some specific application scenarios. For example, it would be reasonable to assume that the eavesdropper's (Eve's) power collection ability is limited due to the size of her aperture in an optical wireless channel from Alice to Bob. In [26,27], geometrical optics restricted eavesdropping analysis was proposed, considering the reasonably limited power collection ability of Eve. In [28–33], some of the applications of this restricted Eve model were introduced.

In this invited paper, we present some of the applications of the geometrical optics restricted model. In Section 2, we briefly introduce the power-collection-restricted eavesdropping model and give the lower and upper bound expressions. In Section 3.1, we showcase geometrical optics restricted eavesdropping analysis with a case where the eavesdropper has an aperture of a limited size in the same plane as Bob's while investigating the exclusion zone as one of Bob's defense strategies. In Section 3.2, we further assume that Eve's aperture can be dynamically positioned and provide the results while optimizing this eavesdropping strategy. We conclude that the geometrical optics restricted eavesdropping model is suitable for multiple application scenario analysis.

2. Geometrical Optics Restricted Eavesdropping Model

As is illustrated in Figure 1, instead of assuming that Eve collects all the photons outside of Bob's receiver, only a fraction κ of them is collectable by Eve, denoted here as a wiretap channel with a κ-transmissivity beamsplitter. Here, η is the Alice-to-Bob channel transmissivity, μ is the input mean photon number per mode on Alice's side, and n_e is the noise mean photon number per mode on Eve's side. $\psi^{AA'}$ and $\psi^{EE'}$ in Figure 1 are entanglement pairs. Alice would keep mode A and send mode A' to Bob, and in the most general case, Eve would also use entanglement pairs to eavesdrop, retaining mode E and sending mode E' into the channel. In [26], the lower bound on the achievable key rate for direct and reverse reconciliation is shown below:

$$K_\rightarrow \geq \beta g(n_e(1-\eta) + \eta\mu) - \sum_i g\left(\frac{\nu_{y_i}^{ER} - 1}{2}\right) - \beta g(n_e(1-\eta)) + g(n_e(1-\eta\kappa)), \quad (1)$$

$$K_\leftarrow \geq \beta g(\mu) - \sum_i g\left(\frac{\nu_{y_i}^{ER} - 1}{2}\right) - \beta g\left(\mu - \frac{\eta\mu(1+\mu)}{1 + n_e - n_e\eta + \eta\mu}\right) + \sum_i g\left(\frac{\nu_{y_i}^{ER} - 1}{2}\right), \quad (2)$$

$$g(x) = (x+1)\log_2(x+1) - x\log_2 x \quad (3)$$

with detailed expressions of $\nu_{y_i}^{ER}$ available in [26]. Here, β is the reconciliation efficiency, which is set to $\beta = 1$ throughout this paper.

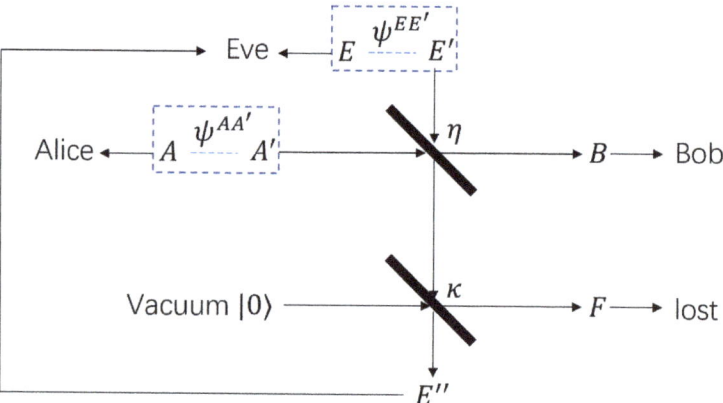

Figure 1. Geometrical optics restricted model wiretap channel notation [26].

The upper bound in a pure loss channel ($n_e = 0$) is shown to be [26]

$$K \leq \log_2 \frac{\eta + \kappa(1-\eta)}{\kappa(1-\eta)}, \quad (4)$$

while the upper bound in a thermal noise channel does not have a closed form expression. Detailed calculations can be found in Appendix A of [26].

3. Applications on Satellite-to-Satellite Secret Key Distillation

In this section, we study some applications of the geometrical optics restricted model analysis that would be common in satellite-to-satellite links where Eve's collecting ability would be naturally limited due to the radius of her receiver aperture, which usually ranges from centimeters to decimeters for traditional free-space communication. If we take existing space applications into account for an upper-bounding estimation of Eve's aperture size, the Giant Magellan Telescope, one of the largest optical observatories, has a primary mirror of a 12.5-m radius [34]. Other known aperture sizes of satellite-based applications are much smaller, such as the 1.2-m-radius primary mirror for the Hubble Space Telescope [35] and the 20-cm-radius aperture for NASA's "Wide-field Infrared Survey Explorer" infrared telescope [36].

We analyze both the communication parties' and Eve's strategy by starting with a defense strategy from Bob's side called an exclusion zone, under the aforementioned assumptions and considering the case where Eve's aperture is in the same plane with Bob's in Section 3.1. Then, in Section 3.2, we move forward from that and assume that Eve's aperture can be dynamically positioned, concluding Eve's strategy for eavesdropping. In this section, we assume that a Gaussian beam with a beam waist W_0 and wavelength $\lambda = 1550$ nm is transmitted. The space temperature is set to $T = 3$ K, and we calculate the noise mean photon number using the black body radiation equation:

$$n_e = \frac{1}{e^{\frac{hf}{kT}} - 1}, \tag{5}$$

where h is the Planck constant, f is the transmission center frequency, and k is the Boltzmann constant. We then calculate the power transmitted by Alice P_{Alice}, the power received by Bob P_{Bob}, the power received by Eve P_{Eve}, and the channel transmissivity η, and the restriction factor on Eve κ can be expressed as

$$\eta = \frac{P_{Bob}}{P_{Alice}}, \tag{6}$$

$$\kappa = \frac{P_{Eve}}{P_{total}(1-\eta)}, \tag{7}$$

In this section, we calculate the lower bound as the maximum of the direct reconciliation lower bound and the reverse reconciliation lower bound.

3.1. Bob's Defense Strategy: Exclusion Zone

In this subsection, we introduce the problem set-up of one of the most straightforward defense strategies of the communication parities: the so-called exclusion zone. In principle, the closer Eve is to the beam transmission axis from Alice to Bob, the more likely the legitimate communication parities would detect the eavesdropper's presence (e.g., with a naïve approach such as a visible or infrared telescope or even radar to detect the eavesdropper's presence and abort communication if a possible eavesdropper is detected within a certain range to the communication parities). In free-space channels such as the satellite links, it is also possible for Bob to have opaque material around his receiver to absorb any photons that might have arrived outside of his receiver's aperture, preventing them from further propagation and possibly ending up in Eve's receiver aperture. As is illustrated in Figure 2, the exclusion zone is denoted with a dashed circle around Bob's receiver, excluding potential eavesdroppers to collect photons that arrive in this region. By definition, Bob's aperture area is also part of the exclusion zone, since the photons arriving at Bob's aperture would not be collectable by Eve. Here, more specifically, we say that Bob is setting up an exclusion zone if the area of the exclusion zone (A_{ex}) is larger than his receiver aperture area (A_{Bob} or A_b). Other specified parameters include L being the transmission distance and A_{Alice} (A_a) and A_{Eve} (A_e) being the area of Alice's aperture (radius r_a) and Eve's aperture (radius r_e), respectively. The radii of Bob's aperture and the exclusion zone are denoted as r_b and r_{ex} ($r_{ex} \geq r_b$). Here, the limited size of Eve's aperture is placed in the same plane as Bob's, since that would be the worst-case scenario for the purpose of our study under this exclusion zone assumption if Eve is not allowed between the Alice-to-Bob line of sight.

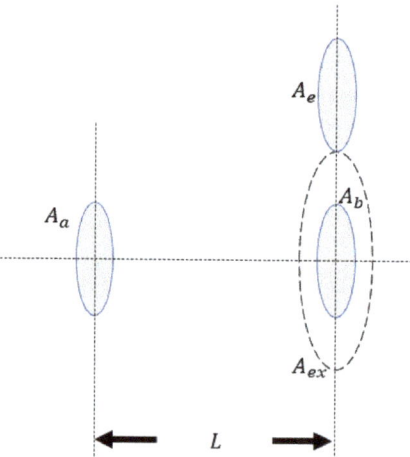

Figure 2. Limited size aperture of Eve in the same plane as Bob's. Here, Bob is setting an exclusion zone around his receiver as a defense strategy.

To start with, we set $r_{ex} = r_b$ (no additional exclusion zone) and investigate how Eve's aperture size would affect the achievable secure key rate lower bound (LB) and upper bound (UB), as shown in Figure 3. Here, we can see that under these parameters, the lower bound was quite close to the upper bound, which gave us the capacity in this scenario. As Eve's aperture size increased, the achievable rate went down and saturated but still outperformed the unrestricted case capacity. The reason for this convergence is that the transmitted beam intensity was the strongest at its center and weakened fast in the outer regions. As such, up to some point, increasing Eve's aperture size would only be able to gather photons from the regions far away from the beam center, thus making it ineffective in increasing Eve's advantage. As a result of that, in the figure below, we only set Eve's aperture radius to be 10 cm, equal to r_a and r_b, for a fair comparison.

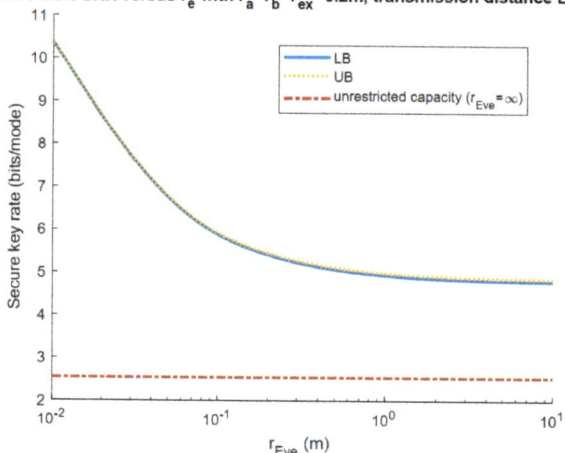

Figure 3. Achievable secure key rate lower and upper bound as functions of Eve's aperture radius r_e, with $r_{ex} = r_b$. The unrestricted case (infinite-sized aperture on Eve's side) is also included. Here, $W_0 = r_a = r_b = r_{ex} = 20$ cm.

In Figure 4, we set the exclusion zone radius to be $r_{ex} = 15$ cm and 20 cm to compare the achievable rate lower bounds (LB) and upper bounds (UB) for the case without an additional exclusion zone. Here, we can see that with an aperture of a limited size on Eve's side, the achievable secure key rate outperformed that of the unrestricted case. The lower bound and upper bound were quite close, which gave the range for the capacity. We can also see that an exclusion zone helped increase the key rate when the transmission distance was not too large. However, when the transmission distance was sufficiently large, the lower and upper bounds became constant, as proved in [30], when the collecting ability of Bob and Eve became proportional to their aperture sizes:

$$\lim_{L \to \infty} \frac{P_{Eve}}{P_{Bob}} = \frac{A_e}{A_b}, \tag{8}$$

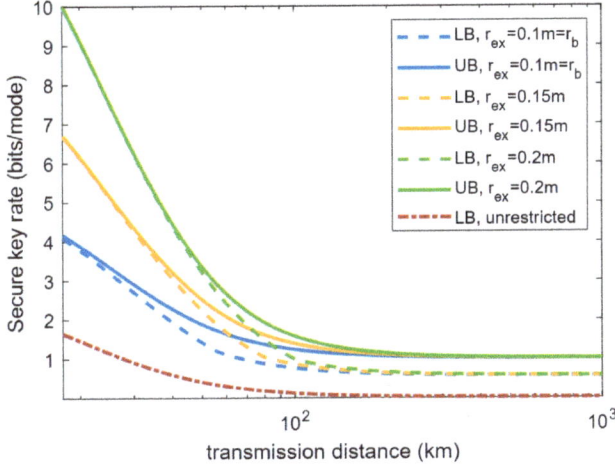

Figure 4. Achievable secure key rate lower and upper bounds as functions of the transmission distance. The unrestricted case (infinite size aperture on Eve's side with $r_{ex} = r_b$) is also included. Here, $W_0 = r_a = r_b = r_e = 10$ cm.

Here, we can see that an exclusion zone would not affect this saturation very much, as at a large transmission distance, the collecting ability of Bob and Eve became proportional to their aperture sizes as in Equation (8) when the area of an exclusion zone was not significantly larger than the receiver aperture sizes of Bob and Eve.

3.2. Eavesdropper's Strategy: A Dynamically Positioned Aperture

In this subsection, we introduce and analyze one of the eavesdropper's possible strategies with a dynamically positioned aperture, which would apply to the geometrical optics restricted model, where Eve could dynamically position her aperture behind Bob's. As is illustrated in Figure 5, $A_{Alice}(A_a)$, $A_{Bob}(A_b)$, and $A_{Eve}(A_e)$ are the area of Alice's aperture (radius r_a), Bob's aperture (radius r_b), and Eve's aperture (radius r_e), respectively. L_{AB} is the distance between Alice's and Bob's aperture planes, while L_{BE} is the distance between Bob's and Eve's aperture planes. D is the distance between Eve's aperture center and the beam propagation line-of-sight path.

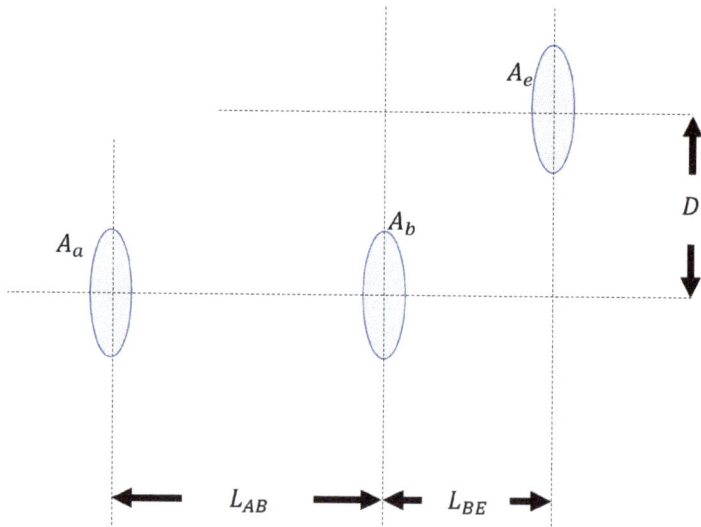

Figure 5. Eavesdropper dynamic positioning set-up.

As was proven in Equation (44) of [33], when L_{AB} was sufficiently large, the optimal strategy for Eve was to set $L_{BE} = L_{AB}$ and $D = 0$. Thus, we set $L_{BE} = L_{AB}$, $D = 0$ and obtained the lower and upper bounds on the achievable secure key rate as in Figure 6. It is shown that in this case, the rate increased with the increase in W_0 as this decreased the divergence angle, making the beam more focused on Bob's aperture plane. We can also see that Eve suppressed Alice and Bob's achievable key rate compared with the similar distance range in Figure 4 by applying this strategy.

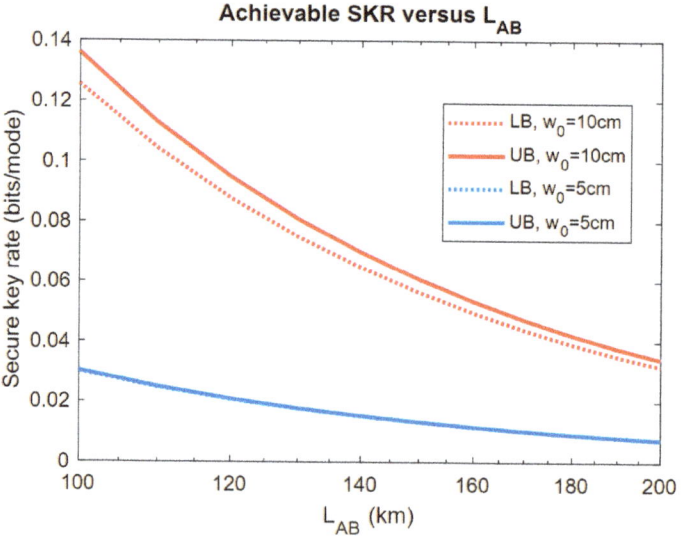

Figure 6. Lower and upper bounds of the achievable secure key rate versus L_{AB} with $L_{BE} = L_{AB}$ and $D = 0$. Bob's and Eve's aperture radii are $r_b = r_e = 10$ cm.

4. Discussion

In this invited paper, we briefly introduced the geometrical optics restricted model and presented a few cases applying this model to some common cases in free-space optical links such as the satellite-to-satellite channel. We showcased the achievable secure key rate lower and upper bounds and compared them to the unrestricted case. Furthermore, we investigated the strategy from both the communication parties' side and Eve's side within this model.

Funding: National Science Foundation (1828132, 1907918).

Acknowledgments: The authors thankfully acknowledge helpful discussions with Saikat Guha, Kaushik P. Seshadreesan and John Gariano from the University of Arizona, Jeffrey H. Shapiro from the Massachusetts Institute of Technology and William Clark and Mark R. Adcock from General Dynamics.

Conflicts of Interest: The authors declare no conflict of interest.

References

1. Charles, H.B.; Brassard, G. Quantum cryptography: Public key distribution and coin tossing. *arXiv* **2020**, arXiv:2003.06557.
2. Dominic, M.; Andrew, C.-C.Y. Quantum Cryptography with Imperfect Apparatus. In Proceedings of the IEEE Symposium on Foundations of Computer Science (FOCS), Palo Alto, CA, USA, 8–11 November 1998.
3. Jonathan, B.; Hardy, L.; Kent, A. No signaling and quantum key distribution. *Phys. Rev. Lett.* **2005**, *95*, 010503.
4. Pironio, S.; Acín, A.; Brunner, N.; Gisin, N.; Massar, S.; Scarani, V. Device-independent quantum key distribution secure against collective attacks. *New J. Phys.* **2009**, *11*, 045021. [CrossRef]
5. McKague, M. Device independent quantum key distribution secure against coherent attacks with memoryless measurement devices. *New J. Phys.* **2009**, *11*, 103037. [CrossRef]
6. Mafu, M.; Dudley, A.; Goyal, S.; Giovannini, D.; McLaren, M.; Padgett, M.J.; Konrad, T.; Petruccione, F.; Lütkenhaus, N.; Forbes, A. Higher-dimensional orbital-angular-momentum-based quantum key distribution with mutually unbiased bases. *Phys. Rev. A* **2013**, *88*, 032305. [CrossRef]
7. Ziwen, P.; Cai, J.; Wang, C. Quantum key distribution with high order fibonacci-like orbital angular momentum states. *Int. J. Theor. Phys.* **2017**, *56*, 2622–2634.
8. Ivan, B.D. Deep-space and near-Earth optical communications by coded orbital angular momentum (OAM) modulation. *Opt. Express* **2011**, *19*, 14277–14289.
9. Tittel, W.; Brendel, J.; Zbinden, H.; Gisin, N. Quantum cryptography using entangled photons in energy-time Bell states. *Phys. Rev. Lett.* **2000**, *84*, 4737. [CrossRef]
10. Bing, Q. Single-photon continuous-variable quantum key distribution based on the energy-time uncertainty relation. *Opt. Lett.* **2006**, *31*, 2795–2797.
11. Wang, X.-B. Decoy-state protocol for quantum cryptography with four different intensities of coherent light. *Phys. Rev. A* **2005**, *72*, 012322. [CrossRef]
12. Lo, H.-K.; Ma, X.; Chen, K. Decoy State Quantum Key Distribution. *Phys. Rev. Lett.* **2005**, *94*, 230504. [CrossRef] [PubMed]
13. Ma, X.; Qi, B.; Zhao, Y.; Lo, H.-K. Practical decoy state for quantum key distribution. *Phys. Rev. A* **2005**, *72*, 012326. [CrossRef]
14. Lutkenhaus, N. Security against individual attacks for realistic quantum key distribution. *Phys. Rev. A* **2000**, *61*, 052304. [CrossRef]
15. Cerf, N.J.; Lévy, M.; Van Assche, G. Quantum distribution of Gaussian keys using squeezed states. *Phys. Rev. A* **2001**, *63*, 052311. [CrossRef]
16. Grosshans, F.; Grangier, P. Continuous Variable Quantum Cryptography Using Coherent States. *Phys. Rev. Lett.* **2002**, *88*, 057902. [CrossRef] [PubMed]
17. Braunstein, S.L.; Van Loock, P. Quantum information with continuous variables. *Rev. Mod. Phys.* **2005**, *77*, 513–577. [CrossRef]
18. Maurer, U.M. Secret key agreement by public discussion from common information. *IEEE Trans. Inf. Theory* **1993**, *39*, 733–742. [CrossRef]
19. Michał, H.; Horodecki, P.; Horodecki, R. Unified approach to quantum capacities: Towards quantum noisy coding theorem. *Phys. Rev. Lett.* **2000**, *85*, 433.
20. Devetak, I.; Winter, A. Distillation of secret key and entanglement from quantum states. *Proc. R. Soc. A Math. Phys. Eng. Sci.* **2005**, *461*, 207–235. [CrossRef]
21. Renato, R.; Cirac, J.I. de Finetti representation theorem for infinite-dimensional quantum systems and applications to quantum cryptography. *Phys. Rev. Lett.* **2009**, *102*, 110504.
22. García-Patrón, R.; Pirandola, S.; Lloyd, S.; Shapiro, J.H. Reverse Coherent Information. *Phys. Rev. Lett.* **2009**, *102*, 210501. [CrossRef]
23. Pirandola, S.; García-Patrón, R.; Braunstein, S.L.; Lloyd, S. Direct and Reverse Secret-Key Capacities of a Quantum Channel. *Phys. Rev. Lett.* **2009**, *102*, 050503. [CrossRef]

24. Masahiro, T.; Guha, S.; Wilde, M.M. Fundamental rate-loss tradeoff for optical quantum key distribution. *Nat. Commun.* **2014**, *5*, 1–7.
25. Pirandola, S.; Laurenza, R.; Ottaviani, C.; Banchi, L. Fundamental limits of repeaterless quantum communications. *Nat. Commun.* **2017**, *8*, 15043. [CrossRef] [PubMed]
26. Pan, Z.; Seshadreesan, K.P.; Clark, W.; Adcock, M.R.; Djordjevic, I.B.; Shapiro, J.H.; Guha, S. Secret-Key Distillation across a Quantum Wiretap Channel under Restricted Eavesdropping. *Phys. Rev. Appl.* **2020**, *14*, 024044. [CrossRef]
27. Pan, Z.; Seshadreesan, K.P.; Clark, W.; Adcock, M.R.; Djordjevic, I.B.; Shapiro, J.H.; Guha, S. Secret key distillation over a pure loss quantum wiretap channel under restricted eavesdropping. In Proceedings of the 2019 IEEE International Symposium on Information Theory (ISIT), Paris, France, 7–12 July 2019.
28. Pan, Z.; Djordjevic, I.B. Security of satellite-based cv-qkd under realistic assumptions. In Proceedings of the 2020 22nd International Conference on Transparent Optical Networks (ICTON), Bari, Italy, 19–23 July 2020; pp. 1–4.
29. Pan, Z.; Gariano, J.; Djordjevic, I.B. Secret key distillation over satellite-to-satellite free-space channel with eavesdropper dynamic positioning. In *Signal Processing in Photonic Communications*; Optical Society of America: Washington, DC, USA, 2020; p. SpTu3I-4.
30. Pan, Z.; Djordjevic, I.B. Secret key distillation over satellite-to-satellite free-space optics channel with a limited-sized aperture eavesdropper in the same plane of the legitimate receiver. *Opt. Express* **2020**, *28*, 37129–37148. [CrossRef] [PubMed]
31. Pan, Z.; Gariano, J.; Clark, W.; Djordjevic, I.B. Secret key distillation over realistic satellite-to-satellite free-space channel. In *Quantum 2.0*; Optical Society of America: Washington, DC, USA, 2020; p. QTh7B-15.
32. Pan, Z.; Djordjevic, I.B. Secret key distillation over realistic satellite-to-satellite free-space channel: Exclusion zone analysis. *arXiv* **2020**, arXiv:2009.05929.
33. Pan, Z.; Djordjevic, I.B. Secret Key Distillation over Satellite-to-satellite Free-space Optics Channel with Eavesdropper Dynamic Positioning. *arXiv* **2020**, arXiv:2012.13865.
34. Johns, M.; McCarthy, P.; Raybould, K.; Bouchez, A.; Farahani, A.; Filgueira, J.; Jacoby, G.; Shectman, S.; Sheehan, M. Giant magellan telescope: Overview. In *Ground-Based and Airborne Telescopes IV, Volume 8444*; International Society for Optics and Photonics: Amsterdam, The Netherlands, 2012; p. 84441H.
35. Montagnino, L.A. Test and evaluation of the hubble space telescope 2.4-meter primary mirror. In *Large Optics Technology, Volume 571*; International Society for Optics and Photonics: San Diego, CA, USA, 1985; pp. 182–190.
36. Wright, E.L.; Eisenhardt, P.R.M.; Mainzer, A.K.; Ressler, M.E.; Cutri, R.; Jarrett, T.; Kirkpatrick, D.; Padgett, D.; McMillan, R.S.; Skrutskie, M.; et al. The wide-field infrared survey explorer (wise): Mission description and initial on-orbit performance. *Astron. J.* **2010**, *140*, 1868–1881. [CrossRef]

Perspective

On Global Quantum Communication Networking

Ivan B. Djordjevic

Department of Electrical and Computer Engineering, University of Arizona, Tucson, AZ 85721, USA; ivan@email.arizona.edu; Tel.: +1-520-626-5119

Received: 29 June 2020; Accepted: 28 July 2020; Published: 29 July 2020

Abstract: Research in quantum communications networks (QCNs), where multiple users desire to generate or transmit common quantum-secured information, is still in its beginning stage. To solve for the problems of both discrete variable- and continuous variable-quantum key distribution (QKD) schemes in a simultaneous manner as well as to enable the next generation of quantum communication networking, in this Special Issue paper we describe a scenario where disconnected terrestrial QCNs are coupled through low Earth orbit (LEO) satellite quantum network forming heterogeneous satellite–terrestrial QCN. The proposed heterogeneous QCN is based on the cluster state approach and can be used for numerous applications, including: (i) to teleport arbitrary quantum states between any two nodes in the QCN; (ii) to enable the next generation of cyber security systems; (iii) to enable distributed quantum computing; and (iv) to enable the next generation of quantum sensing networks. The proposed QCNs will be robust against various channel impairments over heterogeneous links. Moreover, the proposed QCNs will provide an unprecedented security level for 5G+/6G wireless networks, Internet of Things (IoT), optical networks, and autonomous vehicles, to mention a few.

Keywords: quantum key distribution (QKD); discrete variable (DV)-QKD; continuous variable (CV)-QKD; postquantum cryptography (PQC); quantum communications networks (QCNs)

---

1. Introduction

Quantum communication (QuCom) employs quantum information theory concepts, in particular the no-cloning theorem and the theorem of indistinguishability of arbitrary quantum states, to implement the distribution of keys with verifiable security, commonly referred to as quantum key distribution (QKD), where security is guaranteed by the fundamental laws of physics as opposed to unproven mathematical assumptions employed in computational security-based cryptography [1–3]. Despite the appealing features of QuComs, there are some fundamental and technical challenges that need to be addressed prior to its widespread application. For instance, both the rate and distance of QuCom are fundamentally limited by channel loss, which is specified by the rate-loss tradeoff. To overcome the rate-distance limit of discrete variable (DV)-QKD protocols, two predominant approaches have been pursued recently: (i) the development of quantum relays and (ii) the employment of trusted relays. Quantum relays require the use of long-duration quantum memories and high-fidelity entanglement distillation [4], which are not yet widely available. On the other hand, the trusted-relay methodology assumes that the relay between two users can be trusted [5]; unfortunately, this assumption is difficult to verify in practice. The measurement device independent (MDI)-QKD approach [6] was able to close the detection loopholes; however, its secret-key rate (SKR) is still bounded by $O(T)$-dependence (with T standing for transmissivity). Recently, twin-field (TF) QKD has been proposed to overcome the rate-distance limit [7], whose SKR scales with the square-root of transmittance, which represents a promising approach to extend the transmission distance. Another key limitation of DV-QKD is the deadtime of single-photon detectors (SPDs), which limits the baud rate and consequently the SKRs. To solve for this problem, a continuous variable (CV)-QKD can be used instead [1,8–10], which employs homodyne/heterodyne detection instead and thus does not exhibit the SPDS' deadtime limitation problem. In particular, the discrete modulation (DM)-based CV-QKD protocols offer much better reconciliation efficiency compared to that of Gaussian modulation (GM)-based CV-QKD protocols. Unfortunately, the security proofs of DM-based CV-QKD schemes for collective and coherent attacks are still incomplete. To overcome key challenges for DV-QKD, such as low SKR values and limited distance, as well as for DM-based CV-QKD, such as incompleteness of security proofs, the following approaches have been proposed in our recent papers: (1) discretized GM (DGM)-CV-QKD [11], (2) optimized CV-QKD [12], and (3) hybrid DV-CV QKD [13]. An alternative approach to QKD is post-quantum cryptography (PQC) [14]. PQC is typically referred to by various cryptographic algorithms that are thought to be secure against any quantum computer-based attack. Unfortunately, PQC is also based on unproven assumptions and some of the PQC algorithms will be broken in the future by developing more sophisticated quantum algorithms.

Modern classical communication networks consist of multiple nodes connected by various types of channels, including free-space optical (FSO) links, optical fibers, ground–satellite links, wireless RF, and coaxial cables. Such a heterogeneous architecture would be equally important for QCNs, as quantum nodes may access a QCN via different kinds of channels. Indeed, quantum communications have been individually validated in free-space, optical fibers, and between a satellite and a ground station, but a combined heterogeneous QCN employing multiple types of channels remains elusive. Unlike in the point-to-point communication case, the fundamental quantum communication rate limits are not well known. Several QKD testbeds have been reported so far, including the DARPA QKD network [15], Tokyo QKD network [16], and secure communication based on quantum cryptography (SECOQC) network [17]. The QKD can also be used to establish QKD-based campus-to-campus virtual private networks employing the IPsec protocol [18] as well as to establish the network setup for using transport-layer security (TLS) based on QKD [19]. However, all of these networks employ the dark fiber infrastructure. Quantum communication over satellite links has already been demonstrated; see for example [20,21].

In this Special Issue paper, we propose to implement the multipartite QCN by employing the cluster state-based concept [22]. The proposed quantum network can be used to: (i) perform distributed quantum computing, (ii) teleport quantum states between any two nodes in the network, and (iii) enable the next generation of cyber security systems. The cluster states can be described by using the stabilizer formalism and as such they can easily be certified by simple syndrome measurements. In this formalism, the cluster states can be interpreted as codewords of a corresponding quantum error correction code, while corresponding errors can be corrected for by simple syndrome decoding, among others. By performing simple Y and Z measurements on properly selected nodes we can straightforwardly establish the Einstein–Podolsky–Rosen (EPR) pair between any two nodes in the network. Moreover, multiple EPR pairs can be established simultaneously. We further propose a cluster state-based quantum network of satellites that enables global coverage. The quantum satellite network would be composed of quantum subnetworks comprised of low Earth orbit (LEO) satellites. Some of these LEO satellite-based quantum subnetworks can be connected to a subnetwork of medium Earth orbit (MEO)/ geostationary orbit (GEO) satellites. The LEO satellites should be used to interconnect terrestrial cluster state-based quantum networks. This quantum global network can also be used to distribute the entangled states for quantum sensing applications and to enable distributed quantum computing on a global scale. SDN concepts should be used to reconfigure the proposed QCN.

The paper is organized as follows. In Section 2, we describe the proposed cluster states-based QCN concept. In Section 3, we describe potential approaches to extend the transmission distance between QCN nodes. In Section 4, we describe the QCN that is currently under development at the University of Arizona. Finally, in Section 5, we provide some relevant concluding remarks.

2. Proposed Cluster States-Based Quantum Communications Networks

To enable the next generation of quantum communication networking, we envision a scenario in which disconnected terrestrial cluster states-based QCNs are coupled through the LEO satellite (cluster state) quantum network, thus providing global coverage. The proposed quantum network will be highly robust against turbulence encountered by FSO links, as the envisioned quantum satellite network will communicate to ground nodes only through the LEO satellite-to-ground links, exhibiting a vertical downlink profile through vacuum followed by a turbulence layer with strength that is altitude-dependent.

The cluster states belong to the class of the graph states, which also include Bell states, Greenberger–Horne–Zeilinger (GHZ) states, W-states, and various entangled states used in quantum error correction [22]. When the cluster C is defined as a connected subset on a d-dimensional lattice, it obeys the set of eigenvalue equations $S_a|\phi\rangle_C = |\phi\rangle_C$, $S_a = X_a \bigotimes_{b \in N(a)} Z_b$, where S_a are *stabilizer operators* with $N(a)$ denoting the neighborhood of $a \in C$. To create a 2-D cluster state, the approach proposed by Gilbert et al. [23] is applicable; it employs linear states, generated by spontaneous parametric down conversion (SPDC), local unitaries, and type I fusion to create the desired 2-D cluster state. The type I fusion is illustrated in Figure 1, based on [23]. The vertical photon is reflected by the polarization beam splitter (PBS), while the horizontal photon is transmitted through the PBS. Given the probabilistic nature of the PBS, with the photons present at both the left and right input ports, there are four possible outcomes, each occurring with probability 0.25. Two outcomes correspond to the desired fusion operators, and the success probability of the fusion is 0.5. When a single photon is detected by the detector, a successful fusion is declared. The procedure to create the T-shape cluster state is described in Figure 2. To create the box-cluster state, we start with a four-qubit linear cluster state, re-label the qubits 2 and 3, and apply the Hadamard gates to qubits 2 and 3, which effectively establish the bond between qubits 1 and 4. Namely, relabeling the qubits is equivalent to the SWAP gate action. To create the box-on-chain cluster state, we start with a longer linear chain of qubits and apply the same approach as in a box-state creation. Two T-shape cluster states can be fused together to get the H-shape cluster state, etc.

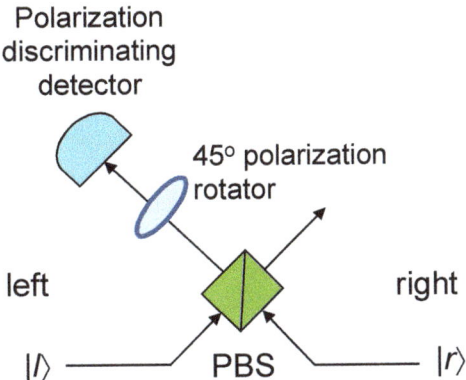

Figure 1. Illustrating the type I fusion process. PBS: polarization beam splitter.

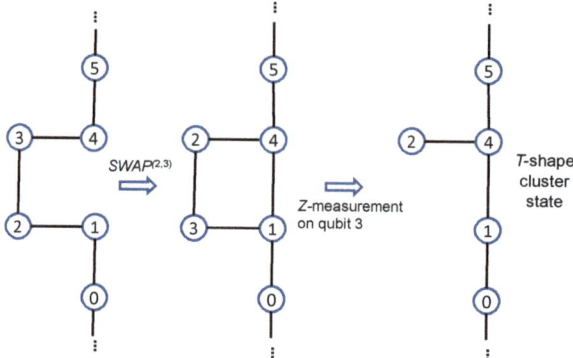

Figure 2. Gilbert's approach to create the *T*-shape cluster state.

Once the 2-D cluster state of nodes is created, we can use properly selected *Y* and *Z* measurements to create the EPR pair between any two arbitrary nodes in the quantum network. As a reminder, the role of the *Z* measurement is to remove the particular node (qubit) from the cluster, whereas the role of *Y* measurement is to remove a given node and link neighboring nodes. As an illustration, the 2-D cluster state with nine nodes is shown in Figure 3. Let us assume that we are interested in establishing EPR pairs between nodes 3 and 7 as well as nodes 1 and 9. We first perform *Y* measurements in the following order: Y_8, Y_5, and Y_6 to get the intermediate stage. We then perform *Z*-measurement on node 2 and *Y* measurement on node 4 to get the two desired EPR pairs. Given that the 2-D cluster state is universal, it is possible to use the same network architecture for both QCN and distributed quantum computing. We also imagine the scenario in which each node is equipped with multiple qubits, wherein several layers of 2-D cluster states are active at the same time, which will allow us to simultaneously perform QCN and distributed quantum computing. Moreover, when several 2-D cluster states are run in parallel on the same set of network nodes, we will be able to reconfigure the QCN as needed. This can be done with the help of the SDN concept. The SDN has been introduced to separate the control plane and data plane, manage network services through the abstraction of higher-level functionality, and implement new applications and algorithms efficiently. It has already been studied to enable the coexistence of classical and quantum communication channels. Our SDN-based QCN architecture is composed of three layers, namely an application layer, a control layer, and a QCN layer. Users send their requests from the application layer with the help of the northbound interface to the SDN controller. The SDN controller allocates the QCN resources with the help of its global map through the southbound interface. The QCN layer would be composed of dense wavelength-division multiplexing (DWDM) FSO/single-mode fiber (SMF)/few-mode fiber (FMF) links and QCN nodes. Any two nodes in the QCN can communicate through either through a dedicated SMF/FSO/FMF link or through a wavelength channel. The SDN control should also determine sequence of measurements to be performed in order to establish desired EPR pairs. To deal with time-varying channel conditions over heterogeneous links, we should adapt the system configuration based on both application requirement and link condition.

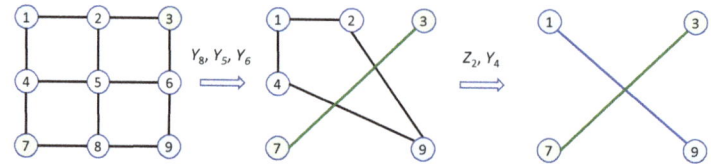

Figure 3. Establishing EPR pairs between nodes 1 and 9 as well as between nodes 3 and 7.

3. Extending the Distance between Nodes in QCN

The DV-QKD can be used to build QKD networks, as discussed in the introduction. Unfortunately, the DV-QKD is affected by the deadtime of SPDs. Moreover, even if Eve cannot get the key because DV-QKD is used, she can prevent parties from creating secure keys, which is similar to the Denial of Service (DoS) attack. Further, since SKRs for DV-QKD are low, the quantum key pool, storing the secure keys, will often be empty, hampering the operation of QKD networks. To solve for this problem we propose to use the hybrid QKD-PQC protocols, in which QKD is used for raw key transmission and PQC in information reconciliation to reduce the leakage during the error reconciliation stage, which is illustrated in Figure 4. As mentioned in the introduction, the PQC is typically referred to in various cryptographic algorithms that are thought to be secure against any quantum computer-based attack. Unfortunately, the PQC is also based on unproven assumptions and some of the QPC algorithms might be broken in the future by developing advanced quantum algorithms. For this reason we propose to use the PQC algorithms only in the information reconciliation phase so as to limit the leakage due to transmission of parity bits over an authenticated classical channel (in conventional QKD). The quantum algorithms to be developed (not yet known), which will be capable of breaking the PQC algorithms, will have certain complexity expressed in terms of the number of operations L. By ensuring that the number of parity bits $N-K$ is shorter than the number of secure PQC bits $\log_2 L$, the proposed cryptographic scheme will be secure. Evidently, the proposed cryptographic scheme exploits the complexity of corresponding quantum algorithms used to break the PQC protocols. Given that the McEliece cryptosystem based on quasi cyclic (QC)-low-density parity-check (LDPC) coding is straightforward to implement as shown in [24], whereas the corresponding LDPC encoders and decoders have been already implemented in field-programmable gate array (FPGA) [25], it represents an excellent candidate to be used for the transmission of parity bits in the TF-QKD scheme. As an illustration, the secret fraction that can be achieved with the BB84 protocol is lower bounded by [1]:

$$r = q^{(Z)}\left[1 - h_2\left(e^{(X)}\right)\right] - q^{(Z)} f_e h_2\left(e^{(Z)}\right), \tag{1}$$

where $q^{(Z)}$ denotes the probability of declaring a successful result when Alice sent a single-photon and Bob detected it in the Z-basis, f_e denotes the error correction inefficiency ($f_e \geq 1$), $e^{(X)}$ [$e^{(Z)}$] denotes the QBER in the X-basis (Z-basis), and $h_2(x)$ is the binary entropy function $h_2(x) = -x\log_2(x) - (1-x)\log_2(1-x)$. The second term $q^{(Z)} h_2[e^{(X)}]$ denotes the amount of information Eve was able to learn during the raw key transmission, and this information can be removed from the final key during the privacy amplification phase. The third term $q^{(Z)} f_e h_2[e^{(Z)}]$ represents the amount of information revealed during the error correction stage. By sending the parity bits over the PQC channel this term can be effectively eliminated and the SKR can be increased.

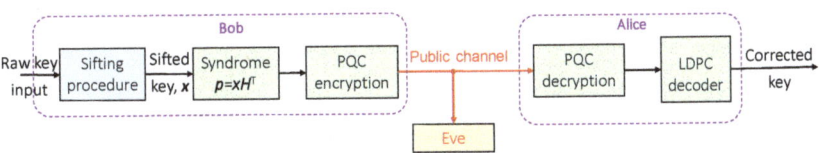

Figure 4. Illustration of post-quantum cryptography-based information reconciliation.

By using this approach, as illustrated in Figure 5, the transmission distance between two nodes in QCN can be significantly extended. Here we provide comparisons of the joint TF-QKD-McEliece encryption scheme against the phase-matching (PM) TF-QKD protocol introduced in [26], the MDI-QKD protocol [6], and the decoy-state-based BB84 protocol [27]. The system parameters are selected as follows: the detector efficiency $\eta_d = 0.25$, reconciliation inefficiency $f_e = 1.15$, the dark count rate $p_d = 8 \times 10^{-8}$, the misalignment error $e_d = 1.5\%$, and the number of phase slices for PM TF-QKD is set to $M = 16$. Regarding the transmission medium, it is assumed that recently reported ultra-low-loss fiber of attenuation 0.1419 dB/km (at 1560 nm) is employed [28]. In the same Figure, the Pirandola–Laurenza–Ottaviani–Banchi (PLOB) bound on a linear key rate is provided as well. Both PM TF-QKD and joint TF-QKD-McEliece encryption schemes outperform the decoy-state BB84 protocol for distances larger than 162 km, while simultaneously outperforming the MDI-QKD protocol for all distances, and exceed the PLOB bound at a distance of 322 km. The PM TF-QKD protocol can achieve the maximum distance of 623 km. The proposed joint TF-QKD-McEliece encryption scheme is able to achieve the distance of even 1127 km, thus significantly outperforming all other schemes. Even though the operating wavelength was 1560 nm, other suitable wavelengths such as 2 µm and 3.9 µm can be used as well.

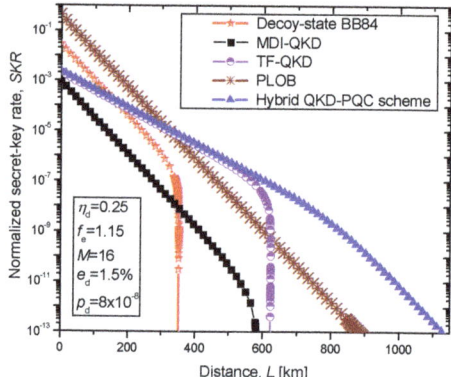

Figure 5. Proposed hybrid QKD-PQC scheme against MDI-QKD and TF-QKD in terms of secret-key rate vs. distance, assuming that ultra-low loss fiber is used.

Now, by connecting the *base stations* to the nodes in the proposed QCNs, we can provide the unconditional security to the 5G+/6G wireless networks. By organizing the base stations in a quantum optical mesh network and employing the proposed hybrid QKD-PQC concept we can provide unconditional security to a large number of users. The Internet of Things (IoT) architecture will comprise widely distributed nodes connected via different types of channels to enable new functionalities in communication, sensing, and computing. Communication security in such a giant network is of paramount importance. Our proposed QCNs will underpin the unconditional physical-layer security of the IoT given that it will allow any two arbitrary nodes to securely transmit data at a high rate via an optical link. Critically, the security of such a network will not rest upon the trusted-node assumption, and a compromised node will not affect the security of other nodes. As such, the proposed QCNs will lead to a substantially stronger security level for the IoT. To enable security for future 6G wireless networks at a reasonable cost, the proposed joint satellite–terrestrial QCN can be based on the Cubesat satellites.

For satellite-to-satellite quantum communications, in addition to the proposed hybrid QKD-PQC concept, it also possible to employ our recent restricted eavesdropping concept [29], which offers a significant increase in SKRs. This concept was presented in the ICTON 2020 paper [30]. Alternatively, the hybrid QKD can also be applied [13].

4. QCN under Development

The terrestrial QCN to be developed at the University of Arizona is shown in Figure 6; it will exploit the existing NSF MRI INQUIRE quantum network, representing the quantum hub (QuHub) to share entangled photons and SPDs among different labs across the campus. The outdoor FSO bidirectional link, connecting the Electrical and Computer Engineering and Optical Sciences buildings, has already been established, with the FSO transceiver shown in Figure 7. We will also create the mesh network as well as the hybrid network composed of mesh, optical star, and ring network segments. The deployed heterogeneous QCNs will allow us to test novel quantum-networking theories and develop experimental tools for counteracting various channel impairments. To deal with atmospheric turbulence effects, the adaptive optics (AO) subsystem, composed of a wavefront sensor (WFS) and deformable mirror will be used. The AO will be combined with adaptive LDPC coding.

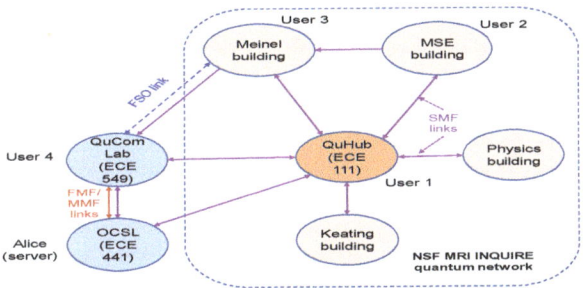

Figure 6. Terrestrial quantum communication network to be developed at the University of Arizona.

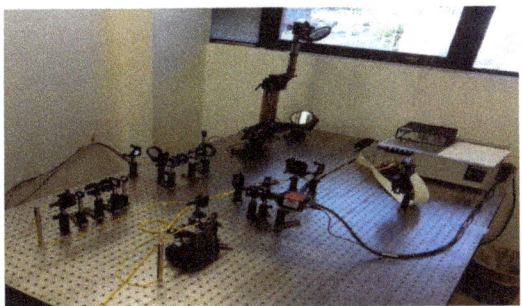

Figure 7. Free-space optical transceiver used in outdoor FSO link.

To provide global coverage, we envision a scenario in which disconnected terrestrial QCNs, such as the one shown in Figure 6, are coupled through the LEO satellite quantum network. We have recently shown that a Bessel–Gaussian (BG) beam, carrying an orbital angular momentum mode, exhibits better tolerance to atmospheric turbulence effects compared to Gaussian beams for distances up to a few kilometers [31]. However, for LEO satellite-to-ground QuCom links, BG beams diffract much faster than Gaussian beams for such long-distance applications. Hence, we need to use pure Bessel beams to overcome this problem, as we have shown in our recent paper [32]. To enable robustness against turbulence encountered by FSO links, the envisioned quantum satellite QCN should communicate to ground nodes only through the LEO satellite-to-ground links, exhibiting a vertical downlink profile through vacuum followed by a turbulence layer with altitude-dependent strength. In principle. MEO/GEO satellite QCNs can be created above LEO QCNs to provide the planetary coverage.

5. Concluding Remarks

To enable the next generation of quantum-enabled cyber security systems, we proposed a quantum network of satellites that will provide the global coverage. The quantum satellite network will be composed of quantum subnetworks comprised of LEO satellites. Some of these LEO satellite-based quantum subnetworks will be connected to a subnetwork of MEO satellites. The MEO satellite subnetworks will then be interconnected to the global network of GEO satellites. The LEO/MEO satellites will also be used to interconnect terrestrial quantum networks. Each quantum communication subnetwork will be based on the cluster state concept. This quantum global network will allow us to establish EPR pairs between any two nodes in the global network. It can also be used to distribute the entangled states for quantum-sensing applications and to enable distributed quantum computing on a global scale.

Funding: This research received no external funding.

Conflicts of Interest: The author declares no conflict of interest.

References

1. Djordjevic, I.B. *Physical-Layer Security and Quantum Key Distribution*; Springer Nature Switzerland: Cham, Switzerland, 2019.
2. Pljonkin, A.P. Features of the Photon Pulse Detection Algorithm in the Quantum Key Distribution System. In Proceedings of the 2017 International Conference on Cryptography, Security and Privacy (ICCSP '17), Wuhan, China, 17–19 March 2017; Association for Computing Machinery: New York, NY, USA, 2017; pp. 81–84. [CrossRef]
3. Pljonkin, A.P. Vulnerability of the synchronization process in the quantum key distribution system. *Int. J. Cloud Appl. Comput.* **2019**, *9*, 4. [CrossRef]
4. Duan, L.-M.; Lukin, M.; Cirac, J.I.; Zoller, P. Long-distance quantum communication with atomic ensembles and linear optics. *Nature* **2001**, *414*, 413–418. [CrossRef]
5. Qiu, J. Quantum communications leap out of the lab. *Nature* **2014**, *508*, 441–442. [CrossRef]
6. Lo, H.-K.; Curty, M.; Qi, B. Measurement-device-independent quantum key distribution. *Phys. Rev. Lett.* **2012**, *108*, 130503. [CrossRef]
7. Lucamarini, M.; Yuan, Z.L.; Dynes, J.F.; Shields, A.J. Overcoming the rate–distance limit of quantum key distribution without quantum repeaters. *Nature* **2018**, *557*, 400–403. [CrossRef]
8. Fossier, S.; Diamanti, E.; Debuisschert, T.; Tualle-Brouri, R.; Grangier, P. Improvement of continuous-variable quantum key distribution systems by using optical preamplifiers. *J. Phys. B* **2009**, *42*, 114014. [CrossRef]
9. Qu, Z.; Djordjevic, I.B. Four-dimensionally multiplexed eight-state continuous-variable quantum key distribution over turbulent channels. *IEEE Photonics J.* **2017**, *9*, 7600408. [CrossRef]
10. Ralph, T.C. Continuous variable quantum cryptography. *Phys. Rev. A* **1999**, *61*, 010303. [CrossRef]
11. Djordjevic, I.B. On the Discretized Gaussian Modulation (DGM)-based Continuous Variable-QKD. *IEEE Access* **2019**, *7*, 65342–65346. [CrossRef]
12. Djordjevic, I.B. Optimized-Eight-State CV-QKD Protocol Outperforming Gaussian Modulation Based Protocols. *IEEE Photonics J.* **2019**, *11*, 4500610. [CrossRef]
13. Djordjevic, I.B. Hybrid QKD Protocol Outperforming both DV- and CV-QKD Protocols. *IEEE Photonics J.* **2020**, *12*, 7600108. [CrossRef]
14. Bernstein, D.J.; Buchmann, J.; Dahmen, E. *Post-Quantum Cryptography*; Springer: Berlin, Germany, 2009.
15. Elliott, C.; Colvin, A.; Pearson, D.; Pikalo, O.; Schlafer, J.; Yeh, H. Current status of the DARPA quantum network (Invited Paper). In Proceedings of the SPIE 5815, Quantum Information and Computation III, Defense and Security, Orlando, FL, USA, 25 May 2005.
16. Sasaki, M.; Fujiwara, M.; Ishizuka, H.; Klaus, W.; Wakui, K.; Takeoka, M.; Miki, S.; Yamashita, T.; Wang, Z.; Tanaka, A.; et al. Field test of quantum key distribution in the Tokyo QKD Network. *Opt. Express* **2011**, *19*, 10387–10409. [CrossRef] [PubMed]
17. Alléaume, R.; Branciard, C.; Bouda, J.; Debuisschert, T.; Dianati, M.; Gisin, N.; Godfrey, M.; Grangier, P.; Länger, T.; Lütkenhaus, N.; et al. Using quantum key distribution for cryptographic purposes. *J. Theor. Comput. Sci.* **2014**, *560*, 62–81. [CrossRef]
18. Nagayama, S.; Van Meter, R. Internet-Draft: IKE for IPsec with QKD. 2009. Available online: https://tools.ietf.org/html/draft-nagayama-ipsecme-ipsec-with-qkd-01 (accessed on 28 July 2020).
19. Mink, A.; Frankel, S.; Perlner, R. Quantum Key Distribution (QKD) and Commodity Security Protocols: Introduction and Integration. *Intern. J. Netw. Secur. Appl.* **2009**, *1*, 101–112.
20. Yin, J.; Cao, Y.; Li, Y.H.; Liao, S.K.; Zhang, L.; Ren, J.G.; Cai, W.Q.; Liu, W.Y.; Li, B.; Dai, H.; et al. Satellite-based entanglement distribution over 1200 kilometers. *Science* **2017**, *356*, 1140–1144. [CrossRef] [PubMed]
21. Dequal, D.; Vallone, G.; Bacco, D.; Gaiarin, S.; Luceri, V.; Bianco, G.; Villoresi, P. Experimental single-photon exchange along a space link of 7000 km. *Phys. Rev. A* **2016**, *93*, 010301. [CrossRef]

22. Briegel, H.J. Cluster States. In *Compendium of Quantum Physics*; Greenberger, D., Hentschel, K., Weinert, F., Eds.; Springer: Berlin/Heidelberg, Germany, 2009; pp. 96–105.
23. Gilbert, G.; Hamrick, M.; Weinstein, Y.S. Efficient construction of photonic quantum-computational clusters. *Phys. Rev. A* **2006**, *73*, 064303. [CrossRef]
24. Baldi, M.; Bianchi, M.; Chiaraluce, F. Security and complexity of the McEliece cryptosystem based on QC LDPC codes. *IET Inf. Secur.* **2013**, *7*, 212–220. [CrossRef]
25. Sun, X.; Zou, D.; Qu, Z.; Djordjevic, I.B. Run-time reconfigurable adaptive LDPC coding for optical channels. *Opt. Express* **2018**, *26*, 29319–29329. [CrossRef]
26. Ma, X.; Zeng, P.; Zhou, H. Phase-matching quantum key distribution. *Phys. Rev. X* **2018**, *8*, 031043. [CrossRef]
27. Lo, H.-K.; Ma, X.; Chen, K. Decoy state quantum key distribution. *Phys. Rev. Lett.* **2005**, *94*, 230504. [CrossRef] [PubMed]
28. Tamura, Y.; Sakuma, H.; Morita, K.; Suzuki, M.; Yamamoto, Y.; Shimada, K.; Honma, Y.; Sohma, K.; Fujii, T.; Hasegawa, T.; et al. The First 0.14-dB/km loss optical fiber and its impact on submarine transmission. *J. Lightw. Technol.* **2018**, *36*, 44–49. [CrossRef]
29. Pan, Z.; Seshadreesan, K.P.; Clark, W.; Adcock, M.R.; Djordjevic, I.B.; Shapiro, J.H.; Guha, S. Secret Key Distillation over a Pure Loss Quantum Wiretap Channel under Restricted Eavesdropping. In Proceedings of the 2019 IEEE International Symposium on Information Theory (ISIT 2019), Paris, France, 7–12 July 2019; pp. 3032–3036.
30. Pan, Z.; Djordjevic, I.B. Security of Satellite-Based CV-QKD under Realistic Assumptions. In Proceedings of the 22nd International Conference on Transparent Optical Networks ICTON 2020, Bari, Italy, 19–23 July 2020.
31. Wang, T.-L.; Gariano, J.; Djordjevic, I.B. Employing Bessel-Gaussian Beams to Improve Physical-Layer Security in Free-Space Optical Communications. *IEEE Photonics J.* **2018**, *10*, 7907113. [CrossRef]
32. Wang, T.-L.; Djordjevic, I.B.; Nagel, J. Laser Beam Propagation Effects on Secure Key Rates for Satellite-to-Ground Discrete Modulation CV-QKD. *Appl. Opt.* **2019**, *58*, 8061–8068. [CrossRef]

© 2020 by the author. Licensee MDPI, Basel, Switzerland. This article is an open access article distributed under the terms and conditions of the Creative Commons Attribution (CC BY) license (http://creativecommons.org/licenses/by/4.0/).

Article

Improving Underwater Continuous-Variable Measurement-Device-Independent Quantum Key Distribution via Zero-Photon Catalysis

Yuang Wang [1,†], Shanhua Zou [1,2,*,†], Yun Mao [1] and Ying Guo [1,2,3,*]

1. School of Automation, Central South University, Changsha 410083, China; wya1759991046@gmail.com (Y.W.); maocsu@sina.com (Y.M.)
2. School of Internet of Things Engineering, Wuxi Taihu University, Wuxi 214064, China
3. State Key Laboratory of Advanced Optical Communication Systems and Networks, Shanghai Jiao Tong University, Shanghai 200240, China
* Correspondence: 000037@wxu.edu.cn (S.Z.); yingguo@csu.edu.cn (Y.G.)
† These authors contributed equally to this work.

Received: 27 March 2020; Accepted: 16 May 2020; Published: 19 May 202

Abstract: Underwater quantum key distribution (QKD) is tough but important for modern underwater communications in an insecure environment. It can guarantee secure underwater communication between submarines and enhance safety for critical network nodes. To enhance the performance of continuous-variable quantum key distribution (CVQKD) underwater in terms of maximal transmission distance and secret key rate as well, we adopt measurement-device-independent (MDI) quantum key distribution with the zero-photon catalysis (ZPC) performed at the emitter of one side, which is the ZPC-based MDI-CVQKD. Numerical simulation shows that the ZPC-involved scheme, which is a Gaussian operation in essence, works better than the single photon subtraction (SPS)-involved scheme in the extreme asymmetric case. We find that the transmission of the ZPC-involved scheme is longer than that of the SPS-involved scheme. In addition, we consider the effects of temperature, salinity and solar elevation angle on the system performance in pure seawater. The maximal transmission distance decreases with the increase of temperature and the decrease of sunlight elevation angle, while it changes little over a broad range of salinity.

Keywords: continuous-variable quantum key distribution; measurement device independent; zero-photon catalysis; underwater channel

---

1. Introduction

Quantum key distribution (QKD) [1–3] is a key part of quantum communications. There are two categories of protocols, that is, the discrete-variable (DV) QKD protocol [4,5] and the continuous variable (CV) QKD protocol [6–8]. DVQKD, which was proposed in 1984 with the proposal of Bennett-Brassard 1984 (BB84) [9], codes on different states of a single photon to convey information. Currently, it has gotten fully developed and has been experimented in free space, optical fiber, and so forth. However, DVQKD can be easily interfered by various factors such as background noise light and noise from components. Besides, because single-photon source is quite hard to realize even nowadays, people use attenuating laser sources for substitution, which could exert bad effects on secret key rate. Fortunately, two decades after BB84 was proposed, CVQKD was born, which was based on the continuity of quantum eigenstate and modulates information on continuous variable of quantum such as phase and amplitude for communications. Compared with DVQKD, CVQKD can automatically filter background noise light with simple light source at the same time. Subsequently, CVQKD is compatible with contemporary optical communication system, which makes it a hot topic in QKD realm quickly. Moreover, in terms of measurement devices, CVQKD relies on homodyne or heterodyne detectors, which are more efficient to achieve higher secret key rates than single-photon detectors. Of course, CVQKD is still imperfect. There exist disadvantages like short transmission distance, but these defects are being overcome by advancing technology.

Currently, there have been several CVQKD protocols in terms of system model, such as the point-to-point (PP) CVQKD and measurement-device-independent [10,11] (MDI) CVQKD [12]. PP-CVQKD, as literally interpreted, is conducted between two parties, Alice and Bob, directly. It is vulnerable to attacks aimed at detector imperfection. However, in MDI-CVQKD, Alice and Bob first prepare and transmit coherent states to the third party Charlie. Subsequently, Charlie interferes the received states to make Bell measurement and announces measurement results publicly. Finally, the secret key can be shared between Alice and Bob after post-processing. Compared with PP-CVQKD, MDI-CVQKD is born to solve the flaw of detector imperfection. It can resist side-channel attacks such as the local oscillator calibration attack [13], the wavelength attack [14], and the detector saturation attack [15].

At present, CVQKD is always conducted through free space and fiber channel, both of which are meaningful but challenging. Light transmission in air channel can be disturbed by natural environment like atmospheric turbulence [16–18], rain, fog, sunlight, and so forth. Fiber channel seems immune to external disturbance, but it is difficult to be wired up and could be easily destroyed. Underwater CVQKD may be more meaningful than air or fiber channel in a sense. Common QKD methods for two underwater vehicles nowadays are using periscopes and satellite link. However, these methods require underwater vehicles to rise to the sea surface. Fortunately, CVQKD can be feasibly implemented through underwater channel in practice, which provide a more convenient scheme for underwater vehicles to communicate safely. However, the realization of underwater CVQKD is more difficult considering attenuation caused by ocean current, molecular impact, microorganism, scattering, and so forth. These factors could exert adverse effects on entanglement between quantum, thus leading to short transmission distance. In what follows, we consider something different as the effects of temperature, salinity and sun elevation angle.

Recently, there have been several works for QKD underwater. For example, John proposed the underwater BB84 protocol using pairs of polarization entangled photons [19]. Bouchard suggested a high dimensional BB84 protocol with twisted photons in outdoor conditions [20]. After that Ruan proposed a method to estimate parameters to improve CVQKD performance [21]. However, the implementation of MDI-QKD underwater has been waiting for some researches to fill the gaps. Note that despite the absolute device security of MDI-QKD, its transmission distance is unsatisfactory, and thus it is difficult to be implemented in harsh environments like seawater. Fortunately, to lengthen the transmission distance, the non-Gaussian operations [22] like single photon subtraction (SPS) [23] and zero-photon catalysis (ZPC) [24] are the most commonly used means. One article has put forward a plan of operating single photon subtraction (SPS) in the fiber-based CVQKD [25]. In this paper, we dedicate to lengthen the transmission distance of underwater CVQKD via the Gaussian operations. Motivated by the characteristics of noiseless attenuation, we perform the zero-photon catalysis, which can keep the Gaussian behavior of photon to prolong the maximal transmission distance of the CVQKD system underwater with the achievable high secret key rate.

This paper is structured as follows. In Section 2, we propose the ZPC-based MDI-CVQKD for underwater secure communication. In Section 3, we show the performance improvement of the ZPC-based scheme by using numerical simulations. Finally, a conclusion is drawn in Section 4.

2. The ZPC-Based MDI-CVQKD Protocol

In this section, we suggest the ZPC-based MDI-CVQKD system through underwater channel. Due to the equivalence of prepare-and-measure (PM) scheme and entanglement-based (EB) scheme, we consider the EB ZPC-involved scheme to simplify the security proof of the underwater MDI-CVQKD system.

Figure 1 shows the schematic diagram of the EB ZPC-involved scheme. In this scheme, Alice in deep water aims to establish a secret channel with Bob in shallow water. Note that Alice and Bob may not locate in the same vertical area. For the convenience of demonstration, we suppose that Alice is vertically below Bob, and the transmission distance turns into depth. First, Alice and Bob prepare entanglement resource EPR1 and EPR2 with variances V_A and V_B, respectively. Then, they keep modes A_1 and B_1, and send other modes A_2 and B_2 to an untrusted party Charlie through water channel. To simplify equipment, we assume that the ZPC operation is conducted by David on Alice's side, which turns mode A_2 into mode $\widetilde{A_2}$. After that, Charlie receives modes $\widetilde{A_2}$ and B_2, and performs BSM (Bell state measurement)-based detection and announces measurement results P_{C_2} and X_{C_1} publicly through a classical channel. Ultimately, Bob modifies mode B_1 to mode $\widetilde{B_1}$ through operation $D(\alpha)$, where $D(\alpha)$ is a displacement operation. In this way, Alice and Bob obtain two mode A_1, $\widetilde{B_1}$ for heterodyne detection to get data (X_A, P_A) and (X_B, P_B), which can be used for estimation of channel parameter, coordinate information, and so forth. After series of post-processing, secret key will be achieved successfully.

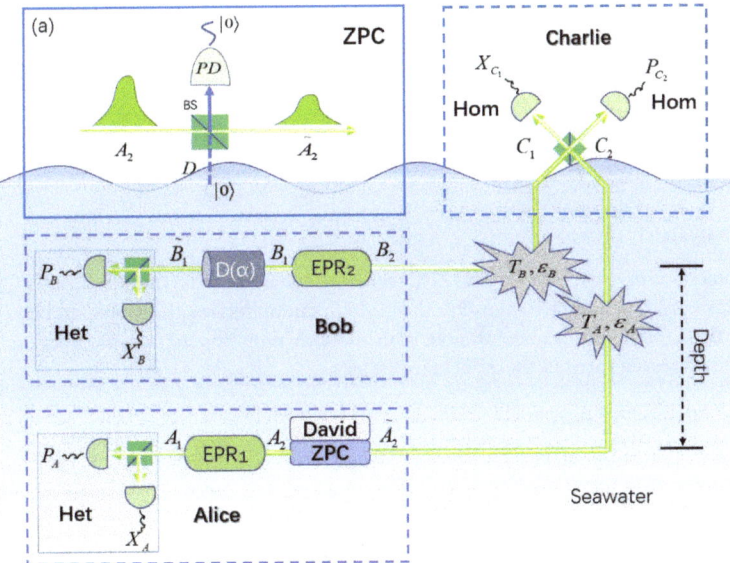

Figure 1. Schematic diagram of the zero-photon catalysis (ZPC) based measurement-device-independent-continuous-variable quantum key distribution (MDI-CVQKD) through underwater channel. Hom: homodyne detection, Het: heterodyne detection, PD: photon detector, BS: beam splitter.

As for the ZPC-involved data-processing shown in Figure 1 (a), vacuum state in auxiliary mode D is injected into an input port of beam splitter (BS) with transmittance T, which is detected at the corresponding output port of BS at the same time. That is exactly the ZPC operation. This process is usually represented by an equivalent operator given by

$$\hat{O}_0 \equiv Tr[B(T) \prod_{\text{off}} \hat{}] = {}_D\langle 0| B(T) |0\rangle_D, \tag{1}$$

where $B(T)$ is the operator representing BS with transmittance T and can be described as

$$B(T) = \exp[\sqrt{T} - 1)(a_2^\dagger a_2 + d^\dagger d) + (d^\dagger a_2 - d a_2^\dagger)\sqrt{1-T}], \tag{2}$$

and $\hat{\prod}_{\text{off}}$ is the projection operator in photon detector(PD), which here is an on/off detector. Now we consider how the ZPC operation makes effect. State EPR1 is essentially a two-mode squeezed vacuum state, which can be expressed as

$$|EPR_1\rangle_{A_1A_2} = S_2(r)|0,0\rangle_{A_1A_2}$$
$$= \sqrt{1-\lambda^2}\sum_{l=0}^{\infty}\lambda^l|l,l\rangle_{A_1A_2}, \quad (3)$$

where $\lambda = \sqrt{(V_A-1)(V_A+1)}$. After conducting the ZPC operation, this state turns into $|\psi\rangle_{A_1\widetilde{A_2}}$, which can be described as

$$|\psi\rangle_{A_1\widetilde{A_2}} = \frac{\hat{O}_0}{\sqrt{P_d}}|EPR_1\rangle_{A_1A_2}, \quad (4)$$

where $P_d = 2/(1+T+(1-T)V_A)$, standing for the success probability of the ZPC operation. Subsequently, the covariance matrix of $|\psi\rangle_{A_1\widetilde{A_2}}$ can be calculated as

$$V_{A_1\widetilde{A_2}} = \begin{pmatrix} x\prod & z\sigma_z \\ z\sigma_z & y\prod \end{pmatrix}, \quad (5)$$

where $\sigma_z = \text{diag}(1,-1)$, $x = y = (2V_A - RV_A + R)/(1+T+RV_A)$, and $z = 2\sqrt{T(V_A^2-1)}/(1+T+RV_A)$. We note that the above-mentioned ZPC operation is actually a Gaussian operation in essence, which have an effect on the performance of the underwater CVQKD system.

3. Security Analysis

While demonstrating the effect of the ZPC-involved scheme on the underwater CVQKD system, we consider transmittance of seawater channel, which characterizes the transparency of seawater, thus affecting the ability of light transmission, which is shown in Appendix A. Subsequently, we show the performance improvement of the ZPC-based system.

3.1. Derivation of the Secret Key Rate

As shown in Figure 2, we have an equivalent point-to-point (PP) protocol of the underwater ZPC-based MDI-CVQKD. It should be noticed that the reasonableness of this equivalence has been proved [26]. Thus we use T_c and ε_{th} to represent the transmittance and excess noise of the PP CVQKD protocol given by

$$T_c = g^2 T_A/2, \quad (6)$$

and

$$\varepsilon_{th} = T_B/T_A(\varepsilon_B - 2) + \varepsilon_A + 2/T_A. \quad (7)$$

Taking into account the noise caused by Charlie's imperfect detection, the whole channel noise can be expressed as

$$\chi_{tot} = 1 - T_c/T_c + \varepsilon_{th} + 2\chi_{\text{hom}}/T_A, \quad (8)$$

with $\chi_{\text{hom}} = (\nu_{el}+1-\eta)/\eta$, where ν_{el} stands for electronic noise and η stands for quantum efficiency. The transmittance $T_{A(B)}$ of seawater channel can be expressed as

$$T_{A(B)} = e^{-\alpha(\lambda)D_{AC(BC)}}, \quad (9)$$

where $\alpha(\lambda)$ means attenuation coefficient shown in Appendix A.

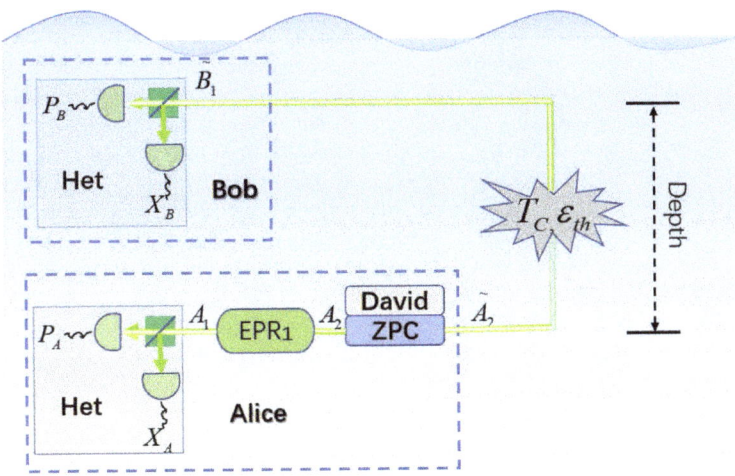

Figure 2. Schematic diagram of the ZPC-based point-to-point (PP) CVQKD system.

Different from non-Gaussian operation, after performing ZPC, the resulting state $|\psi\rangle_{A_1\widetilde{A_2}}$ is still a Gaussian state, thus it is reasonable to derive the secret key rate directly from the conventional Gaussian CVQKD given by

$$K = P_d\{(\beta I(A:B)) - \chi(B:E)\}, \tag{10}$$

where β means the reverse-reconciliation efficiency, $I(A:B)$ represents the mutual information between Alice and Bob, and $\chi(B:E)$ denotes the Holevo bound between Bob and Eve. Assuming $|\psi\rangle_{A_1\widetilde{B_1}}$ denotes the state when $|\psi\rangle_{A_1\widetilde{A_2}}$ passes through the channel in the equivalent PP CVQKD protocol, the covariance matrix of $|\psi\rangle_{A_1\widetilde{B_1}}$ can be described as

$$V_{A_1\widetilde{B_1}} = \begin{pmatrix} X\Pi & Z\sigma_z \\ Z\sigma_z & Y\Pi \end{pmatrix}$$
$$= \begin{pmatrix} x\Pi & \sqrt{T_c}z\sigma_z \\ \sqrt{T_c}z\sigma_z & T_c(x+\chi_{tot})\Pi \end{pmatrix}. \tag{11}$$

Then, $I(A:B)$ can be calculated as

$$I(A:B) = \log_2 \frac{(X+1)(Y+1)}{(X+1)(Y+1)-Z^2}. \tag{12}$$

To calculate $\chi(B:E)$, we assume Eve is aware of David's existence and can purify the whole system $\rho_{A_1\widetilde{B_1}ED}$. Based on this, $\chi(B:E)$ can be described as

$$\chi(B:E) = S(E) - S(E|B)$$
$$= \sum_{i=1}^{2} G(\tfrac{\lambda_i-1}{2}) - G(\tfrac{\lambda_3-1}{2}), \tag{13}$$

where $G(x) = (x+1)\log_2(x+1) - x\log_2 x$, representing the von Neumann entropy, and $\lambda_{1,2}^2 = (\Delta \pm \sqrt{\Delta^2 - 4\omega^2})/2$ with $\omega = XY - Z^2$ and $\Delta = X^2 + Y^2 - 2Z^2$.

3.2. Numerical Simulations

In the following, we show the performance improvement of the ZPC-based MDI-CVQKD in terms of the maximal transmission distance and the secret key rate as well, compared with the SPS-based MDI-CVQKD and the traditional MDI-CVQKD.

In numerical simulations of the secret key rate of the ZPC-based MDI-CVQKD, we set $D_{BC} = 0$, which is the asymmetric case that achieves the longest transmission distance. Moreover, we take into account $\varepsilon_A = \varepsilon_B = 0.01$, $\beta = 0.96$, $\eta = 1$, and $v_{el} = 0$. First of all, we consider the influence of the tunable variance V_A and V_B, where V_A and V_B are significant to system, as shown in Figure 3. For the simplicity, we set $V_A = V_B$. We find that the traditional scheme is sensitive to $V_A(V_B)$, whereas the SPS-based and ZPC-based schemes show the stable transmission depth even when $V_A(V_B)$ changes in a big range in Figure 3a. In addition, the secret key rate decreases fast with the increase of $V_A(V_B)$, as shown in Figure 3b. By contrast, the secret key rate of the other two schemes decrease slowly with the increase of $V_A(V_B)$. This result shows that the ZPC-based and SPS-based schemes have a more flexible application in the underwater CVQKD system.

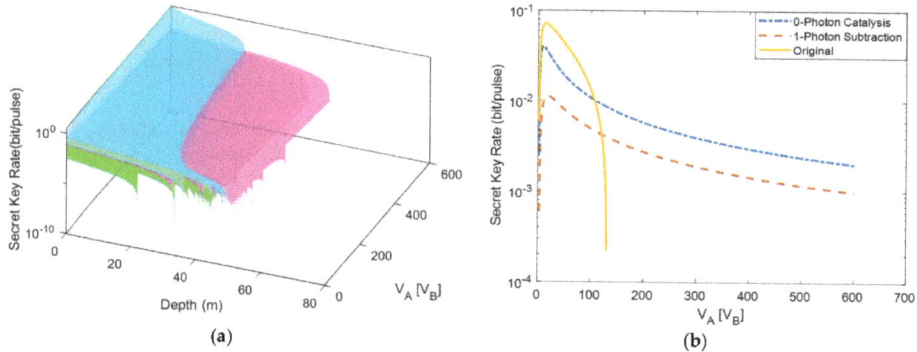

Figure 3. (a) The secret key rate as a function of V_A (V_B) for the traditional scheme (blue surface) and the ZPC-based (magenta surface) and the single photon subtraction (SPS)-based scheme (green surface). (b) A cross section of (a) where depth is set to 30 m for the traditional (yellow), the ZPC-based (blue), and the SPS-based (red).

Note that in practical system, the performance of CVQKD is related to the perfection of components. For example, the Faraday-mirror, which is used for adjusting the polarization angle of signal, is quite sensitive to the rotation angle. The rotation angle should be set as $45°$ accurately to make the polarization angles of signal and local oscillator orthogonal. However, in practice, the rotation angle could not be perfectly set, thus leading to the decrease of secret key rate, especially when transmittance T is small. Fortunately, increasing variance appropriately can provide us an efficient ploy to make up for the defects [27].

In Figure 4, we illustrate the performance of the related schemes in terms of the secret key rate and the maximal transmission depth under different variance. From Figure 4a, when variance V_A (V_B) is small, both underwater ZPC-based and SPS-based schemes show no obvious advantages in terms of depth compared with the condition on land. For the SPS-based scheme, it reaches the longest depth at about 43 m, which is close to that of the traditional scheme. For the ZPC-based scheme, it has the longest transmission distance of 50 m. This phenomenon may be caused by the small transmittance in the sea. Due to the small transmittance of seawater, the secret key rate of all three schemes comes to zero fast, thus giving fewer chances for the SPS-based scheme and ZPC-based scheme to show distance advantages. However, In Figure 4b, it shows a different result. When variance V_A (V_B) is increased, the longest distance of traditional scheme decreases to 30 m, while the performance of the SPS-based and ZPC-based schemes maintain stable. It seems that for the increased modulation variance the SPS-based and ZPC-based schemes show better performance than the traditional protocol, of which the ZPC operation works better. Moreover, it also shows that for the high modulation variance, the ZPC-based scheme is the best among the three schemes discussed above.

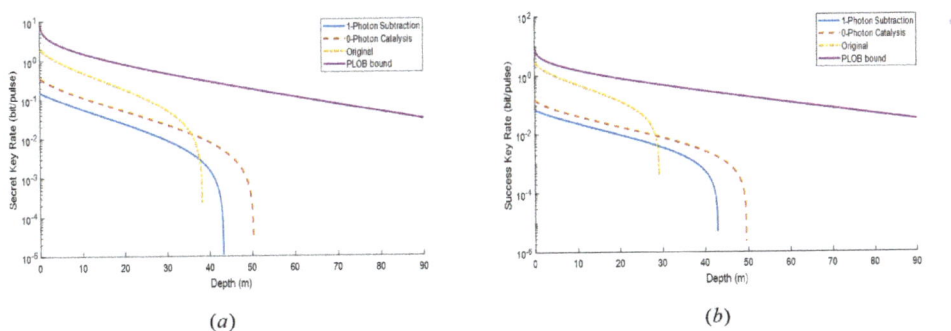

Figure 4. The secret key rate of the MDI-CVQKD system under pure seawater via the ZPC-based scheme, the SPS-based scheme, and the traditional scheme. $T(SPS) = 0.9$. The purple line represents PLOB [28] bound. (**a**). $V_A = V_B = 40$. (**b**). $V_A = V_B = 150$.

To show the advantages of the ZPC-based scheme over the SPS-based scheme, we plot the secret key rate as a function of transmittance (T) of beam splitter (BS) and depth. As shown in Figure 5, the ZPC-based scheme has apparent advantages in terms of both secret key rate and depth compared with the SPS-based scheme. Besides, from this figure, we can get the optimal transmittance (T) of both two schemes. We find that the optimal transmittance (T) is 0.75 for the ZPC-based scheme and 0.72 for the SPS-based scheme. This result proves that the ZPC operation does improve system performance and works better than the SPS operation.

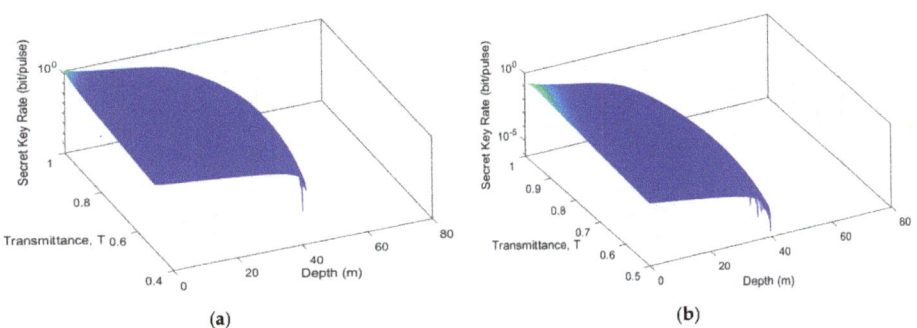

Figure 5. The secret key rate of the MDI-CVQKD system under pure seawater for $V_A = V_B = 40$. (**a**) the ZPC-based scheme, (**b**) the SPS-based scheme.

Subsequently, we consider effects of factors of pure sea water on the ZPC-based MDI-CVQKD system. First of all, we consider the effects of temperature in Figure 6. It shows that the transmission depth changes by about 5 m when the temperature ranges from 0 °C to 40 °C. It seems that the colder the seawater means the better the performance. This characteristic is easily to be comprehended since colder seawater means weaker thermal movement of molecular, thus leading to weaker influence on the performance of the underwater CVQKD system. It should be noticed that this range of change is possible, considering differences in seasons, time in a day and geographical location.

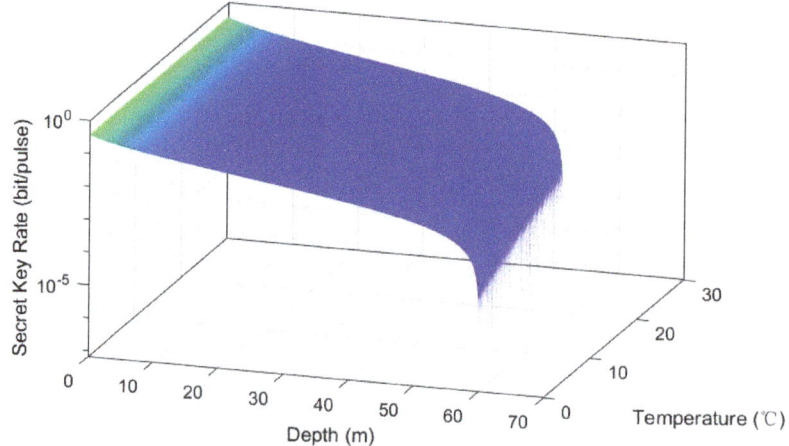

Figure 6. Relationship among secret key rate, transmission depth and temperature for $V_A = V_B = 40$.

Figure 7 shows the effects of sun elevation angle. Here we consider the influence that sunlight exerts on transmittance and omit the influence on the excess noise. The reason for this simplification is based on the assumption that the photon detector is ideal and not affected by background light. It is shown that depth lengthens by about 15 m when the sun elevation angle changes from 70° to 20°. Therefore, we could deduce that the underwater CVQKD system has the best performance around midday and has the worst performance at dusk. This result is quite different from the situation of CVQKD in free space, transmittance of which has little relationship to background light while background noise is influenced profoundly by background solar light.

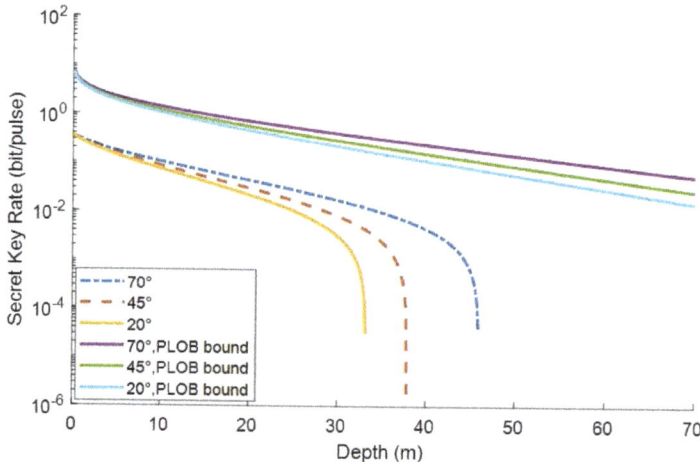

Figure 7. Secret key rate of the ZPC-based MDI-CVQKD in oligotrophic seawater under different sun elevation angle for $V_A = V_B = 40$. The upper three lines represent PLOB bound corresponding different sun elevation angle.

From simulation above, we can find that even if ZPC operation improves the performance of CV-MDI-QKD to some extent, our scheme is still constrained by transmission distance compared with conditions in fiber and open air, which is secure up to at least 100 km. However, its flexibility compared with fiber allows it to become the next generation of optical switch underwater. For example, it can be used as a non-contact optical switch to establish secure net for underwater vehicles. Besides, it can be applied to optical communication system for autonomous underwater robots [29] and remote underwater robot operation [30]. Moreover, the development of underwater wireless optical communication (UWOC) provides another chance for our scheme. Recently, Sun verified the operation of UWOC at tens of gigabits per second or close to a hundred meters of distance [31]. With the help of our proposed scheme, UWOC will be safer and more credible.

4. Conclusions

We have proposed a ZPC-involved scheme for strengthening the security of the underwater MDI-CVQKD system in terms of the secret key rate and the maximal transmission depth. This scheme aims to establish a potential underwater MDI-CVQKD channel between two underwater parties. We consider the influence that the ZPC operation exerts on the MDI-CVQKD system and derive the secret key rate. To make it more persuasive, we compare the ZPC-involved scheme with the SPS-involved and traditional schemes as well. Numerical simulations show that the ZPC-involved scheme has better performance, prolonging the transmission depth by about 5 m. We find that the ZPC-involved scheme shows better performance obviously when the tunable modulation variance is set high. Besides, we consider the possible factors influencing our proposed method. It is found that temperature has a relatively considerable impact on transmission depth while salinity is not an important factor in terms of the maximal transmission depth and the secret key rate. In addition, sun elevation angle influences the system performance to some extent as well, which implies that the performance of the underwater CVQKD system may be changeable with different time.

Author Contributions: Conceptualization, writing–traditional draft preparation, Y.W. and Y.M.; software and validation, Y.M.; formal analysis, Y.W. and Y.M.; Data curation, S.Z.; supervision, Y.G. All authors have read and agreed to the published version of the manuscript.

Funding: This work is supported by the National Natural Science Foundation of China (Grant No. 61871407).

Conflicts of Interest: The authors declare no conflict of interest.

Abbreviations

The following abbreviations are used in this manuscript:

QKD	Quantum key Distribution
DVQKD	Discrete-variable Quantum key Distribution
CVQKD	Continuous-variable Quantum key Distribution
MDI	Measurement-device-independent
TMSV	Two-mode squeezed vacuum
SPS	Single-photon subtraction
ZPC	Zero-photon catalysis
EB	Entanglement-based
PM	Prepare- and-measure
Het	Heterodyne detection
Hom	Homodyne detection
BS	Beam splitter

Appendix A. A: Seawater Channel

Usually, transmittance is a function of distance (here means depth) D and attenuation coefficient $\alpha(\lambda)$. Since the transmission distance of light in seawater is short, seawater channel could be regarded as a linear attenuation model, which can be expressed as

$$T_{sea} = e^{-\alpha(\lambda)D}, \quad (A1)$$

where $\alpha(\lambda)$ is related to wavelength λ. In seawater, the blue-green light (450 nm < λ < 550 nm) has the smallest attenuation coefficient. For the performance improvement, we use 520 nm laser in numerical simulations. The attenuation coefficient $\alpha(\lambda)$ is affected by absorption and scattering [32,33]. Absorption, as it is literally comprehended, means irreversible energy loss of light caused by the interaction of photons and particles, which is a kind of electromagnetic action. However, scattering is a purely physical collision process happening between photons and particles, which just changes the direction of photon movement and does not cause energy degradation. Involving these two factors, the expression of $\alpha(\lambda)$ can be written as

$$\alpha(\lambda) = a(\lambda) + b(\lambda), \tag{A2}$$

where $a(\lambda)$ is absorption coefficient and $b(\lambda)$ is scattering coefficient. More specifically, the parameters $a(\lambda)$ and $b(\lambda)$ consist the effects of seawater and other particles given by [34]

$$a(\lambda) = a_w(\lambda) + a_{CDOM}(\lambda) + a_{phy}(\lambda) + a_{det}(\lambda), \tag{A3}$$

and

$$b(\lambda) = b_w(\lambda) + b_{phy}(\lambda) + b_{det}(\lambda), \tag{A4}$$

where w means pure sea water, $CDOM$ means colored dissolved organic matter, phy means plankton, and det means detritus. Consequently, it is impossible to calculate all impact factors. However, researchers have demonstrated some effects of factors such as chlorophyll, bubbles, and salt, providing us valuable experience. In fact, besides the above-mentioned factors, temperature and sunlight could have potential impacts on $\alpha(\lambda)$ as well. Therefore, we will further consider the mixing effects of temperature and salinity, and the effects of sun elevation angle in the following part of this section. Since the factors we consider have little effects on impurity not belonging to seawater, our security analysis is based on pure seawater.

Appendix A.1. Mixing Effects of Temperature and Salinity

In what follows, we consider the effect of temperature and salinity on the ZPC-based MDI-CVQKD in pure seawater environment. Then the attenuation coefficient α can be simplified to

$$\alpha = a_w + b_w, \tag{A5}$$

where a_w stands for absorption coefficient of seawater and b_w stands for scattering coefficient. Moreover, b_w contains two parts, the fluctuation of the density of pure water (b_{wd}) and the electro shrinkage effect of hydrated ions (b_{we}) given by

$$b_w = b_{we} + b_{wd}, \tag{A6}$$

where b_{we} and b_{wd} can be respectively expressed as

$$b_{we} = \frac{64\pi^5 N R^6 (2+\delta)}{3\lambda^4 (1+\delta)} \left(\frac{\varepsilon_{wa} - \varepsilon_{pw}}{\varepsilon_{wa} + 2\varepsilon_{pw}}\right)^2, \tag{A7}$$

$$b_{wd} = \frac{8\pi^3}{\lambda^4} \left(\rho \frac{\partial n^2}{\partial \rho}\right)^2 k\tau\beta h(\delta), \tag{A8}$$

where λ is light wavelength, N is number of ions in unit volume, δ is solution depolarization, n is the refractive index of pure water, k is Boltzmann constant, β is isothermal compressibility, τ is absolute temperature, ρ is seawater density, R represents hydration radius [35], ε_{wa} and ε_{pw} represent the average dielectric constant of the hydrated ions and the average dielectric constant of pure water respectively, and $h(\delta) = (2+\delta)/(7-7\delta)$. In addition, we take into account $\varepsilon_{pw} = n_w^2$, and $\varepsilon_{wa} = \varepsilon_{hw}(R^3 - r^3)/r^3 + \varepsilon_i r^3/R^3$, where r represents the effective radius of ions [36], ε_i is the Dielectric constant of ions, ε_{hw} denotes the Dielectric constant of water in the first hydrated layer. Both ε_i and ε_{hw} can be obtained from Clausius-Mossotti equation [37].

In Equation (12), it shows that the increase of N (number of ions in unit volume) will lead to the increase of b_{we}, whereas the increase of salinity will lead to the decrease of b_{wd}, as shown in Equation (13). Besides, the increase of temperature will cause the increase of b_{wd}. In reality, it is analyzed that b_{we} acts as the main factor affecting b_w because the increase of salinity also causes the increase of b_w, the trend of which is similar to that of b_{we}. However, b_{we} is quite small and is slightly influenced by salinity [38]. Therefore, we ignore the effect of b_w on the CVQKD system while deriving the secret key rate. Note that the scattering coefficient b_w is also negligible compared with the absorption coefficient a_w in terms of temperature [39].

Therefore, the change of total attenuation coefficient α with temperature and salinity mainly reflects the change of absorption coefficient a_w with temperature and salinity, and the change of attenuation coefficient and absorption coefficient is consistent. Note that the effect of temperature on absorption coefficient in seawater can be expressed as [40]

$$a_w(\lambda, T, S) = a_w(\lambda, T_0, 0) + \psi_S S + \psi_T (T - T_0), \tag{A9}$$

where T and T_0 mean real-time temperature and initial temperature respectively, S means salinity, ψ_S and ψ_T stand for linear salinity slope and temperature slope, respectively. From analysis all above, we obtain the expression of transmittance in pure seawater

$$T_{puresea} = e^{-[a_w(\lambda, T_0, 0) + \psi_S S + \psi_T (T - T_0)]D}. \tag{A10}$$

To show the mixing effects of temperature and salinity visually, we simulate in the pure seawater environment, where attenuation coefficient α is around 0.04. Note that according to Reference [40], when λ = 520 nm, $\psi_S = -0.00002$ and $\psi_T = 0.0002$ for seawater respectively. In Figure A1, we find that temperature has a great influence on the attenuation coefficient α. Specifically, the attenuation coefficient α increases by 0.008 when temperature changes from 0 °C to 40 °C. However, salinity has little influence on the attenuation coefficient α. The range of 40 PSU brings no significant changes.

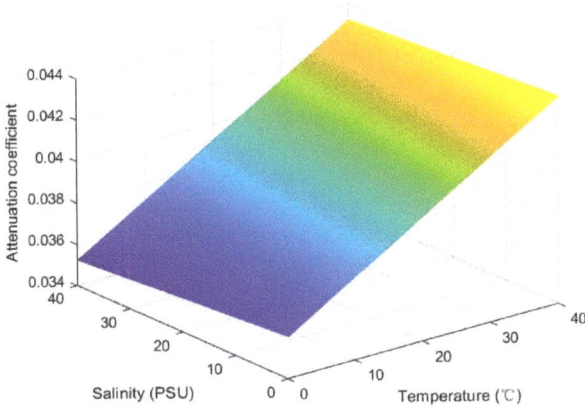

Figure A1. Effects of temperature and salinity on attenuation coefficient.

Appendix A.2. Effects of Sun Elevation Angle

Generally speaking, the intensity of sunlight, which is closely related to sun elevation angle, mainly influences transmittance of seawater and excess noise. In this section, we will have a deep insight into these two effects.

First, we study its influence on transmittance. It is generally admitted that the transparency and color of ocean water are determined by the optical properties of sea water, which are related to sunlight illumination. Thus, the optical properties changed by sunlight could have a certain impact on the underwater ZPC-based MDI-CVQKD system. To have a quantitative elaboration of the impact of sunlight or more specifically, the irradiance on the transmittance of seawater, we consider the effects of sun elevation angle on the performance of the CVQKD system.

Actually, the transmittance of seawater in different depth z relates with sun light through the following equation [41]

$$T_{sea}(z) = [E_d(z) + \mu_s F_s e^{-kz/\mu_s}]/(E_0 + \mu_s F_s), \tag{A11}$$

where $E_d(z)$ is downward irradiance, μ_s is the angle at which sun rays enter the water, and F_s is the irradiance from the sky just below the sea surface given by $F_s = qE_0$ with a parameter q related to characteristics of atmosphere and the air-water interface. In addition, E_0 is the irradiance of the sky diffuse light going into the water and $k = a + 2b_B$, where a is the absorption coefficient, and b_B is the backscattering coefficient. According to the Snellius law, μ_s and sun elevation angle have the following relationship

$$\mu_s = \sqrt{1 - \cos^2 h_s / n_w^2}, \tag{A12}$$

where h_s is the sun elevation angle, and n_w is the refraction coefficient of seawater (usually takes value 1.34). $E_d(z)$ can be calculated through irradiance attenuation coefficient, which takes different value in different depth z, given by

$$k_d(z) = -\frac{1}{E_d(z)} \times \frac{dE_d(z)}{dz}. \tag{A13}$$

Therefore, the relationship among $k_d(z)$, absorption coefficient a and scattering coefficient b can be expressed by [42]

$$k_d(z) = \frac{1}{\mu_0}[a^2 + G(\mu_0)ab]^{\frac{1}{2}}, \tag{A14}$$

where $G(\mu_0) = q_1\mu_0 - q_2$. q_1 and q_2 are related to the average value of $k_d(z)$, which in practice we often take the value of intermediate depth.

From the elaboration of $T(z)$, it is still not easy to get an accurate simulation of the transmittance $T(z)$. Fortunately, we can obtain data directly from the derived chart [41]. For example, the transmittance (520 nm light) of 10 m deep oligotrophic seawater is 62%, 56%, and 52% corresponding sun elevation angle of $70°$, $45°$, and $20°$, respectively. Thus, it is possible to calculate the attenuation coefficient through the equation $\alpha = -\ln T/D$, which are 0.047, 0.057 and 0.065, correspondingly.

Then, we analyze its influence on excess noise. According to Reference [43], the solar background noise underwater is

$$P = L\Omega B\pi r^2, \tag{A15}$$

where $\Omega = \pi$ and L, B, r mean solar radiance, filter bandwidth determined by laser generating local oscillator (LO), radius of virtual telescope on sea surface to receive background light respectively. The parameter L can be calculated by

$$L = \frac{HRL_f e^{-cD}}{\pi}, \tag{A16}$$

where H is downwelling irradiance, $R = 1.25\%$, $L_f = 1$ are underwater reflectance of H and the factor of directional dependence of the underwater radiance. Finally, we derive the expression of excess noise underwater:

$$\varepsilon = \varepsilon_{\lim} + \frac{\tau P}{h\nu}, \tag{A17}$$

where $\varepsilon_{\lim}$ means excess noise limit and is estimated as 0.01 (SNU), $\tau = 1$ ns is the reciprocal of frequency of homodyne detector at Bob's end, h is Planck's constant and ν is the frequency of noise photons, which is in the range of visible light. Note that H ranges from about 0.5 to 2 for clear day time. The according excess noise ranges from 0.01 to 0.012, which is so trivial that could be ignored.

References

1. Vazirani, U.; Vidick, T. Fully Device Independent Quantum Key Distribution. *Commun. ACM* **2019**, *62*, 133. [CrossRef] [CrossRef]
2. Eriksson, T.; Hirano, T.; Puttnam, B.; Rademacher, G.; Luís, R.; Fujiwara, M.; Namiki, R.; Awaji, Y.; Takeoka, M.; Wada, N.; et al. Wavelength division multiplexing of continuous variable quantum key distribution and 18.3 Tbit/s data channels. *Commun. Phys.* **2019**, *2*, 1301–1350. [CrossRef] [CrossRef]
3. Wang, Y.J.; Mao, Y.Y.; Huang, W.T.; Huang, D.; Guo, Y. Optical frequency comb-based multichannel parallel continuous-variable quantum key distribution. *Opt. Express* **2019**, *27*, 25314–25329. [CrossRef] [CrossRef]
4. Gessner, M.; Pezzè, L.; Smerzi, A. Efficient entanglement criteria for discrete, continuous, and hybrid variables. *Phys. Rev. A* **2016**, *94*, 020101. [CrossRef] [CrossRef]
5. Pirandola, S.; Andersen, U.L.; Banchi, L.; Berta, M.; Bunandar, D.; Colbeck, R.; Englund, D.; Gehring, T.; Lupo, C.; Ottaviani, C.; et al. Advances in Quantum Cryptography. *arXiv* **2019**, *1906*, 01645. [CrossRef] [CrossRef]
6. Ye, W.; Zhong, H.; Liao, Q.; Huang, D.; Hu, L.Y.; Guo, Y. Improvement of self-referenced continuous-variable quantum key distribution with quantum photon catalysis. *Opt. Express* **2019**, *27*, 17186–17198. [CrossRef] [CrossRef] [PubMed]
7. Liao, Q.; Guo, Y.; Huang, D.; Huang, P.; Zeng, G. Long-distance continuous-variable quantum key distribution using non-Gaussian state-discrimination detection. *New J. Phys.* **2018**, *20*, 023015. [CrossRef] [CrossRef]
8. Zhao, W.; Guo, Y.; Zhang, L.; Huang, D. Coherent communications; Phase compensation; Phase estimation; Phase noise; Phase shift; Quantum key distribution. *Opt. Express* **2019**, *27*, 1838–1853. [CrossRef] [CrossRef] [PubMed]
9. Shor, P.; Preskill, J. Simple Proof of Security of the BB84 Quantum Key Distribution Protocol. *Phys. Rev. Lett.* **2000**, *85*, 441–444. [CrossRef] [CrossRef]
10. Braunstein, S.; Pirandola, S. Side-Channel-Free Quantum Key Distribution. *Phys. Rev. Lett.* **2012**, *108*, 130502. [CrossRef] [CrossRef]
11. Lo, H.; Curty, M.; Qi, B. Measurement-Device-Independent Quantum Key Distribution. *Phys. Rev. Lett.* **2012**, *108*, 130503. [CrossRef] [CrossRef] [PubMed]
12. Pirandola, S.; Ottaviani, C.; Spedalieri, G.; Weedbrook, C.; Braunstein, S.; Lloyd, S.; Gehring, T.; Jacobsen, C.; Andersen, U. High-rate measurement-device-independent quantum cryptography. *Nat. Photonics* **2015**, *9*, 397–402. [CrossRef] [CrossRef]
13. Ma, X.; Sun, S.; Jiang, M.; Liang, L. Local oscillator fluctuation opens a loophole for Eve in practical continuous-variable quantum-key-distribution systems. *Phys. Rev. A* **2013**, *88*, 022339. [CrossRef] [CrossRef]
14. Huang, J.; Weedbrook, C.; Yin, Z.; Wang, S.; Li, H.; Chen, W.; Guo, G.; Han, Z. Quantum hacking of a continuous-variable quantum-key-distribution system using a wavelength attack. *Phys. Rev. A* **2013**, *87*, 062329. [CrossRef] [CrossRef]
15. Qin, H.; Kumar, R.; Alléaume, R. Quantum hacking: Saturation attack on practical continuous-variable quantum key distribution. *Phys. Rev. A* **2016**, *94*, 012325. [CrossRef] [CrossRef]
16. Paterson, C. Atmospheric Turbulence and Orbital Angular Momentum of Single Photons for Optical Communication. *Phys. Rev. Lett.* **2005**, *94*, 153901. [CrossRef] [CrossRef]
17. Berman, G.; Chumak, A. Photon distribution function for long-distance propagation of partially coherent beams through the turbulent atmosphere. *Phys. Rev. A* **2006**, *74*, 013805. [CrossRef] [CrossRef]
18. Semenov, A.; Töppel, F.; Vasylyev, D.; Gomonay, H.; Vogel, W. Homodyne detection for atmosphere channels. *Phys. Rev. A* **2012**, *85*, 013826. [CrossRef] [CrossRef]
19. Gariano, J.; Djordjevic, I. Theoretical study of a submarine to submarine quantum key distribution systems. *Opt. Express* **2019**, *27*, 3055–3064. [CrossRef] [CrossRef]

20. Bouchard, F.; Sit, A.; Hufnagel, F.; Abbas, A.; Zhang, Y.; Heshami, K.; Fickler, R.; Marquardt, C.; Leuchs, G.; Boyd, R.; et al. Underwater Quantum Key Distribution in Outdoor Conditions with Twisted Photons. *arXiv* **2018**, *1801*, 10299. [CrossRef]
21. Ruan, X.; Zhang, H.; Zhao, W.; Wang, X.; Li, X.; Guo, Y. Discrete-Modulated Continuous-Variable Quantum Key Distribution over Seawater Channel. *Appl. Sci.* **2019**, *9*, 4956. [CrossRef] [CrossRef]
22. Kitagawa, A.; Takeoka, M.; Sasaki, M.; Chefles, A. Entanglement evaluation of non-Gaussian states generated by photon subtraction from squeezed states. *Phys. Rev. A* **2006**, *73*, 042310. [CrossRef] [CrossRef]
23. Guo, Y.; Liao, Q.; Wang, Y.; Huang, D.; Huang, P.; Zeng, G. Performance improvement of continuous-variable quantum key distribution with an entangled source in the middle via photon subtraction. *Phys. Rev. A* **2017**, *95*, 032304. [CrossRef] [CrossRef]
24. Guo, Y.; Ye, W.; Zhong, H.; Liao, Q. Continuous-variable quantum key distribution with non-Gaussian quantum catalysis. *Phys. Rev. A* **2019**, *99*, 032327. [CrossRef] [CrossRef]
25. Peng, Q.; Chen, G.; Li, X.; Liao, Q.; Guo, Y. Performance Improvement of Underwater Continuous-Variable Quantum Key Distribution via Photon Subtraction. *Entropy* **2019**, *21*, 1011. [CrossRef] [CrossRef]
26. Bennett, C.; Brassard, G.; Mermin, N. Quantum cryptography without Bell's theorem. *Phys. Rev. Lett.* **1992**, *68*, 557–559. [CrossRef] [CrossRef]
27. Yang, R.H.; He, G.Q. The Influence of Faraday Mirror's Imperfection in Continuous Variable Quantum Key Distribution System. *Acta Photonica Sinica* **2015**, *44*, 2.
28. Pirandola, S.; Laurenza, R.; Ottaviani, C.; Banchi, L. Fundamental limits of repeaterless quantum communications. *Nat. Commun.* **2017**, *8*, 15043. [CrossRef] [CrossRef]
29. Tian, B.; Zhang, F.; Tan, X. Design and development of an LED-based optical communication system for autonomous underwater robots. In Proceedings of the 2013 IEEE/ASME International Conference on Advanced Intelligent Mechatronics, Wollongong, Australia, 9–12 July 2013; pp. 1558–1563.
30. Doniec, M.;Detweiler, C.; Vasilescu, I.; Rus, D. Using optical communication for remote underwater robot operation. In Proceedings of the 2010 IEEE/RSJ International Conference on Intelligent Robots and Systems, Taipei, Taiwan, 18–22 October 2010; pp. 4017–4022.
31. Sun, X.; Kang, C.; Kong, M.; Alkhazragi, O.; Guo, Y.; Ouhssain, M.; Weng, Y.; Jones, B.; Ng, T.; Ooi, B. A Review on Practical Considerations and Solutions in Underwater Wireless Optical Communication. *OSA* **2020**, *38*, 421–431. [CrossRef] [CrossRef]
32. Wiscombe, W. Improved Mie scattering algorithms. *Appl. Opt.* **1980**, *19*, 1505–1509. [CrossRef] [CrossRef]
33. Lock, J.; Gérard, G. Generalized Lorenz–Mie theory and applications. *J QUANT SPECTROSC RA* **2009**, *110*, 800–807. [CrossRef] [CrossRef]
34. Zeng, Z.; Fu, S.; Zhang, H.; Dong, Y.; Cheng, J. A Survey of Underwater Optical Wireless Communications. *IEEE Commun. Surv. Tutor.* **2017**, *19*, 204–238. [CrossRef]
35. Danielewicz-Ferchmin, I. Phase Diagram of Hydration Shells in Ionic Solutions. *J. Phys. Chem.* **1995**, *99*, 5658–5665. [CrossRef] [CrossRef]
36. Shvab, I. Sadus, R. Structure and polarization properties of water: Molecular dynamics with a nonadditive intermolecular potential. *Phys. Rev. E* **2012**, *85*, 051509. [CrossRef] [CrossRef] [PubMed]
37. Coker, H. Empirical free-ion polarizabilities of the alkali metal, alkaline earth metal, and halide ions. *J. Phys. Chem.* **1976**, *80*, 2078–2084. [CrossRef] [CrossRef]
38. Farinato, R.; Rowell, R. New values of the light scattering depolarization and anisotropy of water. *J. Chem. Phys.* **1976**, *65*, 593. [CrossRef]
39. Duntley, S. Light in the Sea*. *J. Opt. Soc. Am.* **1963**, *53*, 214–233. [CrossRef] [CrossRef]
40. Pegau, W.; Gray, D.; Zaneveld, J. Absorption and attenuation of visible and near-infrared light in water: dependence on temperature and salinity. *OSA* **1997**, *36*, 6035–6046. [CrossRef] [CrossRef]
41. Haltrin, V. Apparent optical properties of the sea illuminated by sun and sky: case of the optically deep sea. *Appl. Opt.* **1998**, *37*, 8336–8340. [CrossRef] [CrossRef]

42. Zaneveld, J.; Barnard, Z.; Boss, E. Theoretical derivation of the depth average of remotely sensed optical parameters. *Opt. Express* **2005**, *13*, 9052–9061. [CrossRef] [CrossRef]
43. Guo, Y.; Xie, C.; Huang, P.; Li, J.; Zhang, L.; Huang, D.; Zeng, G. Channel-parameter estimation for satellite-to-submarine continuous-variable quantum key distribution. *Phys. Rev. A* **2018**, *97*, 052326. [CrossRef]

© 2020 by the authors. Licensee MDPI, Basel, Switzerland. This article is an open access article distributed under the terms and conditions of the Creative Commons Attribution (CC BY) license (http://creativecommons.org/licenses/by/4.0/).

Article

Surface-Codes-Based Quantum Communication Networks

Ivan B. Djordjevic

Department of Electrical and Computer Engineering, University of Arizona, Tucson, AZ 85721, USA; ivan@email.arizona.edu; Tel.: +1-520-626-5119

Received: 8 August 2020; Accepted: 21 September 2020; Published: 22 September 2020

Abstract: In this paper, we propose the surface codes (SCs)-based multipartite quantum communication networks (QCNs). We describe an approach that enables us to simultaneously entangle multiple nodes in an arbitrary network topology based on the SCs. We also describe how to extend the transmission distance between arbitrary two nodes by using the SCs. The numerical results indicate that transmission distance between nodes can be extended to beyond 1000 km by employing simple syndrome decoding. Finally, we describe how to operate the proposed QCN by employing the software-defined networking (SDN) concept.

Keywords: quantum key distribution (QKD); quantum communications networks (QCNs); quantum communications; entanglement; surface codes

1. Introduction

Quantum information processing (QIP) opens up new avenues for reliable communications, high-precision sensing, and high-performance computing [1–20]. Entanglement represents a unique resource for QIP, which allows quantum computers to solve classically intractable problems [7], provides certifiable security [2] for data transmissions, and enables sensors to achieve measurement sensitivities beyond the classical limit [8]. The quantum communication is the key cornerstone to fully exploit the properties of entanglement. The modern classical communications tend to use heterogeneous networks capable of simultaneous data transmission between nodes connected via different types of channels, such as free-space optical (FSO) and fiber-optics links. Nodes in existing quantum communication networks (QCNs), however, have been limited to a single optical medium. Moreover, trusted node assumption [4] is required to operate the current QCNs. As a result, one compromised node in a QCN can undermine the security of the entire QCN. Several quantum key distribution (QKD) testbeds have been reported so far, such as the DARPA QKD network [5], Tokyo QKD network [6], and the secure communication based on quantum cryptography (SECOQC) network [7]. Unfortunately, these different QKD networks employ the dark fiber infrastructure.

In this paper, we propose the multipartite heterogenous QCN employing the surface codes, which does not require the trusted node assumption. The research on multipartite entanglement is getting momentum with numerous experimental demonstrations, such as [8]. The surface codes, typically defined on a 2-D lattice, are closely related to the quantum topological codes on the boundary [1], introduced by Bravyi and Kitaev [11,12]. This class of codes is highly popular in quantum computing [13–15] because only local qubits are involved in stabilizers. In *Litinski's framework* [14], the surface code for quantum computing is represented as a game, played on a board partitioned in a certain number of tiles. On each tile we can place a logical qubit, represented as a *patch*. The edges of qubits represent the logical Pauli operators [1]. The logical qubits correspond to the surface code (SC) patches. By placing the SC patches in nodes of a communication network, and connecting the neighbouring patches by *d* wavelength channels, corresponding to the distance of the underlying surface code, we can create the quantum communication network. The SC patches placed in intermediate nodes can be operated as the SC-based quantum repeaters, thus extending significantly the transmission distance. When the patch edges in the tiles of neighbouring network nodes are different, we can perform the product measurements to entangle them. For instance, the product Z⊗Z between adjacent nodes' patches can be simultaneously measured to introduce the entanglement between two adjacent quantum nodes. Namely, we start with the state $|++\rangle = 0.5(|00\rangle + |11\rangle + |01\rangle + |10\rangle)$ and perform the measurement on Z⊗Z operator. If the result of the measurement is +1, the qubits end up in state $2^{-1/2}(|00\rangle + |11\rangle)$; otherwise, they end up in state $2^{-1/2}(|01\rangle + |10\rangle)$. In either case, the qubits are maximally entangled. This indicates that the proposed SC-based QCN is highly flexible and have numerous applications, including: (i) to teleport quantum states between any two nodes in the network, (ii) to develop the information infrastructure with unprecedented security level, (iii) to enable distributed quantum computing, and (iv) to enable ultra-high precision for quantum sensing applications. To operate such a quantum network, we propose to employ the software-defined networking (SDN) concepts.

The paper is organized as follows. In Section 2, we introduce the surface codes and describe briefly the *Litinski's* formalism needed in incoming sections. In Section 3, we describe the proposed SC-based QCN concept. In Section 4, we describe our approach to extend the transmission distance between QCN nodes. In Section 5, we provide illustrative numerical results. In Section 6, we describe how to operate the proposed SC-based QCN by utilizing the SDN concepts. Finally, in Section 7, we provide some important concluding remarks.

2. Surface Codes for Quantum Networking and Distributed Computing

The surface code belongs to the class of topological codes [1] and it is defined on a 2-D lattice, with one illustrative example provided in Figure 1, with qubits being clearly indicated in Figure 1a. The stabilizers of plaquette type can be defined as provided in Figure 1b. Each plaquette stabilizer denoted by X (Z) is composed of Pauli X (Z)-operators on qubits located in the intersection of edges of corresponding plaquette. As an illustration, the plaquette stabilizer denoted by X related to qubits 1 and 2 will be $X_{1\times 2}$. The plaquette stabilizer denoted by Z, related to qubits 5, 6, 8, and 9, will be $Z_5 Z_6 Z_8 Z_9$. To simplify the notation, we can use the representation provided in Figure 1c, where the shaded plaquettes correspond to all-X containing operators' stabilizers, while the white plaquettes correspond to all-Z containing operators' stabilizers. The stabilizers require only local qubits' interaction, which is not true for other classes of quantum error correction codes.

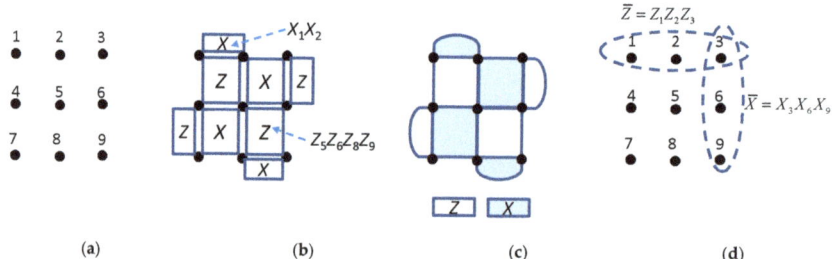

Figure 1. Illustration of a surface code: (**a**) the qubits are located in the lattice positions, (**b**) all-X and all-Z plaquette operators, (**c**) popular representation of surface codes in which stabilizers are clearly indicated, and (**d**) logical operators.

The weight-2 stabilizers are allocated around perimeter, while weight-4 stabilizers are located in the interior. The logical operators for this code are run over both sides of the lattice, as shown in Figure 1d, and can be represented as $\overline{X} = X_3 X_6 X_9$, $\overline{Z} = Z_1 Z_2 Z_3$. The codeword length is determined as the product of side lengths, expressed in number of qubits, and, for the surface code from Figure 1, we have that $n = L_x \times L_z = 3 \times 3 = 9$. On the other hand, the number of information qubits is $k = 1$. The minimum distance of this code is determined as the minimum side length, that is $d = \min(L_x, L_z) = 3$, indicating that this code can correct a single qubit error.

Let us now specify the *rules of the game*, that is the operations that can be applied to the patches (qubits), which can be categorized as [14]: (i) *initialization*, (ii) *qubit measurements*, and (iii) *patch deformations*. Compared to computing only limited number of operations are required in quantum networking. With each of these operations, we associate the cost, expressed in terms of time-steps, with each time-step (t.s.) corresponding to $\sim d$ code cycles (related to the measuring all stabilizers d times), with d being the distance of underlying surface code per tile. One-qubit patches, shown in Figure 2 as $|q_1\rangle$ and $|q_2\rangle$, can be initialized to $|0\rangle$ or $|+\rangle$ states, while two-qubit patches, shown in Figure 2 as $|q_3\rangle$, to $|00\rangle$ or $|++\rangle$ states, with associated cost being 0 t.s. (The logic $|+\rangle$-state indicates that all physical qubits are initialized into $|+\rangle$-state.) In principle, one-qubit patches can be initialized to the arbitrary states, such as the *magic state* $|m\rangle = |0\rangle + \exp(j\pi/4)|1\rangle$; however, an undetected Pauli error [1] can spoil the initialized state. The *single-patch measurements* can be performed in X or Z bases, and after the measurement the corresponding patches get removed from the board, thus freeing up the occupied tiles for future use. The cost associated with single-patch measurements is 0 t.s. For *two-patch measurements*, when the edges in neighboring tiles are different, we can perform the product measurements. As an illustration, the product $Z \otimes Z$ between adjacent patches can be measured as illustrated in Figure 3 (left).

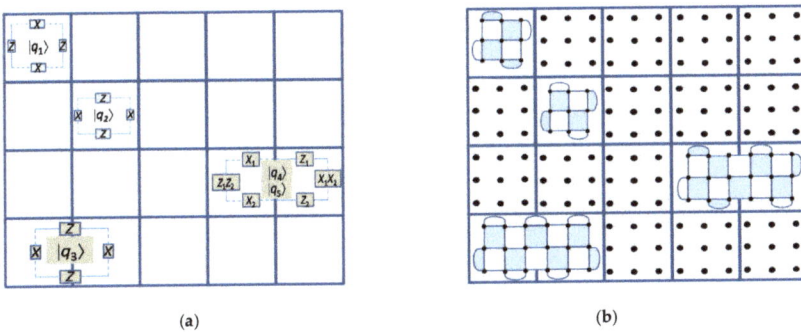

Figure 2. Illustration of one-qubit and two-qubits patches: (a) notation and (b) actual physical implementation.

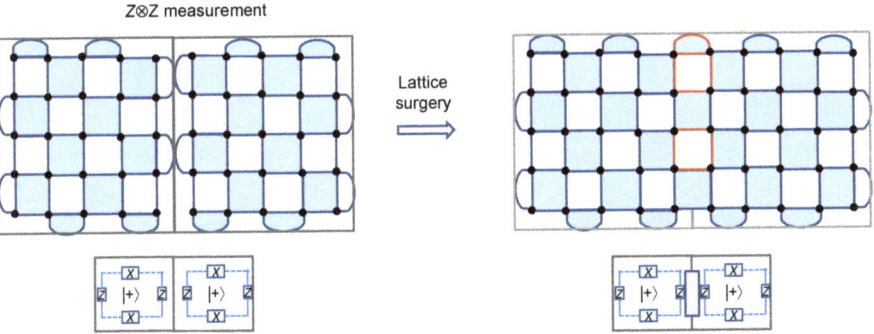

Figure 3. Illustrating the lattice surgery procedure for the measurement on the product $Z \otimes Z$.

In surface codes, this corresponds to the *lattice surgery* [14,15], in which we change the configuration as shown in Figure 3 (right) by introducing the patches with dark-red edges; after that, we measure the stabilizers for d cycles to get the outcome of measurements, and split again. The cost associated with the lattice surgery is 1 t.s. This represents the way to introduce the entanglement between two adjacent patches. Namely, we start with the state $|++\rangle = 0.5(|00\rangle + |11\rangle + |01\rangle + |10\rangle)$ and perform the measurement on $Z \otimes Z$ operator. If the result of the measurement is +1, the qubits end up in state $2^{-1/2}(|00\rangle + |11\rangle)$; otherwise, they end up in state $2^{-1/2}(|01\rangle + |10\rangle)$. In either case, the qubits are maximally entangled. We can apply the similar procedure to the $X \otimes Z$ product operator. Of course, it is also possible to measure the product operator involving the Y operator, which is really not needed in our proposed QCNs. What is even more interesting is that it is possible to measure the product for more than two encoded Pauli operators through *multi-patch measurements* [14].

3. Proposed Surface-Codes-Based Quantum Communications Networks

To enable the next generation of quantum communication networking, we propose to employ the surface codes so that the logical qubits are located at different nodes in the network. The logical qubits are represented by the patches introduced in the previous section. For simplicity, we assume that the surface code is defined on a $d \times d$ grid. The neighboring nodes are connected by employing d wavelengths, as illustrated in Figure 4. Some of the optical links could be FSO links.

By performing the $Z \otimes Z$ measurement, as described in the previous section, the logical qubits create the Einstein–Podolsky–Rosen (EPR) pair. The results of the measurements have been passed to the SDN controller, which will know the exact EPR pair being created. To create the desired QCN, the corresponding product measurements need to be simultaneously performed. As an illustration, let us consider the ring network composed of four nodes, as shown in Figure 5 (left), with each node being equipped with the surface code patch representing the corresponding logical qubits. In principle, one surface patch can be split between multiple nodes, but, to facilitate explanations, we assume that each node contains a single SC patch. By performing the simultaneous product $Z \otimes Z$ measurements between logical qubits q_1 and q_2, q_2 and q_3, q_3 and q_4, q_4 and q_1, we can entangle the nodes 1–4 and thus create the ring QCN. On the other hand, for the four-node mesh network shown in Figure 5 (right), by performing the simultaneous product $Z \otimes Z$ measurements between logical qubits q_1 and q_2, q_2 and q_3, q_3 and q_4, q_4 and q_1 as well as the simultaneous $X \otimes X$ measurements between q_1 and q_3, q_2 and q_4, we can entangle the four qubits into the mesh configuration. By providing the results of the measurements to the SDN control plane, the exact maximum entangled state between nodes in the QCN will be known. Clearly, this approach allows us to entangle the logical qubits in an arbitrary network. The trapped ions-based technology represents a perfect candidate for practical implementation of the proposed QCN. By equipping every node in the proposed QCN by multiple qubit patches, in principle, we can simultaneously perform quantum networking and quantum distributed computing. Instead of wavelength-division multiplexing (WDM), the multicore fiber can also be used to connect the logical qubits [16]. The proposed QCN does not require the trusted node assumption, but it is assumed that Eve does not have access to SDN controller.

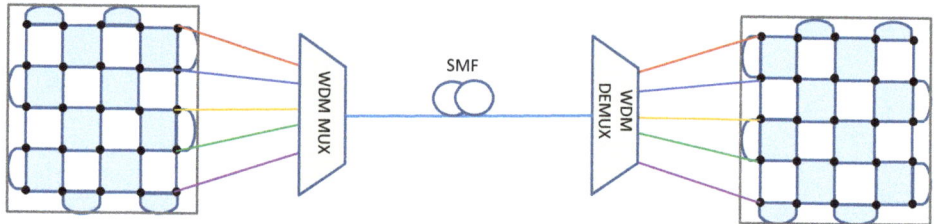

Figure 4. Simplified description of connecting two logical qubits from two neighboring nodes by d wavelengths.

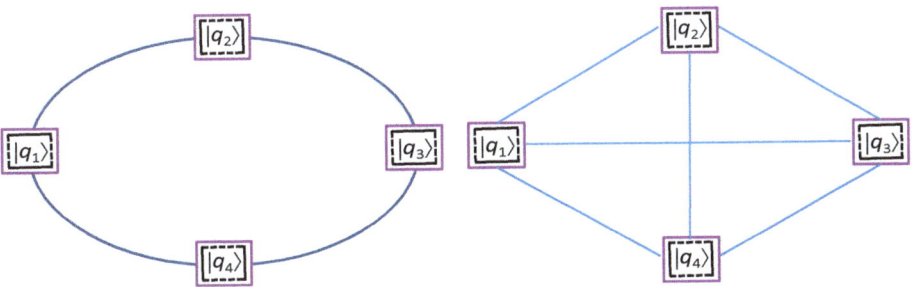

Figure 5. Illustrative four-node ring (**left**) and four-node mesh (**right**) quantum communication networks.

4. Extending the Distance between the Nodes in the Proposed SC-Based QCN

To extend the transmission distance between neighboring nodes in QCN, we propose to use the *quantum error correction (QEC)-based repeaters*. So far, QEC-based repeaters are based on two-dimensional QE-based repeaters, such as the dual-containing Calderbank–Shor–Steane (CSS)-codes-based repeaters [17] and surface-codes-based repeaters [18]. Unfortunately, dual-containing CSS codes are essentially girth-4 quantum low-density parity-check (LDPC) codes with poor error correction performance [19]. On the other hand, the surface codes proposed in [18] introduce large latency and are not compatible with the QCN proposed in the previous section. Here, we propose a different approach to interpret an intermediate node as an SC patch and apply the patch deformation approach due to Litinski and thus extend the logical qubit to two spatially separated patches, which is illustrated in Figure 6. In this example, three wavelengths are needed to interact remote patches. Once the logical qubit is extended to the intermediate node, we further perform product $X \otimes Z$ measurements to entangle the logical qubits q_1 and q_2. This approach is applicable to several intermediate nodes, thus offering the potential to significantly extend the distance between any two desired nodes in the QCN.

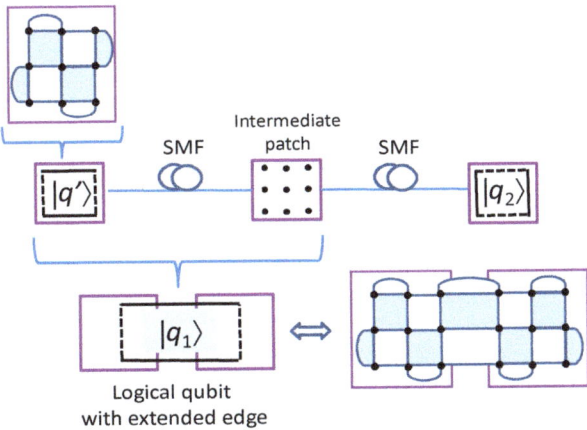

Figure 6. Extending the distance between two nodes in a quantum communication network (QCN) by creating the logical qubit spanning two spatially separated surface code (SC) patches.

5. Illustrative Numerical Results

Although the channel loss dominates the performance of quantum repeaters, there will be quantum errors associated with each stage, which can be represented by using the quantum channel model provided in Figure 7, where X and Z quantum errors occur with the same probability p. The corresponding Kraus representation [1] is given by:

$$\rho_f = \xi(\rho) = (1-2p)\rho + pX\rho X + pZ\rho Z. \qquad (1)$$

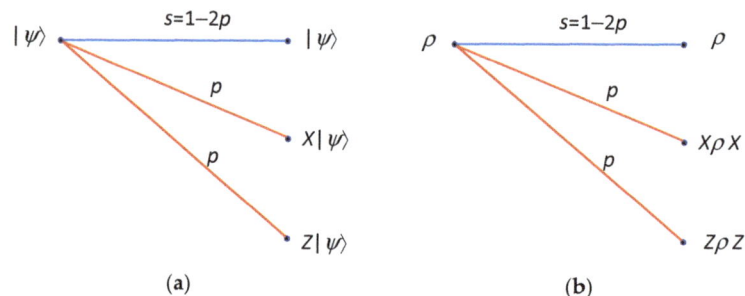

Figure 7. Quantum channel model under study: (**a**) Pauli operator description and (**b**) density operator description.

Let us consider the BB84 protocol by employing the approach introduced in previous section. The corresponding secret-key rate after N sections will be:

$$SKR = \{[1 - P(E)]T\}^N \max\left(1 - h_2\left(q_N^{(Z)}\right) - f_e h_2\left(q_N^{(X)}\right), 0\right), \qquad (2)$$

where f_e denotes the error correction inefficiency ($f_e \geq 1$), $q_N^{(X)}$ $\left[q_N^{(Z)}\right]$ denotes the quantum bit-error rate (QBER) in the X-basis (Z-basis) after N stages, T represents the single link transmissivity, and $h_2(x)$ is the binary entropy function $h_2(x) = -x\log_2(x) - (1-x)\log_2(1-x)$. The term $h_2\left(q_N^{(Z)}\right)$ represents the amount of information Eve was able to learn during the raw key transmission, which can be removed from the final key during the privacy amplification phase. The term $f_e h_2\left(q_N^{(X)}\right)$ represents the amount of information revealed to Eve during the information reconciliation stage. The dark counts, device imperfections, and errors introduced by Eve are all contributed to the Eve and included in transition probability p. The QBER after N stages can be estimated by:

$$q_N = \frac{1 - s^N}{2}, \quad s = 1 - 2p. \qquad (3)$$

The probability of the syndrome decoding error is bounded by [1]:

$$P(E) \leq \sum_{j=\lfloor(d-1)/2\rfloor+1}^{d^2} \binom{d^2}{j}(1-s)^j s^{d^2-j}, \quad s = 1 - 2p, \qquad (4)$$

So, $[1 - P(E)]T$ represents the success probability for the single stage. The total success probability can be estimated by $\{[1 - P(E)]T\}^N$ and is illustrated in Figure 8 by setting the X (Z) qubit error probability to $p = 10^{-2}$ and transmissivity to $T = 1$, for different $d \times d$ surface codes.

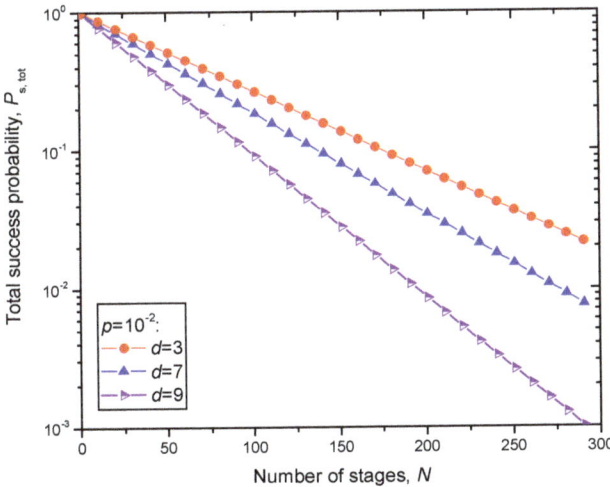

Figure 8. Total success probability defined as $(1 - P(E))^N$, where N is the number of stages, when the $d \times d$ surface code is used, and syndrome decoding is applied.

The numerical results for secret-key rate (SKR) for different transmissivities T (assuming that $f_e = 1$) vs. the number of stages N are summarized in Figures 9 and 10. The channel transmittance in Figure 9 is set to $T = 0.95$, while in Figure 10 it is set to $T = 0.85$. The qubit error transition probability p is used as a parameter. In both figures, the 7×7 surface code is used. Given that the effective transmission distance of the fiber is given by [20]:

$$L_{\text{eff}} = \frac{1 - e^{-\alpha L}}{\alpha} \approx 1/\alpha, \tag{5}$$

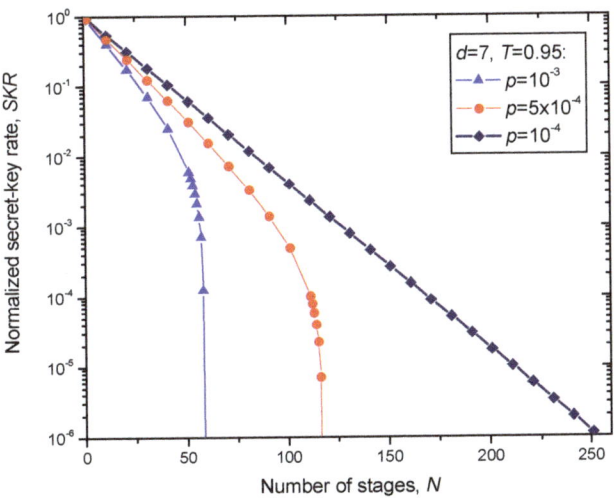

Figure 9. Normalized secret-key rate (SKR) vs. the number of stages N assuming that the 7×7 surface code is used, and single link channel transmittance is $T = 0.95$.

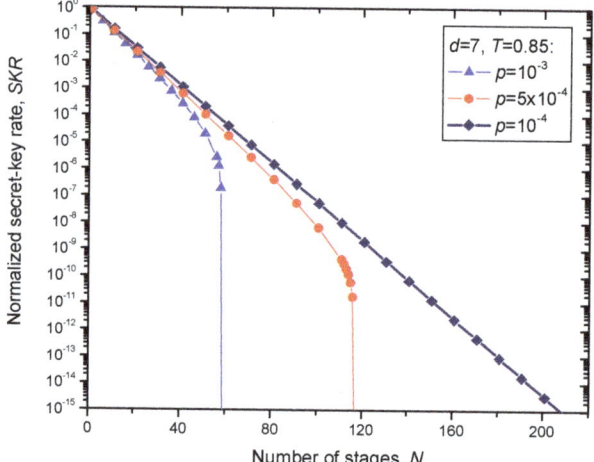

Figure 10. Normalized SKR vs. number of stages N assuming that 7×7 surface code is used, and single link channel transmittance is $T = 0.85$.

For ultra-low loss fiber introduced in [21] with attenuation coefficient $\alpha = 0.1419$ dB/km, we obtain that $L_{eff} = 30.606$ km. The total transmission length can be now estimated by:

$$L_{tot} = NL_{eff}|\ln T|. \tag{6}$$

For $T = 0.95$, by setting the qubit error probability to $p = 10^{-4}$, we can see from Figure 9 that the achievable total transmission distance for normalized SKR of 10^{-6} is $L_{tot} = 252 \times 30.606 \times |\ln 0.95| = 395.61$ km. On the other hand, for $T = 0.85$, by setting the qubit error probability to $p = 10^{-4}$, we can see from Figure 10 that the achievable total transmission distance for normalized SKR of 10^{-15} (typical for discrete variable QKD schemes [2]) is $L_{tot} = 208 \times 30.606 \times |\ln 0.85| = 1034.61$ km, and this results is comparable to the recently proposed hybrid QKD-postquantum cryptography scheme [22,23]. By employing higher complexity quantum sum-product algorithm [1] in each stage, instead of simple syndrome decoding, the total transmission distance well beyond 1000 km can be achieved. Typical QKD transmission distances are significantly shorter, even when the most advanced twin-field QKD schemes are used [24].

6. Operating the Proposed QCN by SDN Control

The SDN has been introduced to separate the control plane and data plane, manage network services through abstraction of higher-level functionality, and implement new applications and algorithms efficiently [25,26]. It has already been studied to enable the coexistence of classical and quantum communication channels [27]. To enhance the security of the software-defined optical networks, authors in [28] proposed a four-layer architecture composed of: application, control, QKD, and data layers. The SDN-based QCN architecture compatible with the proposed QCN should contain three layers only—namely, application layer, control layer, and QCN layer. Users will send their requests from the application layer with the help of northbound interface to the SDN controller. The SDN controller will allocate the QCN resources with the help of its global map through the southbound interface. The QCN layer can be composed of DWDM links and QCN nodes. Each QCN node should contain quantum transceivers, integrated on the same chip, together with a $d \times d$ array of physical qubits. Any two nodes in QCN can communicate through either a dedicated SMF link or by d wavelength channels. To enable so, we could employ our recently proposed bidirectional optical space switch [29], to reconfigure the QCN. Other alternative optical switches can be used as well.

In addition to conventional modules, the application layer should also have modules to provide security management services. On the other hand, the control layer, in addition to controlling the QCN layer, should provide allocation of resources as well as provide services for multiple applications. To deal with time-varying channel conditions over heterogeneous links, we can adapt the channel configuration based on both application requirements and link conditions.

7. Concluding Remarks

To enable the next generation of quantum communication networks, we have proposed to employ the surface-codes-based patches as quantum nodes. We have described how to simultaneously entangle multiple quantum nodes in any quantum network topology by employing the SCs. We have also described how to extend the transmission distance between any two quantum nodes to beyond 1000 km. Finally, we have described how to operate the proposed QCN by employing the SDN concept. The trapped ion technology is an excellent candidate to be used as an enabling technology to implement SC-based QCNs. One important issue will be to implement a portable, rack-mounted ion-trap-based quantum interface, and some progress has already been made by researchers from Duke University in collaboration with ColdQuanta, Inc [30]. To improve the efficiency of the proposed QCNs, the high-dimensional SCs should be employed. By employing high-dimensional-based quantum error correction, we can achieve error correction capability comparable to 2D but with significantly shorter codeword lengths as discussed in [31]. An alternative approach to the proposed QCN will be a recently introduced cluster-state-based QCN [32].

Funding: This research received no external funding.

Conflicts of Interest: The author declares no conflict of interest.

References

1. Djordjevic, I.B. *Quantum Information Processing and Quantum Error Correction: An Engineering Approach*; Elsevier: Amsterdam, The Netherlands; Academic Press: Boston, MA, USA, 2012.
2. Djordjevic, I.B. *Physical-Layer Security and Quantum Key Distribution*; Springer Nature: Cham, Switzerland, 2019.
3. Duan, L.-M.; Lukin, M.; Cirac, J.I.; Zoller, P. Long-distance quantum communication with atomic ensembles and linear optics. *Nature* **2001**, *414*, 413–418. [CrossRef]
4. Qiu, J. Quantum communications leap out of the lab. *Nature* **2014**, *508*, 441–442. [CrossRef]
5. Elliott, C.; Colvin, A.; Pearson, D.; Pikalo, O.; Schlafer, J.; Yeh, H. Current status of the DARPA quantum network (Invited Paper). In Proceedings of the SPIE 5815, Quantum Information and Computation III, Orlando, FL, USA, 25 May 2005.
6. Sasaki, M.; Fujiwara, M.; Ishizuka, H.; Klaus, W.; Wakui, K.; Takeoka, M.; Miki, S.; Yamashita, T.; Wang, Z.; Tanaka, A. Field test of quantum key distribution in the Tokyo QKD Network. *Opt. Express* **2011**, *19*, 10387–10409. [CrossRef]
7. Nagayama, S.; Van Meter, R. Internet-Draft: IKE for IPsec with QKD. 2009. Available online: https://tools.ietf.org/html/draft-nagayama-ipsecme-ipsec-with-qkd-01 (accessed on 21 September 2020).
8. Mccutcheon, W.; Pappa, A.; Bell, B.A.; Mcmillan, A.; Chailloux, A.; Lawson, T.; Mafu, M.; Markham, D.; Diamanti, E.; Kerenidis, I.; et al. Experimental verification of multipartite entanglement in quantum networks. *Nat. Commun.* **2016**, *7*, 13251. [CrossRef] [PubMed]
9. Ekert, A.; Josza, R. Quantum computation and Shor's factoring algorithm. *Rev. Mod. Phys.* **1996**, *68*, 733–753. [CrossRef]
10. The LIGO Scientific Collaboration. A gravitational wave observatory operating beyond the quantum shot-noise limit. *Nat. Phys.* **2011**, *7*, 962–965. [CrossRef]
11. Kitaev, A.Y. Fault-tolerant quantum computation by anyons. *Ann. Phys.* **2003**, *303*, 2–30. [CrossRef]
12. Bravyi, S.B.; Kitaev, A.Y. Quantum Codes on a Lattice with Boundary. Available online: http://arxiv.org/abs/quant-ph/9811052 (accessed on 21 September 2020).

13. Fowler, A.G.; Mariantoni, M.; Martinis, J.M.; Cleland, A.N. Surface codes: Towards practical large-scale quantum computation. *Phys. Rev. A* **2012**, *86*, 32324. [CrossRef]
14. Litinski, D.A. Game of surface codes: Large-scale quantum computing with lattice surgery. *Quantum* **2019**, *3*, 128. [CrossRef]
15. Horsman, C.; Fowler, A.G.; Devitt, S.; Meter, R.V. Surface code quantum computing by lattice surgery. *New J. Phys.* **2012**, *14*, 123011. [CrossRef]
16. Bacco, D.; Da Lio, B.; Cozzolino, D.; Da Ros, F.; Guo, X.; Ding, Y.; Sasaki, Y.; Aikawa, K.; Miki, S.; Terai, H.; et al. Boosting the secret key rate in a shared quantum and classical fibre communication system. *Commun. Phys.* **2019**, *2*, 140. [CrossRef]
17. Jiang, L.; Taylor, J.M.; Nemoto, K.; Munro, W.J.; van Meter, R.; Lukin, D.M. Quantum repeater with encoding. *Phys. Rev. A* **2009**, *79*, 32325. [CrossRef]
18. Fowler, A.G.; Wang, D.S.; Hill, C.D.; Ladd, T.D.; van Meter, R.; Hollenberg, L.C.L. Surface code quantum communication. *Phys. Rev. Lett.* **2010**, *104*, 180503. [CrossRef] [PubMed]
19. Djordjevic, I.B. Quantum LDPC Codes from Balanced Incomplete Block Designs. *IEEE Commun. Lett.* **2008**, *12*, 389–391. [CrossRef]
20. Djordjevic, I.B. *Advanced Optical and Wireless Communications Systems*; Springer International Publishing: Basel, Switzerland, 2017.
21. Tamura, Y.; Sakuma, H.; Morita, K.; Suzuki, M.; Yamamoto, Y.; Shimada, K.; Honma, Y.; Sohma, K.; Fujii, T.; Hasegawa, T.; et al. The First 0.14-dB/km loss optical fiber and its impact on submarine transmission. *J. Lightwave Technol.* **2018**, *36*, 44–49. [CrossRef]
22. Djordjevic, I.B. Secure, global quantum communications networks (Invited). In Proceedings of the 22nd International Conference on Transparent Optical Networks ICTON 2020, Bari, Italy, 19–23 July 2020.
23. Djordjevic, I.B. Joint QKD-Post-Quantum Cryptosystems. *IEEE Access* **2020**, *8*, 154708–154712. [CrossRef]
24. Ma, X.; Zeng, P.; Zhou, H. Phase-matching quantum key distribution. *Phys. Rev. X* **2018**, *8*, 31043. [CrossRef]
25. Yang, M.; Rastegarfar, H.; Djordjevic, I.B. Probabilistically coded modulation formats for 5G Mobile Fronthaul Networks. *J. Lightwave Technol.* **2019**, *37*, 3882–3892. [CrossRef]
26. Yang, M.; Rastegarfar, H.; Djordjevic, I.B. Physical-layer adaptive resource allocation in software-defined data center networks. *OSA/IEEE J. Opt. Commun. Netw.* **2018**, *10*, 1015–1026. [CrossRef]
27. Aguado, A.; Martin, V.; Lopez, D.; Peev, M.; Martinez-Mateo, J.; Rosales, J.L.; de la Iglesia, F.; Gomez, M.; Hugues-Salas, E.; Lord, A. Quantum-aware software defined networks. In Proceedings of the 6th International Conference on Quantum Cryptography, Washington, DC, USA, 12–16 September 2016.
28. Cao, Y.; Zhao, Y.; Yu, X.; Wang, H.; Liu, C.; Li, B.; Zhang, J. Resource allocation in optical networks secured by quantum key distribution. *IEEE Commun. Mag.* **2018**, *56*, 130–137.
29. Yang, M.; Djordjevic, I.B.; Tunc, C.; Hariri, S.; Akoglu, A. An optical interconnect network design for dynamically composable data centers. In Proceedings of the 19th IEEE International Conference on High Performance Computing and Communications (HPCC 2017), Bangkok, Thailand, 18–20 December 2017; pp. 299–306.
30. Cryogenic Ion Trap Package, ColdQuanta. Available online: https://www.coldquanta.com/standard-products/ion-trapping/ (accessed on 21 September 2020).
31. Djordjevic, I.B. Integrated optics modules based proposal for quantum information processing, teleportation, QKD, and quantum error correction employing photon angular momentum. *IEEE Photonics J.* **2016**, *8*, 6600212. [CrossRef]
32. Djordjevic, I.B. On global quantum communication networking. *Entropy* **2020**, *22*, 831. [CrossRef]

© 2020 by the author. Licensee MDPI, Basel, Switzerland. This article is an open access article distributed under the terms and conditions of the Creative Commons Attribution (CC BY) license (http://creativecommons.org/licenses/by/4.0/).

Article

Open-Destination Measurement-Device-Independent Quantum Key Distribution Network

Wen-Fei Cao [1,2], Yi-Zheng Zhen [1,2], Yu-Lin Zheng [1,2], Shuai Zhao [1,2], Feihu Xu [1,2,*], Li Li [1,2,*], Zeng-Bing Chen [3,*], Nai-Le Liu [1,2,*] and Kai Chen [1,2,*]

1. Hefei National Laboratory for Physical Sciences at Microscale and Department of Modern Physics, University of Science and Technology of China, Hefei 230026, China; caowf@mail.ustc.edu.cn (W.-F.C.); yizheng@mail.ustc.edu.cn (Y.-Z.Z.); ylzheng@mail.ustc.edu.cn (Y.-L.Z.); zssa@mail.ustc.edu.cn (S.Z.)
2. CAS Center for Excellence and Synergetic Innovation Center of Quantum Information and Quantum Physics, University of Science and Technology of China, Hefei 230026, China
3. National Laboratory of Solid State Microstructures and School of Physics, Nanjing University, Nanjing 210093, China
* Correspondence: feihuxu@ustc.edu.cn (F.X.); eidos@ustc.edu.cn(L.L.); zbchen@nju.edu.cn(Z.-B.C.); nlliu@ustc.edu.cn(N.-L.L.); kaichen@ustc.edu.cn(K.C.)

Received: 16 August 2020; Accepted: 22 September 2020; Published: 26 September 2020

Abstract: Quantum key distribution (QKD) networks hold promise for sharing secure randomness over multi-parties. Most existing QKD network schemes and demonstrations are based on trusted relays or limited to point-to-point scenario. Here, we propose a flexible and extensible scheme named as open-destination measurement-device-independent QKD network. The scheme enjoys security against untrusted relays and all detector side-channel attacks. Particularly, any users can accomplish key distribution under assistance of others in the network. As an illustration, we show in detail a four-user network where two users establish secure communication and present realistic simulations by taking into account imperfections of both sources and detectors.

Keywords: quantum cryptography; quantum key distribution; quantum network; measurement-device-independent

PACS: 03.67.Dd; 03.67.Hk

---

1. Introduction

Quantum key distribution (QKD) [1–4] provides unconditional security between distant communication parties based on the fundamental laws of quantum physics. In the last three decades, QKD has achieved tremendous progress in both theoretical developments and experimental demonstrations. To extend to a large scale, the QKD network holds promise to establish an unconditionally secure global network. Different topologies for QKD network have been demonstrated experimentally during the past decades [5–11]. However, due to high demanding on security and the relatively low detection efficiency, the realization of large-scale QKD networks is still challenging.

On the one hand, many previous demonstrations of quantum networks heavily rely on the assumption of trusted measurement devices. From security point of view, however, such assumption is challenging in realistic situations, as various kinds of detector side-channel attacks are found due to the imperfections of practical devices [12–16]. Fortunately, measurement-device-independent QKD (MDI-QKD) protocol [17,18] can remove all kinds of attacks in the detector side-channel. Since its security does not rely on any assumptions on measurement devices, MDI-QKD networks are expected to close the security loophole existing in the previous QKD networks. The MDI-QKD network has been discussed theoretically in Ref. [19,20], and a preliminary experimental MDI-QKD network demonstration was realized very recently [21].

On the other hand, most of the existing QKD networks are limited to point-to-point QKD. When expanded to multi-partite QKD case, the complexity increases, and the efficiency decreases significantly. Recent study shows that multi-partite entanglement can speed up QKD in networks [22]. Therefore, it is highly desirable to develop variously novel schemes of QKD networks if assisted by multi-partite entanglement source. Then, an immediate problem comes out: how to design a QKD network enjoying security against untrusted measurement devices and simultaneously offer practical applicability for arbitrary scalability? This is exactly the purpose of this work.

In this paper, we propose a flexible and extensible protocol named as open-destination MDI-QKD network, by combining the idea of open-destination teleportation [23] and MDI-QKD [17,18]. In this protocol, secure communication between any two users in the network can be accomplished under assistance of others. The open-destination feature allows these two-party users share secure keys simultaneously, where we also generalize to the case of C communication users. Remarkably, this feature allows communication users not to be specified before the measurement step, which makes the network flexible and extendable. Furthermore, the MDI feature enables this scheme to be secure against untrusted relays and all detector side-channel attacks. Specially, all users need only trusted state-preparation devices at hand, while the untrusted relay section is made by entangled resources and measurement devices.

2. Open-Destination MDI-QKD Network

Consider an N-party quantum network. We are particularly interested in the case where arbitrary two users want to share secure keys. This scenario is denoted as $(N,2)$ for convenience. To simplify the discussion, here we focus on the star-type network, where both the user and a central source emit quantum signals. The signals are measured by untrusted relays located between each user and the central source.

2.1. Protocol

The $(N,2)$ open-destination MDI-QKD runs as follows. An illustration of the $(4,2)$ example is shown in Figure 1.

Step. 1 **Preparation**: A third party, which may be untrusted, prepares N-partite GHZ state

$$|GHZ\rangle_N = \frac{1}{\sqrt{2}}(|0\rangle^{\otimes N} + |1\rangle^{\otimes N}), \qquad (1)$$

where $|0\rangle$ and $|1\rangle$ denote two eigenstates of the computational basis Z. All users prepare BB84 polarization states, i.e., $|0\rangle$, $|1\rangle$, $|+\rangle$, and $|-\rangle$ with $|\pm\rangle = (|0\rangle \pm |1\rangle)/\sqrt{2}$ being the two eigenstates of the basis X. The third party and all users distribute the prepared quantum states to their relays, which may also be untrusted.

Step. 2 **Measurement**: The relays perform Bell state measurements (BSMs). When using linear optical setups, only two outcomes related to projections on $|\psi^\pm\rangle = (|01\rangle \pm |10\rangle)/\sqrt{2}$ can be distinguished.

Step. 3 **Announcement**: All relays announce their successful BSM results among a public classical authenticated channel. The two communication users announce their photons bases, and other users announce their states prepared in the X basis.

Step. 4 **Sifting**: The two communication user keep the strings where all the relays get successful BSM results and other users use X bases. Then, they discard the strings where different preparation bases are used. To guarantee their strings to be correctly correlated, one of the two users flip or not flip his/her bit according to the corresponding BSM results and other users' prepared states (see Appendix A for details). Then, the two users obtain the raw key bits.

Step. 5 **Post-processing**: The two communication users estimate the quantum phase error and quantum bit error rate (QBER) in Z and X bases, according to which they further perform error correction and privacy amplification to extract correct and secure keys.

In this protocol, the multi-partite GHZ state between distant users can also be established through a prior distributed singlets, following the scheme of Bose et al. [24]. In fact, the open-destination feature allows arbitrary two users in the network to share secure keys based on the same experiment statistics. To accomplish the task of MDI-QKD among arbitrary two users, a natural scheme is to establish direct MDI-QKD between each two users. This requires either the central source to adjust his devices such that EPR pairs (the maximally entangled quantum states of a two qubit system, named after Einsetin, Podolski and Rosen Paradox [25]) are sent along desired directions, or a number $N(N-1)/2$ of two-user combinations to establish direct MDI-QKD using the same number of untrusted relays. The open-destination scheme is an alternative scheme. It does not require the central source to adjust his devices according to the demand of communications, at the same time involve only N untrusted relays. In a practical scenario, all the users can use weak coherent pulses to reduce experimental cost and apply decoy-state techniques [26–28] to avoid photon-number-splitting attack, as well as to estimate the gain and the error rate.

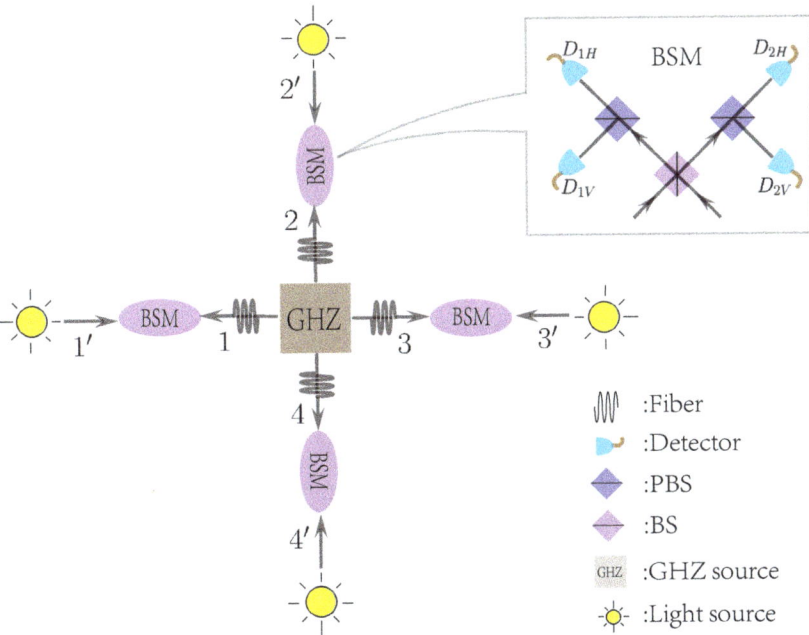

Figure 1. An optical diagram for the polarization-encoding $(4,2)$ open-destination measurement-device-independent quantum key distribution (MDI-QKD) network. The GHZ source outputs 4-partite GHZ entangled state in polarization and the light source outputs BB84 polarization state. The BSM represents the Bell state measurement, where BS is the 50:50 beam splitter, PBS is the polarization beam splitter, and D_{1H}, D_{2H}, D_{1V}, and D_{2V} are single-photon detectors. A click in D_{1H} and D_{2V}, or in D_{1V} and D_{2H}, indicates a projection into the Bell state $|\psi^-\rangle = (|01\rangle - |10\rangle)/\sqrt{2}$, and a click in D_{1H} and D_{1V}, or in D_{2H} and D_{2V}, indicates a projection into the Bell state $|\psi^+\rangle = (|01\rangle + |10\rangle)/\sqrt{2}$.

2.2. Correctness and Security Analysis

We will show the correctness and security of the open-destination MDI-QKD protocol, i.e., the communication users end up with sharing a common key in an honest run and any eavesdropper can only obtain limited information of the final key. The following analysis applies for the $(N,2)$ case. As an illustration, we show a detailed derivation of the $(4,2)$ in Appendix A.

For the correctness of the protocol, we show that after successful BSMs and other users announce the X-basis states, the two communication users can perform flip their bits locally to obtain perfectly correlated sifted keys. We start from rewriting the GHZ state as

$$|GHZ\rangle_N = \frac{1}{\sqrt{2}} \left[|00\rangle_{12} \bigotimes_{k=3...N} \frac{|+\rangle_k + |-\rangle_k}{\sqrt{2}} + |11\rangle_{12} \bigotimes_{k=3...N} \frac{|+\rangle_k - |-\rangle_k}{\sqrt{2}} \right], \quad (2)$$

$$= \left(\frac{1}{\sqrt{2}}\right)^{N-1} \sum_{\chi} (|00\rangle_{12} + (-1)^{\sigma_\chi} |11\rangle_{12}) |\chi\rangle_{3...N}. \quad (3)$$

Here, $\chi \in \{+,-\}^{N-2}$ is a string of $N-2$ bits with bit value "+" or "−" and $\sigma_\chi = 0(1)$ if the number of "−" is even (odd).

We label each user by $1', 2', \ldots, N'$ and let the two communication users be $1'$ and $2'$. In a successful run of the protocol, suppose that users $1'$ and $2'$ prepare states $|\alpha\rangle, |\beta\rangle \in \{0, 1, +, -\}$, respectively, and other users $3', \ldots, N'$ prepare state in the X basis, denoted as a string $\chi' \in \{+,-\}^{N-2}$. In addition, denote the successful BSM results as a string $v \in \{+,-\}^N$, with the kth bit v_k denoting the BSM outcome on the state prepared by the user k' and the k-th particle of the GHZ state. Here, $v_k = \pm$ corresponds to projections $|\psi^\pm\rangle\langle\psi^\pm|$, respectively. Then, when other users send states denoted by $|\chi'\rangle$ and when all untrusted relays announce successful BSM results v, the equivalent measurement $M_{12}^{\chi',v}$ on $1'$ and $2'$ is

$$\sqrt{M_{1'2'}^{\chi',v}} |\alpha\beta\rangle_{1'2'} = \left(\bigotimes_k \langle\psi^{v_k}|_{kk'}\right) |GHZ\rangle_N \otimes |\alpha\beta\rangle_{1'2'} |\chi'\rangle_{3'...N'}, \quad (4)$$

$$= \left(\frac{1}{\sqrt{2}}\right)^{N-1} \sum_\chi \langle\psi^{v_1}|_{11'} \langle\psi^{v_2}|_{22'} (|00\rangle_{12} + (-1)^{\sigma_\chi} |11\rangle_{12}) |\alpha\beta\rangle_{1'2'}$$
$$\times \prod_{k=3...N} \langle\psi^{v_k}|_{kk'} |\chi\rangle_k |\chi'\rangle_{k'}, \quad (5)$$

$$\propto (\langle 00|_{1'2'} + (-1)^\tau \langle 11|_{1'2'}) |\alpha\beta\rangle_{1'2'}. \quad (6)$$

Here, $\tau = \sigma_{\chi' \oplus \tilde{v}} \oplus v_1 \oplus v_2$ with $\tilde{v} = v_3 v_4 \ldots v_N \in \{+,-\}^{N-2}$ and $\sigma_{\chi' \oplus \tilde{v}} = +(-)$ if the number of "−" in $\chi' \oplus \tilde{v}$ is even (odd). Therefore, when the user $1'$ and $2'$ both prepare Z-basis states, or when they both prepare X-basis states with $\tau = 0$, the corresponding strings are correctly correlated; otherwise, when they both prepare X-basis states but $\tau = 1$, their strings are anticorrelated, and one party needs to flip all his/her bits.

For the security of the protocol, here we show that an open-destination MDI-QKD can be equivalent to a standard bipartite MDI-QKD if we only focus on the two communication users. Recall that, in the standard MDI-QKD, two parties, Alice and Bob, prepare and send quantum signals to a remote untrusted relay, which announces a successful BSM result or not. In our scheme, one can treat all parts outside the two users $1'$ and $2'$ as an untrusted relay [29]. That is, the GHZ source, the BSM setups and all other users serve as a big untrusted relay, and the successful BSM results in the standard MDI-QKD corresponds to all BSMs announcing successful measurements together with all other users announcing X-basis states (see Figure A1 as an example of the $(4,2)$ case). In this sense, our scheme is reduced to the MDI-QKD and the two has the same security. Additionally, although we require the preparation device of each user to be trusted in the protocol, the two communication users need not to trust these preparation devices of other users.

2.3. Key Generation Rate

The key generation rate for open-destination MDI-QKD can be derived similarly as the standard MDI-QKD, i.e., by converting it to an entanglement purification scheme. Suppose that the two communication users both have virtual singlets at their hands and then send one particle to the untrusted relays. In a successful run of the protocol, the remaining virtual particles of the two communication users will be entangled. When the entanglement between the virtual particles is sufficiently strong, the monogamy property of entanglement [30–32] guarantees the extraction of information-theoretically secure key bits between the two users. In this sense, the secret key rate can be roughly viewed as the gains of entanglement purification in the asymptotic case. Taking account of imperfections, such as basis misalignment, channel loss, and dark counts of the detectors, the key generation rate is given by the GLLP method [33]

$$R_2 = Q^{ZZ} \left[1 - H\left(e^{XX}\right) - fH\left(e^{ZZ}\right) \right]. \tag{7}$$

Here, we have assumed that the user $1'$ and $2'$ use Z basis to generate keys and use X basis to estimate phase errors. In the equation, Q^{ZZ} denotes the overall gain in the Z basis, and e^{XX} (e^{ZZ}) denotes the phase (bit) error rate, $f > 1$ is the error correction inefficiency for the error correction process, and $H(x) = -x \log_2(x) - (1-x) \log_2(1-x)$ is the binary Shannon entropy function. In a realistic experiment, if using weak coherent pulses and adopting decoy-state techniques, Q^{ZZ}, e^{ZZ}, and e^{XX} can be efficiently estimated [27,28].

2.4. Comparison with the Standard MDI-QKD

The open-destination MDI-QKD network is different from the conventional MDI-QKD. The main difference comes from the open-destination feature, which in fact allows the all 2-party users in the network generate their own secure keys independently and simultaneously. There are in fact $N(N-1)/2$ combinations of such two-party users. If one uses the conventional MDI-QKD scheme, the same number of untrusted relays are required. To increase the communication distance, one may further add the same number of relays and EPR sources to construct the user-relay-EPR source-relay-user structure. Such construction of quantum network could be expensive considering the number of devices required. One could also use the optical switches to reduce the number of relays; however, in this case the communication would be arranged in time order and some users have to wait. In the open-destination scheme, N untrusted relays are sufficient to connect each other supplied with good-quality GHZ central source. Although the distribution of GHZ states may lead to other technological challenges, the open-destination scheme can reduce the number of devices significantly in constructing the network. As for the performance, the two schemes in fact have similar performance in the ideal case. The difference is that the open-destination scheme generates secure keys for any two-party users in one round of implementation while the bipartite MDI-QKD scheme costs $N(N-1)/2$ rounds. Furthermore, the open-destination scheme also establishes conference key agreements among arbitrary users, which can not be accomplished directly via the bipartite MDI-QKD. We will discuss this case in the next section.

3. Numerical Simulation

As an example, we will analyze the secure key rate for the $(4,2)$ open-destination MDI-QKD (see Appendices B and C for details). For simplicity, the single-photon source and the asymptotic approximations are assumed. We let the BSM setups be located in each user's side, although, in a realistic experiment, the BSM setups can be located in anywhere to increase the communication distance. We suppose that quantum channels are identically depolarizing such that untrusted relays receive the GHZ state in a mixture form [34]:

$$\rho = p \left| GHZ \right\rangle \left\langle GHZ \right|_4 + \frac{1-p}{16} \mathbb{I}_{16}, \tag{8}$$

where $0 \leq p \leq 1$. We also assume that all detectors are identical, i.e., they have the same dark count rates and the same detection efficiencies. After numerical simulation, the lower bound of secure key rates with respective to communication distance between user and central source are shown in Figure 2.

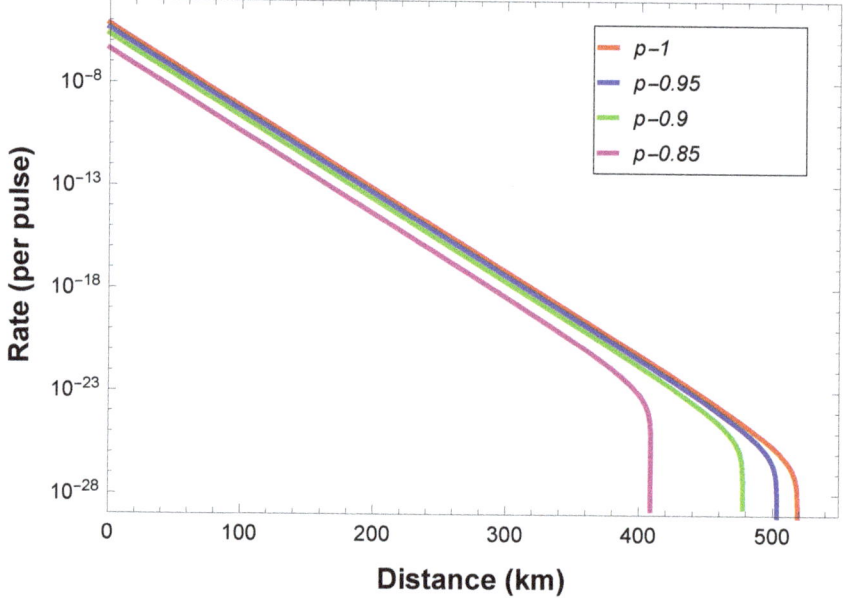

Figure 2. Lower bound on the secret key rate R versus communication distance between communication users using Werner-like states source. The red line denotes $p = 1$, i.e., the perfect GHZ source. The parameters are chosen according to experiments [35] : the detection efficiency $\eta_d = 40\%$, the misalignment-error probability of the system $e_d = 2\%$, the dark count rate of the detector $p_d = 8 \times 10^{-8}$, the error correction efficiency $f = 1.16$, the intrinsic loss coefficient of the standard telecom fiber channel $\alpha = 0.2$ dB/km.

The simulation shows that the secure key rate and the largest communication distance decrease when p decreases. To implement open-destination MDI-QKD efficiently, good-quality GHZ sources and single-photon sources are necessary. If such requirements are satisfied, our scheme can tolerate a high loss of more than 500 km of optical fibers, i.e., 100 dB, using perfect GHZ source and single-photon source, even when the BSM setups are located in every user's side. One can double the communication distance by putting the BSM setups in the middle of the users and the GHZ source, which is similar with the case in MDI-QKD [17,18]. For the realistic case where weak coherent pulses are used, our analysis can be generalized by considering the decoy state method [27,28] and following the procedures in Refs. [36,37].

4. Generalization to The (N,C) Case

As aforementioned, the complete analysis has been focused on the $(N, 2)$ open-destination MDI-QKD case. Here, we show that the case of two communication users can also generalized to the case of C communication users. Note that the open-destination feature enables any C users to generate secure keys at the same time.

Suppose that, in an N-party quantum network with users $1, 2, \cdots, N$, the communication users are denoted by the subset $\mathcal{C} = \{i_1, i_2, \ldots, i_C\}$, where $C = |\mathcal{C}|$. The auxiliary set denoted by $\mathcal{A}$ consists of auxiliary users, i.e., users that assist communication users to generate secure keys, with $A = |\mathcal{A}| = N - C$ users. According to Equation (3), for a general C communication users case, the GHZ state can be rewritten as

$$|GHZ\rangle_N = \frac{1}{\sqrt{2}} \left[|00\cdots 0\rangle_{12\cdots C} \bigotimes_{k=C+1\ldots N} \frac{|+\rangle_k + |-\rangle_k}{\sqrt{2}} + |11\cdots 1\rangle_{12\cdots C} \bigotimes_{k=C+1\ldots N} \frac{|+\rangle_k - |-\rangle_k}{\sqrt{2}} \right], \quad (9)$$

$$= \left(\frac{1}{\sqrt{2}}\right)^{N-1} \sum_{\chi} (|00\cdots 0\rangle_{12\cdots C} + (-1)^{\sigma_\chi} |11\cdots 1\rangle_{12\cdots C}) |\chi\rangle_{C+1\ldots N}. \quad (10)$$

Here, $\chi \in \{+, -\}^{N-C}$ is a string of $N - C$ bits with bit value "+" or "−" and $\sigma_\chi = 0(1)$ if the number of "−" is even (odd). Intuitively, with the assistance of $N - C$ auxiliary users, C-qubit GHZ states are shared among arbitrary C communication users. Meanwhile, based on the C-qubit GHZ state, the communication users can complete different quantum information tasks with the merit of open destination, such as quantum conference key agreement [24,34,38–40] and quantum secret sharing [39,41–43]. In general, we call it the (N, C) open-destination quantum communication task. When $C = 2$, and the aim is to establish QKD, the task is reduced to the $(N, 2)$ open-destination MDI-QKD network discussed above.

For instance, in the general case of (N, C) open-destination quantum conference key agreement, all users prepares and sends BB84 states to their respective untrusted relays. The central source simultaneously distribute the GHZ state, which is measured together with the state from user on the untrusted relay. When the relays announce successful BSM outcomes and when all auxiliary users announce their prepared states in X-basis, the communication users virtually share a multipartite entangled state, as the same of the $(N, 2)$ case. After suitable local operations of bit flips, all communication users share correctly correlated bits.

By slightly modifying the scheme, the experimental cost, especially the number of detectors can be reduced significantly. For instance, when all users announce their preparation basis X for assisting others while keep the bits corresponding to Z basis for distill the key, any C users can share secure keys simultaneously. This is because their respective sifted keys corresponds to different portions of the raw data. If one insists on using the conventional two-party QKD and multi-party conference key agreement scheme to realize the same function of the open-destination scheme under discussion, about $(2^N - 2)N$ detectors are required. In the open-destination scheme, the number of detectors is reduced to $4N$, which only increases linearly with the user number N.

As an example, we consider the case of $(N, 3)$ open-destination quantum conference key agreement. From Equation (10), the post-selected 3-party GHZ state is $|\phi^\pm_{\text{3-party}}\rangle = (|000\rangle \pm |111\rangle)/\sqrt{2}$ according to the announcements of the states and the BSM results related with auxiliary users. Meanwhile, as shown in Table 1, an equivalent GHZ analyzer among three communication users can be obtained according to the post-selected GHZ state $|\phi^\pm_{\text{3-party}}\rangle$ and the BSM results of their corresponding relays. Then, according to the MDI-QCC protocol in Ref. [39], $(N, 3)$ open-destination quantum conference key agreement can be directly conducted based on the equivalent GHZ analyzer.

Table 1. The equivalent GHZ analyzer measurement results of three communication users. Here, GHZ^A denotes the post-selected GHZ state from the GHZ source; BSM result 1(2,3) denotes the BSM results of three relays nearby the communication users' side; GHZ analyzer^C denotes the results of corresponding GHZ analyzer among three communication users.

GHZ^A	BSM Result 1	BSM Result 2	BSM Result 3	GHZ Analyzer^C
$\|\phi^+_{3\text{-party}}\rangle$ ($\|\phi^-_{3\text{-party}}\rangle$)	$\|\psi^+\rangle$	$\|\psi^+\rangle$	$\|\psi^+\rangle$	$\|\phi^+_{3\text{-party}}\rangle$ ($\|\phi^-_{3\text{-party}}\rangle$)
$\|\phi^+_{3\text{-party}}\rangle$ ($\|\phi^-_{3\text{-party}}\rangle$)	$\|\psi^+\rangle$	$\|\psi^+\rangle$	$\|\psi^-\rangle$	$\|\phi^-_{3\text{-party}}\rangle$ ($\|\phi^+_{3\text{-party}}\rangle$)
$\|\phi^+_{3\text{-party}}\rangle$ ($\|\phi^-_{3\text{-party}}\rangle$)	$\|\psi^+\rangle$	$\|\psi^-\rangle$	$\|\psi^+\rangle$	$\|\phi^-_{3\text{-party}}\rangle$ ($\|\phi^+_{3\text{-party}}\rangle$)
$\|\phi^+_{3\text{-party}}\rangle$ ($\|\phi^-_{3\text{-party}}\rangle$)	$\|\psi^+\rangle$	$\|\psi^-\rangle$	$\|\psi^-\rangle$	$\|\phi^+_{3\text{-party}}\rangle$ ($\|\phi^-_{3\text{-party}}\rangle$)
$\|\phi^+_{3\text{-party}}\rangle$ ($\|\phi^-_{3\text{-party}}\rangle$)	$\|\psi^-\rangle$	$\|\psi^+\rangle$	$\|\psi^+\rangle$	$\|\phi^-_{3\text{-party}}\rangle$ ($\|\phi^+_{3\text{-party}}\rangle$)
$\|\phi^+_{3\text{-party}}\rangle$ ($\|\phi^-_{3\text{-party}}\rangle$)	$\|\psi^-\rangle$	$\|\psi^+\rangle$	$\|\psi^-\rangle$	$\|\phi^+_{3\text{-party}}\rangle$ ($\|\phi^-_{3\text{-party}}\rangle$)
$\|\phi^+_{3\text{-party}}\rangle$ ($\|\phi^-_{3\text{-party}}\rangle$)	$\|\psi^-\rangle$	$\|\psi^-\rangle$	$\|\psi^+\rangle$	$\|\phi^+_{3\text{-party}}\rangle$ ($\|\phi^-_{3\text{-party}}\rangle$)
$\|\phi^+_{3\text{-party}}\rangle$ ($\|\phi^-_{3\text{-party}}\rangle$)	$\|\psi^-\rangle$	$\|\psi^-\rangle$	$\|\psi^-\rangle$	$\|\phi^-_{3\text{-party}}\rangle$ ($\|\phi^+_{3\text{-party}}\rangle$)

Similar to the open-destination MDI-QKD in Section (2) of the $(N,2)$ case, the security of the $(N,3)$ open-destination quantum conference key agreement is also based on the entanglement purification discussion [39,44,45]. According to the multi-partite entanglement purification scheme [46], the secret key rate can be written as follows [34,39,40]:

$$R_3 = Q^Z\{1 - f \cdot \max[H(E^Z_{12}), H(E^Z_{13})] - H(E^X)\}, \tag{11}$$

where Q^Z is the overall gains when three communication users send out quantum states in Z basis, E^Z_{12} (E^Z_{13}) is the marginal quantum bit error rate between user 1 and user 2 (3) in Z basis, E^X is the overall quantum bit error rate in X basis, f is the error correction efficiency, and $H(x) = -x\log_2(x) - (1-x)\log_2(1-x)$ is the binary Shannon entropy function. Q^Z, E^X, E^Z_{12}, and E^Z_{13} can be gotten directly from the experimental results. Meanwhile, the estimation of key rate can be slightly different if the sources of users are weak coherent states [33].

5. Conclusions

As a conclusion, we proposed a flexible and extensible scheme of the $(N,2)$ open-destination MDI-QKD network. We proved the correctness and security of the protocol, and derived practical key generation rate formula. For an illustration, we studied a specific network where two of four users want to distill quantum secure keys. For the scenario, we presented a polarization-encoding scheme for experimental implementation and offered in detail a simulation by taking the imperfections in both source and detectors into account. The simulation results show that the scheme enjoys a promising structure and performance in real-life situation.

A significant virtue of our scheme is the security against untrustful relays and all detector side-channel attacks. Moreover, the open-destination feature enables any two users to establish MDI-QKD without changing the network structures. In fact, one can establish MDI-QKD among arbitrary users even after the entangled source have been distributed and all the measurements have been completed. Furthermore, following the multi-entanglement swapping scheme, the network can be extended into a large scale by adding shared multi-partite GHZ states.

We would like to remark that currently the efficiency was relatively low (seen from Figure 2). This can be overcome by taking optimization in network topology, basis selections, and measurements for both the auxiliary and communication parties, as well as considering asymmetric loss for various channels, etc., like techniques adopted in Ref. [47]. Any future improvement on distributing multipartite entanglement efficiently and effectively will definitely benefit the proposed scheme and push it forward practical applications.

Author Contributions: Conceptualization, K.C.; methodology, F.X., L.L., N.-L.L., and K.C.; software, W.-F.C. and Y.-L.Z.; validation, Y.-Z.Z., Y.-L.Z., and K.C.; investigation, W.-F.C., Y.-Z.Z.; Writing—Original draft preparation, W.-F.C., Z.-Y.Z., and S.Z.; Writing—Review and editing, F.X., L.L., Z.-B.C., N.-L.L., and K.C.; visualization, W.-F.C., N.-L.L., and K.C.; supervision, F.X., L.L., Z.-B.C., N.-L.L., and K.C.; All authors have read and agreed to the published version of the manuscript.

Funding: This research was funded by the Chinese Academy of Science, the National Fundamental Research Program, the National Natural Science Foundation of China (Grants No. 11575174, No. 11374287, No. 61125502, No. 11574297, and No. 61771443), as well as the Fundamental Research Funds for the Central Universities (WK2340000083).

Acknowledgments: We thank Yu-Ao Chen and Qiang Zhang for valuable and enlightening discussions.

Conflicts of Interest: The authors declare no conflict of interest.

Appendix A. Sifting Procedure of The (4,2) Case

In this section, we describe the sifting procedure of open-destination MDI-QKD in detail for the $(4,2)$ case. We will show that such scenario can be reduced to the standard MDI-QKD scenario. The general case can be proved in a similar way, as shown in the main text. The schematic diagram is depicted in Figure A1a.

We start by writing the GHZ state as

$$|GHZ\rangle_4 = \frac{1}{2\sqrt{2}}[(|00\rangle + |11\rangle)(|++\rangle + |--\rangle) \\ + (|00\rangle - |11\rangle)(|+-\rangle + |-+\rangle)]. \tag{A1}$$

Up to the announcement of the quantum state of users $3'$ and $4'$, the BSM(s) of relays 3 and 4 on the received quantum state from GHZ source and quantum state from users $3'(4')$ can be treated as an equivalent projective measurement on the whole GHZ state. Specifically, if the relays 3 and 4 perform the BSM and obtain equivalent projective measurement results $|00\rangle$ or $|11\rangle$ ($|01\rangle$ or $|10\rangle$), the photons received by relays 1 and 2 will be projected into state $|\phi^+\rangle = (|00\rangle + |11\rangle)/\sqrt{2}$ ($|\phi^-\rangle = (|00\rangle - |11\rangle)\sqrt{2}$) according to Equation (A1). After announcement of the successful BSM results and the quantum states of auxiliary users $3'$ and $4'$, the projected state received by relays 1 and 2 can be determined. So, one can treat the GHZ source, the BSM setups of relays 3 and 4 and the quantum state of auxiliary user $3'$ and $4'$ as a virtual entanglement source, which outputs different Bell states. The protocol is thus directly equivalent to MDI-QKD with an entangled source in the middle [29] as illustrated in Figure A1b. Since the virtual Bell state with two BSMs along each side can be equivalent to a virtual BSM, the scheme is finally equivalent to implement MDI-QKD between users $1'$ and $2'$ as showed in Figure A1c. Therefore, in an honest run, the protocol is reduced to the honest standard MDI-QKD scenario, and the parties will end up with sharing a common key.

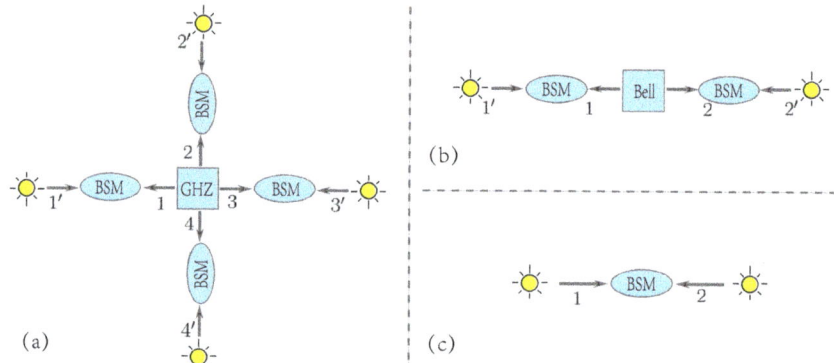

Figure A1. (**a**) The schematic diagram for the (4, 2) open-destination MDI-QKD scheme. Users $1'$ and $2'$ denote communication users, while users $3'$ and $4'$ denote auxiliary users. (**b**) The equivalent topological schematic diagram when users $1'$ and $2'$ communicate with each other. According to BSM results of relays 3 and 4 and quantum states of auxiliary users $3'$ and $4'$, the GHZ state is projected to a virtual Bell state. (**c**) The final equivalent topological schematic diagram that users $1'$ and $2'$ perform MDI-QKD, according to the BSM results and the virtual Bell state.

Firstly, notice that the projection measurement of two systems onto one Bell state can be viewed as a POVM (positive operator valued measure) on one system if one knows the state of the other system. For example, as shown in Figure A1a, a successful BSM result of $|\psi^-\rangle$ of the relay 3 with auxiliary photons from auxiliary $3'$ in the state $|\alpha\rangle'_3$ can be viewed as a POVM $\mathrm{tr}_{3'}\left[|\psi^-\rangle\langle\psi^-|_{33'}|\alpha\rangle\langle\alpha|_{3'}\right]$ on the state 3. In the open-destination scheme, we have $|\alpha\rangle \in \{|+\rangle, |-\rangle\}$ and the BSM results $\{|\psi^+\rangle, |\psi^-\rangle\}$. The correspondence between the POVM on the system k and the untrusted relay announces a successful BSM together with auxiliary state are listed in Table A1.

Table A1. The correspondence between the POVM on state labeled k and the BSM result labeled by kk' with auxiliary state labeled by k'.

State of System k'	BSM Result on Systems kk'	POVM on System k
$\|+\rangle$	$\|\psi^-\rangle$	$\|-\rangle\langle-\|/2$
$\|-\rangle$	$\|\psi^-\rangle$	$\|+\rangle\langle+\|/2$
$\|+\rangle$	$\|\psi^+\rangle$	$\|+\rangle\langle+\|/2$
$\|-\rangle$	$\|\psi^+\rangle$	$\|-\rangle\langle-\|/2$

Secondly, when the two auxiliary users prepare X-basis photons and the corresponding relays get successful BSM results, according to Table A1, the total GHZ state collapses into one of the maximally entangled states $|\phi^\pm\rangle = \frac{1}{\sqrt{2}}(|HH\rangle \pm |VV\rangle)$ at the side of two communication users.

Thirdly, at the sides of the two communication users, according to the post-selected Bell state $|\phi^\pm\rangle$ and the BSM results of their corresponding relays, a BSM between two communication users can be obtained. Such correspondence is listed in Table A2.

Table A2. The equivalent BSM results of two communication users. Here, Bell^A denotes the post-selected Bell state from the GHZ source; BSM result 1(2) denotes the BSM results of the two relays nearby the communication users' side; BSM^C denotes the results of corresponding BSM between two communication users.

Bell^A	BSM Result 1	BSM Result 2	BSM^C
$\|\phi^+\rangle$	$\|\psi^+\rangle$	$\|\psi^+\rangle$	$\|\phi^+\rangle$
$\|\phi^+\rangle$	$\|\psi^+\rangle$	$\|\psi^-\rangle$	$\|\phi^-\rangle$
$\|\phi^+\rangle$	$\|\psi^-\rangle$	$\|\psi^+\rangle$	$\|\phi^-\rangle$
$\|\phi^+\rangle$	$\|\psi^-\rangle$	$\|\psi^-\rangle$	$\|\phi^+\rangle$
$\|\phi^-\rangle$	$\|\psi^+\rangle$	$\|\psi^+\rangle$	$\|\phi^-\rangle$
$\|\phi^-\rangle$	$\|\psi^+\rangle$	$\|\psi^-\rangle$	$\|\phi^+\rangle$
$\|\phi^-\rangle$	$\|\psi^-\rangle$	$\|\psi^+\rangle$	$\|\phi^+\rangle$
$\|\phi^-\rangle$	$\|\psi^-\rangle$	$\|\psi^-\rangle$	$\|\phi^-\rangle$

Finally, as shown in Table A3, according to the final equivalent BSM result and the preparation bases, one of the communication users apply a bit flip or not such that their keys can be correlated. In fact, only when both communication users select X basis and the final equivalent BSM result is $|\phi^-\rangle$, one of them needs to apply a bit flip. After many rounds, they obtain enough raw key bits that can be used in the following data post-processing process.

Table A3. Flip table according to the preparation bases and the equivalent BSM result at communication users side.

Basis	$\|\phi^+\rangle$	$\|\phi^-\rangle$
Z-basis	No Flip	No Flip
X-basis	No Flip	Flip

Appendix B. Detector Analysis

Since the BSM with the auxiliary photon is equivalent to an probabilistic projective measurement, one can use an equivalent detector to replace the BSM device with the corresponding light source in the key rate analysis. Here, we develop a method to derive the equivalent detector parameters, i.e., the detection efficiency and the dark count of the equivalent detector. We use the BSM setup with polarization encoding as illustrated in Figure A2.

In H/V basis, suppose that Alice and Bob encode the same polarization states; then, the state becomes as follows after the BS:

$$a_H^\dagger b_H^\dagger |vac\rangle \rightarrow (a_{1H}^{\dagger 2} - a_{2H}^{\dagger 2})|vac\rangle, \tag{A2}$$

where $a^\dagger$ ($b^\dagger$) denotes creation operators, and $|vac\rangle$ denotes vacuum state. The probability of the successful BSM when the input states are $|H\rangle$ and $|H\rangle$, is given by

$$P_{HH} = 2p_d(1-p_d)^2(1-(1-p_d)(1-\eta_d)^2), \tag{A3}$$

where η_d is the detection efficiency, and p_d is the dark count. Suppose that Alice and Bob encode different polarization state; then, after the BS, the state becomes as follows:

$$\begin{aligned}a_H^\dagger b_V^\dagger |vac\rangle \rightarrow &(a_{1H}^\dagger a_{1V}^\dagger - a_{2H}^\dagger a_{2V}^\dagger)|vac\rangle \\ &+ (a_{2H}^\dagger a_{1V}^\dagger - a_{1H}^\dagger a_{2V}^\dagger)|vac\rangle.\end{aligned} \tag{A4}$$

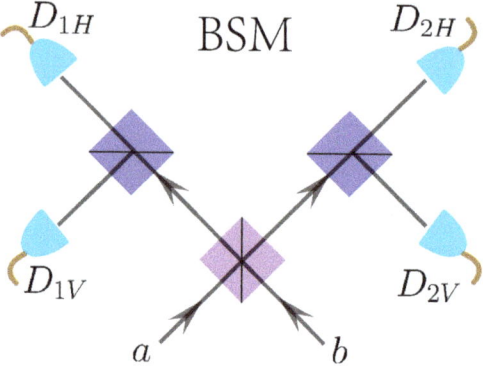

Figure A2. The BSM setup with polarization encoding. BS denotes beam splitter, PBS denotes polarization beam splitter, and H and V denote, respectively, horizontal and vertical linear polarizations, and D_{1H}, D_{2H}, D_{1V}, D_{2V} denote single-photon detectors. A click in D_{1H} and D_{2V}, or in D_{1V} and D_{2H}, indicates a projection into the Bell state $|\psi^-\rangle = (|HV\rangle - |VH\rangle)/\sqrt{2}$, and a click in D_{1H} and D_{1V}, or in D_{2H} and D_{2V}, indicates a projection into the Bell state $|\psi^+\rangle = (|HV\rangle + |VH\rangle)/\sqrt{2}$.

The probability of the successful BSM when the input states are $|H\rangle$ and $|V\rangle$ is given by

$$P_{HV} = (1-p_d)^2(1-(1-p_d)(1-\eta_d))^2. \tag{A5}$$

Thus, the equivalent detection probability when the input state is $|H\rangle$ is given by

$$\begin{aligned}\eta'_H =& \frac{1}{2}(1-p_d)^2[2p_d(1-(1-p_d)(1-\eta_d)^2) \\ & + (1-(1-p_d)(1-\eta_d))^2].\end{aligned} \tag{A6}$$

Due to symmetry, the equivalent detection probability when the input state is $|V\rangle$ has the same form with the case that the input state is $|H\rangle$, i.e., one has $\eta'_V = \eta'_H$. Similarly, by using the transformation relation under $\{+,-\}$ basis

$$\begin{aligned}a^\dagger_+ b^\dagger_+ |vac\rangle &\to (a^\dagger_{1H} a^\dagger_{1V} - a^\dagger_{2H} a^\dagger_{2V})|vac\rangle \\ a^\dagger_+ b^\dagger_- |vac\rangle &\to (a^\dagger_{1H} a^\dagger_{2V} - a^\dagger_{1V} a^\dagger_{2H})|vac\rangle,\end{aligned} \tag{A7}$$

one can ontain the equivalent detection probability when the input state is $|+\rangle$ as follows:

$$\eta'_+ = (1-p_d)^2(1-(1-p_d)(1-\eta_d))^2. \tag{A8}$$

Due to symmetry, one has $\eta'_- = \eta'_+$.

We consider practical experimental parameters, which are listed in Table A4. For the experimental parameters, one arrives at

$$\eta'^Z_d = 0.08, \quad \eta'^X_d = 0.16, \tag{A9}$$

where η'^Z_d denotes the equivalent detection efficiency for H/V basis, i.e., Z basis, and η'^X_d denotes the equivalent detection efficiency for $+/-$ basis, i.e., X basis.

Table A4. List of experimental parameters used for simulation. η_d is the detection efficiency; e_d is the misalignment-error probability of the system; p_d is the dark count rate of the detector; f is error correction efficiency; α is the intrinsic loss coefficient of the standard telecom fiber channel.

η_d	e_d	p_d	f	α (dB/km)
40%	2%	8×10^{-8}	1.16	0.2

To calculate the parameters for equivalent dark count, one should consider the case in which there was no incoming photon. Suppose the local photon being $|H\rangle$, and the incoming photon being vacumm state, the states become as follows after the BS:

$$b_H^\dagger |vac\rangle \to \frac{i}{\sqrt{2}} a_{1H}^\dagger + \frac{1}{\sqrt{2}} a_{2H}^\dagger, \quad (A10)$$

where $b_H^\dagger$ denotes the creation operator of local photon. So, one can get the probability of the successful BSM as follows:

$$P_H = 2p_d(1-p_d)^2 \eta_d. \quad (A11)$$

Due to symmetry, one has that $P_+ = P_- = P_V = P_H$. Here, P_x denotes the probability of the successful BSM result when the local photon is $|x\rangle$ and there is no incoming photon. So, one can get the equivalent dark count as

$$p_d' = 2p_d(1-p_d)^2 \eta_d. \quad (A12)$$

For the experimental parameters given in Table A4, one arrives at

$$p_d' = 6.4 \times 10^{-8}. \quad (A13)$$

Finally, one can achieve the parameters for the equivalent detectors shown in Table A5.

Table A5. List of the parameters for the equivalent detectors. $\eta_d'^Z$ ($\eta_d'^X$) denotes the equivalent detection efficiency for Z (X) basis, and p_d' denotes the equivalent dark count.

$\eta_d'^Z$	$\eta_d'^X$	p_d'
8%	16%	6.4×10^{-8}

Appendix C. Simulation for (4,2)-Scenario

For simulation purposes, one can assume practically that the source has the form of Werner-like states

$$\rho = p |GHZ\rangle \langle GHZ|_4 + \frac{1-p}{16} \mathbb{I}, \quad (A14)$$

in which $|GHZ\rangle_4 = (|HHHH\rangle + |VVVV\rangle)/\sqrt{2}$ is the 4-partite GHZ states, $\mathbb{I}/16$ is the 4-partite maximal mixed states, and $0 \le p \le 1$. As proven in the previous section, according to the measurement results of auxiliary side, the photons received by communication side will be projected into different Bell states. Here, we consider the case in which auxiliary side get the $|+\rangle \otimes |+\rangle$ results, due to the symmetry. When auxiliary side get the $|+\rangle \otimes |+\rangle$ result, the particles received by communication side will collapse into

$$\rho_{AB} = p |\phi^+\rangle \langle \phi^+| + \frac{1-p}{4} \mathbb{I}, \quad (A15)$$

where $\phi^+ = (|HH\rangle + |VV\rangle)/\sqrt{2}$ is one of the Bell states. So, it is equivalent with the case in which the two communication users (denoted by Alice and Bob) perform an entanglement-based QKD using the two-qubit Werner states ρ_{AB} as a source and the equivalent detectors as detection device, as illustrated in Figure A3, from the perspective of key rate analysis.

Taking these imperfections of the source and detectors into account, the key generation rate in a realistic setup will be given by

$$R = Q_{11}^{ZZ}(1 - H(e_{11}^{XX})) - Q_{\mu\nu}^{ZZ} \cdot f \cdot H(E_{\mu\nu}^{ZZ}). \tag{A16}$$

In the following, we discuss how one can derive each quantity in this key rate formula, i.e., Q_{11}^{ZZ}, e_{11}^{XX}, $Q_{\mu\nu}^{ZZ}$, and $E_{\mu\nu}^{ZZ}$.

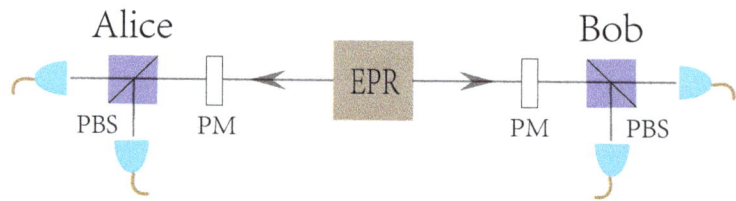

Figure A3. Equivalent setup for Alice and Bob when tracing the BSM results of the auxiliary users. PBS denotes polarization beam splitter, PM denotes polarization modulator, and EPR denotes EPR source.

Yield. Denote the yield of single-photon pair as Y_{11}, i.e., the conditional probability of a coincidence detection event given that the entanglement source emits an single-photon pair. Then, Y_{11} is given by

$$Y_{11} = [1 - (1 - Y_{0A})(1 - \eta_A)][1 - (1 - Y_{0B})(1 - \eta_B)], \tag{A17}$$

where $Y_{0A} = Y_{0B} = p'_d$ are the background count rates on Alice's and Bob's sides in the Z basis, and $\eta_A = \eta_B = \eta_d'^Z \times 10^{-\alpha L/20}$ denotes the total detection efficiency considering the channel loss. Equation (A17) is also applicable to the X basis. Then, the gain of the single photon part and the overall gain are given by

$$Q_{\mu\nu}^{ZZ} = Q_{11}^{ZZ} = Y_{11}. \tag{A18}$$

Error Rate. The error rate of single-photon pair in the X basis e_{11}^{XX} has three main contributions taking some imperfections into account: (i) *The imperfections of entanglement source*, i.e., the maximal mixed states component, which brings 50% error rate $e_0 = 1/2$; (ii) *Background counts*, which are random noises $e_0 = 1/2$; (iii) *Intrinsic detector error e_d*, which characterizes the alignment and stability of the optical system. So, the error rate of single-photon pair e_{11}^{XX} is given as follows:

$$e_{11}^{XX} Y_{11} = pe_0(Y_{11} - \eta_A \eta_B) + pe_d \eta_A \eta_B + (1-p)e_0 Y_{11}, \tag{A19}$$

where the first item comes from background counts, the second term comes from intrinsic errors, and the third term comes from the mixed part of the source. So, one achieves the error rate of single-photon pair e_{11}^{XX} as follows:

$$e_{11}^{XX} = e_0 - \frac{p\eta_A\eta_B(e_0 - e_d)}{Y_{11}}. \tag{A20}$$

Similarly, the error rate in the Z basis is given by

$$E_{\mu\nu}^{ZZ} = e_0 - \frac{p\eta_A\eta_B(e_0 - e_d)}{Y_{11}}. \tag{A21}$$

Reference

1. Bennett, C.H.; Brassard, G. Quantum cryptography: Public key distribution and coin tossing. In *Proceedings of IEEE International Conference on Computer System and Signal Processing*; IEEE: New York, NY, USA, 1984; p. 175.
2. Ekert, A.K. Quantum cryptography based on Bell's theorem. *Phys. Rev. Lett.* **1991**, *67*, 661–663. [CrossRef] [PubMed]
3. Gisin, N.; Ribordy, G.; Tittel, W.; Zbinden, H. Quantum cryptography. *Rev. Mod. Phys.* **2002**, *74*, 145–195. [CrossRef]
4. Scarani, V.; Bechmann-Pasquinucci, H.; Cerf, N.J.; Dušek, M.; Lütkenhaus, N.; Peev, M. The security of practical quantum key distribution. *Rev. Mod. Phys.* **2009**, *81*, 1301–1350. [CrossRef]
5. Elliott, C. The DARPA quantum network. In *Quantum Communications and Cryptography*; CRC Press: Boca Raton, FL, USA, 2005; pp. 83–102.
6. Peev, M.; Pacher, C.; Alléaume, R.; Barreiro, C.; Bouda, J.; Boxleitner, W.; Debuisschert, T.; Diamanti, E.; Dianati, M.; Dynes, J.; et al. The SECOQC quantum key distribution network in Vienna. *New J. Phys.* **2009**, *11*, 075001. [CrossRef]
7. Chen, T.Y.; Wang, J.; Liang, H.; Liu, W.Y.; Liu, Y.; Jiang, X.; Wang, Y.; Wan, X.; Cai, W.Q.; Ju, L.; et al. Metropolitan all-pass and inter-city quantum communication network. *Opt. Express* **2010**, *18*, 27217–27225. [CrossRef]
8. Sasaki, M.; Fujiwara, M.; Ishizuka, H.; Klaus, W.; Wakui, K.; Takeoka, M.; Miki, S.; Yamashita, T.; Wang, Z.; Tanaka, A.; et al. Field test of quantum key distribution in the Tokyo QKD Network. *Opt. Express* **2011**, *19*, 10387–10409. [CrossRef]
9. Fröhlich, B.; Dynes, J.F.; Lucamarini, M.; Sharpe, A.W.; Yuan, Z.; Shields, A.J. A quantum access network. *Nature* **2013**, *501*, 69. [CrossRef]
10. Qiu, J. Quantum communications leap out of the lab. *Nature (London)* **2014**, *508*, 441. [CrossRef]
11. Liao, S.K.; Cai, W.Q.; Handsteiner, J.; Liu, B.; Yin, J.; Zhang, L.; Rauch, D.; Fink, M.; Ren, J.G.; Liu, W.Y.; et al. Satellite-Relayed Intercontinental Quantum Network. *Phys. Rev. Lett.* **2018**, *120*, 030501. [CrossRef]
12. Qi, B.; Fung, C.H.F.; Lo, H.K.; Ma, X. Time-shift Attack in Practical Quantum Cryptosystems. *Quantum Inf. Comput.* **2007**, *7*, 073.
13. Zhao, Y.; Fung, C.H.F.; Qi, B.; Chen, C.; Lo, H.K. Quantum hacking: Experimental demonstration of time-shift attack against practical quantum-key-distribution systems. *Phys. Rev. A* **2008**, *78*, 042333. [CrossRef]
14. Lydersen, L.; Wiechers, C.; Wittmann, C.; Elser, D.; Skaar, J.; Makarov, V. Hacking commercial quantum cryptography systems by tailored bright illumination. *Nat. Photonics* **2010**, *4*, 686–689. [CrossRef]
15. Gerhardt, I.; Liu, Q.; Lamas-Linares, A.; Skaar, J.; Kurtsiefer, C.; Makarov, V. Full-field implementation of a perfect eavesdropper on a quantum cryptography system. *Nat. Commun.* **2011**, *2*, 349. [CrossRef] [PubMed]
16. Weier, H.; Krauss, H.; Rau, M.; Fürst, M.; Nauerth, S.; Weinfurter, H. Quantum eavesdropping without interception: An attack exploiting the dead time of single-photon detectors. *New J. Phys.* **2011**, *13*, 073024. [CrossRef]
17. Lo, H.K.; Curty, M.; Qi, B. Measurement-Device-Independent Quantum Key Distribution. *Phys. Rev. Lett.* **2012**, *108*, 130503. [CrossRef]
18. Braunstein, S.L.; Pirandola, S. Side-Channel-Free Quantum Key Distribution. *Phys. Rev. Lett.* **2012**, *108*, 130502. [CrossRef]
19. Xu, F.; Curty, M.; Qi, B.; Qian, L.; Lo, H.K. Discrete and continuous variables for measurement-device-independent quantum cryptography. *Nat. Photonics* **2015**, *9*, 772. [CrossRef]
20. Pirandola, S.; Ottaviani, C.; Spedalieri, G.; Weedbrook, C.; Braunstein, S.L.; Lloyd, S.; Gehring, T.; Jacobsen, C.S.; Andersen, U.L. Reply to Discrete and continuous variables for measurement-device-independent quantum cryptography. *Nat. Photonics* **2015**, *9*, 773. [CrossRef]
21. Tang, Z.; Wei, K.; Bedroya, O.; Qian, L.; Lo, H.K. Experimental measurement-device-independent quantum key distribution with imperfect sources. *Phys. Rev. A* **2016**, *93*, 042308. [CrossRef]
22. Epping, M.; Kampermann, H.; Macchiavello, C.; Bruß, D. Multi-partite entanglement can speed up quantum key distribution in networks. *New J. Phys.* **2017**, *19*, 093012. [CrossRef]

23. Zhao, Z.; Chen, Y.A.; Zhang, A.N.; Yang, T.; Briegel, H.J.; Pan, J.W. Experimental demonstration of five-photon entanglement and open-destination teleportation. *Nature* **2004**, *430*, 54–58. [CrossRef] [PubMed]
24. Bose, S.; Vedral, V.; Knight, P.L. Multiparticle generalization of entanglement swapping. *Phys. Rev. A* **1998**, *57*, 822–829. [CrossRef]
25. Einstein, A.; Podolsky, B.; Rosen, N. Can Quantum-Mechanical Description of Physical Reality Be Considered Complete? *Phys. Rev.* **1935**, *47*, 777. [CrossRef]
26. Hwang, W.Y. Quantum Key Distribution with High Loss: Toward Global Secure Communication. *Phys. Rev. Lett.* **2003**, *91*, 057901. [CrossRef]
27. Lo, H.K.; Ma, X.; Chen, K. Decoy State Quantum Key Distribution. *Phys. Rev. Lett.* **2005**, *94*, 230504. [CrossRef]
28. Wang, X.B. Beating the Photon-Number-Splitting Attack in Practical Quantum Cryptography. *Phys. Rev. Lett.* **2005**, *94*, 230503. [CrossRef]
29. Xu, F.; Qi, B.; Liao, Z.; Lo, H.K. Long distance measurement-device-independent quantum key distribution with entangled photon sources. *Appl. Phys. Lett.* **2013**, *103*, 061101. [CrossRef]
30. Koashi, M.; Winter, A. Monogamy of quantum entanglement and other correlations. *Phys. Rev. A* **2004**, *69*, 022309. [CrossRef]
31. Osborne, T.J.; Verstraete, F. General Monogamy Inequality for Bipartite Qubit Entanglement. *Phys. Rev. Lett.* **2006**, *96*, 220503. [CrossRef]
32. Ou, Y.C.; Fan, H.; Fei, S.M. Proper monogamy inequality for arbitrary pure quantum states. *Phys. Rev. A* **2008**, *78*, 012311. [CrossRef]
33. Gottesman, D.; Lo, H.K.; Lütkenhaus, N.; Preskill, J. Security of quantum key distribution with imperfect devices. *Quantum Inf. Comput.* **2004**, *4*, 325.
34. Chen, K.; Lo, H.K. Multi-partite quantum cryptographic protocols with noisy GHZ states. *Quantum Inf. Comput.* **2007**, *7*, 689.
35. Tang, Y.L.; Yin, H.L.; Chen, S.J.; Liu, Y.; Zhang, W.J.; Jiang, X.; Zhang, L.; Wang, J.; You, L.X.; Guan, J.Y.; et al. Measurement-Device-Independent Quantum Key Distribution over 200 km. *Phys. Rev. Lett.* **2014**, *113*, 190501. [CrossRef] [PubMed]
36. Curty, M.; Xu, F.; Cui, W.; Lim, C.C.W.; Tamaki, K.; Lo, H.K. Finite-key analysis for measurement-device-independent quantum key distribution. *Nat. Commun.* **2014**, *5*, 3732. [CrossRef]
37. Xu, F.; Xu, H.; Lo, H.K. Protocol choice and parameter optimization in decoy-state measurement-device-independent quantum key distribution. *Phys. Rev. A* **2014**, *89*, 052333. [CrossRef]
38. Chen, K.; Lo, H.K. Conference key agreement and quantum sharing of classical secrets with noisy GHZ states. In Proceedings of the International Symposium on Information Theory (ISIT 2005), Adelaide, SA, Australia, 4–9 September 2005; pp. 1607–1611. [CrossRef]
39. Fu, Y.; Yin, H.L.; Chen, T.Y.; Chen, Z.B. Long-Distance Measurement-Device-Independent Multiparty Quantum Communication. *Phys. Rev. Lett.* **2015**, *114*, 090501. [CrossRef]
40. Zhao, S.; Zeng, P.; Cao, W.F.; Xu, X.Y.; Zhen, Y.Z.; Ma, X.; Li, L.; Liu, N.L.; Chen, K. Phase-Matching Quantum Cryptographic Conferencing. *Phys. Rev. Appl.* **2020**, *14*, 024010. [CrossRef]
41. Hillery, M.; Bužek, V.; Berthiaume, A. Quantum secret sharing. *Phys. Rev. A* **1999**, *59*, 1829–1834. [CrossRef]
42. Cleve, R.; Gottesman, D.; Lo, H.K. How to Share a Quantum Secret. *Phys. Rev. Lett.* **1999**, *83*, 648–651. [CrossRef]
43. Chen, Y.A.; Zhang, A.N.; Zhao, Z.; Zhou, X.Q.; Lu, C.Y.; Peng, C.Z.; Yang, T.; Pan, J.W. Experimental Quantum Secret Sharing and Third-Man Quantum Cryptography. *Phys. Rev. Lett.* **2005**, *95*, 200502. [CrossRef]
44. Lo, H.K.; Chau, H.F. Unconditional security of quantum key distribution over arbitrarily long distances. *Science* **1999**, *283*, 2050–2056. [CrossRef] [PubMed]
45. Shor, P.W.; Preskill, J. Simple proof of security of the BB84 quantum key distribution protocol. *Phys. Rev. Lett.* **2000**, *85*, 441. [CrossRef] [PubMed]

46. Maneva, E.N.; Smolin, J.A. Improved two-party and multi-party purification protocols. *Contemp. Math.* **2002**, *305*, 203–212.
47. Wang, W.; Xu, F.; Lo, H.K. Asymmetric Protocols for Scalable High-Rate Measurement-Device-Independent Quantum Key Distribution Networks. *Phys. Rev. X* **2019**, *9*, 041012. [CrossRef]

© 2020 by the authors. Licensee MDPI, Basel, Switzerland. This article is an open access article distributed under the terms and conditions of the Creative Commons Attribution (CC BY) license (http://creativecommons.org/licenses/by/4.0/).

Article
Distinguishability and Disturbance in the Quantum Key Distribution Protocol Using the Mean Multi-Kings' Problem

Masakazu Yoshida [1,*], **Ayumu Nakayama** [2] **and Jun Cheng** [3]

1. Faculty of Design Technology, Osaka Sangyo University, 3-1-1 Daito-shi, Osaka 574-8530, Japan
2. Independent Researcher, Chiba 263-8522, Japan; chiba.u.nakayama@gmail.com
3. Faculty of Science and Engineering, Doshisha University, 1-3 Kyotanabe-shi, Kyoto 610-0394, Japan; jcheng@mail.doshisha.ac.jp
* Correspondence: yoshida@ise.osaka-sandai.ac.jp

Received: 7 October 2020; Accepted: 9 November 2020; Published: 11 November 2020

Abstract: We introduce a quantum key distribution protocol using mean multi-kings' problem. Using this protocol, a sender can share a bit sequence as a secret key with receivers. We consider a relation between information gain by an eavesdropper and disturbance contained in legitimate users' information. In BB84 protocol, such relation is known as the so-called information disturbance theorem. We focus on a setting that the sender and two receivers try to share bit sequences and the eavesdropper tries to extract information by interacting legitimate users' systems and an ancilla system. We derive trade-off inequalities between distinguishability of quantum states corresponding to the bit sequence for the eavesdropper and error probability of the bit sequence shared with the legitimate users. Our inequalities show that eavesdropper's extracting information regarding the secret keys inevitably induces disturbing the states and increasing the error probability.

Keywords: quantum key distribution; mean-king's problem; mean multi-kings' problem; information disturbance theorem

1. Introduction

In the quantum state discrimination problems, one tries to discriminate the quantum states by performing the single measurement. Several strategies exist, e.g., in [1–3] and Section 9.1.4 in [4]. On the other hand, in the mean-king's problem [5], one can use not the single measurement but also post-information. Specific setting of the mean-king's problem is often told as a tale [6] of a king and a physicist Alice. In the tale, Alice prepares a qubit in an initial state at first. The king performs a measurement with one of observables $\sigma_x, \sigma_y, \sigma_z$ on the qubit and obtains an outcome. Then, Alice obtains an outcome by performing a measurement on the qubit. After the measurement, the king reveals the observable he has measured as the post-information. Then, Alice tries to guess king's outcome by using her outcome and the post-information. A solution to the problem is a pair of the initial state and Alice's measurement such that she can guess king's outcome correctly. Using Aharonov–Bergman–Lebowitz rule [7], a solution which consists of Bell state and a measurement on a bipartite system has been shown [5]. As an application of the solution to the mean-king's problem, a quantum key distribution protocol (QKD) has been shown [8]. In this protocol, Alice and the king employ the guessing result as a secret key, and security analysis of the protocol has been considered [8–11].

A QKD protocol by using mean multi-kings' problem has been shown [12] (see Section 2 for details). In this protocol, Alice and kings (called $King_1, King_2, ..., King_n$) are legitimate users. Alice guesses each king's measurement outcome by using her measurement outcome and post-information from each king; then, each guessing result is shared as a secret key between Alice and each king. The protocol has superior aspects, such as the number of measurements, state preparation and key discarding, to several realizations (whose components are the QKD protocol by using the mean-king's problem or BB84 protocol [13]) for Alice and each king to share the secret key. In the case of $n = 2$, security analysis against a simple attack so called intercept-resend attack has been considered and error rate of bits shared between Alice and the kings has been shown.

In this paper, we consider a relation between information gain by an eavesdropper (called Eve) and disturbance contained in the legitimate users' information in the QKD protocol by using the mean multi-kings' problem. In BB84 protocol, such relation is known as the so-called information disturbance theorem [14–18]. According to the theorem, Eve's information gain in a basis inevitably induces disturbance contained in the legitimate users' information in the conjugate basis. Therefore, the theorem is also regarded as an information theoretical version of the uncertainty relation. The theorem also plays an important role in the proof of the unconditional security [19]. We consider that Eve tries to extract information by employing an attack which she performs any measurement on her quantum system at any time after interacting the quantum system with kings' qubits after their measurements in the case of $n = 2$. In this setting, we give trade-off inequalities between distinguishability of quantum states corresponding to the bit sequences for Eve and error probability of the bit sequences shared with Alice and the kings. Our inequalities show that Eve's extracting information regarding the secret keys inevitably induces disturbing the states of kings' qubits and increasing the error probability even though the post-information and Alice's qubit are used in the guessing step, unlike BB84 protocol.

This paper is organized as follows. In the next section, we review a description of the quantum key distribution protocol by using the mean multi-kings' problem. In Section 3, we give the description of the protocol in the case of $n = 2$. In Section 4, we give the outline of the attack and the trade-off inequalities between distinguishability and disturbance. Finally, we summarize this paper in Section 5.

2. Protocol

Let us start by introducing the essence of the mean multi-kings' problem and the QKD by using it. Alice and $King_1$, $King_2$, ... , $King_n$ are the characters in this problem. The problem can be summarized as follows. Alice prepares a composite system, which consists of her system and n systems for kings, in an initial state. Each king performs a measurement on his system and obtains an outcome. After kings' measurement, Alice performs a measurement on the composite system and obtains an outcome. Furthermore, each king reveals post-information: the measurement type he has performed. Immediately, Alice guesses kings' outcomes by using her outcome and the post-information from each king. A solution to the problem is defined as a three-tuple of the initial state, Alice's measurement, and a guessing function such that she can guess kings' outcomes correctly. In this problem, the initial state will be changed depending on the kings' measurements and outcomes. In general, it is impossible to distinguish the changed states correctly. Therefore, Alice tries to get some potential answers by performing the measurement and to narrow down the correct outcome from them by using the guessing function of her outcome and the post-information.

We can construct the QKD protocol by using a setting of the mean multi-kings' problem and a solution to it, i.e., Alice and each king share the guessing result as a secret key. Figure 1 is a graphically demonstrated protocol. Let us consider a setting that Alice prepares a composite system which consists of $n + 1$ qubits and each king performs one of two fixed measurements on his qubit. Then, two solutions where the initial states are multipartite entangled states can be shown as described below; therefore, we can also construct the QKD protocol by using those solutions. In the QKD, Alice and each king try to share secret keys while she switches the solutions.

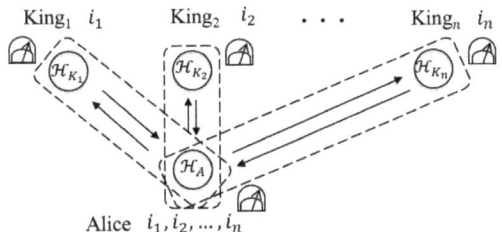

Figure 1. The QKD protocol by using the mean multi-kings' problem.

Before introducing details of the QKD protocol, we introduce some preliminary definitions, the setting of the mean multi-kings' problem, and the solutions to it. Define

$$Z_0 := |0\rangle\langle 0|, Z_1 := |1\rangle\langle 1|, X_0 := |\bar{0}\rangle\langle\bar{0}|, X_1 := |\bar{1}\rangle\langle\bar{1}| \tag{1}$$

for $|0\rangle := (1,0)^T, |1\rangle := (0,1)^T, |\bar{0}\rangle := \frac{1}{\sqrt{2}}(1,1)^T, |\bar{1}\rangle := \frac{1}{\sqrt{2}}(1,-1)^T$. Define an outcome set

$$\mathcal{K} := \{(s_1, t_1, s_2, t_2, \ldots, s_n, t_n) \mid s_j, t_j \in \{0,1\}\}, \tag{2}$$

operators for $(s_1, t_1, s_2, t_2, \ldots, s_n, t_n) \in \mathcal{K}$

$$E^{(Z)}_{(s_1,t_1,s_2,t_2,\ldots,s_n,t_n)} := X_{s_1} Z_{t_1} \otimes X_{s_2} Z_{t_2} \otimes \cdots \otimes X_{s_n} Z_{t_n}, \tag{3}$$

$$E^{(X)}_{(s_1,t_1,s_2,t_2,\ldots,s_n,t_n)} := Z_{s_1} X_{t_1} \otimes Z_{s_2} X_{t_2} \otimes \cdots \otimes Z_{s_n} X_{t_n}, \tag{4}$$

and an index set

$$S^{(W)}_{(J_j,i_j)_{j=1}^n} = S^{(W)}_{(J_1,i_1,J_2,i_2,\ldots,J_n,i_n)} := S^{(W)}_{(J_1,i_1)} \times S^{(W)}_{(J_2,i_2)} \times \cdots \times S^{(W)}_{(J_n,i_n)} \tag{5}$$

($W \in \{Z, X\}$) which consists of direct product of

$$S^{(Z)}_{(J,i)} := \begin{cases} \{(0,i),(1,i)\} & (J=0, i \in \{0,1\}) \\ \{(i,0),(i,1)\} & (J=1, i \in \{0,1\}), \end{cases} \tag{6}$$

$$S^{(X)}_{(J,i)} := \begin{cases} \{(i,0),(i,1)\} & (J=0, i \in \{0,1\}) \\ \{(0,i),(1,i)\} & (J=1, i \in \{0,1\}). \end{cases} \tag{7}$$

We define the setting of the mean multi-kings' problem. Alice prepares the composite system $(n+1$ qubits) $\tilde{\mathcal{H}} := \mathcal{H}_A \otimes \mathcal{H}_{K_1} \otimes \mathcal{H}_{K_2} \otimes \cdots \otimes \mathcal{H}_{K_n} \simeq (\mathbb{C}^2)^{\otimes n+1}$ in an initial state. Each King$_j$ performs one of the measurements on $\mathcal{H}_{K_j}$

$$M^{(J_j)} = (M^{(J_j)}_0, M^{(J_j)}_1) \ (J_j \in \{0,1\}), \tag{8}$$

where $M^{(0)} := (M^{(0)}_0 := Z_0, M^{(0)}_1 := Z_1)$ and $M^{(1)} := (M^{(1)}_0 := X_0, M^{(1)}_1 := X_1)$, and obtains an outcome $i_j \in \{0,1\}$. Alice performs a measurement on $\tilde{\mathcal{H}}$ and obtains an outcome. After Alice's measurement, the kings reveal $(J_j)_{j=1}^n$ as the post-information. Then, Alice tries to guess kings' outcomes by using her outcome and the post-information.

Here, we show two solutions to the problem. In this case, Alice can guess the kings' outcomes correctly by employing one of

$$|\Phi^{(Z)}\rangle := \frac{1}{\sqrt{2}}(|00\cdots 0\rangle + |11\cdots 1\rangle) \tag{9}$$

$$|\Phi^{(X)}\rangle := \frac{1}{\sqrt{2}}(|\bar{0}\bar{0}\cdots \bar{0}\rangle + |\bar{1}\bar{1}\cdots \bar{1}\rangle) \tag{10}$$

as an initial state, a measurement depending on the initial state $|\Phi^{(W)}\rangle$

$$P^{(W)} := \left(P_k^{(W)} := 2^{n+1}|(\mathbb{I}\otimes E_k^{(W)})\Phi^{(W)}\rangle\langle(\mathbb{I}\otimes E_k^{(W)})\Phi^{(W)}|\right)_{k\in\mathcal{K}} \tag{11}$$

and a guessing function $s(k, (J_j)_{j=1}^n, \Phi^{(W)})$ of her outcome $k \in \mathcal{K}$, the post-information $(J_j)_{j=1}^n$, and the initial state $|\Phi^{(W)}\rangle$, where $s(k, (J_j)_{j=1}^n, \Phi^{(W)})$ is defined as $(i_j)_{j=1}^n$ satisfying $k \in S_{(J_j, i_j)_{j=1}^n}^{(W)}$ (we regard $k = (s_1, t_1, s_2, t_2, \ldots, s_n, t_n)$ in the same light as $((s_1, t_1), (s_2, t_2), \ldots, (s_n, t_n))$).

We clear the number of non-zero matrices in her measurement and their orthogonality. We can observe

$$\begin{aligned}|(\mathbb{I}\otimes E_k^{(Z)})\Phi^{(Z)}\rangle &= (\mathbb{I}\otimes X_{s_1}Z_{t_1}\otimes\cdots\otimes X_{s_n}Z_{t_n})\frac{1}{\sqrt{2}}(|00\cdots 0\rangle+|11\cdots 1\rangle)\\ &= \frac{1}{\sqrt{2}}(\delta_{t_1 0}\cdots\delta_{t_n 0}|0\rangle X_{s_1}|0\rangle\otimes X_{s_2}|0\rangle\otimes\cdots\otimes X_{s_n}|0\rangle \\ &\quad+\delta_{t_1 1}\cdots\delta_{t_n 1}|1\rangle\otimes X_{s_1}|1\rangle\otimes X_{s_2}|1\rangle\otimes\cdots\otimes X_{s_n}|1\rangle).\end{aligned} \tag{12}$$

Then, the number of non-zero vectors is equal to 2^{n+1}. It leads to the conclusion that the number of non-zero matrices in $P^{(Z)}$ is equal to 2^{n+1}. Furthermore, we observe

$$\begin{aligned}&\langle(\mathbb{I}\otimes E_k^{(Z)})\Phi^{(Z)}|(\mathbb{I}\otimes E_{k'}^{(Z)})\Phi^{(Z)}\rangle\\&=\langle(\mathbb{I}\otimes X_{s_1}Z_{t_1}\otimes\cdots\otimes X_{s_n}Z_{t_n})\Phi^{(Z)}|(\mathbb{I}\otimes X_{s'_1}Z_{t'_1}\otimes\cdots\otimes X_{s'_n}Z_{t'_n})\Phi^{(Z)}\rangle\\&=\frac{1}{2^{n+1}}(\delta_{t_1 0}\delta_{t_2 0}\cdots\delta_{t_n 0}+\delta_{t_1 1}\delta_{t_2 1}\cdots\delta_{t_n 1})\delta_{kk'}.\end{aligned} \tag{13}$$

It implies that $P^{(Z)}$ is an orthogonal measurement on $\tilde{\mathcal{H}}$. When Z is switched to X, we have the same result in the case of $W = X$.

Next, we show that Alice can correctly guess kings' outcomes. We observe

$$S_{(J_j, i_j)_{j=1}^n}^{(W)} \cap S_{(J_j, i'_j)_{j=1}^n}^{(W)} = \emptyset \tag{14}$$

for any J_j and $(i_1, i_2, \ldots, i_n) \neq (i'_1, i'_2, \ldots, i'_n)$, and

$$M_{i_1}^{(J_1)} \otimes M_{i_2}^{(J_2)} \otimes \cdots \otimes M_{i_n}^{(J_n)} = \sum_{k \in S_{(J_j, i_j)_{j=1}^n}^{(W)}} E_k^{(W)} \tag{15}$$

holds for any J_j and i_j. When King$_j$ performs the measurement $M^{(J_j)}$ and obtains an outcome i_j, by Equation (15), the post-measurement state is proportional to

$$|(\mathbb{I}\otimes M_{i_1}^{(J_1)}\otimes M_{i_2}^{(J_2)}\otimes\cdots\otimes M_{i_n}^{(J_n)})\Phi^{(W)}\rangle \in \bigoplus_{k\in S_{(J_j, i_j)_{j=1}^n}^{(W)}} \mathcal{A}_k, \tag{16}$$

where $\mathcal{A}_k$ is a subspace spanned by $|(\mathbb{I}\otimes E_k^{(W)})\Phi^{(W)}\rangle$. $\mathcal{A}_k$ and $\mathcal{A}_{k'}$ are orthogonal for any $k \neq k'$ and $P^{(W)}$ is composed of orthogonal projections onto each subspace $\mathcal{A}_k$ by Equation (13). If Alice obtains an outcome k by performing $P^{(W)}$ and the post-information $(J_j)_{j=1}^n$ from the kings, then kings' outcomes

$(i_j)_{j=1}^n$ should satisfy $k \in S_{(J_j, i_j)_{j=1}^n}^{(W)}$. However, by Equation (14), such $(i_j)_{j=1}^n$ uniquely exists. Thus, Alice can correctly guess kings' outcomes.

A description of the QKD protocol by using the mean multi-kings' problem is as follows.

1. Alice prepares a composite system ($n + 1$ qubits) $\tilde{\mathcal{H}} = \mathcal{H}_A \otimes \mathcal{H}_{K_1} \otimes \mathcal{H}_{K_2} \otimes \cdots \otimes \mathcal{H}_{K_n} \simeq (\mathbb{C}^2)^{\otimes n+1}$ in the initial state $|\Phi^{(W)}\rangle$ ($W \in \{Z, X\}$) with probability $\frac{1}{2}$. Then, she sends the qubit $\mathcal{H}_{K_j}$ to King$_j$ ($j = 1, 2, \ldots, n$).
2. Each King$_j$ performs the measurement $M^{(J_j)} = (M_0^{(J_j)}, M_1^{(J_j)})$ ($J_j \in \{0,1\}$) with probability $\frac{1}{2}$ on $\mathcal{H}_{K_j}$ and obtains an outcome $i_j \in \{0,1\}$. After the measurement, each King$_j$ returns $\mathcal{H}_{K_j}$ to Alice.
3. Alice performs the measurement $P^{(W)} = (P_k^{(W)})_{k \in \mathcal{K}}$ ($W \in \{Z, X\}$) on $\tilde{\mathcal{H}}$ when the initial state was $|\Phi^{(W)}\rangle$. Then, she obtains an outcome $k \in \mathcal{K}$.
4. After the measurement, each King$_j$ announces post-information J_j to Alice.
5. Alice obtains a sequence $s(k, (J_j)_{j=1}^n, \Phi^{(W)})$ from the outcome k, the post-information $(J_j)_{j=1}^n$, and the initial state $|\Phi^{(W)}\rangle$.
6. They repeat the above process. After that, Alice randomly chooses sequences $(i_j^{\prime 1})_{j=1}^n, (i_j^{\prime 2})_{j=1}^n, \ldots, (i_j^{\prime r})_{j=1}^n$ from all sequences. Similarly, kings work together to choose sequences $(i_j^1)_{j=1}^n, (i_j^2)_{j=1}^n, \ldots, (i_j^r)_{j=1}^n$ which are the same positions as the positions Alice chose. Then, Alice and kings work together to calculate error rate $\frac{\sum_{u=1}^r (1 - \delta_{(i_j^{\prime u})_{j=1}^n, (i_j^u)_{j=1}^n})}{r}$.

The rest of the process is the same as for ordinary QKD protocols, such as BB84 protocol. If the error rate is too large, the protocol is aborted. Otherwise, the leftover sequences are performed with error-correction and privacy amplification [20].

Remark that Alice and each King$_j$ can share the secret key when they employ the QKD protocol using the mean-king's problem or BB84 protocol. In the case of employing the QKD using the mean-king's problem (see left hand side of Figure 2), Alice prepares 2 qubits in the Bell state and performs a single measurement on the 2 qubits for each King$_j$. Therefore, she needs to prepare $2n$ qubits and perform n measurements to share the secret key with n kings. On the other hand, in the QKD protocol using the mean multi-kings' problem, Alice only prepares $n + 1$ qubits in $|\Phi^{(Z)}\rangle$ or $|\Phi^{(X)}\rangle$ and performs the single measurement $P^{(Z)}$ or $P^{(X)}$. In the case where the BB84 protocol is employed (see right hand side of Figure 2), Alice just prepares n qubits in one of the states $|0\rangle, |1\rangle, |\bar{0}\rangle, |\bar{1}\rangle$ and no performing the measurement is required. Then, Alice and King$_j$ discard the raw key where their bases do not match before calculating error rate. On the other hand, in the QKD protocol using the mean multi-kings' problem, there is not such discarding step before calculating error rate.

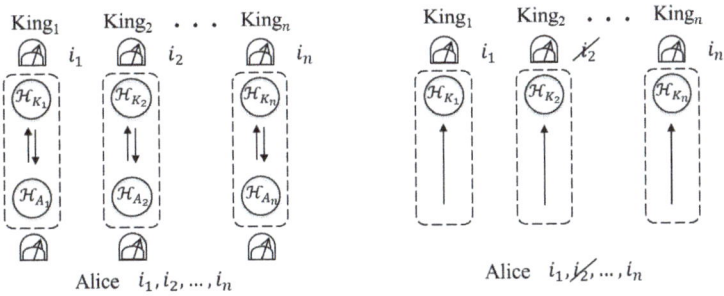

Figure 2. The QKD protocols using the mean-king's problem (**left hand side**) and BB84 protocols (**right hand side**) for Alice and the kings to share the secret key.

3. Protocol: $n = 2$

We describe the working of the protocol in the case of $n = 2$ by focusing on the case of $W = Z$ to reduce cumbersome notations.

By Equation (2), the index set takes the following form,

$$\mathcal{K} = \{(s_1, t_1, s_2, t_2) \mid s_j, t_j \in \{0, 1\}\}. \tag{17}$$

And by Equation (3), the operator $E_k^{(Z)}$ for $k \in \mathcal{K}$ takes the following form,

$$E_k^{(Z)} = E_{(s_1,t_1,s_2,t_2)}^{(Z)} = X_{s_1} Z_{t_1} \otimes X_{s_2} Z_{t_2} \quad (k = (s_1, t_1, s_2, t_2) \in \mathcal{K}). \tag{18}$$

Similarly, we can observe the operators for $W = X$. By Equation (5), we observe the index sets $S_{(J_1,i_1,J_2,i_2)}^{(W)}$ for $J_1 = 0, J_2 = 0, i_1, i_2 \in \{0, 1\}$, and $W = Z$:

$$
\begin{aligned}
S_{(0,0,0,0)}^{(Z)} &= S_{(0,0)}^{(Z)} \times S_{(0,0)}^{(Z)} \\
&= \{((0,0),(0,0)), ((0,0),(1,0)), ((1,0),(0,0)), ((1,0),(1,0))\} \\
&= \{(0,0,0,0), (0,0,1,0), (1,0,0,0), (1,0,1,0)\} \qquad (19)\\
S_{(0,0,0,1)}^{(Z)} &= S_{(0,0)}^{(Z)} \times S_{(0,1)}^{(Z)} \\
&= \{((0,0),(0,1)), ((0,0),(1,1)), ((1,0),(0,1)), ((1,0),(1,1))\} \\
&= \{(0,0,0,1), (0,0,1,1), (1,0,0,1), (1,0,1,1)\} \qquad (20)\\
S_{(0,1,0,0)}^{(Z)} &= S_{(0,1)}^{(Z)} \times S_{(0,0)}^{(Z)} \\
&= \{((0,1),(0,0)), ((0,1),(1,0)), ((1,1),(0,0)), ((1,1),(1,0))\} \\
&= \{(0,1,0,0), (0,1,1,0), (1,1,0,0), (1,1,1,0)\} \qquad (21)\\
S_{(0,1,0,1)}^{(Z)} &= S_{(0,1)}^{(Z)} \times S_{(0,1)}^{(Z)} \\
&= \{((0,1),(0,1)), ((0,1),(1,1)), ((1,1),(0,1)), ((1,1),(1,1))\} \\
&= \{(0,1,0,1), (0,1,1,0), (1,1,0,1), (1,1,1,1)\}, \qquad (22)
\end{aligned}
$$

where we regard $((l_1, l_2), (l_3, l_4))$ in the same light as (l_1, l_2, l_3, l_4). Similarly, we can observe the index sets for other $J_1, J_2, i_1, i_2,$ and W.

Let us consider that Alice prepares the qubits $\tilde{\mathcal{H}} = \mathcal{H}_A \otimes \mathcal{H}_{K_1} \otimes \mathcal{H}_{K_2}$ in the initial state

$$|\Phi^{(Z)}\rangle = \frac{1}{\sqrt{2}}(|000\rangle + |111\rangle). \tag{23}$$

Let us consider that King$_1$ and King$_2$ choose the same measurement $M^{(0)}$ and obtain the same outcome 0, i.e., $J_1 = 0, J_2 = 0$ and $i_1 = 0, i_2 = 0$. After kings' measurement, Alice performs the measurement $P^{(Z)} = (P_k^{(Z)})_{k \in \mathcal{K}}$ on $\tilde{\mathcal{H}}$, where

$$
\begin{aligned}
P_k^{(Z)} &= 8|(\mathbb{I} \otimes E_k^{(Z)}) \Phi^{(Z)}\rangle \langle (\mathbb{I} \otimes E_k^{(Z)}) \Phi^{(Z)}|r \\
&= 8|(\mathbb{I} \otimes X_{s_1} Z_{t_1} \otimes X_{s_2} Z_{t_2}) \Phi^{(Z)}\rangle \langle (\mathbb{I} \otimes X_{s_1} Z_{t_1} \otimes X_{s_2} Z_{t_2}) \Phi^{(Z)}|.
\end{aligned} \tag{24}
$$

After the measurement, King$_1$ and King$_2$ announce the post-information $J_1 = 0$ and $J_2 = 0$ to Alice. When Alice obtains an outcome $k = (0, 0, 0, 0)$, she is assured that kings' outcome (i_1, i_2) is $(0, 0)$, because (i_1, i_2) satisfying $k = (0, 0, 0, 0) \in S_{(J_1,i_1,J_2,i_2)}^{(W)} = S_{(0,i_1,0,i_2)}^{(Z)}$ is $(0, 0)$. In Table 1, we summarize Alice's guessing rule by using her outcome and the post-information from the kings.

Table 1. The relationship among kings' measurements J_1, J_2, Alice's outcome k, and kings' outcomes i_1, i_2 when she chooses $|\Phi^{(W)}\rangle$. In this table, NA means that probability of obtaining the corresponding outcome k is zero unless Eve performs an attack because the corresponding matrix $P_k^{(W)}$ is a zero matrix. An example of Alice's guessing: Alice is assured that kings' outcome (i_1, i_2) is $(0,0)$ when $W = Z, J_1 = 0, J_2 = 0$, and $k = (0,0,0,0)$.

$W = Z, J_1 = 0, J_2 = 0$ $W = X, J_1 = 1, J_2 = 1$		$W = Z, J_1 = 0, J_2 = 1$ $W = X, J_1 = 1, J_2 = 0$		$W = Z, J_1 = 1, J_2 = 0$ $W = X, J_1 = 0, J_2 = 1$		$W = Z, J_1 = 1, J_2 = 1$ $W = X, J_1 = 0, J_2 = 0$	
k	(i_1, i_2)	k	(i_1, i_2)	k	(i_1, i_2)	k	(i_1, i_2)
(0,0,0,0)	(0,0)	(0,0,0,0)	(0,0)	(0,0,0,0)	(0,0)	(0,0,0,0)	(0,0)
(0,0,0,1) NA	—	(0,0,0,1) NA	—	(0,0,0,1) NA	—	(0,0,0,1) NA	—
(0,0,1,0)	(0,0)	(0,0,1,0)	(0,1)	(0,0,1,0)	(0,0)	(0,0,1,0)	(0,1)
(0,0,1,1) NA	—	(0,0,1,1) NA	—	(0,0,1,1) NA	—	(0,0,1,1) NA	—
(0,1,0,0) NA	—	(0,1,0,0) NA	—	(0,1,0,0) NA	—	(0,1,0,0) NA	—
(0,1,0,1)	(1,1)	(0,1,0,1)	(1,0)	(0,1,0,1)	(0,1)	(0,1,0,1)	(0,0)
(0,1,1,0) NA	—	(0,1,1,0) NA	—	(0,1,1,0) NA	—	(0,1,1,0) NA	—
(0,1,1,1)	(1,1)	(0,1,1,1)	(1,1)	(0,1,1,1)	(0,1)	(0,1,1,1)	(0,1)
(1,0,0,0)	(0,0)	(1,0,0,0)	(0,0)	(1,0,0,0)	(1,0)	(1,0,0,0)	(1,0)
(1,0,0,1) NA	—	(1,0,0,1) NA	—	(1,0,0,1) NA	—	(1,0,0,1) NA	—
(1,0,1,0)	(0,0)	(1,0,1,0)	(0,1)	(1,0,1,0)	(1,0)	(1,0,1,0)	(1,1)
(1,0,1,1) NA	—	(1,0,1,1) NA	—	(1,0,1,1) NA	—	(1,0,1,1) NA	—
(1,1,0,0) NA	—	(1,1,0,0) NA	—	(1,1,0,0) NA	—	(1,1,0,0) NA	—
(1,1,0,1)	(1,1)	(1,1,0,1)	(1,0)	(1,1,0,1)	(1,1)	(1,1,0,1)	(1,0)
(1,1,1,0) NA	—	(1,1,1,0) NA	—	(1,1,1,0) NA	—	(1,1,1,0) NA	—
(1,1,1,1)	(1,1)	(1,1,1,1)	(1,1)	(1,1,1,1)	(1,1)	(1,1,1,1)	(1,1)

In the case of $n = 2$, the following simple attack so called intercept-resend attack can be considered. An eavesdropper (called Eve) intercepts $\mathcal{H}_{K_j}$ returned to Alice from King$_j$ (step 2 in the protocol) and performs the measurement $M^{(0)}$ or $M^{(1)}$ probabilistically on $\mathcal{H}_{K_j}$. After the measurement, she resends $\mathcal{H}_{K_j}$ to Alice. When Eve performs the intercept-resend attack to only $\mathcal{H}_{K_1}$, the probability which the error occurs is $\frac{1}{8}$, where the error means the event: $\delta_{(i_j^u)_{j=1}^2, (i_j^u)_{j=1}^2} = 0$. When Eve performs the intercept-resend attack to both $\mathcal{H}_{K_1}$ and $\mathcal{H}_{K_2}$, the probability which the error occurs is $\frac{1}{32}(p_1 + p_2 - 2p_1 p_2 + 7)$, where p_j denotes the probability, which Eve performs the measurement $M^{(0)}$ on $\mathcal{H}_{K_j}$ ($j \in \{1, 2\}$). The minimum value of the probability is 0.21875 when $(p_1 = 1, p_2 = 1)$ or $(p_1 = 0, p_2 = 0)$ and the maximum value of the probability is 0.25 when $(p_1 = 1, p_2 = 0)$ or $(p_1 = 0, p_2 = 1)$.

4. Distinguishability vs. Disturbance

In this section, let us consider two types of the attacks and let us see whether Eve can extract information by employing the attacks without disturbing contained in legitimate users' information in the case of $n = 2$. First, Eve tries to gain information from the qubit returned to Alice by King$_1$ (step 2 in the protocol) by interacting the qubit $\mathcal{H}_{K_1}$ with her quantum system $\mathcal{H}_E$ (see Figure 3). Second, she tries to gain information from the qubits $\mathcal{H}_{K_j}$ returned to Alice by King$_j$ (step 2 in the protocol) by interacting $\mathcal{H}_{K_1} \otimes \mathcal{H}_{K_2}$ with her quantum system $\mathcal{H}_E$ (see Figure 4). In both of the attacks, Eve performs any measurement on her quantum system $\mathcal{H}_E$ at any time.

We can consider an attack that Eve interacts her quantum system with the qubits sent to the kings by Alice. However, in this attack, the qubits are not encoded because the kings have not measured the qubits. Especially, in the case of $n = 1$, the setting of the attack can be considered as monogamy of entanglement [21,22]. Moreover, we can also consider an attack that Eve interacts her quantum system with both of the qubits sent to the kings by Alice and the qubits returned to Alice by the kings. However, the setting of the attack is different from one for discussing the information disturbance theorem. In the setting for the theorem, Eve tries to information extract from only the encoded qubits. Therefore, we concentrate on the above two attacks that Eve tries to extract information from the qubits sent to Alice by the kings.

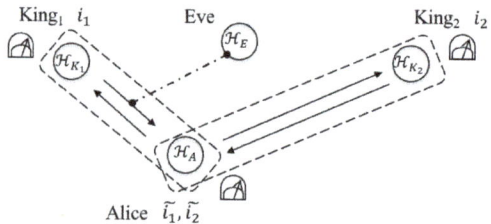

Figure 3. The interaction $\mathcal{H}_{K_1}$ with $\mathcal{H}_E$.

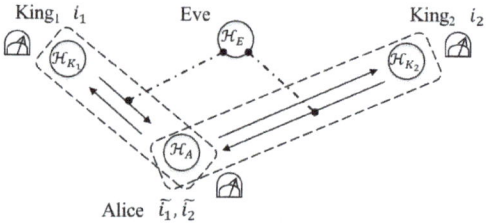

Figure 4. The interaction $\mathcal{H}_{K_1} \otimes \mathcal{H}_{K_2}$ with $\mathcal{H}_E$.

In the beginning, we define error probability which represents probability that Alice cannot guess king's outcomes correctly by using her outcome and the post-information. Remark that the error probability is different from the error rate (step 6 in the protocol). Let $P^{(W)}(k \mid J_1; i_1, J_2; i_2)$ be the probability that Alice obtains an outcome k when she chooses $|\Phi^{(W)}\rangle$ and King$_j$ obtains an outcome i_j with the measurement $M^{(J_j)}$ ($j \in \{1,2\}$). We define

$$P^{(W)}_{\text{suc}(J_1;i_1,J_2;i_2)} := \sum_{k \in S^{(W)}_{(J_j,i_j)_{j=1}^2}} P^{(W)}(k \mid J_1; i_1, J_2; i_2) \qquad (25)$$

and

$$P_{\text{suc}(J_1;i_1,J_2;i_2)} := \frac{1}{2} \sum_{W \in \{X,Z\}} P^{(W)}_{\text{suc}(J_1;i_1,J_2;i_2)}. \qquad (26)$$

Then, we define the error probability when King$_j$ obtains an outcome i_j with the measurement $M^{(J_j)}$:

$$P_{\text{err}(J_1;i_1,J_2;i_2)} := 1 - P_{\text{suc}(J_1;i_1,J_2;i_2)}. \qquad (27)$$

Equation (27) represents probability that Alice's sequence and kings' sequence do not match when King$_j$ obtains an outcome i_j with the measurement $M^{(J_j)}$, i.e., Alice cannot guess kings' outcomes correctly by using her outcome and the post-information.

Let us consider that Eve tries to extract information from $\mathcal{H}_{K_1}$. Eve prepares her own quantum system $\mathcal{H}_E$ in a quantum state Ω. She intercepts $\mathcal{H}_{K_1}$ in the state $\rho^{(K_1)}$ returned to Alice by King$_1$ and interacts it with $\mathcal{H}_E$. Let us denote the interaction by

$$T^*(\rho^{(K_1)}) := U \rho^{(K_1)} \otimes \Omega U^\dagger, \qquad (28)$$

where U is a unitary operator on $\mathcal{H}_{K_1} \otimes \mathcal{H}_E$. Moreover, we denote the local state of $\mathcal{H}_E$ (resp. $\mathcal{H}_{K_1}$) by partial trace over the $\mathcal{H}_{K_1}$ (resp. $\mathcal{H}_E$)

$$T^*_E(\rho^{(K_1)}) := \text{tr}_{\mathcal{H}_{K_1}} T^*(\rho^{(K_1)}) \quad \left(\text{resp. } T^*_{K_1}(\rho^{(K_1)}) := \text{tr}_{\mathcal{H}_{K_E}} T^*(\rho^{(K_1)}) \right). \qquad (29)$$

Let us consider that King$_1$ obtains an outcome i with a measurement $M^{(1)}$. Then, the state of $\mathcal{H}_{K_1}$ before the interaction is $\rho^{(K_1)} = |\bar{i}\rangle\langle\bar{i}|$. Eve tries to extract information regarding to the secret key by distinguishing $T_E^*(|\bar{0}\rangle\langle\bar{0}|)$ and $T_E^*(|\bar{1}\rangle\langle\bar{1}|)$.

We employ trace distance as a measure for distinguishability of the states. Trace norm between a state ρ and a state σ is defined as $||\rho - \sigma||_1 := \sup_{||A||=1} |\text{tr}(\rho - \sigma)A|$, where $||\cdot||$ denotes operator norm. Trace distance is defined as follows,

$$D(\rho, \sigma) := \frac{1}{2}||\rho - \sigma||_1. \tag{30}$$

It takes a value from 0 to 1. In addition, $D(\rho, \sigma) = 0$ if and only if $\rho = \sigma$, and $D(\rho, \sigma) = 0$ if and only if $\text{tr}(\rho\sigma) = 0$. Let us remind the definition of fidelity [23,24]. Fidelity between ρ and σ is defined as $F(\rho, \sigma) := \text{tr} \sqrt{\rho^{1/2}\sigma\rho^{1/2}}$. The following alternative expression of fidelity [25,26] has been shown,

$$F(\rho, \sigma) = \inf_{(M_a)_a: \text{POVM}} \sum_a \sqrt{p(a|\rho)p(a|\sigma)}, \tag{31}$$

where $p(a|\rho)$ and $p(a|\sigma)$ are defined as $p(a|\rho) := \text{tr}(M_a\rho)$ and $p(a|\sigma) := \text{tr}(M_a\sigma)$.

Lemma 1. *The following relation between trace distance and fidelity holds,*

$$\frac{1}{2}||T_E^*(|\bar{0}\rangle\langle\bar{0}|) - T_E^*(|\bar{1}\rangle\langle\bar{1}|)||_1 \leq F(T_{K_1}^*(|0\rangle\langle0|), T_{K_1}^*(|1\rangle\langle1|)). \tag{32}$$

Proof of Lemma 1. From Lemma 3 in [27], we have

$$|\langle 0|T(\mathbb{I} \otimes A)|1\rangle| \leq ||A|| F(T_{K_1}^*(|0\rangle\langle0|), T_{K_1}^*(|1\rangle\langle1|)) \tag{33}$$

for any operator A on $\mathcal{H}_E$, where T is defined as $\text{tr}\,T^*(\rho)X = \text{tr}\,\rho T(X)$. By using Equation (33), we observe

$$\begin{aligned}
\left|\text{tr}\left[\left\{T_E^*(|\bar{0}\rangle\langle\bar{0}|) - T_E^*\left(\tfrac{1}{2}\mathbb{I}\right)\right\}A\right]\right| &= \left|\text{tr}\left\{\left(|\bar{0}\rangle\langle\bar{0}| - \tfrac{1}{2}\mathbb{I}\right)T(\mathbb{I} \otimes A)\right\}\right| \\
&= \left|\text{tr}\left\{\tfrac{1}{2}(|0\rangle\langle 1| + |1\rangle\langle 0|)T(\mathbb{I} \otimes A)\right\}\right| \\
&\leq \tfrac{1}{2}\{|\langle 1|T(\mathbb{I}\otimes A)|0\rangle| + |\langle 0|T(\mathbb{I}\otimes A)|1\rangle|\} \\
&\leq ||A|| F(T_{K_1}^*(|0\rangle\langle0|), T_{K_1}^*(|1\rangle\langle1|)).
\end{aligned} \tag{34}$$

Then,

$$\begin{aligned}
\tfrac{1}{2}||T_E^*(|\bar{0}\rangle\langle\bar{0}|) - T_E^*(|\bar{1}\rangle\langle\bar{1}|)||_1 &= \left\|T_E^*(|\bar{0}\rangle\langle\bar{0}|) - T_E^*\left(\tfrac{1}{2}\mathbb{I}\right)\right\|_1 \\
&= \sup_{||A||=1}\left|\text{tr}\left[\left\{(T_E^*(|\bar{0}\rangle\langle\bar{0}|) - T_E^*\left(\tfrac{1}{2}\mathbb{I}\right)\right\}A\right]\right| \\
&\leq F(T_{K_1}^*(|0\rangle\langle0|), T_{K_1}^*(|1\rangle\langle1|))
\end{aligned} \tag{35}$$

holds. □

Theorem 1. *The following trade-off inequality holds,*

$$D(T_E^*(|\bar{0}\rangle\langle\bar{0}|), T_E^*(|\bar{1}\rangle\langle\bar{1}|)) \leq \sqrt{2P_{\text{err}(0;0,0;0)}} + \sqrt{2P_{\text{err}(0;1,0;1)}}. \tag{36}$$

The left hand side of the inequality represents distinguishability for Eve, and the right hand side is the sum of the error probabilities which represent probability that Alice's sequence and kings' sequence are not equal when the kings obtain the corresponding outcomes with the corresponding measurements, i.e., Alice cannot guess kings' sequence correctly by using her outcome and the post-information. This theorem shows that Eve's extracting information regarding King$_1$'s key related with the measurement $M^{(1)}$ inevitably induces disturbing the states and increases the error probability when both of kings choose the measurement $M^{(0)}$. This implies that the more Eve extracts information, the more possibility for Alice and the kings to detect the existence of the attack increases. In particular, Eve cannot extract information about the key at all (i.e., trace distance is zero) when the corresponding error probabilities are zero. Remark that similar inequalities between distinguishability of other pairs of states and the error probabilities can be proven in the similar way as below.

Proof of Theorem 1. Before obtaining the inequalities, let us observe the error probability. Define $\rho_i := T^*_{K_1}(|i\rangle\langle i|)$. By direct calculations (see Appendix A for details), we have the following probability,

$$P_{\text{err}(0;i,0;i)} = \frac{1}{2}(1 - \langle i|\rho_i i\rangle). \tag{37}$$

By using Equations (31) and (37), we have

$$\begin{aligned}
F(\rho_0, \rho_1) &= \inf_{(M_a)_a:\text{POVM}} \sum_a \sqrt{\text{tr}(M_a\rho_0)\,\text{tr}(M_a\rho_1)} \\
&\leq \sqrt{\text{tr}(|0\rangle\langle 0|\rho_0)\,\text{tr}(|0\rangle\langle 0|\rho_1)} + \sqrt{\text{tr}(|1\rangle\langle 1|\rho_0)\,\text{tr}(|1\rangle\langle 1|\rho_1)} \\
&= \sqrt{\langle 0|\rho_0 0\rangle(1 - \langle 1|\rho_1 1\rangle)} + \sqrt{(1 - \langle 0|\rho_0 0\rangle)\langle 1|\rho_1 1\rangle} \\
&\leq \sqrt{1 - \langle 1|\rho_1 1\rangle} + \sqrt{1 - \langle 0|\rho_0 0\rangle} \\
&= \sqrt{2P_{\text{err}(0;0,0;0)}} + \sqrt{2P_{\text{err}(0;1,0;1)}},
\end{aligned} \tag{38}$$

where we employ $(|0\rangle\langle 0|, |1\rangle\langle 1|)$ as a POVM in the first inequality. Then, we have the trade-off inequality by the definition of trace distance, Equations (32) and (38). □

Let us consider that Eve tries to extract information from $\mathcal{H}_{K_1}$ and $\mathcal{H}_{K_2}$. Eve prepares a quantum systems $\mathcal{H}_E$ in a quantum state Ω. She intercepts $\mathcal{H}_{K_1} \otimes \mathcal{H}_{K_2}$ in the state $\rho^{(K_1,K_2)}$ returned to Alice by King$_1$ and King$_2$. Then, she interacts both systems with $\mathcal{H}_E$. Let us denote the interaction by

$$K^*(\rho^{(K_1,K_2)}) := V\rho^{(K_1,K_2)} \otimes \Omega V^\dagger, \tag{39}$$

where V is a unitary operator on $\mathcal{H}_{K_1} \otimes \mathcal{H}_{K_2} \otimes \mathcal{H}_E$. And we denote the local state of $\mathcal{H}_E$ (resp. $\mathcal{H}_{K_1} \otimes \mathcal{H}_{K_2}$) by partial trace over the $\mathcal{H}_{K_1} \otimes \mathcal{H}_{K_2}$ (resp. $\mathcal{H}_E$)

$$K^*_E(\rho^{(K_1,K_2)}) := \text{tr}_{\mathcal{H}_{K_1} \otimes \mathcal{H}_{K_2}} K^*(\rho^{(K_1,K_2)}) \quad \left(\text{resp. } K^*_{K_1,K_2}(\rho^{(K_1,K_2)}) := \text{tr}_{\mathcal{H}_{K_E}} K^*(\rho^{(K_1,K_2)})\right). \tag{40}$$

Let us consider that King$_1$ and King$_2$ perform the same measurement $M^{(1)}$ and obtain the same outcome i. Then, the state of $\mathcal{H}_{K_1} \otimes \mathcal{H}_{K_2}$ before the interaction is $|\bar{i}\bar{i}\rangle\langle\bar{i}\bar{i}|$. Eve tries to extract information regarding to the secret key by distinguishing $K^*_E(|\bar{0}\bar{0}\rangle\langle\bar{0}\bar{0}|)$ and $K^*_E(|\bar{1}\bar{1}\rangle\langle\bar{1}\bar{1}|)$.

Lemma 2. *The following relation between trace distance and fidelity holds,*

$$\begin{aligned}
\|K^*_E(|\bar{0}\bar{0}\rangle\langle\bar{0}\bar{0}|) - K^*_E(|\bar{1}\bar{1}\rangle\langle\bar{1}\bar{1}|)\|_1 &\leq \sum_{i\in\{0,1\}} F(K^*_{K_1K_2}(|ii\rangle\langle ii|), K^*_{K_1K_2}(|01\rangle\langle 01|)) \\
&\quad + \sum_{i\in\{0,1\}} F(K^*_{K_1K_2}(|ii\rangle\langle ii|), K^*_{K_1K_2}(|10\rangle\langle 10|)).
\end{aligned} \tag{41}$$

Proof of Lemma 2. From Lemma 3 in [27], we have

$$|\langle i_1 i_2|K(I \otimes A)|i'_1 i'_2\rangle| \leq \|A\| F(K^*_{K_1K_2}(|i_1 i_2\rangle\langle i_1 i_2|), K^*_{K_1K_2}(|i'_1 i'_2\rangle\langle i'_1 i'_2|)) \tag{42}$$

for any operator A on $\mathcal{H}_E$, where K is defined as $\operatorname{tr} K^*(\rho)X = \operatorname{tr} \rho K(X)$. By using Equation (42), we observe

$$
\begin{aligned}
|\operatorname{tr}[\{K_E^*(|\bar{0}\bar{0}\rangle\langle\bar{0}\bar{0}|) - K_E^*(|\bar{1}\bar{1}\rangle\langle\bar{1}\bar{1}|)\}A]| &= |\operatorname{tr}\{(|\bar{0}\bar{0}\rangle\langle\bar{0}\bar{0}| - |\bar{1}\bar{1}\rangle\langle\bar{1}\bar{1}|)K(\mathbb{I}\otimes A)\}| \\
&= \left|\operatorname{tr}\left\{\tfrac{1}{2}(|00\rangle\langle 01| + |00\rangle\langle 10| + |01\rangle\langle 00| + |01\rangle\langle 11| \right.\right. \\
&\quad\left.\left. + |10\rangle\langle 00| + |10\rangle\langle 11| + |11\rangle\langle 01| + |11\rangle\langle 10|)K(\mathbb{I}\otimes A)\right\}\right| \\
&\leq \sum_{i\in\{0,1\}} |\langle ii|K(\mathbb{I}\otimes A)|01\rangle| + \sum_{i\in\{0,1\}} |\langle ii|K(\mathbb{I}\otimes A)|10\rangle| \\
&\leq \|A\|\left\{\sum_{i\in\{0,1\}} F(K_{K_1K_2}^*(|ii\rangle\langle ii|), K_{K_1K_2}^*(|01\rangle\langle 01|)) \right. \\
&\quad\left. + \sum_{i\in\{0,1\}} F(K_{K_1K_2}^*(|ii\rangle\langle ii|), K_{K_1K_2}^*(|10\rangle\langle 10|))\right\}.
\end{aligned}
\tag{43}
$$

In Equation (43), we take supreme over all A such that $\|A\| = 1$, then we have Equation (41). □

Theorem 2. *The following trade-off inequality holds,*

$$
D(K_E^*(|\bar{0}\bar{0}\rangle\langle\bar{0}\bar{0}|), K_E^*(|\bar{1}\bar{1}\rangle\langle\bar{1}\bar{1}|)) < \sum_{i_1,i_2\in\{0,1\}} \sqrt{2P_{\operatorname{err}(0;i_1,0;i_2)}}.
\tag{44}
$$

Although Eve tries to distinguish the states on $\mathcal{H}_{K_1}\otimes\mathcal{H}_{K_2}$, this theorem gives the same claim as the one of Theorem 1. This theorem shows that Eve's extracting information regarding kings' keys related with the measurement $M^{(1)}$ inevitably induces disturbing the states and increases the error probability when both of kings choose the measurement $M^{(0)}$. Remark that similar inequalities between distinguishability of other pairs of states and the error probabilities can be proven in the similar way as below.

Proof of Theorem 2. In the same manner, let us observe the error probability. Define $\rho_{i_1i_2} := K_{K_1K_2}^*(|i_1i_2\rangle\langle i_1i_2|)$. By direct calculations (see Appendix B for details), we have the following probability,

$$
P_{\operatorname{err}(0;i_1,0;i_2)} = \begin{cases} \tfrac{1}{2}(1 - \langle i_1i_2|\rho_{i_1i_2}|i_1i_2\rangle) & (i_1 = i_2) \\ 1 - \tfrac{1}{2}\langle i_1i_2|\rho_{i_1i_2}|i_1i_2\rangle & (i_1 \neq i_2). \end{cases}
\tag{45}
$$

By using Equations (31) and (45), we have

$$
\begin{aligned}
F(\rho_{00},\rho_{01}) &= \inf_{(M_a)_a:\text{POVM}} \sum_a \sqrt{\operatorname{tr}(M_a\rho_{00})\operatorname{tr}(M_a\rho_{01})} \\
&\leq \sqrt{\operatorname{tr}\{(|11\rangle\langle 11| + |01\rangle\langle 01|)\rho_{00}\}\operatorname{tr}\{(|00\rangle\langle 00| + |01\rangle\langle 01|)\rho_{01}\}} \\
&\quad + \sqrt{\operatorname{tr}\{(|00\rangle\langle 00| + |10\rangle\langle 10|)\rho_{00}\}\operatorname{tr}\{(|00\rangle\langle 00| + |10\rangle\langle 10|)\rho_{01}\}} \\
&< \sqrt{\operatorname{tr}\{(|11\rangle\langle 11| + |01\rangle\langle 01|)\rho_{00}\}} + \sqrt{\operatorname{tr}\{(|00\rangle\langle 00| + |10\rangle\langle 10|)\rho_{01}\}} \\
&= \sqrt{1 - \langle 00|\rho_{00}|00\rangle - \langle 10|\rho_{00}|10\rangle} + \sqrt{1 - \langle 01|\rho_{01}|01\rangle - \langle 11|\rho_{01}|11\rangle} \\
&< \sqrt{1 - \langle 00|\rho_{00}|00\rangle} + \sqrt{2 - \langle 01|\rho_{01}|01\rangle} \\
&= \sqrt{2P_{\operatorname{err}(0;0,0;0)}} + \sqrt{2P_{\operatorname{err}(0;0,0;1)}}.
\end{aligned}
\tag{46}
$$

where we employ $(|11\rangle\langle 11| + |01\rangle\langle 01|, |00\rangle\langle 00| + |10\rangle\langle 10|)$ as a POVM in the first inequality. In the same manner, we have

$$
F(\rho_{ii},\rho_{01}) < \sqrt{2P_{\operatorname{err}(0;i,0;i)}} + \sqrt{2P_{\operatorname{err}(0;0,0;1)}},
\tag{47}
$$

$$
F(\rho_{ii},\rho_{10}) < \sqrt{2P_{\operatorname{err}(0;i,0;i)}} + \sqrt{2P_{\operatorname{err}(0;1,0;0)}} \quad (i\in\{0,1\}).
\tag{48}
$$

Then, we have the trade-off inequality by the definition of trace distance, Equations (41) and (48). □

5. Summary

In this paper, we discussed the quantum key distribution protocol using the mean multi-kings' problem. By using the protocol, Alice can share the secret key with King$_j$ ($j = 1, 2, \ldots, n$). In the case of $n = 2$, we considered whether Eve can extract information when she can performs the interaction between her own quantum system and the qubit returned by King$_j$ and can performs any measurement on her quantum system at any time. We employed trace distance as a measure for distinguishability of the states for Eve. Furthermore, we gave the trade-off inequalities between trace distance of the quantum states corresponding to the secret key for Eve and the error probability which represents probability that the bit sequences shared by the legitimate users do not match. In BB84, such relation is know as the information disturbance theorem and the theorem is also regarded as an information theoretical version of the uncertainty relation. Our inequalities showed that Eve's extracting information regarding kings' keys inevitably induces disturbing the states and increases the error probability even though Alice can use the post-information to guess kings' outcomes. This implies that the information gain by Eve increases possibility for the legitimate users to detect the existence of the attacks. In particular, when the corresponding error probability is zero, Eve cannot extract any information.

Author Contributions: Conceptualization, M.Y.; investigation, A.N. and J.C. All authors have read and agreed to the published version of the manuscript.

Funding: This research received no external funding.

Conflicts of Interest: The authors declare no conflict of interest.

Appendix A

We provide a direct calculation for obtaining the error probabilities in the proof of Theorem 1. Let us consider that the initial state is $|\Phi^{(W)}\rangle$, King$_j$ ($j \in \{1, 2\}$) obtains an outcome i_j with $M^{(J_j)}$, and Eve performs the interaction on $\mathcal{H}_{K_1} \otimes \mathcal{H}_E$. Let $\rho^{(W)}_{(J_1;i_1,J_2;i_2)}$ be a state of the composite system before Alice's measurement. The state takes one of the following forms,

$$\rho^{(Z)}_{(0;i_1,0;i_1)} = |i_1\rangle\langle i_1| \otimes \rho_{i_1} \otimes |i_1\rangle\langle i_1|, \tag{A1}$$

$$\rho^{(Z)}_{(0;i_1,1;i_2)} = |i_1\rangle\langle i_1| \otimes \rho_{i_1} \otimes |\bar{i}_2\rangle\langle \bar{i}_2|, \tag{A2}$$

$$\rho^{(Z)}_{(1;i_1,0;i_2)} = |i_2\rangle\langle i_2| \otimes \rho_{\bar{i}_1} \otimes |i_2\rangle\langle i_2|, \tag{A3}$$

$$\rho^{(Z)}_{(1;i_1,1;i_2)} = |\bar{i}_1\rangle\langle \bar{i}_1| \otimes \rho_{\bar{i}_1} \otimes |\bar{i}_2\rangle\langle \bar{i}_2|, \tag{A4}$$

$$\rho^{(X)}_{(0;i_1,0;i_2)} = |i_1 \oplus i_2\rangle\langle i_1 \oplus i_2| \otimes \rho_{i_1} \otimes |i_2\rangle\langle i_2|, \tag{A5}$$

$$\rho^{(X)}_{(0;i_1,1;i_2)} = |\bar{i}_2\rangle\langle \bar{i}_2| \otimes \rho_{i_1} \otimes |\bar{i}_2\rangle\langle \bar{i}_2|, \tag{A6}$$

$$\rho^{(X)}_{(1;i_1,0;i_2)} = |\bar{i}_1\rangle\langle \bar{i}_1| \otimes \rho_{\bar{i}_1} \otimes |i_2\rangle\langle i_2|, \tag{A7}$$

$$\rho^{(X)}_{(1;i_1,1;i_1)} = |\bar{i}_1\rangle\langle \bar{i}_1| \otimes \rho_{\bar{i}_1} \otimes |\bar{i}_1\rangle\langle \bar{i}_1|, \tag{A8}$$

where $\rho_i := T^*_{K_1}(|i\rangle\langle i|)$, $\rho_{\bar{i}} := T^*_{K_1}(|\bar{i}\rangle\langle \bar{i}|)$, and $\oplus$ denotes exclusive or.

By direct calculation of

$$P^{(W)}_{\text{suc}(J_1;i_1,J_2;i_2)} = \sum_{k \in S^{(W)}_{(J_j;i_j)_{j=1}^2}} \operatorname{tr}\left(P^{(W)}_k \rho^{(W)}_{(J_1;i_1,J_2;i_2)}\right), \tag{A9}$$

we have the following probabilities,

$$P^{(Z)}_{\text{suc}(0;i_1,0;i_1)} = P^{(Z)}_{\text{suc}(0;i_1,1;i_2)} = 1, \tag{A10}$$

$$P^{(Z)}_{\text{suc}(1;i_1,0;i_2)} = P^{(Z)}_{\text{suc}(1;i_1,1;i_2)} = \langle \bar{i}_1 | \rho_{\bar{i}_1} \bar{i}_1 \rangle, \tag{A11}$$

$$P^{(X)}_{\text{suc}(0;i_1,0;i_2)} = P^{(X)}_{\text{suc}(0;i_1,1;i_2)} = \langle i_1 | \rho_{i_1} i_1 \rangle, \tag{A12}$$

$$P^{(X)}_{\text{suc}(1;i_1,0;i_2)} = P^{(X)}_{\text{suc}(1;i_1,1;i_1)} = 1, \tag{A13}$$

where we can find out the index set $S^{(W)}_{(J_j,i_j)^2_{j=1}}$ in Table 1. By the definition of $P_{\text{suc}(J_1;i_1,J_2;i_2)}$, we have the following probabilities,

$$P_{\text{suc}(0;i_1,0;i_2)} = \begin{cases} \frac{1}{2}(\langle i_1|\rho_{i_1}i_1\rangle + 1) & (i_1 = i_2) \\ \frac{1}{2}\langle i_1|\rho_{i_1}i_1\rangle & (i_1 \neq i_2), \end{cases} \tag{A14}$$

$$P_{\text{suc}(0;i_1,1;i_2)} = \frac{1}{2}\langle i_1|\rho_{i_1}i_1\rangle, \tag{A15}$$

$$P_{\text{suc}(1;i_1,0;i_2)} = \frac{1}{2}\langle \bar{i}_1|\rho_{\bar{i}_1}\bar{i}_1\rangle, \tag{A16}$$

$$P_{\text{suc}(1;i_1,1;i_2)} = \begin{cases} \frac{1}{2}(\langle \bar{i}_1|\rho_{\bar{i}_1}\bar{i}_1\rangle + 1) & (i_1 = i_2) \\ \frac{1}{2}\langle \bar{i}_1|\rho_{\bar{i}_1}\bar{i}_1\rangle & (i_1 \neq i_2). \end{cases} \tag{A17}$$

Then, we can observe the error probabilities from these probabilities.

Appendix B

We provide a direct calculation for obtaining the error probabilities in the proof of Theorem 2. Let us consider that the initial state is $|\Phi^{(W)}\rangle$, King$_j$ ($j \in \{1,2\}$) obtains an outcome i_j with $M^{(J_j)}$, and Eve performs the interaction on $\mathcal{H}_{K_1} \otimes \mathcal{H}_{K_2} \otimes \mathcal{H}_{E_j}$. Let $\rho'^{(W)}_{(J_1;i_1,J_2;i_2)}$ be a state of the composite system before Alice's measurement. The state takes one of the following forms,

$$\rho'^{(Z)}_{(0;i_1,0;i_1)} = |i_1\rangle\langle i_1| \otimes \rho_{i_1 i_1}, \tag{A18}$$

$$\rho'^{(Z)}_{(0;i_1,1;i_2)} = |i_1\rangle\langle i_1| \otimes \rho_{i_1 \bar{i}_2}, \tag{A19}$$

$$\rho'^{(Z)}_{(1;i_1,0;i_2)} = |i_2\rangle\langle i_2| \otimes \rho_{\bar{i}_1 i_2}, \tag{A20}$$

$$\rho'^{(Z)}_{(1;i_1,1;i_2)} = |\bar{i}_1\rangle\langle \bar{i}_1| \otimes \rho_{\bar{i}_1 \bar{i}_2}, \tag{A21}$$

$$\rho'^{(X)}_{(0;i_1,0;i_2)} = |i_1 \oplus i_2\rangle\langle i_1 \oplus i_2| \otimes \rho_{i_1 i_2}, \tag{A22}$$

$$\rho'^{(X)}_{(0;i_1,1;i_2)} = |\bar{i}_2\rangle\langle \bar{i}_2| \otimes \rho_{\bar{i}_1 i_2}, \tag{A23}$$

$$\rho'^{(X)}_{(1;i_1,0;i_2)} = |\bar{i}_1\rangle\langle \bar{i}_1| \otimes \rho_{\bar{i}_1 i_2}, \tag{A24}$$

$$\rho'^{(X)}_{(1;i_1,1;i_1)} = |\bar{i}_1\rangle\langle \bar{i}_1| \otimes \rho_{\bar{i}_1 \bar{i}_1}, \tag{A25}$$

where $\rho_{ij} := K^*_{K_1 K_2}(|ij\rangle\langle ij|)$ ($i,j \in \{0,1,\bar{0},\bar{1}\}$).

By direct calculation of

$$P^{(W)}_{\text{suc}(J_1;i_1,J_2;i_2)} = \sum_{k \in S^{(W)}_{(J_j,i_j)^2_{j=1}}} \text{tr}\left(P^{(W)}_k \rho'^{(W)}_{(J_1;i_1,J_2;i_2)}\right), \tag{A26}$$

we have the following probabilities,

$$P^{(Z)}_{\text{suc}(0;i_1,0;i_1)} = 1, \tag{A27}$$

$$P^{(Z)}_{\text{suc}(0;i_1,1;i_2)} = \langle \bar{i}_1\bar{i}_2|\rho_{i_1 i_2}|\bar{i}_1\bar{i}_2\rangle + \langle \overline{\bar{i}_1\oplus 1 \bar{i}_2}|\rho_{i_1 i_2}|\overline{\bar{i}_1\oplus 1 \bar{i}_2}\rangle, \tag{A28}$$

$$P^{(Z)}_{\text{suc}(1;i_1,0;i_2)} = \langle \bar{i}_1\bar{i}_2|\rho_{\bar{i}_1 i_2}|\bar{i}_1\bar{i}_2\rangle + \langle \overline{\bar{i}_1\bar{i}_2\oplus 1}|\rho_{\bar{i}_1 i_2}|\overline{\bar{i}_1\bar{i}_2\oplus 1}\rangle, \tag{A29}$$

$$P^{(Z)}_{\text{suc}(1;i_1,1;i_2)} = \langle \bar{i}_1\bar{i}_2|\rho_{\bar{i}_1 \bar{i}_2}|\bar{i}_1\bar{i}_2\rangle, \tag{A30}$$

$$P^{(X)}_{\text{suc}(0;i_1,0;i_2)} = \langle i_1 i_2|\rho_{i_1 i_2}|i_1 i_2\rangle, \tag{A31}$$

$$P^{(X)}_{\text{suc}(0;i_1,1;i_2)} = \langle i_1 i_2|\rho_{i_1 \bar{i}_2}|i_1 i_2\rangle + \langle i_1 i_2 \oplus 1|\rho_{i_1 \bar{i}_2}|i_1 i_2 \oplus 1\rangle, \tag{A32}$$

$$P^{(X)}_{\text{suc}(1;i_1,0;i_2)} = \langle i_1 i_2|\rho_{\bar{i}_1 i_2}|i_1 i_2\rangle + \langle i_1 \oplus 1 i_2|\rho_{\bar{i}_1 i_2}|i_1 \oplus 1 i_2\rangle, \tag{A33}$$

$$P^{(X)}_{\text{suc}(1;i_1,1;i_1)} = 1. \tag{A34}$$

By the definition of $P_{\text{suc}(J_1;i_1,J_2;i_2)}$, we have the following probabilities,

$$P_{\text{suc}(0;i_1,0;i_2)} = \begin{cases} \frac{1}{2}(\langle i_1 i_2|\rho_{i_1 i_2}|i_1 i_2\rangle + 1) & (i_1 = i_2) \\ \frac{1}{2}\langle i_1 i_2|\rho_{i_1 i_2}|i_1 i_2\rangle & (i_1 \neq i_2), \end{cases} \tag{A35}$$

$$P_{\text{suc}(0;i_1,1;i_2)} = \frac{1}{2}(\langle \bar{i}_1\bar{i}_2|\rho_{i_1 i_2}|\bar{i}_1\bar{i}_2\rangle + \langle \overline{\bar{i}_1\oplus 1 \bar{i}_2}|\rho_{i_1 i_2}|\overline{\bar{i}_1\oplus 1 \bar{i}_2}\rangle$$
$$+ \langle i_1 i_2|\rho_{i_1 \bar{i}_2}|i_1 i_2\rangle + \langle i_1 i_2 \oplus 1|\rho_{i_1 \bar{i}_2}|i_1 i_2 \oplus 1\rangle), \tag{A36}$$

$$P_{\text{suc}(1;i_1,0;i_2)} = \frac{1}{2}(\langle \bar{i}_1\bar{i}_2|\rho_{\bar{i}_1 i_2}|\bar{i}_1\bar{i}_2\rangle + \langle \overline{\bar{i}_1\bar{i}_2\oplus 1}|\rho_{\bar{i}_1 i_2}|\overline{\bar{i}_1\bar{i}_2\oplus 1}\rangle$$
$$+ \langle i_1 i_2|\rho_{\bar{i}_1 i_2}|i_1 i_2\rangle + \langle i_1 \oplus 1 i_2|\rho_{\bar{i}_1 i_2}|i_1 \oplus 1 i_2\rangle), \tag{A37}$$

$$P_{\text{suc}(1;i_1,1;i_2)} = \begin{cases} \frac{1}{2}(\langle \bar{i}_1\bar{i}_2|\rho_{\bar{i}_1 \bar{i}_2}|\bar{i}_1\bar{i}_2\rangle + 1) & (i_1 = i_2) \\ \frac{1}{2}\langle \bar{i}_1\bar{i}_2|\rho_{\bar{i}_1 \bar{i}_2}|\bar{i}_1\bar{i}_2\rangle & (i_1 \neq i_2). \end{cases} \tag{A38}$$

Then, we can observe the error probabilities from those probabilities.

References

1. Chefles, A. Quantum state discrimination. *Contemp. Phys.* **2000**, *41*, 401–424. [CrossRef]
2. Bergou, J.A.; Herzog, U.; Hillery, M. *Quantum State Estimation, 11 Discrimination of Quantum States*; Lecture Notes in Physics; Springer: Berlin/Heidelberg, Germany, 2007; Volume 649.
3. Qiu, D.; Li, L. Relation between minimum-error discrimination and optimum unambiguous discrimination. *Phys. Rev. A* **2010**, *82*, 032333. [CrossRef]
4. Wilde, M. *Quantum Information Theory*; Cambridge University Press: Cambridge, UK, 2017.
5. Vaidman, L.; Aharonov, Y.; Albert, D.Z. How to ascertain the values of σ_x, σ_y, and σ_z of a spin-1/2 particle. *Phys. Rev. Lett.* **1987**, *58*, 1385–1387. [CrossRef] [PubMed]
6. Englert, B.-G.; Aharonov, Y. The mean-kings' problem: prime degrees of freedom. *Phys. Lett. A* **2001**, *284*, 1–5. [CrossRef]
7. Aharonov, Y.; Bergmann, P.G.; Lebowitz, J.L. Time Symmetry in the Quantum Process of Measurement. *Phys. Rev.* **1964**, *134*, B1410. [CrossRef]
8. Bub, J. Secure key distribution via pre- and postselected quantum states. *Phys. Rev. A* **2001**, *63*, 032309. [CrossRef]
9. Werner, A.H.; Franz, T.; Werner, R.F. Quantum Cryptography as a Retrodiction Problem. *Phys. Rev. Lett.* **2009**, *103*, 220504. [CrossRef] [PubMed]
10. Yoshida, M.; Miyadera, T.; Imai, H. Quantum Key Distribution using Mean King Problem with Modified Measurement Schemes. In Proceedings of the International Symposium on Information Theory and Its Applications 2012, Honolulu, HI, USA, 28–31 October 2012; pp. 317–321.

11. Azuma, H.; Ban, M. The intercept/resend attack and the collective attack on the quantum key distribution protocol based on the pre- and post-selection effect. *arXiv* **2018**, arXiv:quant-ph/1811.07282.
12. Nakayama, A.; Yoshida, M.; Cheng, J. Quantum Key Distribution using Extended Mean King's Problem. In Proceedings of the International Symposium on Information Theory and Its Applications 2018, Singapore, 28–31 October 2018; pp. 339–343.
13. Bennett, C.H.; Brassard, G. Quantum Cryptography: Public Key Distribution And Coin Tossing. In Proceedings of the IEEE International Conference on Computers Systems and Signal Processing, Bangalore, India, 9–12 December 1984; pp. 175–179.
14. Fuchs, C.A.; Jacobs, K. Information-tradeoff relations for finite-strength quantum measurements. *Phys. Rev. A* **2001**, *63*, 062305. [CrossRef]
15. Boykin, P.O.; Roychowdhury, V.P. Information vs. Disturbance in Dimension D. *Quantum Inf. Comput.* **2005**, *5*, 396–412.
16. Miyadera, T.; Imai, H. Information-disturbance theorem for mutually unbiased observables. *Phys. Rev. A* **2006**, *73*, 042317. [CrossRef]
17. Miyadera, T.; Imai, H. Information-Disturbance theorem and Uncertainty Relation. *arXiv* **2007**, arXiv:quant-ph/0707.4559.
18. Busch, P. *No Information Without Disturbance: Quantum Limitations of Measurement*; Springer: Berlin/Heidelberg, Germany, 2009; pp. 229–256.
19. Biham, E.; Boyer, M.; Boykin, P.O.; Mor, T.; Roychowdhury, V. A proof of security of quantum key distribution. In Proceedings of the 32nd Annual ACM Symposium on Theory of Computing, Portland, OR, USA, 21–23 May 2000; pp. 715–724.
20. Bennett, C.H.; Brassard, G.; Crépeau, C.; Maurer, U.M. Generalized Privacy Amplification. *IEEE Trans. Inf. Theory* **1995**, *41*, 1915–1923. [CrossRef]
21. Deutsch, D.; Ekert, A.; Jozsa, R.; Macchiavello, C.; Popescu, S.; Sanpera, A. Quantum Privacy Amplification and the Security of Quantum Cryptography over Noisy Channels. *Phys. Rev. Lett.* **1996**, *77*, 2818–2821. [CrossRef] [PubMed]
22. Lo, H.-K.; Chau, H.F. Unconditional Security of Quantum Key Distribution over Arbitrarily Long Distances. *Science* **1999**, *283*, 2050–2056. [CrossRef] [PubMed]
23. Uhlmann, A. The "transition probability" in the state space of a ∗-algebra. *Rep. Math. Phys.* **1976**, *9*, 273–279. [CrossRef]
24. Jozsa, R. Fidelity for Mixed Quantum States. *J. Mod. Opt.* **1994**, *41*, 2315–2323. [CrossRef]
25. Fuchs, C.A.; Caves, C.M. Mathematical techniques for quantum communication theory. *Open Syst. Inf. Dyn.* **1995**, *3*, 345–356. [CrossRef]
26. Barnum, H.; Caves, C.M.; Fuchs, C.A.; Jozsa, R.; Schumacher, B. Noncommuting Mixed States Cannot Be Broadcast. *Phys. Rev. Lett.* **1996**, *76*, 2818–2821. [CrossRef] [PubMed]
27. Miyadera, T.; Imai, H. State collapse in Information Transfer and its applications. In Proceedings of the 2008 Symposium on Cryptography and Information Security, Miyazaki, Japan, 22–25 January 2008; p. 2D2-4.

Publisher's Note: MDPI stays neutral with regard to jurisdictional claims in published maps and institutional affiliations.

© 2020 by the authors. Licensee MDPI, Basel, Switzerland. This article is an open access article distributed under the terms and conditions of the Creative Commons Attribution (CC BY) license (http://creativecommons.org/licenses/by/4.0/).

Article

Beyond the Limits of Shannon's Information in Quantum Key Distribution

Luis Adrián Lizama-Pérez [1,*], J. Mauricio López R. [2] and Emmanuel H. Samperio [1]

[1] Dirección de Investigación, Innovación y Posgrado, Universidad Politécnica de Pachuca, Ex-Hacienda de Santa Bárbara, Zempoala, Hidalgo 43830, Mexico; esamperio593@micorreo.upp.edu.mx

[2] Cinvestav Querétaro, Libramiento Norponiente 2000, Real de Juriquilla, Santiago de Querétaro, Querétaro 76230, Mexico; jm.lopez@cinvestav.mx

* Correspondence: luislizama@upp.edu.mx

Abstract: We present a new post-processing method for Quantum Key Distribution (QKD) that raises cubically the secret key rate in the number of double matching detection events. In Shannon's communication model, information is prepared at Alice's side, and it is then intended to pass it over a noisy channel. In our approach, secret bits do not rely in Alice's transmitted quantum bits but in Bob's basis measurement choices. Therefore, measured bits are publicly revealed, while bases selections remain secret. Our method implements sifting, reconciliation, and amplification in a unique process, and it just requires a round iteration; no redundancy bits are sent, and there is no limit in the correctable error percentage. Moreover, this method can be implemented as a post-processing software into QKD technologies already in use.

Keywords: QKD; distillation; amplification; reconciliation

1. Introduction

To put it in historical context, fiber-optic telecommunications over long distances was not possible until manufacturing techniques that improved drastically its efficiency were developed. Fibers had been used to see inside the body, but they remained unusable for long-distance information transfer because too much light was lost along the way. However, in the 1960s, Charles Kao introduced a new disruptive approach based on pure glass fibers and laser technology with transcendent achievements [1].

In the quantum era, Quantum Key Distribution (QKD) is one of the most promising technologies to secure the information intended to cross data networks. However, the development of new techniques for the rapid establishment of secret key information using quantum pulses over long distances has become unpostponable [2–6].

Unfortunately, some factors prevent QKD of becoming a widely used technology as its inability to reach long-distances and produce large keys at high speed. The greatest weakness of QKD technology lies in its ability to gain useful information to establish a secret key despite the noise in the quantum channel [7,8]. On the one hand, noise provides the possibility for an attacker to disguise themselves, and, on the other hand, it imposes severe difficulties to correct errors produced during transmission in order to derive two identical cryptographic keys at both sides of the quantum link [9,10]. In the case of BB84 protocol, it has been estimated that a secure key can be distilled when the quantum bit error rate (QBER) is less than 11% [11].

In the few past years, we have developed a new scheme for QKD quantum called quantum flows [12–14] capable of resisting challenging attacks [15–25]. In quantum flows approach, Alice sends to Bob a pair of quantum states, parallel or non-orthogonal, which is chosen randomly. Bob measures the two quantum states with the same measurement basis, X or Z under active basis selection. If Bob obtains the same result, a single bit has been transmitted from Alice to Bob. Quantum flows have allowed us to formulate

a new method for QKD distillation based on binary structures called frames. Framed reconciliation integrates the regular QKD stages of sifting, reconciliation, and amplification in a unique process. This property makes our method unique in the context of QKD distillation; moreover, it accelerates convergence and produces a key that grows cubically in the number of double detection events.

In this work, we enhance the framed reconciliation method showed previously for 2×2 frames [14], and we discuss that framed reconciliation can surpass Shannon's information bounds for noisy channels. We strongly recommend that the reader consults our previous work on Quantum Key Distillation Using Binary Frames, so that we can keep the present article concise, as far as possible. Basic concepts comprise quantum flows, non-orthogonal quantum states, quantum photonic gains, binary frames, and matching results (MR). Having introduced 2×2 frames, which are the frames with the minimum size, we discuss here 3×2 frames. Throughout the article, we will compare both schemes.

2. Communication Model

Classical theory of communication, as it was established by Claude Shannon in 1948, defines a general communication system where Alice (the information source) prepares an information signal, that she sends over a noisy channel, but it corrupts at least in part due to the presence of noise in the channel [26,27]. At the other side, Bob receives this information signal, but Alice and Bob must implement a processing method to recover from the errors produced during transmission [28–32].

Shannon's theory imposes a limit to the highest transmission speed over a noisy channel because it can never surpass the channel capacity. The coding rate is computed as the number of message symbols divided by the number of transmitted signals. A higher coding rate means higher transmission speed. When the efficiency of the codes approximates to the channel capacity by increasing the number of transmitted signals, it is known that these codes approach to the Shannon limit. However, a coding rate too high makes it impossible to achieve a decoding error probability close to zero because the optimum channel capacity is achievable just by letting the number of transmitted signals reach infinity [33]. We claim our method goes beyond this limit because it does not require the number of transmitted signals to be increased. In fact, the coding rate reaches unity. The QKD protocol in Reference [34] exhibits a total efficiency of the communication to come up to 100%, but it does not define an error correction algorithm.

On the other side, if e is the probability that a transmitted 0 bit is received as a 1 and $1-e$ is the probability to be received as a 0, Shannon theory implies that, in case that $e=0.5$, one can never say anything about the original message [35,36] because the entropy is maximized when the two possible outcomes are equally probable. Since our method corrects errors when $e=0.5$, we claim that it goes beyond the limits implied by Shannon's theory.

In our approach, we call active (or real) information that which is derived from Shannon's model viewpoint because information is first prepared by Alice, then transmitted through the (quantum) channel, and, finally, recovered by Bob after it has been measured and proven to be correct. Conversely, in our scheme, information is not enclosed in the transmitted quantum pulses but in the quantum bases (X or Z) that Bob chooses at the other side. In fact, measured bits are publicly announced but the measurement bases are never revealed. We designated reactive information to this communication paradigm that we introduced to the sifting QKD procedure.

Reactive bits are computed using Bob's measurement bases, so errors produced in the quantum channel are easily detected by Alice because such bits are publicly revealed by Bob. Remarkably, in the presence of the unit error rate, information can still be recovered since errors give reactive information by themselves. For the same reason, not all of Alice's information can be recovered, even in the absence of errors produced by the quantum channel.

Two reconciliation approaches have been conceived in QKD: direct and reverse reconciliation. In reverse reconciliation (RR), Alice must infer Bob's outcomes, rather than Bob guessing Alice's encodings, known as direct reconciliation (DR). Under this classification frame, reconciliation is RR, so let us briefly contrast our approach with RR which was introduced in the context of continuous variable QKD [31,37].

It has been demonstrated that RR reconciliation achieves longer distances even beyond the 3dB limit of previous CV-QKD works [38]. RR reconciliation has been implemented over LDPC basis [39], and it was shown that LDPC codes can reach within 0.0045 dB of the Shannon limit. Unfortunately, it requires large block lengths (10^7) [40]. Even more, decoding LDPC has larger computational and memory requirements than either Cascade or Winnow algorithms [41]. In contrast, our method does not require additional bits which reduces the coding rate. Our experimental simulations show complete efficiency in detecting/correcting errors. Moreover, the secret throughput grows cubically in the number of double detection events.

Before we introduce 3×2 frames, we will explain quantum communication based on frames through a simple example about our reconciliation method. To facilitate its exposition, we use 2×2 frames in this example. Then, to simplify exposition we discuss the role of auxiliary frames in the 2×2 case. In Section 3, we address the research methodology for 3×2 frames and then we detail the QKD distillation protocol. To make the discussion more effective, we have placed tables of 3×2 protocol in the Appendix A. Finally, in Section 4, we analyze the efficiency and the security of the 3×2 protocol against different attacks as the Intercept-Resend (IR) attack and the Photon Number Splitting (PNS) attack.

2.1. Quantum Communication

In the BB84 protocol [42–45], a quantum state $|i_X\rangle$ (or $|i_Z\rangle$), where i represents the encoded bit ($i = 0, 1$), is useful to be distilled whenever it has been measured in the proper (compatible) quantum basis, basis X for $|i_X\rangle$ (or Z for $|i_Z\rangle$). Otherwise, a non-compatible measurement is produced, the bit derived from this measurement is ambiguous, and it must be discarded. However, in the quantum flows scheme, ambiguous cases can still be used for the following reasons [14]:

- The states are grouped by non-orthogonal pairs $(|i_X\rangle, |i_Z\rangle)$ or $(|i_X\rangle, |(i-1)_Z\rangle)$, where $i = 0, 1$.
- A non-orthogonal pair is measured with the same quantum basis X or Z. Both measurements yield the same result half of the times, i.e., if measuring $(|i_X\rangle, |i_Z\rangle)$ with X (or Z) gives i, or measuring $(|i_X\rangle, |(i-1)_Z\rangle)$ with X (or Z) gives i or $1 - i$, in both cases. We call those cases double matching detection event. Then, non-compatible measurements never occur.
- It implies that the bit encoded in the X or Z basis is transmitted from Alice to Bob. This communication model defines two communication channels, channel X and channel Z, because there are two bits enclosed in a non-orthogonal quantum pair: one bit over channel X and other bit in channel Z. Bob just chooses which channel he wants to use. Provided a double matching detection event is generated, both measurements are equally useful.

2.2. Example of Error Correction

In order to better introduce our communication model, let us illustrate it with a simple example to contrast it with Shannon's model. To see the effect of the errors instead of the losses in the channel, let us assume a conservative quantum channel. Table 1 shows an hypothetical QKD protocol possibly based on BB84, where Alice has sent 18 quantum states (in practical implementations, some sifted bits must be sacrificed to estimate the error rate of the channel). In this example, a 30% error rate (e) is produced; therefore, the QKD distillation process must be declined because prominent reconciliation algorithms, such as Cascade, Winnow, or LDPC, cannot work with this high error rate.

Table 1. In this example of a running Quantum Key Distribution (QKD), 6 errors (underlined at Bob's column) among 18 measured quantum states are produced, so it gives an error rate of 30%. According to Shannon's limit, it yields a transmission rate of 0.0817. It is known that, at 50%, there is no reconcilable information.

Alice	Bob
$\|0_X\rangle_2, \|0_Z\rangle_1,$ $\|1_X\rangle_4, \|0_Z\rangle_3,$ $\|1_X\rangle_6, \|1_Z\rangle_5,$ $\|0_X\rangle_8, \|1_Z\rangle_7,$ $\|1_X\rangle_{10}, \|0_Z\rangle_9,$ $\|0_X\rangle_{12}, \|1_Z\rangle_{11},$ $\|1_X\rangle_{14}, \|1_Z\rangle_{13},$ $\|1_X\rangle_{16}, \|0_Z\rangle_{15},$ $\|0_X\rangle_{18}, \|1_Z\rangle_{17}$	$\|0_X\rangle_2, \|0_Z\rangle_1,$ $\|1_X\rangle_4, \underline{\|1_Z\rangle_3},$ $\|1_X\rangle_6, \underline{\|1_Z\rangle_5},$ $\|1_X\rangle_8, \|1_Z\rangle_7,$ $\underline{\|0_X\rangle_{10}}, \|0_Z\rangle_9,$ $\underline{\|0_X\rangle_{12}}, \|0_Z\rangle_{11},$ $\|1_X\rangle_{14}, \|1_Z\rangle_{13},$ $\underline{\|0_X\rangle_{16}}, \|0_Z\rangle_{15},$ $\underline{\|1_X\rangle_{18}}, \|1_Z\rangle_{17}$

Let us suppose that the same errors are produced using the framed reconciliation method as it is illustrated in Figure 1. In this example, we ignored the losses due to double detection events and the amplification gain produced by the amount of combinations between double matching detection events (we will discuss them later). The reconciliation based on frames can process this error rate; in fact, it can reconcile any error rate that e has in the channel, so there is no need to estimate e wasting bits for this purpose. To simplify the exposition, in this example, we used 2×2 frames, but we will discuss 3×2 frames in the Distillation Method section.

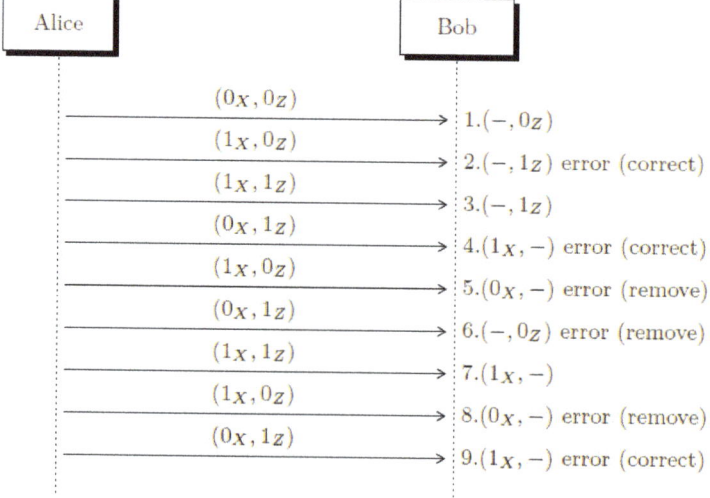

Figure 1. Using frame reconciliation, all errors are detected and corrected (or removed). Each double detection event has been enumerated to follow them into the frames (see Tables 2 and 3).

Table 2. Alice receives the Sifting String (SS) from Bob, which she knows belongs to f_2, f_3, and f_4, respectively, but they are ambiguous, so she uses the auxiliary frames f_{10}, f_9, and f_9, respectively, to identify the error and then correct it.

	MR = 01			MR = 01	
f_2 $\begin{matrix}2.\\3.\end{matrix}$	$\begin{pmatrix}-\\-\end{pmatrix}$	$\begin{pmatrix}\|1_Z\rangle\\\|1_Z\rangle\end{pmatrix}$	f_{10} $\begin{matrix}2.\\1.\end{matrix}$	$\begin{pmatrix}-\\-\end{pmatrix}$	$\begin{pmatrix}\|1_Z\rangle\\\|0_Z\rangle\end{pmatrix}$
	SS = 00, 11			SS = 01, 10	
	MR = 10			MR = 10	
f_3 $\begin{matrix}4.\\3.\end{matrix}$	$\begin{pmatrix}\|1_X\rangle\\-\end{pmatrix}$	$\begin{pmatrix}-\\\|1_Z\rangle\end{pmatrix}$	f_9 $\begin{matrix}4.\\1.\end{matrix}$	$\begin{pmatrix}\|1_X\rangle\\-\end{pmatrix}$	$\begin{pmatrix}-\\\|0_Z\rangle\end{pmatrix}$
	SS = 11, 11			SS = 10, 10	
	MR = 00			MR = 10	
f_4 $\begin{matrix}7.\\9.\end{matrix}$	$\begin{pmatrix}\|1_X\rangle\\\|1_X\rangle\end{pmatrix}$	$\begin{pmatrix}-\\-\end{pmatrix}$	f_9 $\begin{matrix}9.\\1.\end{matrix}$	$\begin{pmatrix}\|1_X\rangle\\-\end{pmatrix}$	$\begin{pmatrix}-\\\|0_Z\rangle\end{pmatrix}$
	SS = 00, 11			SS = 10, 10	

Table 3. After Alice receives these SS, she determines that the respective frames must be eliminated because ambiguity cannot be removed.

	MR = 10			MR = 01			MR = 00	
f_2 $\begin{matrix}5.\\3.\end{matrix}$	$\begin{pmatrix}\|0_X\rangle\\-\end{pmatrix}$	$\begin{pmatrix}-\\\|1_Z\rangle\end{pmatrix}$	f_3 $\begin{matrix}6.\\3.\end{matrix}$	$\begin{pmatrix}-\\-\end{pmatrix}$	$\begin{pmatrix}\|0_Z\rangle\\\|1_Z\rangle\end{pmatrix}$	f_6 $\begin{matrix}8.\\7.\end{matrix}$	$\begin{pmatrix}\|0_X\rangle\\\|1_X\rangle\end{pmatrix}$	$\begin{pmatrix}-\\-\end{pmatrix}$
	SS = 01, 01			SS = 01, 01			SS = 10, 01	

2.3. Auxiliary Frames

A major component of the framed reconciliation method relies in the auxiliary frames. There are two types of auxiliary frames: zero frames and testing frames. Every quantum state of a zero frame is $|0_X\rangle$ or $|0_Z\rangle$. Identifying measurement errors in a zero frame is easy, as we will see later. A testing frame contains one row that is under evaluation because it presumably contains error, and the rest of the rows come from a zero verified frame.

To compute the sifting string (SS), we follow the next procedure: A sifting string is constructed concatenating the bits that result after the $\oplus$ logical operation is applied to each column of the frame (a blank space is treated as a zero bit) and putting the measured bits that are produced by the optical detectors. The secret bits are derived from the code that is assigned to the arrangement of measurements inside the frame. We call measurement results (MR) to this arrangement. To see the role of auxiliary frames, let us assume that we intend to apply the framing algorithm to the Shannon's model; thus, several zero bits are interleaved between the secret bits to be used as auxiliary correcting bits.

1. To achieve reconciliation in Shannon's model, the first step is to ensure that auxiliary zero bits are error-free. However, Shannon's 2×1 frames does not allow to identify errors in two consecutive zero bits (at least in one round iteration) as indicated by the following relations:

$$\begin{pmatrix}0\\\oplus\\0\end{pmatrix} = \begin{pmatrix}1\\\oplus\\1\end{pmatrix} = 0 \text{ (SS)}.$$

In addition, when using 2×1 frames, there is a unique possible matching result (MR), that is written below; therefore, no secret information can be derived from MRs in Shannon's model.

$$\begin{pmatrix} |\bullet\rangle \\ |\bullet\rangle \end{pmatrix}.$$

2. By contrast, using 2 × 2 frames, errors in the auxiliary frames can be easily identified. Here, we list the error-free zero frames:

$$\begin{pmatrix} |0_X\rangle & - \\ \oplus & \\ - & |0_Z\rangle \end{pmatrix} = \begin{pmatrix} - & |0_Z\rangle \\ \oplus & \\ |0_X\rangle & - \end{pmatrix} = \begin{pmatrix} |0_X\rangle & - \\ \oplus & \\ |0_X\rangle & - \end{pmatrix} = \begin{pmatrix} - & |0_Z\rangle \\ \oplus & \\ - & |0_Z\rangle \end{pmatrix} = 00,00 \quad (SS),$$

which can be compared, for illustrative purposes, to the erroneous cases:

$$\begin{pmatrix} |1_X\rangle & - \\ \oplus & \\ - & |1_Z\rangle \end{pmatrix} = \begin{pmatrix} - & |1_Z\rangle \\ \oplus & \\ |1_X\rangle & - \end{pmatrix} = 11,11 \quad (SS),$$

$$\begin{pmatrix} |1_X\rangle & - \\ \oplus & \\ |1_X\rangle & - \end{pmatrix} = \begin{pmatrix} - & |1_Z\rangle \\ \oplus & \\ - & |1_Z\rangle \end{pmatrix} = 00,11 \quad (SS).$$

3. Ambiguous SS are produced in regular frames. For example, to the left, we indicate that Alice sends the frame f_2 to Bob, who measures it using MR = 11. However, when applying the Z measurement basis, the photo-detector yields an error reporting $|1_Z\rangle$ instead $|0_Z\rangle$; so, we have:

$$f_{2_a} = \begin{pmatrix} |1_X\rangle & |0_Z\rangle \\ |1_X\rangle & |1_Z\rangle \end{pmatrix}, f_{2_b} = \begin{pmatrix} - & |1_Z\rangle \\ \oplus & \\ |1_X\rangle & - \end{pmatrix} = 11,11 \quad (SS).$$

When Alice receives the string SS = 11,11 which belongs to f_2, she knows it implies two possibilities: either SS comes from the error-free string $SS_{24} = 11,11$ under MR = 10 in f_2 or an error is produced in the first measured bit that actually corresponds to the string $SS_{23} = 10,01$ under MR = 11 in f_2. To disambiguate it, Alice uses the auxiliary frame f_{10}. Thus, she looks at a frame f_{10} where the ambiguous row $(-, |1_Z\rangle)$ is allocated. Remember that each row is combined with each other. Previously, the second row of f_{10}, i.e., $(|0_X\rangle, -)$, was verified as a zero frame. Then, suppose Alice finds the following f_{10} case:

$$f_{10} = \begin{pmatrix} - & |1_Z\rangle \\ \oplus & \\ |0_X\rangle & - \end{pmatrix} = 10,10.$$

The sifting string 10,10 reveals that an error exists in the row that is under evaluation; therefore, Alice decides SS_{23}. Then, the pair (SS_{23}, f_2) determines Alice's secret bit. It must be highlighted that the sifting strings of auxiliary frames cannot be distinguished from other identical SS from regular frames, so privacy is guaranteed. In fact, it is ensured that each SS can proceed equally from each bit.

2.4. One-Time Pad XOR Equivalency

It is known that the XOR one-time pad encryption method is a perfect cryptosystem provided the crypto key achieves the same number of bits as the plaintext. Let us show that the framing method actually behaves as one-time encryption. First, in Table 4, we can see the logical XOR ($\oplus$) function. Each encrypted bit c could be produced by each key bit denoted as k.

Table 4. The logical XOR function.

c	$k \oplus b$
0	$0 \oplus 0$
	$1 \oplus 1$
1	$0 \oplus 1$
	$1 \oplus 0$

As specified in the framed reconciliation method [14], Bob must reveal the sifting bits along the measured bits. However, each SS maps two different MRs, as can be verified in Table 5. Since secret bits are enclosed in MRs, we proved that secret bits of the framing protocol are equivalent to the secret bits of the XOR one-time pad cryptosystem. The same analysis can be applied to the 3×2 frames.

Table 5. The XOR function for 2×2 frames; matching results (MR) is the measurement result, and sb denotes the final secret bit.

c	$k \oplus b$	MR	Frames	sb
00	$(\lvert 0_X\rangle,-) \oplus (-,\lvert 0_Z\rangle)$	10	f_1	0
	$(-,\lvert 0_Z\rangle) \oplus (\lvert 0_X\rangle,-)$	11	f_5	1
	$(\lvert 1_X\rangle,-) \oplus (\lvert 1_X\rangle,-)$	00	f_2, f_6	0
	$(-,\lvert 1_Z\rangle) \oplus (-,\lvert 1_Z\rangle)$	01	f_3, f_4	1
01	$(-,\lvert 1_Z\rangle) \oplus (-,\lvert 0_Z\rangle)$	01	f_1, f_6	0
	$(-,\lvert 1_Z\rangle) \oplus (\lvert 0_X\rangle,-)$	11	f_4	1
	$(\lvert 0_X\rangle,-) \oplus (-,\lvert 1_Z\rangle)$	10	f_3	0
	$(-,\lvert 0_Z\rangle) \oplus (-,\lvert 1_Z\rangle)$	01	f_2, f_5	1
10	$(\lvert 1_X\rangle,-) \oplus (\lvert 0_X\rangle,-)$	00	f_4, f_5	0
	$(\lvert 1_X\rangle,-) \oplus (-,\lvert 0_Z\rangle)$	10	f_6	1
	$(\lvert 0_X\rangle,-) \oplus (\lvert 1_X\rangle,-)$	00	f_1, f_3	0
	$(-,\lvert 0_Z\rangle) \oplus (\lvert 1_X\rangle,-)$	11	f_2	1
11	$(-,\lvert 1_Z\rangle) \oplus (\lvert 1_X\rangle,-)$	11	f_1, f_3, f_6	0
	$(\lvert 1_X\rangle,-) \oplus (-,\lvert 1_Z\rangle)$	10	f_2, f_4, f_5	1

3. Distillation Method with 3×2 Frames

Before we detail the steps of the distillation method for 3×2 frames, let us describe the research methodology we applied:

1. The 3×2 frames must be identified: there are $4^3 = 64$ binary 3×2 frames.
2. The measurement results (MR) must be specified: in 3×2 frames, there are 8 MR. Those MR are illustrated in Table A2 of Appendix A.
3. Frames are classified as usable and useless frames: a usable frame is a frame that produces a distinct SS under each MR. In 3×2 frames, there are 8 distinct SS per frame and 24 usable frames. Sifting bits are written in Table A4 of Appendix A. Remember that Sifting Strings (SS) are composed by the sifting bits and the measured bits: SS = 1st sifting bit || 2nd sifting bit|| 3th sifting bit, 1st measured bit || 2nd measured bit || 3th measured bit. The 3th sifting bit is appended to achieve discrimination, and it can be considered as a parity sifting bit.
4. Auxiliary frames which are intended to catch errors produced in regular frames must be identified. In 3×2 frames, there are 3 auxiliary frames labeled as f_{25}, f_{26}, and f_{27}. The frame f_{25} is the zero frame and is used to verify the two (below) rows of the testing frames f_{26} and f_{27}. The upper row of f_{26} and f_{27} is the row that is being tested. In the end, Alice will include the auxiliary frames inside the set of frames that Bob must remove. Auxiliary frames are listed in Table A1 of Appendix A.
5. All usable frames under each MR must be expanded to analyze all possible errors through SS, from single to multiple errors. Then, ambiguous SS that can be corrected

under the auxiliary frames must be detected. In addition, all the SS that cannot be disambiguated must be identified and the corresponding frames must be removed. We show in Table A5 the cases that can be successfully disambiguated.

6. At Bob's side, each (SS, MR) pair defines a secret bit (sb). For Alice, the same secret bit results from the pair (SS, f_i) because she knows the frame that is behind each SS. It must be guaranteed that each SS can be produced equally by both bits. In addition, it must be ensured that each secret bit proceeds from the same number of frames, so that the bit probability of each SS is the same in order to reduce the eavesdropper's information gain (SS are publicly transmitted over the classical channel). This action may involve removing some extra SS. Alice sends to Bob the set of SS of all the frames that must be eliminated including auxiliary frames. Table A3 of Appendix A enlists SS, MR, frames, and sb.

Now, we can proceed to summarize the steps of the distillation method for 3×2 frames that comprises sifting, reconciliation, and privacy amplification. The overall steps of the process are indicated in Figure 2:

1. Alice sends some non-orthogonal quantum pairs either $(|i_X\rangle, |i_Z\rangle)$ or $(|i_X\rangle, |(1-i)_Z\rangle)$ where $i = 0, 1$. Although quantum non-orthogonal pairs can be mutually interleaved they are numbered, so each pair can be identified by Alice and Bob
2. Bob measures each quantum pair using the same measurement basis (X or Z) which is chosen randomly (under active basis measurement). Some double detection events are produced. Bob informs Alice the tag number of such quantum pairs.
3. Alice computes all usable frames including null frames and auxiliary frames. She communicates to Bob the frame arrangement information. We call this step privacy amplification.
4. Bob computes the Sifting String (SS) of each frame. He returns the set of Siting Strings he obtained to Alice.
5. Alice analyzes the SS received from Bob:

    She generates frames f_{25} to prepare the auxiliary frames.

    Using auxiliary frames, Alice removes ambiguity. Alice gets the secret bits using the relation (SS, f_i) and Table A3 of Appendix A.

    Alice informs Bob of the cases that must be eliminated (because they cannot be disambiguated).
6. Bob removes the frames identified by Alice to reach Alice's secret bit string. Bob's secret bits are derived from (SS, MR) and Table A3 of Appendix A.

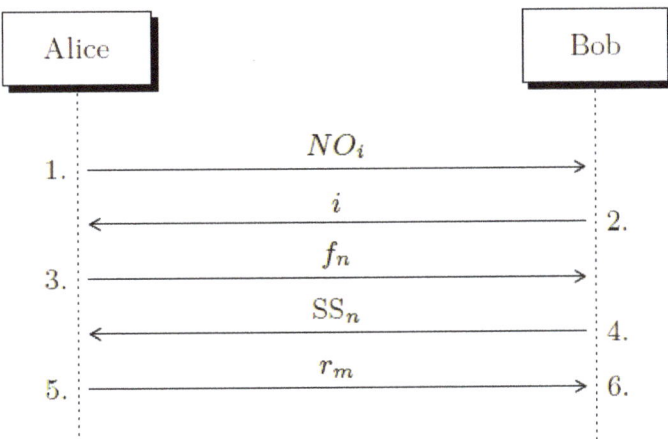

Figure 2. The frame distillation runs in one iteration: Alice sends pairs of non-orthogonal states (NO_i). Bob informs to Alice which cases produced double matching detection events (i). Alice generates all possible frames and sends to Bob the frame arrangement information (f_n). Bob returns back the sifting strings (SS_n). Finally, Alice tells Bob which cases he must delete (r_m). Step 1 is executed over the quantum channel, while steps 2 to 5 are completed using the classical channel.

4. Secret Rate

The secret rate of the framed reconciliation method can be derived directly from frames without recurring to quantum physics mathematical relations. First off, we must enlist the Sifting String (SS) generated by all the frames classified by Measurement Result (MR) and separate the error-free SS from the erroneous SS (single and multiple errors). According to the size of frames (2×2 or 3×2), the error could be in the first bit, second bit, third bit, two bits, two of three bits, and three bits simultaneously. Then, we proceed to identify ambiguous SS, (because they appear simultaneously as error-free SS and erroneous SS for a given frame). Then, we identify the SS that can still be used after they are inspected under auxiliary frames. We call those cases unequivocal SS cases.

We calculate the secret rate (in absence of eavesdropping) as the sum up of the information derived from the unequivocal error-free rate and the amount of information derived from the unequivocal erroneous rate (unequivocal error-free rate is obtained as the number of unequivocal error-free SS under the total number of error-free SS; conversely, the unequivocal error rate is obtained as the rate of unequivocal erroneous SS over the total erroneous SS cases). As mentioned earlier, unequivocal means that ambiguity can be removed using auxiliary frames. The bits from remaining SS must be eliminated since they do not contribute to the secret rate.

In Table 6, we detail the deduction of the secret rate. Each SS contributes with a single bit. In 2×2 frames, we have 4 usable frames, and each one generates 4 SS; to compute the unequivocal erroneous rate, we have 2 SS per frame that can be recovered from 12 SS per frame yields $\frac{1}{6}$. On the other hand, to derive the unequivocal error-free rate, we have 2 SS per frame that can be recovered from 4 SS per frame it yields $\frac{1}{2}$. The unequivocal erroneous rate in 3×2 frames yields $\frac{1}{3}$, and the unequivocal error-free rate gives $\frac{1}{21}$ (see Figure 3).

Table 6. The secret rate is indicated without taking the framing gain for each frame size. The secret rate is shown when $e = 0$ and $e = 1$.

$I_{ab_{(2\times 2)}}$	$I_{ab_{(3\times 2)}}$
$\frac{1}{2}(1-e) + \frac{1}{6}e$	$\frac{1}{3}(1-e) + \frac{1}{21}e$
$\frac{1}{2} - \frac{1}{3}e$	$\frac{1}{3} - \frac{2}{7}e$
$e = 0 \rightarrow I_{ab_{(2\times 2)}} = \frac{1}{2}$	$e = 0 \rightarrow I_{ab_{(3\times 2)}} = \frac{1}{3}$
$e = 1 \rightarrow I_{ab_{(2\times 2)}} = \frac{1}{6}$	$e = 1 \rightarrow I_{ab_{(3\times 2)}} = \frac{1}{21}$

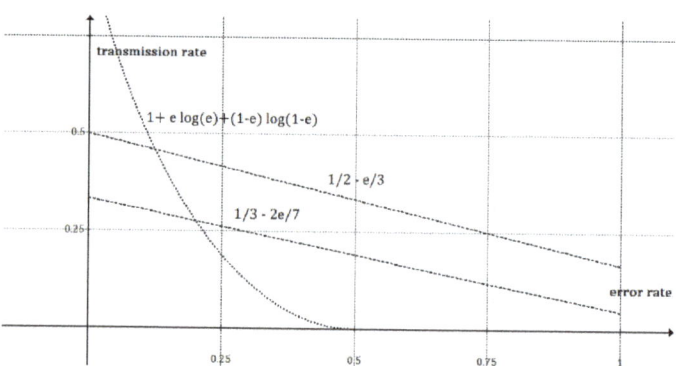

Figure 3. The theoretical transmission rate is plotted as a function of the quantum bit error rate (QBER) e; we show the 2 × 2 and 3 × 2 lines and the Shannon's reference function. When $e = 1$, the secret rate achieves 0.16 for 2 × 2 frames and 0.047 for 3 × 2 frames.

4.1. Secret Throughput

One of the main advantages of the reconciliation method based on frames is the total number of secret bits that results when the framing gain is applied. Remarkably, framing gain results from the amount of total combinations among double matching detection events. We call this process privacy pre-amplification (or amplification in short). Therefore, we compute the secret throughput multiplying the secret rate by the framing gain. In the case of 2 × 2 frames, we have 4 usable frames under 16 total frames, so the framing gain is $\frac{1}{4}\binom{n}{2}$. Conversely, in 3 × 2 frames, there are 24 over 64 frames, so the framing gain is $\frac{3}{8}\binom{n}{3}$. Equation (2) describes the secret throughput for each case.

$$\begin{aligned} I_{ab_{(2x2)}} &= \frac{1}{4}\binom{n}{2}\left(\frac{1}{2} - \frac{1}{3}e\right) \\ I_{ab_{(3x2)}} &= \frac{3}{8}\binom{n}{3}\left(\frac{1}{3} - \frac{2}{7}e\right) \end{aligned} \quad (1)$$

Just to appreciate the growth rate of each frame size, we compute, in Table 7, some values of the secret throughput as a function of n and e. As it can be inferred, 3 × 2 frames have a visible advantage to produce secret bits, e.g., when $n = 10^3$, it raises the secret throughput to $n = 10^8$ bits.

Table 7. The theoretical secret throughput (bits) as a function of n and e for each frame size.

n	$e = 0$		$e = 0.5$		$e = 1$	
	$I_{ab_{(2\times2)}}$	$I_{ab_{(3\times2)}}$	$I_{ab_{(2\times2)}}$	$I_{ab_{(3\times2)}}$	$I_{ab_{(2\times2)}}$	$I_{ab_{(3\times2)}}$
100	618	20,212	412	11,550	206	2887
500	15,593	2,588,562	10,395	1,479,178	5197	369,794
1000	62,437	20,770,875	41,625	11,869,071	20,812	2,967,267

4.2. Rate Code

The rate code r_{ab} is the relation between the secret information and the total bits generated to achieve reconciliation. In the case of 2×2 frames, the total information is $4\binom{n}{2}$, while the total number is $6\binom{n}{3}$ in 3×2 frames. The rate code for each size of frame is written in Equation (2).

$$r_{ab_{(2\times2)}} = \frac{1}{16}\left(\frac{1}{2} - \frac{1}{3}e\right)$$
$$r_{ab_{(3\times2)}} = \frac{1}{16}\left(\frac{1}{3} - \frac{2}{7}e\right) \quad (2)$$

4.3. Secret Key Rate

In the case of frame reconciliation, the eavesdropper has a great disadvantage since they do not know Bob's bases selection because they are not revealed over the classical channel. Even if the eavesdropper captures some copies of the quantum pulses, they must deal with the double detection events and the basis choices. Moreover, although the eavesdropper could replicate some double detection events, Alice performs all combinations between double detection events. As a consequence of the privacy amplification process, the eavesdropper's information reduces even more.

4.3.1. The Intercept and Resend Attack (IR)

In the Intercept and Resend (IR) attack, the eavesdropper first measures each pair of non-orthogonal quantum pulses in the quantum channel, and then they send another pair of quantum pulses to Bob prepared according to the same quantum states.

Since secret bits are derived only from double matching detection events, Eve must produce first a double matching detection event using the quantum states she intercepts in the quantum channel because no useful information could be extracted from double non-matching detection events nor even single detection events.

In addition, Eve must guarantee that both states she resends to Bob's station achieve his optical detectors, which imposes a severe difficulty because vacuum or single detection events are more probable than double detection events. However, suppose Eve forces both quantum states to arrive Bob's receiver station. We can derive the efficiency of the IR attack using the following example:

— Alice sends the non-orthogonal pair $(|0_X\rangle, |0_Z\rangle)$ to Bob over the quantum channel. Eve measures them using Z basis, and let us assume she obtains a double matching detection event, say $(|0_Z\rangle, |0_Z\rangle)$.
— Eve prepares and sends the quantum pair $(|0_Z\rangle, |0_Z\rangle)$ to Bob.
— Suppose Eve can force both quantum pulses to arrive to Bob's optical station. There are two quantum measurement bases (X or Z) and five possible outcomes:
  – $\frac{1}{2}$ due to Bob's Z basis: $(|0_Z\rangle, |0_Z\rangle)$.
  – $\frac{1}{2}$ due to Bob's X basis: $\{(|0_X\rangle, |0_X\rangle), (|1_X\rangle, |1_X\rangle), (|1_X\rangle, |0_X\rangle), (|0_X\rangle, |1_X\rangle)\}$.

To match Eve's double detection event $(|0_Z\rangle, |0_Z\rangle)$, Bob must choose the Z basis which occurs with $\frac{1}{2}$ probability, so Eve's final probability is $\frac{1}{4}$.

The overall scheme is depicted in the following diagram, where $Q_{(+,+)}$ represents Alice's pairs of non-orthogonal states:

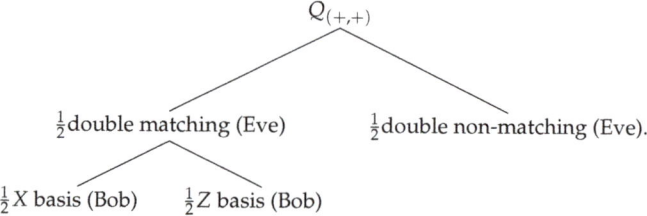

4.3.2. The Photon Number Splitting Attack (PNS)

The eavesdropper has a copy of all the quantum states that arrive to Bob's station because Alice sends attenuated (multi-photon) quantum pulses, and the eavesdropper is equipped with a sufficiently large quantum memory. However, the eavesdropper's probability of getting a double matching detection event is $\frac{1}{2}$. In addition, Eve must measure choosing between two different measurement basis (X or Z); thus, his final probability is $\frac{1}{4}$:

- $\frac{1}{2}$ because of the probability to get a double matching detection event.
- $\frac{1}{2}$ due to basis matching. Eve must measure choosing between two different measurement basis (X or Z).

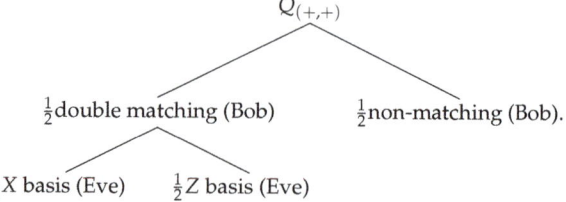

4.3.3. The Bases Choice Attack (BC)

The eavesdropper would decide to apply another quantum measurement bases to gain more information, and then they use the measurement bases $X + Z$ or $X - Z$. First, consider that the eavesdropper chooses between the measurement bases ($X + Z$ or $X - Z$) with 0.5 probability. However, non-matching detection events are ambiguous for the eavesdropper, which occur with $\frac{6}{16}$ probability. In contrast, they get a double matching event with $\frac{9}{16}$ probability. As a result, the chance to get Bob's information is $\frac{9}{32}$.

Equation (3) shows the relation to compute the secret key rate for each frame size. It is written as the secret information multiplied by the rate between the total frames produced by Alice and those the eavesdropper duplicates.

$$\Delta I_{(2X2)} = \left[\frac{1}{2} - \frac{1}{3}e\right]\left[1 - \frac{\binom{R \cdot n}{2}}{\binom{n}{2}}\right]$$
$$\Delta I_{(3X2)} = \left[\frac{1}{3} - \frac{2}{7}e\right]\left[1 - \frac{\binom{R \cdot n}{3}}{\binom{n}{3}}\right]. \quad (3)$$

Table 8 shows the final secret key information for each attack: Intercept and Resend attack (IR), Photon Number Splitting attack (PNS), and Basis Choice attack (BC). In the case of 2×2 frames, we have ignored the linear term n that is generated in $\binom{n}{2}$ because the quadratic term n^2 is dominant. In the same way, we omitted the quadratic and linear terms produced by $\binom{n}{3}$ because of the high order of the cubic term.

Table 8. The secret key rate is computed as $\Delta I = I_{ab} - I_{ae}$ for each attack.

IR	PNS	BC
$\left(1-\left(\frac{1}{4}\right)^2\right)\cdot I_{ab_{(2\times 2)}}$	$\left(1-\left(\frac{1}{4}\right)^2\right)\cdot I_{ab_{(2\times 2)}}$	$\left(1-\left(\frac{9}{32}\right)^2\right)\cdot I_{ab_{(2\times 2)}}$
$\left(1-\left(\frac{1}{4}\right)^3\right)\cdot I_{ab_{(3\times 2)}}$	$\left(1-\left(\frac{1}{4}\right)^3\right)\cdot I_{ab_{(3\times 2)}}$	$\left(1-\left(\frac{9}{32}\right)^3\right)\cdot I_{ab_{(3\times 2)}}$

As it can be deduced from Table 8, the secret key rate is affected slightly by the eavesdropper's behavior. This new scenario opens the possibility to employ less attenuated pulses as in CV-QKD to achieve, on one hand, long-distances quantum links or, on the other, portable QKD in closed buildings [46].

5. Conclusions

We have discussed a new post-processing method for Quantum Key Distribution (QKD) that raises cubically the secret key rate in the number of double matching detection events. Secret bits are derived from reactive bits instead of Shannon information, so Bob's measured bits are publicly revealed, while bases selections remain secret. Our method implements sifting, reconciliation, and amplification in a unique process, and it just requires a round iteration; no redundancy bits are sent, and no limit in the correctable error percentage. Despite the fact that the reconciliation is performed with a unity error channel, the secret rate is kept, at least theoretically, in 16% using 2×2 frames and 4.7% when using 3×2 frames.

It is not difficult to evaluate the security of this method because it can be evaluated directly through the frames. There is no dependency on other security mechanism as hash functions.

The protocol works fast, at least theoretically, convergence is guaranteed, and it can be implemented as a post-processing software into QKD technologies.

Author Contributions: L.A.L.-P. conceived of the presented idea, he developed the theoretical formalism, J.M.L.R. supervised the project and contributed to the interpretation of the results and E.H.S. performed software and numerical simulations. All authors have read and agreed to the published version of the manuscript.

Funding: This research was funded by National Council of Science and Technology of Mexico (CONACyT) and Center for Research and Advanced Studies of the National Polytechnic Institute of Mexico (Cinvestav-IPN).

Informed Consent Statement: Not applicable.

Data Availability Statement: The data presented in this study are available within the article.

Conflicts of Interest: The authors declare no conflict of interest in this article.

Appendix A

This Appendix contains the relevant tables used for the framed methodology:

- Table A1 describes the complete set of 3×2 frames.
- MR are illustrated in Table A2.
- Table A3 enlists SS, MR, frames, and sb.
- Sifting bits are written in Table A4.
- Table A5 shows the cases that can be successfully disambiguated.

Table A1. There are 24 useful frames: f_i, where $i = 1, \ldots, 24$ and 3 Auxiliary frames f_j, where $j = 25, \ldots, 27$.

Useful Frames			Auxiliary Frames
$f_1 = \begin{pmatrix} \lvert 0_X\rangle & \lvert 0_Z\rangle \\ \lvert 0_X\rangle & \lvert 1_Z\rangle \\ \lvert 1_X\rangle & \lvert 0_Z\rangle \end{pmatrix}$	$f_2 = \begin{pmatrix} \lvert 1_X\rangle & \lvert 0_Z\rangle \\ \lvert 0_X\rangle & \lvert 1_Z\rangle \\ \lvert 0_X\rangle & \lvert 0_Z\rangle \end{pmatrix}$	$f_3 = \begin{pmatrix} \lvert 0_X\rangle & \lvert 0_Z\rangle \\ \lvert 1_X\rangle & \lvert 0_Z\rangle \\ \lvert 0_X\rangle & \lvert 1_Z\rangle \end{pmatrix}$	$f_{25} = \begin{pmatrix} \lvert 0_X\rangle & \lvert 0_Z\rangle \\ \lvert 0_X\rangle & \lvert 0_Z\rangle \\ \lvert 0_X\rangle & \lvert 0_Z\rangle \end{pmatrix}$
$f_4 = \begin{pmatrix} \lvert 1_X\rangle & \lvert 0_Z\rangle \\ \lvert 1_X\rangle & \lvert 0_Z\rangle \\ \lvert 1_X\rangle & \lvert 1_Z\rangle \end{pmatrix}$	$f_5 = \begin{pmatrix} \lvert 1_X\rangle & \lvert 1_Z\rangle \\ \lvert 0_X\rangle & \lvert 1_Z\rangle \\ \lvert 0_X\rangle & \lvert 0_Z\rangle \end{pmatrix}$	$f_6 = \begin{pmatrix} \lvert 1_X\rangle & \lvert 0_Z\rangle \\ \lvert 1_X\rangle & \lvert 1_Z\rangle \\ \lvert 0_X\rangle & \lvert 0_Z\rangle \end{pmatrix}$	$f_{26} = \begin{pmatrix} \lvert 0_X\rangle & \lvert 1_Z\rangle \\ \lvert 0_X\rangle & \lvert 0_Z\rangle \\ \lvert 0_X\rangle & \lvert 0_Z\rangle \end{pmatrix}$
$f_7 = \begin{pmatrix} \lvert 0_X\rangle & \lvert 1_Z\rangle \\ \lvert 1_X\rangle & \lvert 0_Z\rangle \\ \lvert 0_X\rangle & \lvert 0_Z\rangle \end{pmatrix}$	$f_8 = \begin{pmatrix} \lvert 0_X\rangle & \lvert 1_Z\rangle \\ \lvert 1_X\rangle & \lvert 0_Z\rangle \\ \lvert 1_X\rangle & \lvert 0_Z\rangle \end{pmatrix}$	$f_9 = \begin{pmatrix} \lvert 1_X\rangle & \lvert 0_Z\rangle \\ \lvert 1_X\rangle & \lvert 0_Z\rangle \\ \lvert 0_X\rangle & \lvert 1_Z\rangle \end{pmatrix}$	$f_{27} = \begin{pmatrix} \lvert 1_X\rangle & \lvert 1_Z\rangle \\ \lvert 0_X\rangle & \lvert 0_Z\rangle \\ \lvert 0_X\rangle & \lvert 0_Z\rangle \end{pmatrix}$
$f_{10} = \begin{pmatrix} \lvert 1_X\rangle & \lvert 1_Z\rangle \\ \lvert 1_X\rangle & \lvert 0_Z\rangle \\ \lvert 1_X\rangle & \lvert 0_Z\rangle \end{pmatrix}$	$f_{11} = \begin{pmatrix} \lvert 0_X\rangle & \lvert 1_Z\rangle \\ \lvert 1_X\rangle & \lvert 1_Z\rangle \\ \lvert 0_X\rangle & \lvert 0_Z\rangle \end{pmatrix}$	$f_{12} = \begin{pmatrix} \lvert 0_X\rangle & \lvert 0_Z\rangle \\ \lvert 1_X\rangle & \lvert 1_Z\rangle \\ \lvert 0_X\rangle & \lvert 1_Z\rangle \end{pmatrix}$	
$f_{13} = \begin{pmatrix} \lvert 0_X\rangle & \lvert 0_Z\rangle \\ \lvert 1_X\rangle & \lvert 0_Z\rangle \\ \lvert 1_X\rangle & \lvert 1_Z\rangle \end{pmatrix}$	$f_{14} = \begin{pmatrix} \lvert 1_X\rangle & \lvert 1_Z\rangle \\ \lvert 1_X\rangle & \lvert 0_Z\rangle \\ \lvert 0_X\rangle & \lvert 0_Z\rangle \end{pmatrix}$	$f_{15} = \begin{pmatrix} \lvert 0_X\rangle & \lvert 0_Z\rangle \\ \lvert 0_X\rangle & \lvert 1_Z\rangle \\ \lvert 1_X\rangle & \lvert 1_Z\rangle \end{pmatrix}$	
$f_{16} = \begin{pmatrix} \lvert 0_X\rangle & \lvert 1_Z\rangle \\ \lvert 0_X\rangle & \lvert 1_Z\rangle \\ \lvert 1_X\rangle & \lvert 0_Z\rangle \end{pmatrix}$	$f_{17} = \begin{pmatrix} \lvert 0_X\rangle & \lvert 1_Z\rangle \\ \lvert 0_X\rangle & \lvert 1_Z\rangle \\ \lvert 1_X\rangle & \lvert 1_Z\rangle \end{pmatrix}$	$f_{18} = \begin{pmatrix} \lvert 0_X\rangle & \lvert 0_Z\rangle \\ \lvert 1_X\rangle & \lvert 1_Z\rangle \\ \lvert 1_X\rangle & \lvert 0_Z\rangle \end{pmatrix}$	
$f_{19} = \begin{pmatrix} \lvert 0_X\rangle & \lvert 1_Z\rangle \\ \lvert 1_X\rangle & \lvert 1_Z\rangle \\ \lvert 1_X\rangle & \lvert 1_Z\rangle \end{pmatrix}$	$f_{20} = \begin{pmatrix} \lvert 1_X\rangle & \lvert 0_Z\rangle \\ \lvert 0_X\rangle & \lvert 1_Z\rangle \\ \lvert 0_X\rangle & \lvert 1_Z\rangle \end{pmatrix}$	$f_{21} = \begin{pmatrix} \lvert 1_X\rangle & \lvert 1_Z\rangle \\ \lvert 0_X\rangle & \lvert 1_Z\rangle \\ \lvert 0_X\rangle & \lvert 1_Z\rangle \end{pmatrix}$	
$f_{22} = \begin{pmatrix} \lvert 1_X\rangle & \lvert 1_Z\rangle \\ \lvert 1_X\rangle & \lvert 1_Z\rangle \\ \lvert 0_X\rangle & \lvert 1_Z\rangle \end{pmatrix}$	$f_{23} = \begin{pmatrix} \lvert 1_X\rangle & \lvert 0_Z\rangle \\ \lvert 1_X\rangle & \lvert 1_Z\rangle \\ \lvert 1_X\rangle & \lvert 1_Z\rangle \end{pmatrix}$	$f_{24} = \begin{pmatrix} \lvert 1_X\rangle & \lvert 1_Z\rangle \\ \lvert 1_X\rangle & \lvert 1_Z\rangle \\ \lvert 1_X\rangle & \lvert 0_Z\rangle \end{pmatrix}$	

Table A2. There exist eight possible Matching Results (MR) for 3 × 2 frames. The bit produced by a double matching event is represented inside the key notation with the symbol •. Additionally, each MR has been identified with a binary code left to each frame. After the sifting process, such MR code will become part of the secret key.

$$\text{MR} = 000 \begin{pmatrix} |\bullet x\rangle & - \\ |\bullet x\rangle & - \\ |\bullet x\rangle & - \end{pmatrix} \qquad \text{MR} = 100 \begin{pmatrix} |\bullet x\rangle & - \\ |\bullet x\rangle & - \\ - & |\bullet z\rangle \end{pmatrix}$$

$$\text{MR} = 001 \begin{pmatrix} - & |\bullet z\rangle \\ - & |\bullet z\rangle \\ - & |\bullet z\rangle \end{pmatrix} \qquad \text{MR} = 101 \begin{pmatrix} - & |\bullet z\rangle \\ - & |\bullet z\rangle \\ |\bullet x\rangle & - \end{pmatrix}$$

$$\text{MR} = 010 \begin{pmatrix} |\bullet x\rangle & - \\ - & |\bullet z\rangle \\ |\bullet x\rangle & - \end{pmatrix} \qquad \text{MR} = 110 \begin{pmatrix} |\bullet x\rangle & - \\ - & |\bullet z\rangle \\ - & |\bullet z\rangle \end{pmatrix}$$

$$\text{MR} = 011 \begin{pmatrix} - & |\bullet z\rangle \\ |\bullet x\rangle & - \\ - & |\bullet z\rangle \end{pmatrix} \qquad \text{MR} = 111 \begin{pmatrix} - & |\bullet z\rangle \\ |\bullet x\rangle & - \\ |\bullet x\rangle & - \end{pmatrix}$$

Table A3. Bob sends to Alice the Sifting Strings (SS) which are constructed with the sifting bits and the measured bits. Alice knows the frames behind each SS, so she can get the secret bit (sb). On his side, Bob uses the SS and the MR to achieve the same bit.

Sifting String		Bob's MR	Alice's Frame	sb	Bob's MR	sb	Alice's Frame
Measured	Sifting						
110	000	000	f_6, f_9, f_{14}, f_{22}	0	001	1	$f_5, f_{11}, f_{16}, f_{24}$
011	000	000	$f_8, f_{13}, f_{18}, f_{19}$	0	001	1	$f_{12}, f_{15}, f_{20}, f_{23}$
011	001	110	$f_{12}, f_{15}, f_{17}, f_{19}$	0	111	1	$f_4, f_{13}, f_{18}, f_{23}$
110	001	100	$f_6, f_{10}, f_{14}, f_{24}$	0	101	1	$f_5, f_{11}, f_{21}, f_{22}$
010	011	110	$f_1, f_{11}, f_{16}, f_{18}$	0	101	1	f_2, f_6, f_{12}, f_{20}
111	011	100	f_4, f_9, f_{22}, f_{23}	0	111	1	$f_8, f_{10}, f_{19}, f_{24}$
001	010	001	f_3, f_4, f_9, f_{13}	0	011	1	f_{15}, f_{20}
100	010	001	f_7, f_8, f_{10}, f_{14}	0	011	1	f_5, f_{16}
010	010	001	f_1, f_2, f_6, f_{18}	0	010	1	f_{11}, f_{12}
111	010	001	$f_{17}, f_{19}, f_{21}, f_{22}$	0	010	1	f_{23}, f_{24}
001	011	110	f_3, f_{13}	0	100	1	f_{15}, f_{17}
100	011	101	f_7, f_{14}	0	111	1	f_5, f_{21}
001	100	000	$f_1, f_{15}, f_{16}, f_{17}$	0	010	1	f_8, f_{13}
100	100	000	f_2, f_5, f_{20}, f_{21}	0	010	1	f_9, f_{14}
010	100	000	f_3, f_7, f_{11}, f_{12}	0	011	1	f_6, f_{18}
111	100	000	$f_4, f_{10}, f_{23}, f_{24}$	0	011	1	f_{19}, f_{22}
001	101	111	f_1, f_{15}	0	101	1	f_4, f_{13}
100	101	100	f_2, f_5	0	110	1	f_{10}, f_{14}
010	101	111	f_3, f_6, f_9, f_{12}	0	100	1	f_7, f_8, f_{11}, f_{18}
111	101	101	$f_{16}, f_{17}, f_{19}, f_{24}$	0	110	1	$f_{20}, f_{21}, f_{22}, f_{23}$
011	110	010	$f_1, f_{15}, f_{16}, f_{17}, f_{18}, f_{19}$	0	011	1	$f_3, f_4, f_9, f_{12}, f_{13}, f_{23}$
110	110	010	$f_2, f_5, f_6, f_{20}, f_{21}, f_{22}$	0	011	1	$f_7, f_8, f_{10}, f_{11}, f_{14}, f_{24}$
011	111	101	$f_1, f_{15}, f_{18}, f_{23}$	0	100	1	$f_3, f_{12}, f_{13}, f_{19}$
110	111	110	f_2, f_5, f_6, f_{24}	0	111	1	$f_7, f_{11}, f_{14}, f_{22}$

Table A4. We list the 24 frames that Alice uses during the distillation process. Bob computes the sifting bits applying the XOR function to each column (they are written at the bottom of each frame) and appending an extra (required) sifting bit. The sifting bits define the set {000, 001, 010, 011, 100, 101, 110, 111} that does not contain redundancy, so that Alice can identify without ambiguity Bob's Matching Results.

Alice		Bob			
$f_1 = \begin{pmatrix} \|0_X\rangle & \|0_Z\rangle \\ \|0_X\rangle & \|1_Z\rangle \\ \|1_X\rangle & \|0_Z\rangle \end{pmatrix}$		$\begin{pmatrix} \|0_X\rangle & - \\ \|0_X\rangle & - \\ \|1_X\rangle & - \end{pmatrix}$ 1 0 0	$\begin{pmatrix} - & \|0_Z\rangle \\ - & \|1_Z\rangle \\ - & \|0_Z\rangle \end{pmatrix}$ 0 1 0	$\begin{pmatrix} \|0_X\rangle & - \\ - & \|1_Z\rangle \\ \|1_X\rangle & - \end{pmatrix}$ 1 1 0	$\begin{pmatrix} - & \|0_Z\rangle \\ \|0_X\rangle & - \\ - & \|0_Z\rangle \end{pmatrix}$ 0 0 0
		$\begin{pmatrix} \|0_X\rangle & - \\ \|0_X\rangle & - \\ - & \|0_Z\rangle \end{pmatrix}$ 0 0 1	$\begin{pmatrix} - & \|0_Z\rangle \\ - & \|1_Z\rangle \\ \|1_X\rangle & - \end{pmatrix}$ 1 1 1	$\begin{pmatrix} \|0_X\rangle & - \\ - & \|1_Z\rangle \\ - & \|0_Z\rangle \end{pmatrix}$ 0 1 1	$\begin{pmatrix} - & \|0_Z\rangle \\ \|0_X\rangle & - \\ \|1_X\rangle & - \end{pmatrix}$ 1 0 1
$f_2 = \begin{pmatrix} \|1_X\rangle & \|0_Z\rangle \\ \|0_X\rangle & \|1_Z\rangle \\ \|0_X\rangle & \|0_Z\rangle \end{pmatrix}$		$\begin{pmatrix} \|1_X\rangle & - \\ \|0_X\rangle & - \\ \|0_X\rangle & - \end{pmatrix}$ 1 0 0	$\begin{pmatrix} - & \|0_Z\rangle \\ - & \|1_Z\rangle \\ - & \|0_Z\rangle \end{pmatrix}$ 0 1 0	$\begin{pmatrix} \|1_X\rangle & - \\ - & \|1_Z\rangle \\ \|0_X\rangle & - \end{pmatrix}$ 1 1 0	$\begin{pmatrix} - & \|0_Z\rangle \\ \|0_X\rangle & - \\ - & \|0_Z\rangle \end{pmatrix}$ 0 0 0
		$\begin{pmatrix} \|1_X\rangle & - \\ \|0_X\rangle & - \\ - & \|0_Z\rangle \end{pmatrix}$ 1 0 1	$\begin{pmatrix} - & \|0_Z\rangle \\ - & \|1_Z\rangle \\ \|0_X\rangle & - \end{pmatrix}$ 0 1 1	$\begin{pmatrix} \|1_X\rangle & - \\ - & \|1_Z\rangle \\ - & \|0_Z\rangle \end{pmatrix}$ 1 1 1	$\begin{pmatrix} - & \|0_Z\rangle \\ \|0_X\rangle & - \\ \|0_X\rangle & - \end{pmatrix}$ 0 0 1
$f_3 = \begin{pmatrix} \|0_X\rangle & \|0_Z\rangle \\ \|1_X\rangle & \|0_Z\rangle \\ \|0_X\rangle & \|1_Z\rangle \end{pmatrix}$		$\begin{pmatrix} \|0_X\rangle & - \\ \|1_X\rangle & - \\ \|0_X\rangle & - \end{pmatrix}$ 1 0 0	$\begin{pmatrix} - & \|0_Z\rangle \\ - & \|0_Z\rangle \\ - & \|1_Z\rangle \end{pmatrix}$ 0 1 0	$\begin{pmatrix} \|0_X\rangle & - \\ - & \|0_Z\rangle \\ \|0_X\rangle & - \end{pmatrix}$ 0 0 0	$\begin{pmatrix} - & \|0_Z\rangle \\ \|1_X\rangle & - \\ - & \|1_Z\rangle \end{pmatrix}$ 1 1 0
		$\begin{pmatrix} \|0_X\rangle & - \\ \|1_X\rangle & - \\ - & \|1_Z\rangle \end{pmatrix}$ 1 1 1	$\begin{pmatrix} - & \|0_Z\rangle \\ - & \|0_Z\rangle \\ \|0_X\rangle & - \end{pmatrix}$ 0 0 1	$\begin{pmatrix} \|0_X\rangle & - \\ - & \|0_Z\rangle \\ - & \|1_Z\rangle \end{pmatrix}$ 0 1 1	$\begin{pmatrix} - & \|0_Z\rangle \\ \|1_X\rangle & - \\ \|0_X\rangle & - \end{pmatrix}$ 1 0 1
$f_4 = \begin{pmatrix} \|1_X\rangle & \|0_Z\rangle \\ \|1_X\rangle & \|0_Z\rangle \\ \|1_X\rangle & \|1_Z\rangle \end{pmatrix}$		$\begin{pmatrix} \|1_X\rangle & - \\ \|1_X\rangle & - \\ \|1_X\rangle & - \end{pmatrix}$ 1 0 0	$\begin{pmatrix} - & \|0_Z\rangle \\ - & \|0_Z\rangle \\ - & \|1_Z\rangle \end{pmatrix}$ 0 1 0	$\begin{pmatrix} \|1_X\rangle & - \\ - & \|0_Z\rangle \\ \|1_X\rangle & - \end{pmatrix}$ 0 0 0	$\begin{pmatrix} - & \|0_Z\rangle \\ \|1_X\rangle & - \\ - & \|1_Z\rangle \end{pmatrix}$ 1 1 0
		$\begin{pmatrix} \|1_X\rangle & - \\ \|1_X\rangle & - \\ - & \|1_Z\rangle \end{pmatrix}$ 0 1 1	$\begin{pmatrix} - & \|0_Z\rangle \\ - & \|0_Z\rangle \\ \|1_X\rangle & - \end{pmatrix}$ 1 0 1	$\begin{pmatrix} \|0_X\rangle & - \\ - & \|0_Z\rangle \\ - & \|1_Z\rangle \end{pmatrix}$ 1 1 1	$\begin{pmatrix} - & \|0_Z\rangle \\ \|1_X\rangle & - \\ \|1_X\rangle & - \end{pmatrix}$ 0 0 1
$f_5 = \begin{pmatrix} \|1_X\rangle & \|1_Z\rangle \\ \|0_X\rangle & \|1_Z\rangle \\ \|0_X\rangle & \|0_Z\rangle \end{pmatrix}$		$\begin{pmatrix} \|1_X\rangle & - \\ \|0_X\rangle & - \\ \|0_X\rangle & - \end{pmatrix}$ 1 0 0	$\begin{pmatrix} - & \|1_Z\rangle \\ - & \|1_Z\rangle \\ - & \|0_Z\rangle \end{pmatrix}$ 0 0 0	$\begin{pmatrix} \|1_X\rangle & - \\ - & \|1_Z\rangle \\ \|0_X\rangle & - \end{pmatrix}$ 1 1 0	$\begin{pmatrix} - & \|1_Z\rangle \\ \|0_X\rangle & - \\ - & \|0_Z\rangle \end{pmatrix}$ 0 1 0
		$\begin{pmatrix} \|1_X\rangle & - \\ \|0_X\rangle & - \\ - & \|0_Z\rangle \end{pmatrix}$ 1 0 1	$\begin{pmatrix} - & \|1_Z\rangle \\ - & \|1_Z\rangle \\ \|0_X\rangle & - \end{pmatrix}$ 0 0 1	$\begin{pmatrix} \|1_X\rangle & - \\ - & \|1_Z\rangle \\ - & \|0_Z\rangle \end{pmatrix}$ 1 1 1	$\begin{pmatrix} - & \|1_Z\rangle \\ \|0_X\rangle & - \\ \|0_X\rangle & - \end{pmatrix}$ 0 1 1

Table A4. Cont.

Alice		Bob							

$f_6 = \begin{pmatrix} |1_X\rangle & |0_Z\rangle \\ |1_X\rangle & |1_Z\rangle \\ |0_X\rangle & |0_Z\rangle \end{pmatrix}$

$\begin{pmatrix} |1_X\rangle & - \\ |1_X\rangle & - \\ |0_X\rangle & - \\ 0 & 0 & 0 \end{pmatrix}$ $\begin{pmatrix} - & |0_Z\rangle \\ - & |1_Z\rangle \\ - & |0_Z\rangle \\ 0 & 1 & 0 \end{pmatrix}$ $\begin{pmatrix} |1_X\rangle & - \\ - & |1_Z\rangle \\ |1_X\rangle & - \\ 1 & 1 & 0 \end{pmatrix}$ $\begin{pmatrix} - & |0_Z\rangle \\ |1_X\rangle & - \\ - & |0_Z\rangle \\ 1 & 0 & 0 \end{pmatrix}$

$\begin{pmatrix} |1_X\rangle & - \\ |1_X\rangle & - \\ - & |0_Z\rangle \\ 0 & 0 & 1 \end{pmatrix}$ $\begin{pmatrix} - & |0_Z\rangle \\ - & |1_Z\rangle \\ |0_X\rangle & - \\ 0 & 1 & 1 \end{pmatrix}$ $\begin{pmatrix} |1_X\rangle & - \\ - & |1_Z\rangle \\ - & |0_Z\rangle \\ 1 & 1 & 1 \end{pmatrix}$ $\begin{pmatrix} |1_X\rangle & - \\ |0_X\rangle & - \\ - & |0_Z\rangle \\ 1 & 0 & 1 \end{pmatrix}$

$f_7 = \begin{pmatrix} |0_X\rangle & |1_Z\rangle \\ |1_X\rangle & |0_Z\rangle \\ |0_X\rangle & |0_Z\rangle \end{pmatrix}$

$\begin{pmatrix} |0_X\rangle & - \\ |1_X\rangle & - \\ |0_X\rangle & - \\ 1 & 0 & 0 \end{pmatrix}$ $\begin{pmatrix} - & |1_Z\rangle \\ - & |0_Z\rangle \\ - & |0_Z\rangle \\ 0 & 1 & 0 \end{pmatrix}$ $\begin{pmatrix} |0_X\rangle & - \\ - & |0_Z\rangle \\ |0_X\rangle & - \\ 0 & 0 & 0 \end{pmatrix}$ $\begin{pmatrix} - & |1_Z\rangle \\ |1_X\rangle & - \\ - & |0_Z\rangle \\ 1 & 1 & 0 \end{pmatrix}$

$\begin{pmatrix} |0_X\rangle & - \\ |1_X\rangle & - \\ - & |0_Z\rangle \\ 1 & 0 & 1 \end{pmatrix}$ $\begin{pmatrix} - & |1_Z\rangle \\ - & |0_Z\rangle \\ |0_X\rangle & - \\ 0 & 1 & 1 \end{pmatrix}$ $\begin{pmatrix} |0_X\rangle & - \\ - & |0_Z\rangle \\ - & |0_Z\rangle \\ 0 & 0 & 1 \end{pmatrix}$ $\begin{pmatrix} - & |1_Z\rangle \\ |1_X\rangle & - \\ |0_X\rangle & - \\ 1 & 1 & 1 \end{pmatrix}$

$f_8 = \begin{pmatrix} |0_X\rangle & |1_Z\rangle \\ |1_X\rangle & |0_Z\rangle \\ |1_X\rangle & |0_Z\rangle \end{pmatrix}$

$\begin{pmatrix} |0_X\rangle & - \\ |1_X\rangle & - \\ |1_X\rangle & - \\ 0 & 0 & 0 \end{pmatrix}$ $\begin{pmatrix} - & |1_Z\rangle \\ - & |0_Z\rangle \\ - & |0_Z\rangle \\ 0 & 1 & 0 \end{pmatrix}$ $\begin{pmatrix} |0_X\rangle & - \\ - & |0_Z\rangle \\ |1_X\rangle & - \\ 1 & 0 & 0 \end{pmatrix}$ $\begin{pmatrix} - & |1_Z\rangle \\ |1_X\rangle & - \\ - & |0_Z\rangle \\ 1 & 1 & 0 \end{pmatrix}$

$\begin{pmatrix} |0_X\rangle & - \\ |1_X\rangle & - \\ - & |0_Z\rangle \\ 1 & 0 & 1 \end{pmatrix}$ $\begin{pmatrix} - & |1_Z\rangle \\ - & |0_Z\rangle \\ |1_X\rangle & - \\ 1 & 1 & 1 \end{pmatrix}$ $\begin{pmatrix} |0_X\rangle & - \\ - & |0_Z\rangle \\ - & |0_Z\rangle \\ 0 & 0 & 0 \end{pmatrix}$ $\begin{pmatrix} - & |1_Z\rangle \\ |1_X\rangle & - \\ |1_X\rangle & - \\ 0 & 1 & 1 \end{pmatrix}$

$f_9 = \begin{pmatrix} |1_X\rangle & |0_Z\rangle \\ |1_X\rangle & |0_Z\rangle \\ |0_X\rangle & |1_Z\rangle \end{pmatrix}$

$\begin{pmatrix} |1_X\rangle & - \\ |1_X\rangle & - \\ |0_X\rangle & - \\ 0 & 0 & 0 \end{pmatrix}$ $\begin{pmatrix} - & |0_Z\rangle \\ - & |0_Z\rangle \\ - & |1_Z\rangle \\ 0 & 1 & 0 \end{pmatrix}$ $\begin{pmatrix} |1_X\rangle & - \\ - & |0_Z\rangle \\ |0_X\rangle & - \\ 1 & 0 & 0 \end{pmatrix}$ $\begin{pmatrix} - & |0_Z\rangle \\ |1_X\rangle & - \\ - & |1_Z\rangle \\ 1 & 1 & 0 \end{pmatrix}$

$\begin{pmatrix} |1_X\rangle & - \\ |1_X\rangle & - \\ - & |1_Z\rangle \\ 0 & 1 & 1 \end{pmatrix}$ $\begin{pmatrix} - & |0_Z\rangle \\ - & |0_Z\rangle \\ |0_X\rangle & - \\ 0 & 0 & 1 \end{pmatrix}$ $\begin{pmatrix} |1_X\rangle & - \\ - & |0_Z\rangle \\ - & |1_Z\rangle \\ 1 & 1 & 1 \end{pmatrix}$ $\begin{pmatrix} - & |0_Z\rangle \\ |1_X\rangle & - \\ |0_X\rangle & - \\ 1 & 0 & 1 \end{pmatrix}$

Table A4. *Cont.*

Alice	Bob				
$f_{10} = \begin{pmatrix} \|1_X\rangle & \|1_Z\rangle \\ \|1_X\rangle & \|0_Z\rangle \\ \|1_X\rangle & \|0_Z\rangle \end{pmatrix}$	$\begin{pmatrix} \|1_X\rangle & - \\ \|1_X\rangle & - \\ \|1_X\rangle & - \\ 1 & 0 & 0 \end{pmatrix}$	$\begin{pmatrix} - & \|1_Z\rangle \\ - & \|0_Z\rangle \\ - & \|0_Z\rangle \\ 0 & 1 & 0 \end{pmatrix}$	$\begin{pmatrix} \|1_X\rangle & - \\ - & \|0_Z\rangle \\ \|1_X\rangle & - \\ 0 & 0 & 0 \end{pmatrix}$	$\begin{pmatrix} - & \|1_Z\rangle \\ \|1_X\rangle & - \\ - & \|0_Z\rangle \\ 1 & 1 & 0 \end{pmatrix}$	
	$\begin{pmatrix} \|1_X\rangle & - \\ \|1_X\rangle & - \\ - & \|0_Z\rangle \\ 0 & 0 & 1 \end{pmatrix}$	$\begin{pmatrix} - & \|1_Z\rangle \\ - & \|0_Z\rangle \\ \|1_X\rangle & - \\ 1 & 1 & 1 \end{pmatrix}$	$\begin{pmatrix} \|1_X\rangle & - \\ - & \|0_Z\rangle \\ - & \|0_Z\rangle \\ 1 & 0 & 1 \end{pmatrix}$	$\begin{pmatrix} - & \|1_Z\rangle \\ \|1_X\rangle & - \\ \|1_X\rangle & - \\ 0 & 1 & 1 \end{pmatrix}$	
$f_{11} = \begin{pmatrix} \|0_X\rangle & \|1_Z\rangle \\ \|1_X\rangle & \|1_Z\rangle \\ \|0_X\rangle & \|0_Z\rangle \end{pmatrix}$	$\begin{pmatrix} \|0_X\rangle & - \\ \|1_X\rangle & - \\ \|0_X\rangle & - \\ 1 & 0 & 0 \end{pmatrix}$	$\begin{pmatrix} - & \|1_Z\rangle \\ - & \|1_Z\rangle \\ - & \|0_Z\rangle \\ 0 & 1 & 0 \end{pmatrix}$	$\begin{pmatrix} \|0_X\rangle & - \\ - & \|1_Z\rangle \\ \|0_X\rangle & - \\ 0 & 1 & 0 \end{pmatrix}$	$\begin{pmatrix} - & \|1_Z\rangle \\ \|1_X\rangle & - \\ - & \|0_Z\rangle \\ 1 & 1 & 0 \end{pmatrix}$	
	$\begin{pmatrix} \|0_X\rangle & - \\ \|1_X\rangle & - \\ - & \|0_Z\rangle \\ 1 & 0 & 1 \end{pmatrix}$	$\begin{pmatrix} - & \|1_Z\rangle \\ - & \|1_Z\rangle \\ \|0_X\rangle & - \\ 0 & 0 & 1 \end{pmatrix}$	$\begin{pmatrix} \|0_X\rangle & - \\ - & \|1_Z\rangle \\ - & \|0_Z\rangle \\ 0 & 1 & 1 \end{pmatrix}$	$\begin{pmatrix} - & \|1_Z\rangle \\ \|1_X\rangle & - \\ \|0_X\rangle & - \\ 1 & 1 & 1 \end{pmatrix}$	
$f_{12} = \begin{pmatrix} \|0_X\rangle & \|0_Z\rangle \\ \|1_X\rangle & \|1_Z\rangle \\ \|0_X\rangle & \|1_Z\rangle \end{pmatrix}$	$\begin{pmatrix} \|0_X\rangle & - \\ \|1_X\rangle & - \\ \|0_X\rangle & - \\ 1 & 0 & 0 \end{pmatrix}$	$\begin{pmatrix} - & \|0_Z\rangle \\ - & \|1_Z\rangle \\ - & \|1_Z\rangle \\ 0 & 0 & 0 \end{pmatrix}$	$\begin{pmatrix} \|0_X\rangle & - \\ - & \|1_Z\rangle \\ \|0_X\rangle & - \\ 0 & 1 & 0 \end{pmatrix}$	$\begin{pmatrix} - & \|0_Z\rangle \\ \|1_X\rangle & - \\ - & \|1_Z\rangle \\ 1 & 1 & 0 \end{pmatrix}$	
	$\begin{pmatrix} \|0_X\rangle & - \\ \|1_X\rangle & - \\ - & \|1_Z\rangle \\ 1 & 1 & 1 \end{pmatrix}$	$\begin{pmatrix} - & \|0_Z\rangle \\ - & \|1_Z\rangle \\ \|0_X\rangle & - \\ 0 & 1 & 1 \end{pmatrix}$	$\begin{pmatrix} \|0_X\rangle & - \\ - & \|1_Z\rangle \\ - & \|1_Z\rangle \\ 0 & 0 & 1 \end{pmatrix}$	$\begin{pmatrix} - & \|0_Z\rangle \\ \|1_X\rangle & - \\ \|0_X\rangle & - \\ 1 & 0 & 1 \end{pmatrix}$	
$f_{13} = \begin{pmatrix} \|0_X\rangle & \|0_Z\rangle \\ \|1_X\rangle & \|0_Z\rangle \\ \|1_X\rangle & \|1_Z\rangle \end{pmatrix}$	$\begin{pmatrix} \|0_X\rangle & - \\ \|1_X\rangle & - \\ \|1_X\rangle & - \\ 0 & 0 & 0 \end{pmatrix}$	$\begin{pmatrix} - & \|0_Z\rangle \\ - & \|0_Z\rangle \\ - & \|1_Z\rangle \\ 0 & 1 & 0 \end{pmatrix}$	$\begin{pmatrix} \|0_X\rangle & - \\ - & \|0_Z\rangle \\ \|1_X\rangle & - \\ 1 & 0 & 0 \end{pmatrix}$	$\begin{pmatrix} - & \|0_Z\rangle \\ \|1_X\rangle & - \\ - & \|1_Z\rangle \\ 1 & 1 & 0 \end{pmatrix}$	
	$\begin{pmatrix} \|0_X\rangle & - \\ \|1_X\rangle & - \\ - & \|1_Z\rangle \\ 1 & 1 & 1 \end{pmatrix}$	$\begin{pmatrix} - & \|0_Z\rangle \\ - & \|0_Z\rangle \\ \|1_X\rangle & - \\ 1 & 0 & 1 \end{pmatrix}$	$\begin{pmatrix} \|0_X\rangle & - \\ - & \|0_Z\rangle \\ - & \|1_Z\rangle \\ 0 & 1 & 1 \end{pmatrix}$	$\begin{pmatrix} - & \|0_Z\rangle \\ \|1_X\rangle & - \\ \|1_X\rangle & - \\ 0 & 0 & 1 \end{pmatrix}$	
$f_{14} = \begin{pmatrix} \|1_X\rangle & \|1_Z\rangle \\ \|1_X\rangle & \|0_Z\rangle \\ \|0_X\rangle & \|0_Z\rangle \end{pmatrix}$	$\begin{pmatrix} \|1_X\rangle & - \\ \|1_X\rangle & - \\ \|0_X\rangle & - \\ 0 & 0 & 0 \end{pmatrix}$	$\begin{pmatrix} - & \|1_Z\rangle \\ - & \|0_Z\rangle \\ - & \|0_Z\rangle \\ 0 & 1 & 0 \end{pmatrix}$	$\begin{pmatrix} \|1_X\rangle & - \\ - & \|0_Z\rangle \\ \|0_X\rangle & - \\ 1 & 0 & 0 \end{pmatrix}$	$\begin{pmatrix} - & \|1_Z\rangle \\ \|1_X\rangle & - \\ - & \|0_Z\rangle \\ 1 & 1 & 0 \end{pmatrix}$	
	$\begin{pmatrix} \|1_X\rangle & - \\ \|1_X\rangle & - \\ - & \|0_Z\rangle \\ 0 & 0 & 1 \end{pmatrix}$	$\begin{pmatrix} - & \|1_Z\rangle \\ - & \|0_Z\rangle \\ \|0_X\rangle & - \\ 0 & 1 & 1 \end{pmatrix}$	$\begin{pmatrix} \|1_X\rangle & - \\ - & \|0_Z\rangle \\ - & \|0_Z\rangle \\ 1 & 0 & 1 \end{pmatrix}$	$\begin{pmatrix} - & \|1_Z\rangle \\ \|1_X\rangle & - \\ \|0_X\rangle & - \\ 1 & 1 & 1 \end{pmatrix}$	

Table A4. *Cont.*

Alice	Bob			
$f_{15} = \begin{pmatrix} \lvert 0_X\rangle & \lvert 0_Z\rangle \\ \lvert 0_X\rangle & \lvert 1_Z\rangle \\ \lvert 1_X\rangle & \lvert 1_Z\rangle \end{pmatrix}$	$\begin{pmatrix} \lvert 0_X\rangle & - \\ \lvert 0_X\rangle & - \\ \lvert 1_X\rangle & - \\ 1 & 0 & 0 \end{pmatrix}$	$\begin{pmatrix} - & \lvert 0_Z\rangle \\ - & \lvert 1_Z\rangle \\ - & \lvert 1_Z\rangle \\ 0 & 0 & 0 \end{pmatrix}$	$\begin{pmatrix} \lvert 0_X\rangle & - \\ - & \lvert 1_Z\rangle \\ \lvert 1_X\rangle & - \\ 1 & 1 & 0 \end{pmatrix}$	$\begin{pmatrix} - & \lvert 0_Z\rangle \\ \lvert 0_X\rangle & - \\ - & \lvert 1_Z\rangle \\ 0 & 1 & 0 \end{pmatrix}$
	$\begin{pmatrix} \lvert 0_X\rangle & - \\ \lvert 0_X\rangle & - \\ - & \lvert 1_Z\rangle \\ 0 & 1 & 1 \end{pmatrix}$	$\begin{pmatrix} - & \lvert 0_Z\rangle \\ - & \lvert 1_Z\rangle \\ \lvert 1_X\rangle & - \\ 1 & 1 & 1 \end{pmatrix}$	$\begin{pmatrix} \lvert 0_X\rangle & - \\ - & \lvert 1_Z\rangle \\ - & \lvert 1_Z\rangle \\ 0 & 0 & 1 \end{pmatrix}$	$\begin{pmatrix} - & \lvert 0_Z\rangle \\ \lvert 0_X\rangle & - \\ \lvert 1_X\rangle & - \\ 1 & 0 & 1 \end{pmatrix}$
$f_{16} = \begin{pmatrix} \lvert 0_X\rangle & \lvert 1_Z\rangle \\ \lvert 0_X\rangle & \lvert 1_Z\rangle \\ \lvert 1_X\rangle & \lvert 0_Z\rangle \end{pmatrix}$	$\begin{pmatrix} \lvert 0_X\rangle & - \\ \lvert 0_X\rangle & - \\ \lvert 1_X\rangle & - \\ 1 & 0 & 0 \end{pmatrix}$	$\begin{pmatrix} - & \lvert 1_Z\rangle \\ - & \lvert 1_Z\rangle \\ - & \lvert 0_Z\rangle \\ 0 & 0 & 0 \end{pmatrix}$	$\begin{pmatrix} \lvert 0_X\rangle & - \\ - & \lvert 1_Z\rangle \\ \lvert 1_X\rangle & - \\ 1 & 1 & 0 \end{pmatrix}$	$\begin{pmatrix} - & \lvert 1_Z\rangle \\ \lvert 0_X\rangle & - \\ - & \lvert 0_Z\rangle \\ 0 & 1 & 0 \end{pmatrix}$
	$\begin{pmatrix} \lvert 0_X\rangle & - \\ \lvert 0_X\rangle & - \\ - & \lvert 0_Z\rangle \\ 0 & 0 & 1 \end{pmatrix}$	$\begin{pmatrix} - & \lvert 1_Z\rangle \\ - & \lvert 1_Z\rangle \\ \lvert 1_X\rangle & - \\ 1 & 0 & 1 \end{pmatrix}$	$\begin{pmatrix} \lvert 0_X\rangle & - \\ - & \lvert 1_Z\rangle \\ - & \lvert 0_Z\rangle \\ 0 & 1 & 1 \end{pmatrix}$	$\begin{pmatrix} - & \lvert 1_Z\rangle \\ \lvert 0_X\rangle & - \\ \lvert 1_X\rangle & - \\ 1 & 1 & 1 \end{pmatrix}$
$f_{17} = \begin{pmatrix} \lvert 0_X\rangle & \lvert 1_Z\rangle \\ \lvert 0_X\rangle & \lvert 1_Z\rangle \\ \lvert 1_X\rangle & \lvert 1_Z\rangle \end{pmatrix}$	$\begin{pmatrix} \lvert 0_X\rangle & - \\ \lvert 0_X\rangle & - \\ \lvert 1_X\rangle & - \\ 1 & 0 & 0 \end{pmatrix}$	$\begin{pmatrix} - & \lvert 1_Z\rangle \\ - & \lvert 1_Z\rangle \\ - & \lvert 1_Z\rangle \\ 0 & 1 & 0 \end{pmatrix}$	$\begin{pmatrix} \lvert 0_X\rangle & - \\ - & \lvert 1_Z\rangle \\ \lvert 1_X\rangle & - \\ 1 & 1 & 0 \end{pmatrix}$	$\begin{pmatrix} - & \lvert 1_Z\rangle \\ \lvert 0_X\rangle & - \\ - & \lvert 1_Z\rangle \\ 0 & 0 & 0 \end{pmatrix}$
	$\begin{pmatrix} \lvert 0_X\rangle & - \\ \lvert 0_X\rangle & - \\ - & \lvert 1_Z\rangle \\ 0 & 1 & 1 \end{pmatrix}$	$\begin{pmatrix} - & \lvert 1_Z\rangle \\ - & \lvert 1_Z\rangle \\ \lvert 1_X\rangle & - \\ 1 & 0 & 1 \end{pmatrix}$	$\begin{pmatrix} \lvert 0_X\rangle & - \\ - & \lvert 1_Z\rangle \\ - & \lvert 1_Z\rangle \\ 0 & 0 & 1 \end{pmatrix}$	$\begin{pmatrix} - & \lvert 1_Z\rangle \\ \lvert 0_X\rangle & - \\ \lvert 1_X\rangle & - \\ 1 & 1 & 1 \end{pmatrix}$
$f_{18} = \begin{pmatrix} \lvert 0_X\rangle & \lvert 0_Z\rangle \\ \lvert 1_X\rangle & \lvert 1_Z\rangle \\ \lvert 1_X\rangle & \lvert 0_Z\rangle \end{pmatrix}$	$\begin{pmatrix} \lvert 0_X\rangle & - \\ \lvert 1_X\rangle & - \\ \lvert 1_X\rangle & - \\ 0 & 0 & 0 \end{pmatrix}$	$\begin{pmatrix} - & \lvert 0_Z\rangle \\ - & \lvert 1_Z\rangle \\ - & \lvert 0_Z\rangle \\ 0 & 1 & 0 \end{pmatrix}$	$\begin{pmatrix} \lvert 0_X\rangle & - \\ - & \lvert 1_Z\rangle \\ \lvert 1_X\rangle & - \\ 1 & 1 & 0 \end{pmatrix}$	$\begin{pmatrix} - & \lvert 0_Z\rangle \\ \lvert 1_X\rangle & - \\ - & \lvert 0_Z\rangle \\ 1 & 0 & 0 \end{pmatrix}$
	$\begin{pmatrix} \lvert 0_X\rangle & - \\ \lvert 1_X\rangle & - \\ - & \lvert 0_Z\rangle \\ 1 & 0 & 1 \end{pmatrix}$	$\begin{pmatrix} - & \lvert 0_Z\rangle \\ - & \lvert 1_Z\rangle \\ \lvert 1_X\rangle & - \\ 1 & 1 & 1 \end{pmatrix}$	$\begin{pmatrix} \lvert 0_X\rangle & - \\ - & \lvert 1_Z\rangle \\ - & \lvert 0_Z\rangle \\ 0 & 1 & 1 \end{pmatrix}$	$\begin{pmatrix} - & \lvert 0_Z\rangle \\ \lvert 1_X\rangle & - \\ \lvert 1_X\rangle & - \\ 0 & 0 & 1 \end{pmatrix}$
$f_{19} = \begin{pmatrix} \lvert 0_X\rangle & \lvert 1_Z\rangle \\ \lvert 1_X\rangle & \lvert 1_Z\rangle \\ \lvert 1_X\rangle & \lvert 1_Z\rangle \end{pmatrix}$	$\begin{pmatrix} \lvert 0_X\rangle & - \\ \lvert 1_X\rangle & - \\ \lvert 1_X\rangle & - \\ 0 & 0 & 0 \end{pmatrix}$	$\begin{pmatrix} - & \lvert 1_Z\rangle \\ - & \lvert 1_Z\rangle \\ - & \lvert 1_Z\rangle \\ 0 & 1 & 0 \end{pmatrix}$	$\begin{pmatrix} \lvert 0_X\rangle & - \\ - & \lvert 1_Z\rangle \\ \lvert 1_X\rangle & - \\ 1 & 1 & 0 \end{pmatrix}$	$\begin{pmatrix} - & \lvert 1_Z\rangle \\ \lvert 1_X\rangle & - \\ - & \lvert 1_Z\rangle \\ 1 & 0 & 0 \end{pmatrix}$
	$\begin{pmatrix} \lvert 0_X\rangle & - \\ \lvert 1_X\rangle & - \\ - & \lvert 1_Z\rangle \\ 1 & 1 & 1 \end{pmatrix}$	$\begin{pmatrix} - & \lvert 1_Z\rangle \\ - & \lvert 1_Z\rangle \\ \lvert 1_X\rangle & - \\ 1 & 0 & 1 \end{pmatrix}$	$\begin{pmatrix} \lvert 0_X\rangle & - \\ - & \lvert 1_Z\rangle \\ - & \lvert 1_Z\rangle \\ 0 & 0 & 1 \end{pmatrix}$	$\begin{pmatrix} - & \lvert 1_Z\rangle \\ \lvert 1_X\rangle & - \\ \lvert 1_X\rangle & - \\ 0 & 1 & 1 \end{pmatrix}$

Table A4. *Cont.*

Alice	Bob			
$f_{20} = \begin{pmatrix} \lvert 1_X\rangle & \lvert 0_Z\rangle \\ \lvert 0_X\rangle & \lvert 1_Z\rangle \\ \lvert 0_X\rangle & \lvert 1_Z\rangle \end{pmatrix}$	$\begin{pmatrix} \lvert 1_X\rangle & - \\ \lvert 0_X\rangle & - \\ \lvert 0_X\rangle & - \end{pmatrix}$ 1 0 0	$\begin{pmatrix} - & \lvert 0_Z\rangle \\ - & \lvert 1_Z\rangle \\ - & \lvert 1_Z\rangle \end{pmatrix}$ 0 0 0	$\begin{pmatrix} \lvert 1_X\rangle & - \\ - & \lvert 1_Z\rangle \\ \lvert 0_X\rangle & - \end{pmatrix}$ 1 1 0	$\begin{pmatrix} - & \lvert 0_Z\rangle \\ \lvert 0_X\rangle & - \\ - & \lvert 1_Z\rangle \end{pmatrix}$ 0 1 0
	$\begin{pmatrix} \lvert 1_X\rangle & - \\ \lvert 0_X\rangle & - \\ - & \lvert 1_Z\rangle \end{pmatrix}$ 1 1 1	$\begin{pmatrix} - & \lvert 0_Z\rangle \\ - & \lvert 1_Z\rangle \\ \lvert 0_X\rangle & - \end{pmatrix}$ 0 1 1	$\begin{pmatrix} \lvert 1_X\rangle & - \\ - & \lvert 1_Z\rangle \\ - & \lvert 1_Z\rangle \end{pmatrix}$ 1 0 1	$\begin{pmatrix} - & \lvert 0_Z\rangle \\ \lvert 0_X\rangle & - \\ \lvert 0_X\rangle & - \end{pmatrix}$ 0 0 1
$f_{21} = \begin{pmatrix} \lvert 1_X\rangle & \lvert 1_Z\rangle \\ \lvert 0_X\rangle & \lvert 1_Z\rangle \\ \lvert 0_X\rangle & \lvert 1_Z\rangle \end{pmatrix}$	$\begin{pmatrix} \lvert 1_X\rangle & - \\ \lvert 0_X\rangle & - \\ \lvert 0_X\rangle & - \end{pmatrix}$ 1 0 0	$\begin{pmatrix} - & \lvert 1_Z\rangle \\ - & \lvert 1_Z\rangle \\ - & \lvert 1_Z\rangle \end{pmatrix}$ 0 1 0	$\begin{pmatrix} \lvert 1_X\rangle & - \\ - & \lvert 1_Z\rangle \\ \lvert 0_X\rangle & - \end{pmatrix}$ 1 1 0	$\begin{pmatrix} - & \lvert 1_Z\rangle \\ \lvert 0_X\rangle & - \\ - & \lvert 1_Z\rangle \end{pmatrix}$ 0 0 0
	$\begin{pmatrix} \lvert 1_X\rangle & - \\ \lvert 0_X\rangle & - \\ - & \lvert 1_Z\rangle \end{pmatrix}$ 1 1 1	$\begin{pmatrix} - & \lvert 1_Z\rangle \\ - & \lvert 1_Z\rangle \\ \lvert 0_X\rangle & - \end{pmatrix}$ 0 0 1	$\begin{pmatrix} \lvert 1_X\rangle & - \\ - & \lvert 1_Z\rangle \\ - & \lvert 1_Z\rangle \end{pmatrix}$ 1 0 1	$\begin{pmatrix} - & \lvert 1_Z\rangle \\ \lvert 0_X\rangle & - \\ \lvert 0_X\rangle & - \end{pmatrix}$ 0 1 1
$f_{22} = \begin{pmatrix} \lvert 1_X\rangle & \lvert 1_Z\rangle \\ \lvert 1_X\rangle & \lvert 1_Z\rangle \\ \lvert 0_X\rangle & \lvert 1_Z\rangle \end{pmatrix}$	$\begin{pmatrix} \lvert 1_X\rangle & - \\ \lvert 1_X\rangle & - \\ \lvert 0_X\rangle & - \end{pmatrix}$ 0 0 0	$\begin{pmatrix} - & \lvert 1_Z\rangle \\ - & \lvert 1_Z\rangle \\ - & \lvert 1_Z\rangle \end{pmatrix}$ 0 1 0	$\begin{pmatrix} \lvert 1_X\rangle & - \\ - & \lvert 1_Z\rangle \\ \lvert 0_X\rangle & - \end{pmatrix}$ 1 1 0	$\begin{pmatrix} - & \lvert 1_Z\rangle \\ \lvert 1_X\rangle & - \\ - & \lvert 1_Z\rangle \end{pmatrix}$ 1 0 0
	$\begin{pmatrix} \lvert 1_X\rangle & - \\ \lvert 1_X\rangle & - \\ - & \lvert 1_Z\rangle \end{pmatrix}$ 0 1 1	$\begin{pmatrix} - & \lvert 1_Z\rangle \\ - & \lvert 1_Z\rangle \\ \lvert 0_X\rangle & - \end{pmatrix}$ 0 0 1	$\begin{pmatrix} \lvert 1_X\rangle & - \\ - & \lvert 1_Z\rangle \\ - & \lvert 1_Z\rangle \end{pmatrix}$ 1 0 1	$\begin{pmatrix} - & \lvert 1_Z\rangle \\ \lvert 1_X\rangle & - \\ \lvert 0_X\rangle & - \end{pmatrix}$ 1 1 1
$f_{23} = \begin{pmatrix} \lvert 1_X\rangle & \lvert 0_Z\rangle \\ \lvert 1_X\rangle & \lvert 1_Z\rangle \\ \lvert 1_X\rangle & \lvert 1_Z\rangle \end{pmatrix}$	$\begin{pmatrix} \lvert 1_X\rangle & - \\ \lvert 1_X\rangle & - \\ \lvert 1_X\rangle & - \end{pmatrix}$ 1 0 0	$\begin{pmatrix} - & \lvert 0_Z\rangle \\ - & \lvert 1_Z\rangle \\ - & \lvert 1_Z\rangle \end{pmatrix}$ 0 0 0	$\begin{pmatrix} \lvert 1_X\rangle & - \\ - & \lvert 1_Z\rangle \\ \lvert 1_X\rangle & - \end{pmatrix}$ 0 1 0	$\begin{pmatrix} - & \lvert 0_Z\rangle \\ \lvert 1_X\rangle & - \\ - & \lvert 1_Z\rangle \end{pmatrix}$ 1 1 0
	$\begin{pmatrix} \lvert 1_X\rangle & - \\ \lvert 1_X\rangle & - \\ - & \lvert 1_Z\rangle \end{pmatrix}$ 0 1 1	$\begin{pmatrix} - & \lvert 0_Z\rangle \\ - & \lvert 1_Z\rangle \\ \lvert 1_X\rangle & - \end{pmatrix}$ 1 1 1	$\begin{pmatrix} \lvert 1_X\rangle & - \\ - & \lvert 1_Z\rangle \\ - & \lvert 1_Z\rangle \end{pmatrix}$ 1 0 1	$\begin{pmatrix} - & \lvert 0_Z\rangle \\ \lvert 1_X\rangle & - \\ \lvert 1_X\rangle & - \end{pmatrix}$ 0 0 1
$f_{24} = \begin{pmatrix} \lvert 1_X\rangle & \lvert 1_Z\rangle \\ \lvert 1_X\rangle & \lvert 1_Z\rangle \\ \lvert 1_X\rangle & \lvert 0_Z\rangle \end{pmatrix}$	$\begin{pmatrix} \lvert 1_X\rangle & - \\ \lvert 1_X\rangle & - \\ \lvert 1_X\rangle & - \end{pmatrix}$ 1 0 0	$\begin{pmatrix} - & \lvert 1_Z\rangle \\ - & \lvert 1_Z\rangle \\ - & \lvert 0_Z\rangle \end{pmatrix}$ 0 0 0	$\begin{pmatrix} \lvert 1_X\rangle & - \\ - & \lvert 1_Z\rangle \\ \lvert 1_X\rangle & - \end{pmatrix}$ 0 1 0	$\begin{pmatrix} - & \lvert 1_Z\rangle \\ \lvert 1_X\rangle & - \\ - & \lvert 0_Z\rangle \end{pmatrix}$ 1 1 0
	$\begin{pmatrix} \lvert 1_X\rangle & - \\ \lvert 1_X\rangle & - \\ - & \lvert 0_Z\rangle \end{pmatrix}$ 0 0 1	$\begin{pmatrix} - & \lvert 1_Z\rangle \\ - & \lvert 1_Z\rangle \\ \lvert 1_X\rangle & - \end{pmatrix}$ 1 0 1	$\begin{pmatrix} \lvert 1_X\rangle & - \\ - & \lvert 1_Z\rangle \\ - & \lvert 0_Z\rangle \end{pmatrix}$ 1 1 1	$\begin{pmatrix} - & \lvert 1_Z\rangle \\ \lvert 1_X\rangle & - \\ \lvert 1_X\rangle & - \end{pmatrix}$ 0 1 1

Table A5. We list the cases that can be successfully disambiguated. Zero cases refer to the error-free SS.

Frame	MR	SS	Disambiguated Bits
f_1	010 101	011,110 011,111	2nd & 3rd
f_2	010 110	110,110 110,111	1st & 2nd
f_3	011 100	011,110 011,111	2nd & 3rd
f_4	100	111,011	zero & 1st
f_5	001 010 101 110	110,000 110,110 110,001 110,111	zero & 2nd
f_6	000 010 100 110	110,000 110,110 110,001 110,111	zero & 1st
f_7	011 111	110,110 110,111	1st & 2nd
f_8	111	111,011	1st & 3rd
f_9	100	111,011	1st & 3rd
f_{10}	111	111,011	zero & 3rd
f_{11}	001 011 101 111	110,000 110,110 110,001 110,111	zero & 1st
f_{12}	001 011 100 110	011,000 011,110 011,111 011,001	zero & 3rd
f_{13}	000 011 100 111	011,000 011,110 011,111 011,001	zero & 2nd
f_{14}	000 011 100 111	110,000 110,110 110,001 110,111	zero & 2nd
f_{15}	001 010 101 110	011,000 011,110 011,111 011,001	zero & 2nd
f_{16}	101	111,101	1st & 3rd
f_{17}	101	111,101	zero & 1st

Table A5. *Cont.*

Frame	MR	SS	Disambiguated Bits
f_{18}	000 010 101 111	011,000 011,110 011,111 011,001	zero & 3rd
f_{19}	001 011 101 111	111,010 111,100 111,101 111,011	zero & 1st
f_{20}	110	111,101	1st & 3rd
f_{21}	110	111,101	zero & 3rd
f_{22}	001 011 100 110	111,010 111,100 111,011 111,101	zero & 3rd
f_{23}	000 010 100 110	111,100 111,010 111,011 111,101	zero & 1st
f_{24}	000 010 101 111	111,100 111,010 111,101 111,011	zero & 3rd

References

1. Kao, K.C.; Hockham, G.A. Dielectric-fibre surface waveguides for optical frequencies. In *Proceedings of the Institution of Electrical Engineers*; IET: London, UK, 1966; Volume 113, pp. 1151–1158.
2. Pirandola, S.; Andersen, U.L.; Banchi, L.; Berta, M.; Bunandar, D.; Colbeck, R.; Englund, D.; Gehring, T.; Lupo, C.; Ottaviani, C.; et al. Advances in quantum cryptography. *Adv. Opt. Photonics* **2020**, *12*, 1012–1236. [CrossRef]
3. Xu, F.; Ma, X.; Zhang, Q.; Lo, H.; Pan, J. Secure quantum key distribution with realistic devices. *Rev. Mod. Phys.* **2020**, *92*, 025002. [CrossRef]
4. Mehic, M.; Niemiec, M.; Rass, S.; Ma, J.; Peev, M.; Aguado, A.; Martin, V.; Schauer, S.; Poppe, A.; Pacher, C.; et al. Quantum key distribution: A networking perspective. *ACM Comput. Surv. CSUR* **2020**, *53*, 1–41. [CrossRef]
5. Lovic, V. Quantum key distribution: Advantages, challenges and policy. *Camb. J. Sci. Policy* **2020**, *1*, e8410270193. [CrossRef]
6. Razavi, M.; Leverrier, A.; Ma, X.; Qi, B.; Yuan, Z. Quantum key distribution and beyond: Introduction. *JOSA B* **2019**, *36*, QKD1–QKD2. [CrossRef]
7. Geihs, M.; Nikiforov, O.; Demirel, D.; Sauer, A.; Butin, D.; Günther, F.; Alber, G.; Walther, T.; Buchmann, J. The status of quantum-key-distribution-based long-term secure internet communication. *IEEE Trans. Sustain. Comput.* **2019**. [CrossRef]
8. Kong, P. A review of quantum key distribution protocols in the perspective of smart grid communication security. *IEEE Syst. J.* **2020**. [CrossRef]
9. Pearson, D. High-speed qkd reconciliation using forward error correction. In *AIP Conference Proceedings*; American Institute of Physics: Melville, NY, USA, 2004; Volume 734, pp. 299–302.
10. Runser, R.J.; Chapuran, T.; Toliver, P.; Peters, N.A.; Goodman, M.S.; Kosloski, J.T.; Nweke, N.; McNown, S.R.; Hughes, R.J.; Rosenberg, D.; et al. Progress toward quantum communications networks: Opportunities and challenges. In *Optoelectronic Integrated Circuits IX*; International Society for Optics and Photonics: Red Hook, NY, USA, 2007; Volume 6476, p. 64760I.
11. Lütkenhaus, N. Estimates for practical quantum cryptography. *Phys. Rev. A* **1999**, *59*, 3301. [CrossRef]
12. Lizama-Pérez, L.A.; López, J.M.; Carlos-López, E.D.; Venegas-Andraca, S.E. Quantum flows for secret key distribution in the presence of the photon number splitting attack. *Entropy* **2014**, *16*, 3121–3135. [CrossRef]
13. Lizama-Pérez, L.A.; López, J.M.; De Carlos López, E. Quantum key distribution in the presence of the intercept-resend with faked states attack. *Entropy* **2016**, *19*, 4. [CrossRef]
14. Lizama-Pérez, L.A.; Lopez, M. Quantum key distillation using binary frames. *Symmetry* **2020**, *12*, 1053. [CrossRef]

15. Fung, C.H.F.; Qi, B.; Tamaki, K.; Lo, H.K. Phase-remapping attack in practical quantum-key-distribution systems. *Phys. Rev. A* **2007**, *75*, 032314. [CrossRef]
16. Xu, F.; Qi, B.; Lo, H.-K. Experimental demonstration of phase-remapping attack in a practical quantum key distribution system. *New J. Phys.* **2010**, *12*, 113026. [CrossRef]
17. Makarov, V.; Hjelme, D.R. Faked states attack on quantum cryptosystems. *J. Mod. Opt.* **2005**, *52*, 691–705. [CrossRef]
18. Makarov, V.; Anisimov, A.; Skaar, J. Effects of detector efficiency mismatch on security of quantum cryptosystems. *Phys. Rev. A* **2006**, *74*, 022313. [CrossRef]
19. Makarov, V.; Skaar, J. Faked states attack using detector efficiency mismatch on sarg04, phase-time, dpsk, and ekert protocols. *Quantum Inf. Comput.* **2008**, *8*, 622–635.
20. Qi, B.; Fung, C.F.; Lo, H.; Ma, X. Time-shift attack in practical quantum cryptosystems. *arXiv* **2005**, arXiv:quant-ph/0512080.
21. Lydersen, L.; Wiechers, C.; Wittmann, C.; Elser, D.; Skaar, J.; Makarov, V. Hacking commercial quantum cryptography systems by tailored bright illumination. *Nat. Photonics* **2010**, *4*, 686–689. [CrossRef]
22. Gerhardt, I.; Liu, Q.; Lamas-Linares, A.; Skaar, J.; Kurtsiefer, C.; Makarov, V. Full-field implementation of a perfect eavesdropper on a quantum cryptography system. *Nat. Commun.* **2011**, *2*, 349. [CrossRef]
23. Wiechers, C.; Lydersen, L.; Wittmann, C.; Elser, D.; Skaar, J.; Marquardt, C.; Makarov, V.; Leuchs, G. After-gate attack on a quantum cryptosystem. *New J. Phys.* **2011**, *13*, 013043. [CrossRef]
24. Weier, H.; Krauss, H.; Rau, M.; Fuerst, M.; Nauerth, S.; Weinfurter, H. Quantum eavesdropping without interception: An attack exploiting the dead time of single-photon detectors. *New J. Phys.* **2011**, *13*, 073024. [CrossRef]
25. Scarani, V.; Acin, A.; Ribordy, G.; Gisin, N. Quantum cryptography protocols robust against photon number splitting attacks for weak laser pulse implementations. *Phys. Rev. Lett.* **2004**, *92*, 057901. [CrossRef] [PubMed]
26. Shannon, C.E. A mathematical theory of communication. *Bell Syst. Tech. J.* **1948**, *27*, 379–423. [CrossRef]
27. Verdu, S. Fifty years of shannon theory. *IEEE Trans. Inf. Theory* **1998**, *44*, 2057–2078. [CrossRef]
28. Kuritsyn, K. Modification of error reconciliation scheme for quantum cryptography. In *First International Symposium on Quantum Informatics*; International Society for Optics and Photonics: Red Hook, NY, USA, 2003; Volume 5128, pp. 91–94.
29. Brassard, G.; Salvail, L. Secret-key reconciliation by public discussion. In *Workshop on the Theory and Application of Cryptographic Techniques*; Springer: Berlin/Heidelberg, Germany, 1993; pp. 410–423.
30. Buttler, W.T.; Lamoreaux, S.K.; Torgerson, J.R.; Nickel, G.H.; Donahue, C.H.; Peterson, C.G. Fast, efficient error reconciliation for quantum cryptography. *Phys. Rev. A* **2003**, *67*, 052303. [CrossRef]
31. Van Assche, G.; Cardinal, J.; Cerf, N.J. Reconciliation of a quantum-distributed gaussian key. *IEEE Trans. Inf. Theory* **2004**, *50*, 394–400. [CrossRef]
32. Bennett, C.H.; Brassard, G.; Crépeau, C.; Maurer, U.M. Generalized privacy amplification. *IEEE Trans. Inf. Theory* **1995**, *41*, 1915–1923. [CrossRef]
33. Muramatsu, J. Transmission of messages to the efficiency limit-implementation of tractable channel code achieving the shannon limit. *NTT Tech. Rev.* **2019**, *17*, 34–39.
34. Yuan, H.; Song, J.; Han, L.; Hou, K.; Shi, S. Improving the total efficiency of quantum key distribution by comparing bell states. *Opt. Commun.* **2008**, *281*, 4803–4806. [CrossRef]
35. Abou Jaoude, A. The paradigm of complex probability and claude shannon's information theory. *Syst. Sci. Control Eng.* **2017**, *5*, 380–425. [CrossRef]
36. Wagner, N.R. The Laws of Cryptography with Java Code. 2003. Available online: https://www.csshl.net/sites/default/files/_downloadable/crypto/laws_of_cryptography_with_java_code.pdf (accessed on 18 December 2020).
37. Grosshans, F.; Van Assche, G.; Wenger, J.; Brouri, R.; Cerf, N.J.; Grangier, P. Quantum key distribution using gaussian-modulated coherent states. *Nature* **2003**, *421*, 238–241. [CrossRef]
38. Grosshans, F.; Grangier, P. Reverse reconciliation protocols for quantum cryptography with continuous variables. *arXiv* **2002**, arXiv:quant-ph/0204127.
39. Wang, X.; Zhang, Y.; Yu, S.; Guo, H. High speed error correction for continuous-variable quantum key distribution with multi-edge type ldpc code. *Sci. Rep.* **2018**, *8*, 1–7. [CrossRef] [PubMed]
40. Chung, S.; Forney, G.D.; Richardson, T.J.; Urbanke, R. On the design of low-density parity-check codes within 0.0045 db of the shannon limit. *IEEE Commun. Lett.* **2001**, *5*, 58–60. [CrossRef]
41. Mehic, M.; Niemiec, M.; Siljak, H.; Voznak, M. Error reconciliation in quantum key distribution protocols. *Lect. Notes Comput. Sci.* **2020**, *12070*, 222–236.
42. Bennett, C.H.; Brassard, G. Quantum cryptography: Public key distribution and coin tossing. In Proceedings of the International Conference on Computers, Systems & Signal Processing, Bangalore, India, 9–12 December 1984.
43. Van Assche, G. *Quantum Cryptography and Secret-Key Distillation*; Cambridge University Press: Cambridge, UK, 2006.
44. Hughes, R.; Nordholt, J.; Rarity, J. *Summary of Implementation Schemes for Quantum Key Distribution and Quantum Cryptography—A Quantum Information Science and Technology Roadmap*; United States Government: New York, NY, USA, 2004.
45. Bennett, C.H.; Bessette, F.; Brassard, G.; Salvail, L.; Smolin, J. Experimental quantum cryptography. *J. Cryptol.* **1992**, *5*, 3–28. [CrossRef]
46. Kumar, V.V.; Karthikeyan, T.; Praveen Sundar, P.V.; Magesh, G.; Balajee, J.M. A quantum approach in lifi security using quantum key distribution. *Int. J. Adv. Sci. Technol.* **2020**, *29*, 2345–2354.

Article
An Attack on Zawadzki's Quantum Authentication Scheme

Carlos E. González-Guillén [1,†], María Isabel González Vasco [2,†], Floyd Johnson [3,*,†] and Ángel L. Pérez del Pozo [2,†]

1. Departamento de Matemática Aplicada a la Ingeniería Industrial, Universidad Politécnica de Madrid, 28040 Madrid, Spain; carlos.gguillen@upm.es
2. MACIMTE, Universidad Rey Juan Carlos, 28933 Madrid, Spain; mariaisabel.vasco@urjc.es (M.I.G.V.); angel.perez@urjc.es (Á.L.P.d.P.)
3. Department of Mathmatical Sciences, Florida Atlantic University, Boca Raton, FL 33431, USA
* Correspondence: johnsonf2017@fau.edu
† Authors names listed alphabetically.

Abstract: Identification schemes are interactive cryptographic protocols typically involving two parties, a prover, who wants to provide evidence of their identity and a verifier, who checks the provided evidence and decides whether or not it comes from the intended prover. Given the growing interest in quantum computation, it is indeed desirable to have explicit designs for achieving user identification through quantum resources. In this paper, we comment on a recent proposal for quantum identity authentication from Zawadzki. We discuss the applicability of the theoretical impossibility results from Lo, Colbeck and Buhrman et al. and formally prove that the protocol must necessarily be insecure. Moreover, to better illustrate our insecurity claim, we present an attack on Zawadzki's protocol and show that by using a simple strategy an adversary may indeed obtain relevant information on the shared identification secret. Specifically, through the use of the principal of conclusive exclusion on quantum measurements, our attack geometrically reduces the key space resulting in the claimed logarithmic security being reduced effectively by a factor of two after only three verification attempts.

Keywords: quantum identity authentication; private equality tests; conclusive exclusion

1. Introduction

One of the major goals of cryptography is authentication in different flavours, namely, providing guarantees that certain interaction is actually involving some specific parties from a designated presumed set of users. In the two party scenario, cryptographic constructions towards this goal are called identity authentication schemes, and have been extensively studied in classical cryptography [1,2]. Classically, there are different ways of defining so-called identification schemes, for mutual authentication of peers, mainly depending on whether the involved parties share some secret information (such as a password) or should rely on different (often certified) keys provided by a trusted third party. The advent of quantum computers may suggest the end for many of these protocols however.

Since Wiesner proposed using quantum mechanics in cryptography in the 1970s, multiple directions using this concept have undergone serious research. One major role quantum mechanics has played in cryptography is the development of quantum key distribution (QKD) where two parties can securely share a one time pad using quantum mechanics, for example, the seminal protocol BB84 [3]. Among protocols providing entity authentication and strictly quantum in nature, some of them, such as those in [4–6], are based on entanglement, while more recently [7,8] do not rely on entanglement but rather propose to obtain identity authentication evidence from only the common knowledge of a shared secret. These approaches are known as quantum identity authentication (QIA) protocols (see also the related papers [9–14]). Due to the existence of quantum protocols such as BB84 that do not rely on entanglement it would be more appealing to not rely on entanglement for entity authentication purposes.

The QIA constructions in which authentication is intended from the common knowledge of a shared secret, often called QIA schemes (or just quantum identification schemes), are closely related to protocols for quantum equality tests and quantum private comparison. All these constructions are concrete examples of two-party computations with asymmetric output, i.e., allowing only one of the two parties involved to learn the result of a computation on two private inputs. Without imposing restrictions on an adversary it was shown by Lo [15], Colbeck [16] and Buhrman et al. [17] that these kind of constructions are impossible, even in a quantum setting. As a consequence, constructions for generic unrestricted adversaries in the quantum setting are doomed to failure.

While there are many things in common in the frameworks for developing QKD protocols and identification schemes built as private comparison tests, we make note of the following key differences in cryptographic considerations. Most QKD setups involve an authenticated classical channel, thus the recipients may safely compare check bits to see if there is an unintended observer. This however may not be the case in an authentication scheme (like the one considered in this paper), so there may be no way for the legitimate parties to determine if an eavesdropper is present. Thus, if the states obtained by the authenticating party are not as expected, the authentication fails without the users knowing if it is due to an adversarial presence or an attempted impersonator. For this reason the traditional so called intercept-and-resend attack is completely irrelevant for authentication as the adversary is always capable of sending messages as if coming from Alice or Bob, though without the correct private value the protocol is overwhelming likely to fail. The closest equivalent constraint is that the authenticating party may only make a single measurement on a qubit before the state collapses. This constraint bars the adversary from making many measurements on the same state in order to fully receive the private value. This however does not exclude the possibility that many different calls of the authentication protocol are made. Unlike key distribution protocols, where after a failure the key is discarded, both classical and quantum authentication protocols must be secure after being run multiple times with the same shared secret though with different random inputs [1]. We make special note here that the objectives of QKD and QIA schemes are very different. With this in mind readers should be cautious to apply the results of this work to any current or future scheme if and only if its objectives and methods fall within certain parameters.

1.1. Our Contribution

Recently, an original work about authentication without entanglement by Hong et al. in [8] was improved by Zawadzki using tools from classical cryptography in [7]. In Zawadzki's protocol, there are two parties, Alice and Bob, who share a common secret bitstring k. In order to achieve entity authentication from Alice to Bob, they run a non-interactive protocol in which Alice first computes a hash value h_a, which depends on k and a random nonce r; then Alice sends r to Bob so he can reproduce the computation obtaining a hash value h_b (which must equal h_a if there is no adversarial interference). Next Alice sequentially sends quantum states to Bob, which she prepares as a function of consecutive pairs of bits of h. At reception, Bob measures these states choosing each time a basis which depends on the value h. If all measures' outcomes are the expected ones, Bob concludes that the other party must know k and, therefore, identifies it as being Alice.

Our theoretical analysis of the protocol shows its insecurity, but in a non-constructive way (e.g., it does not help finding a concrete successful adversarial strategy). However, we are in addition able to show an explicit attack against the protocol, based on conclusive exclusion on quantum measurements, which we describe in Section 4. There we analyze in detail how the attack halves the size of the key space after only three verification attempts.

Note that, when analyzing Zawadzki's protocol, we deal only with its theoretical design. Both the impossibility results we invoke and our attack do not take advantage of physical aspects, such as distance or timing, they hold independently of the implementation. It is indeed interesting to study in depth how identification protocols could be practically deployed in the real world, and what weaknesses could be exploited, but this is beyond the scope of this work. These physical issues, present in attacks against QKD, such as, for example, time-shift attacks [18], phase-remapping attacks [19] or synchronization attacks [20], would also naturally arise for quantum identification protocols.

Finally, we discuss the applicability of the impossibility results and the explicit attack to other QIA protocols, such as [4,5,8,21–24]. For instance, we point out that the protocol from Hong et al. [8], in which Zawadzki's protocol is based upon, is vulnerable to the same attack we describe against the latter. On the other hand, the rest of the protocols cited, for different reasons discussed later, are neither affected by the impossibility results nor vulnerable to our attack.

The main contribution that arises from this work is that our theoretical analysis evidences an implication of the proven impossibility of identification schemes, such as Zawadzki's design. Thus, we stress that fundamental changes in the original proposal, beyond preventing our particular attack, would be needed in order to derive a secure identification scheme.

1.2. Paper Roadmap

We start this contribution by summarizing in Section 2 the impossibility results from Lo [15], Colbeck [16] and Buhrman et al. [17], concerning generic quantum two party protocols. Further, we present and discuss the Zawadzki protocol in Section 3, evidencing it actually fits the framework considered in the impossibility results from Section 2, and thus concluding it must necessarily be insecure. Moreover, we outline a simple explicit attack which we describe in Section 4. Finally we discuss how other QIA protocols are affected by our results in Section 5 and provide some conclusions in Section 6.

2. Quantum Equality Tests Are Impossible

A one sided equality test is a cryptographic protocol in which one party, Alice, convinces another party, Bob, that they share a common key by revealing nothing to them but equality (or inequality) of their inputs. Formally we define a key space K and a function $F : K^2 \to \{0, 1\}$ which checks for equality. Let $i \in K$ be Alice's key and $j \in K$ be Bob's key. The goals of a one sided equality test are as follows:

(1) $F(i, j) = 1$ if and only if $i = j$.
(2) Alice learns nothing about j nor about $F(i, j)$.
(3) Bob learns $F(i, j)$ with certainty. If $F(i, j) = 0$ then Bob learns nothing about i besides that $i \neq j$.

The above is a specific case of a one-sided two-party secure computation protocol as described in [15], as only one side, Bob, learns the output of the computation. In this work, a very general result is proven indicating that any protocol realising a one-sided two-party secure computation task is impossible, even in a quantum setting. In particular, Lo shows in [15] that if a protocol satisfies (1) and (2) then Bob can know the output of $F(i, j)$ for any j. Furthermore, a one sided equality test with some small relaxations on points (1) and (3) is also proven impossible. Hence, any one-sided QIA protocol which validates identities using equality tests by use of quantum mechanics is impossible without imposing restrictions on the adversary.

Note that the above argument says nothing about protocols with built in adversarial assumptions such as those presented in [25,26]. Further, note that many of QIA schemes in the literature include a final round where Bob accepts or rejects, which makes Alice aware of the success or failure of the protocol. Indeed, those schemes can be straightforwardly turned into one-sided equality tests by suppressing Bob's final message announcing the result. Hence, they are clearly insecure against a dishonest Bob. However, note that if any such protocol can be modified so that Alice may obtain information on the identification output at some point before the last protocol round, it is unclear how Lo's impossibility result would apply. However, if they are built upon equality tests we can get impossibility from another well know result by Buhrman el al. [17]. Certainly, two-sided QIA schemes, in which both Alice and Bob learn the result of the protocol, are a particular case of two-sided two-party computations. It is shown in [17] that a correct quantum protocol for a classical two-sided two-party computation that is secure against one of the parties is completely insecure against the other. For equality tests, if one of the parties, say Alice, learns nothing else than $F(i,j)$, the other party, Bob, will indeed be able to compute $F(i,j)$ for all possible inputs j. Thus, any two-sided QIA protocol which validates identities using equality tests is also impossible without imposing further restrictions on the adversary.

Both total insecurity results are valid for protocols that compute a deterministic function F, and admit relaxed versions for computations that implement approximate versions of F. For a non-deterministic function F, Colbeck [16] showed that in a correct one-sided or two-sided two-party computation for F, one of the parties can always access more information about the other party's input than it is supposed to, where the analysis is only done quantitatively for dychotomic values of i,j, and extended trivially to the general case, yielding a qualitative more than a quantitative result.

3. Insecurity of Zawadzki's QIA Protocol

In this section, we outline the protocol proposed in [7] and show that it must be insecure on Alice's side by the results discussed in Section 2. Moreover, we consider minor changes to the protocol to evidence that making it more "in line" with classical authentication does not help, as the protocol remains insecure. Indeed, the changes introduced do not fundamentally alter the protocol, namely both the changed and unchanged protocols allow for the attack we outline in Section 4 to provide information leakage.

The protocol proposed in [7] can be described as follows: suppose Alice and Bob have keys k_a and k_b, respectively, and agree on some universal hash function (universal hash functions are to be understood as families $\mathcal{H}$ of functions providing a nice collision-resistance property, i.e., given inputs $x \neq y$, the probability of $h(x) = h(y)$ can be proven negligible if h is chosen at random from $\mathcal{H}$ (see [27]). In an abuse of notation, is it typical to treat them as individual functions, as we do above) $H : \{0,1\}^N \to \{0,1\}^{2d}$. Bob wishes to verify that $k_b = k_a$ without leaking any information about k_b or k_a. Alice randomly generates a nonce r_a from a designated domain and calculates the value $h_a = H(r_a || k_a)$. Alice sends Bob r_a. Bob receives r_b (which in principle should be equal to r_a) then calculates the value $h_b = H(r_b || k_b)$. Note that if $k_a = k_b$ and the nonces are received as constructed, then $h_a = h_b$. Alice then acts on pairs of bits in h_a with an embedding function $Q : \{0,1\}^2 \to \mathbb{C}^2$. This function Q uses the first of the two binary values to determine the measurement basis (horizontal/vertical or diagonal/antidiagonal) and the second to determine the specific qubit in $\{|0\rangle, |1\rangle, |+\rangle, |-\rangle\}$. More precisely, $Q(0,0) = |0\rangle$, $Q(0,1) = |1\rangle$, $Q(1,0) = |+\rangle$ and $Q(1,1) = |-\rangle$. Applying Q to the pairs of bits in h_a Alice prepares and sends d qubits to Bob over the quantum channel one by one with a constant speed known to Bob.

Using the first bit of each pair Bob decides in which base he measures the quantum states and insures he obtains the correct qubit according to the second bit of the pair. If the loss of qubits is very high or the rate of bits measured by Bob that disagree with the even bits of h_b is over a certain threshold then Bob rejects Alice's challenge. Otherwise he accepts her challenge. See Figure 1 for a schematic overview of the protocol.

For the sake of simplicity we restrict the security analysis to the case where there are no losses in the communication and the bit error rate is set to 0.

The Zawadzki protocol is claimed to be leakage resistant when considering an adversary measuring in a random basis. The reasoning behind this is that unless an adversary, Eve, correctly guesses the correct basis for each round, she will obtain different values for at least one of the bits of the hash. Now suppose an adversary is capable of computing preimages of hash functions through brute force with unbounded classical computational power or through dictionary attacks with unbounded classical memory. In this case it is unlikely that there will exist a $k_e \in K$ such that $H(r_e || k_e)$ matches what Eve measured. In the event there does exist such a k_e then with overwhelming probability $k_e \neq k_a = k_b$ and Eve will not be able to falsify authentication of Alice or Bob.

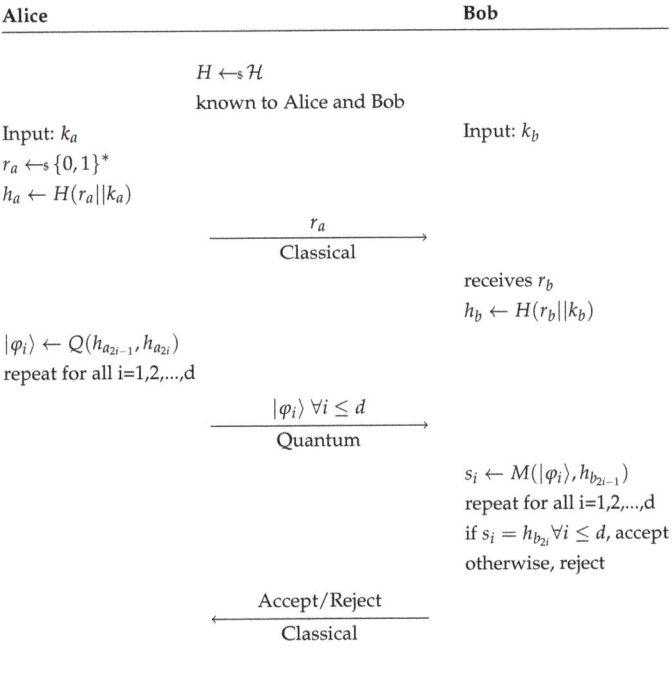

Figure 1. The protocol presented in [7].

Unfortunately, Zawadzki's protocol implemets a two-sided equality test (one-sided if the last accept/reject round is omitted) for the secrets, with a relaxation on the correctness, that is, the condition $F(i,j) = 1$ if and only if $i = j$ (in this case i is h_a and j is h_b). Suppose, for the sake of reasoning, that the protocol were a correct two-sided equality test, then all the results summarized in Section 2 apply and the protocol has necessary leakage. As Bob is sending nothing but the final bit, we know that nothing can possibly leak from h_b. Thus, any potential leakage comes from h_a and in fact it is completely leaked. Although Eve may not be able to determine any exact bit of k_a, due to collisions of the hash function, she may drastically reduce the number of possible options for k_a to those k such that $h_a = H(r_a||k)$ and hence construct a proper subset of K such that the true value for k_a is contained in this subset.

However, Zawadzki's protocol is not perfectly correct. Whenever Alice and Bob secrets, h_a and h_b, differ in the measurement bits (the ones associated to the measurements basis), there is some probability of the computation returning value 1 and thus Bob accepting Alice's input as valid. This probability is exponentially small in the number of different measurement bits between h_a and h_b, that is, for a large majority of the cases this probability is very small. Thus, the reasoning made in the approximate case of the relaxation of the correctness in the one-sided case in [15] can be applied to Zawadzki's protocol (without the last round) in these cases. That is, when Bob chooses a secret that differs in many measurement bits from Alice's secret, what will happen for a random choice of the secret, he will be able not only to compute with some probability (close to 1) the equality test for (h_a, h_b), but to compute the equality test with some different probabilities (close to 1) for every (h_a, h'_b) such that the output of the computation has large probability of being the value of the equality test. Thus, he will obtain partial (but close to full) information about many different secrets at the same time.

The approximate version of the result of Buhrman et al. [17] does not straightforwardly say anything in this case as their notion of approximate correctness requires that the function F should be computed correctly for every input with probability close to 1. Whereas in Zawadzki's proposal the pairs of secrets (h_a, h_b) that only differ in one of the measurement bits has probability of computing correctly the equality test equals $1/2$. However, it may be possible to give a version of the result of Buhrman et al. with a different notion of approximate correctness.

Finally, the result of Colbeck does apply when considering the non deterministic function F to be the actual computation of the secrets h_a and h_b implemented by the protocol. Thus, the function implemented by the protocol is not secure and a dishonest Bob could learn information about the implemented function for more than one secret h_b at a time, acquiring more information than following the protocol honestly.

Next we analyze what happens if some minor changes are done to make the protocol more in line with classical authentication schemes. Unfortunately, we conclude that these changes do not fundamentally modify the protocol and as will be clear the previous reasoning still holds. Moreover, both the changed and unchanged protocols still allow for the particular attack outlined in Section 4 to provide information leakage by allowing an adversary to learn about many h_a simultaneously as predicted by the results of Lo and Colbeck.

Changes made to the protocol are as follows: (1) Bob generates r and H, this is done to thwart a simple attack discussed later; (2) the hash function changes between trials, this has no impact on the security of the protocol due to the public nature of the hash in both instances; and finally (3) here we assume for simplicity that Alice and Bob obtain the same nonce r with certainty, using classical error correction techniques one can be relatively certain both parties obtain the same nonce. See Figure 2 below for a schematic overview of the modified protocol.

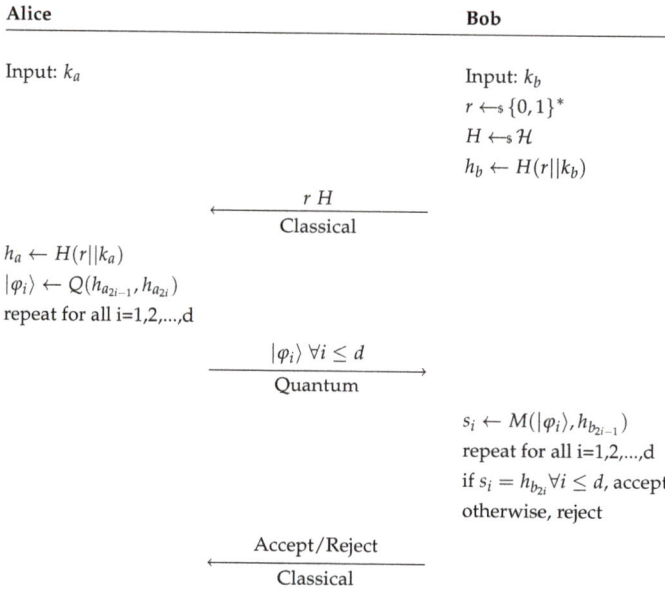

Figure 2. Modified protocol.

The reason we force Bob to generate the randomness instead of Alice is that an adversary with unbounded quantum memory may impersonate Bob but not make a measurement. Suppose an adversary does not know the key but requests Alice to identify herself. If Alice generates and sends r, H with the string of states $|\varphi_i\rangle$ then the adversary may record r, H and hold in memory, but not measure, the qubits. At a later time an honest participant may ask the adversary to identify themselves, in this case the adversary may send r, H and the qubits in memory. Thus, the adversary correctly forges an authentication. Note that as we have presented the algorithm an adversary may still make this impersonation by waiting between Alice and Bob then passing the information between the two. The difference is that as long as Bob generates the nonce then this attack must only be done while Alice and Bob are both online, whereas if Alice generates and sends the nonce then an adversary may hold the states for as long as is technologically feasible.

Unfortunately, the changes introduced do not alter the validity of the impossibility results discussed before. This updated version is still a two-sided equality test (one-sided if the last accept/reject round is omitted) for the secrets with a relaxation on the correctness, as no changes have been introduced after the generation of the secrets.

Thus, both the original and the modified protocols have necessary leakage and due to the non-interactive nature of Bob we know that k_b has no leakage, thus we know there must exist some leakage on k_a. Although Eve may not be able to determine any exact bit of k_a she may drastically reduce the number of possible options for k_a and hence construct a proper subset of K such that the true value for k_a is contained in this subset. An attack exemplifying this phenomenon is described in the next section.

4. A Key Space Reduction Attack on Zawadzki's Protocol

Before discussing the specific attack, let B be a set of orthogonal bases in $\mathbb{C}^2$ and consider the following fact. If a quantum state is prepared in a basis $b \in B$ with value $v \in \{0,1\}$, then an adversary may always remove one possible combination of b and v with a single measurement. Upon measuring in basis $b' \in B$ an adversary obtains $v' \in \{0,1\}$. The adversary is then certain the original pair (b, v) was not $(b', 1 \oplus v')$, as when measured in the basis b the qubit prepared by b and v will yield v with certainty. Note that the adversary cannot say with certainty how the qubit was prepared, but he can always remove one possible option. This is an example of conclusive exclusion discussed in [28] in the case of two measurement bases.

Suppose now that instead of sampling at random for b and v, the qubit is prepared using a private key $k \in K$ and a set of public parameters p, namely $b = b(k, p)$ and $v = v(k, p)$. An adversary once again measures in basis $b' \in B$ (chosen or taken at random) to obtain $v' \in \{0, 1\}$, they may then determine a basis/value pair in which the qubit was not prepared. Because the adversary is assumed to be computationally unbounded they may then compute $b(\hat{k}, p)$ and $v(\hat{k}, p)$ for all $\hat{k} \in K$. Whenever these computations output the impossible pair k', v' the adversary becomes aware that $\hat{k} \neq k$, hence reducing the key space. The extent to which the key space is reduced depends on the number of basis in B. If the distribution of basis choices in B is low entropy the attack may be accomplished as described while if B is high entropy then a probabilistic version decreases the space of likely keys. The assumption that the adversary is computationally unbounded may be lifted if k is low entropy (for he can then indeed test all possible values for k—given there are only a polynomial set of candidates), however assuming a computationally bounded adversary immediately removes unconditional security as an end goal.

Let us now apply this key space reduction to the QIA protocol proposed in [7], in this case the private key is k and the public parameters are r and H. Suppose an Eve has no a priori knowledge of the key except its existence in K. After receiving r and H over the classical channel she measures all qubits $|\varphi_i\rangle$ received from Alice in the horizontal/vertical basis and records the outputs as M. In the case where Eve is utilizing man-in-the-middle, she is done. If she is impersonating Bob, she accepts or rejects the protocol.

After the protocol finishes the adversary may then compute $h_{\hat{k}} = H(r||\hat{k})$ for all $\hat{k} \in K$. Suppose the first qubit Eve measured in M was $|0\rangle$. She now examines the first two bits of each $h_{\hat{k}}$, those that begin 00, 10, or 11 are all possible of obtaining the qubit $|0\rangle$ after measurement. The first of these three tuples will yield $|0\rangle$ with certainty and the later two with a probability of 0.5. The final tuple 01 however is not possible as that would imply that the qubit started in the state $|1\rangle$ and measured in $|0\rangle$. Thus, Eve knows that any $\hat{k}$ such that $h_{\hat{k}}$ begins 01 is not the key. The hash function is assumed to be independent and identically distributed so this removes approximately $\frac{1}{4}$ of all possible keys. Repeat this process for all qubits. After completion of all hash and check operations the adversary has obtained a subset of the key space which contains the key, hence causing information leakage. Specifically, the adversary knows the key is in subset S defined by

$$S = \{s \in K : h_{s_{2i}} = M_i \text{ and } h_{s_{2i-1}} = 0 \; \forall i \leq d\}.$$

Note that the true key $k \in S$ and $|S| \approx (\frac{3}{4})^d |K|$.

After running this attack on a single attempted authentication the proposed ideal (brute force) security of $2^{2d} = 2^N$ drops to $3^d = 2^{\log_2(3)/2 N} \approx 2^{0.792N}$. Recall that authentication protocols must remain secure given many attempts. Thus, an adversary is allowed to receive multiple authentication attempts, possibly claiming that the received hash of the shared secret is denied due to interference from a third party. The logarithm of the security parameter drops geometrically at a rate of $\frac{\log_2(3)}{2} \approx 0.792$ after every authentication the adversary receives, meaning that once an adversary obtains the third authentication (all with different random values or even different hash functions) the brute force security has been reduced to brute force on a string of half the length. This trend continues with every authentication attempt.

5. Other QIA Protocols

It is worth pointing out that the attack described in Section 4 also applies to the protocol by Hong et al. [8], which Zawadzki [7] modifies. In more detail, the protocol in [8] is similar to Zawadzki's, but does not use a hash function. Instead, whenever Alice transmits the qubits sequentially and, before sending each qubit, she randomly decides if she is going to use security mode or authentication mode. In the first case, she sends a decoy state while in the second one, a qubit encoding two bits of the authentication string is sent, similarly to [7]. After Bob's reception, Alice announces which mode she just has used. Therefore an adversary using the same strategy described in our attack in Section 4 and collecting the information obtained whenever Alice announces authentication mode, will be able to shrink the size of the key space in the same way we have previously stated.

On the other hand, other quantum identification protocols proposed in the literature are not vulnerable to our attack neither contradict the impossibility results mentioned in Section 2. For instance, some of them [4,5,21] are aided by the presence of a trusted third party, therefore not being real two-party protocols. Another type of protocols, such as [22–24], make use of an entangled quantum state shared between both parties. In [22], the users, in addition, share a bitstring used as a password; both parties measures their part of the entangled state to produce a one time key that one of the users XORs with the password and sends the result to the other who checks for consistency. The downside of this approach is that to repeat the identification process the parties need to be provided again with new entangled states. In [23,24], the users do not share any classical secret, they just use the entangled state to identify themselves.

6. Conclusions

The protocol given by Zawadzki in [7] may be secure against hash preimage attacks when attempting to find an exact match; however, when considering impossible results from quantum measurements we see some hashed key values are not possible. Proverbially, the forest may be secure but each of the trees reveals enough information to reconstruct the possible forests. By eliminating approximately one quarter of the key options from each qubit we see that by measuring all the individual qubits in a random basis does in fact reveal a great deal about the key. This attack does not concern quantum memory but rather relies heavily on classical computational power. Hence, unlike [25,26] where the authors consider a bounded quantum storage model, the only way to make this protocol secure without greatly changing its construction is to constrict adversarial computational power.

No solution is presented to the problem outlined in this paper. The reason for this is that any solution presented which does not impose more fundamental restrictions such as limited quantum memory or polynomial time restriction will inevitably fail due to the results of Lo [15], Colbeck [16] and Buhrman et al. [17]. Regardless of the restriction imposed, implementation of this and any other "prepare and measure" authentication scheme must find a way to contend with key space reductions posed by conclusive exclusion.

Author Contributions: Conceptualization—all authors equally; original draft preparation—F.J.; review, editing and final draft writing—all authors equally. All authors have read and agreed to the published version of the manuscript.

Funding: This research was sponsored in part by the NATO Science for Peace and Security Programme under grant G5448, in part by Spanish MINECO under grants MTM2016-77213-R and MTM2017-88385-P, and in part by Programa Propio de I+D+i of the Universidad Politécnica de Madrid.

Conflicts of Interest: The authors declare no conflict of interest.

References

1. Bellare, M.; Rogaway, P. Entity authentication and key distribution. In *Annual International Cryptology Conference*; Springer: Berlin/Heidelberg, Germany, 1993; pp. 232–249.
2. Zuccherato, R., Entity Authentication. In *Encyclopedia of Cryptography and Security*; van Tilborg, H.C.A., Ed.; Springer: Boston, MA, USA, 2005; pp. 203–203. [CrossRef]
3. Bennett, C.H.; Brassard, G. Quantum cryptography: public key distribution and coin tossing. *Theor. Comput. Sci.* **2014**, *560*, 7–11. [CrossRef]
4. Penghao, N.; Yuan, C.; Chong, L. Quantum authentication scheme based on entanglement swapping. *Int. J. Theor. Phys.* **2016**, *55*, 302–312. [CrossRef]
5. Zeng, G.; Zhang, W. Identity verification in quantum key distribution. *Phys. Rev. A* **2000**, *61*, 022303. [CrossRef]
6. Huang, P.; Zhu, J.; Lu, Y.; Zeng, G.H. Quantum identity authentication using Gaussian-modulated squeezed states. *Int. J. Quantum Inf.* **2011**, *9*, 701–721. [CrossRef]
7. Zawadzki, P. Quantum identity authentication without entanglement. *Quantum Inf. Process.* **2019**, *18*, 7. [CrossRef]
8. ho Hong, C.; Heo, J.; Jang, J.G.; Kwon, D. Quantum identity authentication with single photon. *Quantum Inf. Process.* **2017**, *16*, 236. [CrossRef]
9. Doosti, M.; Kumar, N.; Delavar, M.; Kashefi, E. Client-Server Identification Protocols with Quantum PUF. *arXiv* **2020**, arXiv:2006.04522.
10. Fladung, L.; Nikolopoulos, G.M.; Alber, G.; Fischlin, M. Intercept-Resend Emulation Attacks against a Continuous-Variable Quantum Authentication Protocol with Physical Unclonable Keys. *Cryptography* **2019**, *3*, 25. [CrossRef]
11. Nikolopoulos, G.M. Continuous-variable quantum authentication of physical unclonable keys: Security against an emulation attack. *Phys. Rev. A* **2018**, *97*, 012324. [CrossRef]
12. Gianfelici, G.; Kampermann, H.; Bruß, D. Theoretical framework for physical unclonable functions, including quantum readout. *Phys. Rev. A* **2020**, *101*, 042337. [CrossRef]
13. Nikolopoulos, G.D.E. Continuous-variable quantum authentication of physical unclonable keys. *Sci. Rep.* **2017**, *7*, 46047. [CrossRef] [PubMed]
14. Kang, M.; Heo, J.; Hong, C.; Yang, H.J.; Han, S.; Moon, S. Controlled mutual quantum entity authentication with an untrusted third party. *Quantum Inf. Process.* **2018**, *17*, 159. [CrossRef]
15. Lo, H.K. Insecurity of quantum secure computations. *Phys. Rev. A* **1997**, *56*, 1154. [CrossRef]
16. Colbeck, R. Impossibility of secure two-party classical computation. *Phys. Rev. A* **2007**, *76*, 062308. [CrossRef]
17. Buhrman, H.; Christandl, M.; Schaffner, C. Complete Insecurity of Quantum Protocols for Classical Two-Party Computation. *Phys. Rev. Lett.* **2012**, *109*, 160501. [CrossRef] [PubMed]
18. Zhao, Y.; Fung, C.H.F.; Qi, B.; Chen, C.; Lo, H.K. Quantum hacking: Experimental demonstration of time-shift attack against practical quantum-key-distribution systems. *Phys. Rev. A* **2008**, *78*, 042333. [CrossRef]
19. Fung, C.H.F.; Qi, B.; Tamaki, K.; Lo, H.K. Phase-remapping attack in practical quantum-key-distribution systems. *Phys. Rev. A* **2007**, *75*, 032314. [CrossRef]
20. Pljonkin, A. Vulnerability of the synchronization process in the quantum key distribution system. *Int. J. Cloud Appl. Comput. (IJCAC)* **2019**, *9*, 50–58. [CrossRef]

21. Yang, Y.G.; Wang, H.Y.; Jia, X.; Zhang, H. A quantum protocol for (t, n)-threshold identity authentication based on greenberger-horne-zeilinger states. *Int. J. Theor. Phys.* **2013**, *52*, 524–530. [CrossRef]
22. Mihara, T. Quantum identification schemes with entanglements. *Phys. Rev. A* **2002**, *65*, 052326. [CrossRef]
23. Shi, B.S.; Li, J.; Liu, J.M.; Fan, X.F.; Guo, G.C. Quantum key distribution and quantum authentication based on entangled state. *Phys. Lett. A* **2001**, *281*, 83–87. [CrossRef]
24. Zhang, Y.S.; Li, C.F.; Guo, G.C. Quantum authentication using entangled state. *arXiv* **2000**, arXiv:quant-ph/0008044.
25. Damgård, I.B.; Fehr, S.; Salvail, L.; Schaffner, C. Secure identification and QKD in the bounded-quantum-storage model. In *Annual International Cryptology Conference*; Springer: Berlin/Heidelberg, Germany, 2007; pp. 342–359.
26. Bouman, N.J.; Fehr, S.; González-Guillén, C.; Schaffner, C. An All-But-One Entropic Uncertainty Relation, and Application to Password-Based Identification. In *Theory of Quantum Computation, Communication, and Cryptography*; Springer: Berlin/Heidelberg, Germany, 2013; pp. 29–44.
27. Carter, L.; Wegman, M.N. Universal Classes of Hash Functions (Extended Abstract). In Proceedings of the 9th Annual ACM Symposium on Theory of Computing, Boulder, CO, USA, 4–6 May 1977; Hopcroft, J.E., Friedman, E.P., Harrison, M.A., Eds.; ACM: New York, NY, USA, 1977; pp. 106–112. [CrossRef]
28. Bandyopadhyay, S.; Jain, R.; Oppenheim, J.; Perry, C. Conclusive exclusion of quantum states. *Phys. Rev. A* **2014**, *89*. [CrossRef]

Article

Phase-Matching Quantum Key Distribution with Discrete Phase Randomization

Xiaoxu Zhang [1,2,3], Yang Wang [1,2,*], Musheng Jiang [1,2], Yifei Lu [1,2], Hongwei Li [1,2], Chun Zhou [1,2] and Wansu Bao [1,2]

[1] Henan Key Laboratory of Quantum Information and Cryptography, SSF IEU, Zhengzhou 450001, China; zxx@qiclab.cn (X.Z.); jms@qiclab.cn (M.J.); lyf@qiclab.cn (Y.L.); lhw@qiclab.cn (H.L.); zc@qiclab.cn (C.Z.); bws@qiclab.cn (W.B.)
[2] Synergetic Innovation Center of Quantum Information and Quantum Physics, University of Science and Technology of China, Hefei 230026, China
[3] Basic Department, SSF IEU, Zhengzhou 450001, China
* Correspondence: wy@qiclab.cn

Abstract: The twin-field quantum key distribution (TF-QKD) protocol and its variations have been proposed to overcome the linear Pirandola–Laurenza–Ottaviani–Banchi (PLOB) bound. One variation called phase-matching QKD (PM-QKD) protocol employs discrete phase randomization and the phase post-compensation technique to improve the key rate quadratically. However, the discrete phase randomization opens a loophole to threaten the actual security. In this paper, we first introduce the unambiguous state discrimination (USD) measurement and the photon-number-splitting (PNS) attack against PM-QKD with imperfect phase randomization. Then, we prove the rigorous security of decoy state PM-QKD with discrete phase randomization. Simulation results show that, considering the intrinsic bit error rate and sifting factor, there is an optimal discrete phase randomization value to guarantee security and performance. Furthermore, as the number of discrete phase randomization increases, the key rate of adopting vacuum and one decoy state approaches infinite decoy states, the key rate between discrete phase randomization and continuous phase randomization is almost the same.

Keywords: twin-field quantum key distribution; phase-matching; discrete phase randomization; intrinsic bit error rate

1. Introduction

Quantum key distribution (QKD) can offer information theoretically secure means to distribute secret keys between two remote parties [1], but the performance is restricted by the fundamental rate-loss limit [2,3]. Recently, a novel twin-field QKD (TF-QKD) protocol [4] is proposed to surpass the linear Pirandola–Laurenza–Ottaviani–Banchi (PLOB) bound [2], which shows the superiority relation between key rate and channel transmittance, $R \sim O(\sqrt{\eta})$. However, the security proof is not completed in the original TF-QKD protocol [4]. In order to present a more rigorous security proof, various variations [5–10] of the original TF-QKD protocol have been proposed. The related experimental works have also been extensively studied [11–20].

All of these variant TF-QKD protocols have their own advantages. The no-phase-post-selection TF-QKD (NPP-TF-QKD) protocol [5,6] provides better key rate performance in closer-to-mid distance, but it needs phase locking and pre-phase feedback in the experiment, so it is hard to implement [5,6,21]. The sending-or-not-sending TF-QKD (SNS-TF-QKD) protocol [10] can tolerate large misalignment errors and provide better performance in long distance [10,21]. The phase-matching QKD (PM-QKD) protocol [8] has no phase locking with phase slices and employs a phase post-compensation technique, so it can be easily experimentally implemented without pre-phase feedback [13,21].

In reality, the decoy state method is adopted to ensure the security of imperfect single photon source [22–25] in the actual QKD system. An important theoretical premise and assumption of the method is that the global phase of coherent sources should be continuously randomized [26–28]. However, perfect phase randomization is very difficult to achieve. In an actual experiment, there are two means to randomize the global phase. One means is to turn the laser on and off by controlling the current, but it is not suitable for PM-QKD with the phase post-compensation technique—the reason for this is that we do not know the precise phase slices. Moreover, experiments show that residual phase correlations may exist between adjacent pulses [29]. The other one is to actively modulate the phase of coherent sources controlled by a phase modulator with a true random number generator; this method is suitable for PM-QKD, but the phase randomization is not continuous. Thus, neither of these two means satisfy the assumption of the decoy state method, which may introduce a potential loophole that threatens the security of the actual protocol [30]. Then, the unambiguous state discrimination (USD) measurement [31] and the photon-number-splitting (PNS) attack [32] can be used against the imperfect phase randomization.

An earlier security analysis of discrete phase randomization appears in the decoy state Bennet-Brassard-1984 (BB84) in Reference [33], which points out, when the number of discrete phase values is larger, that the performance of discrete phase randomization is close to that of continuous phase randomization, and the number is said to be ten [33]. Similar security analysis methods are used for several other protocols, the measurement-device-independent (MDI) QKD in Reference [34], the NPP-TF-QKD in References [35,36], the SNS-TF-QKD in Reference [37], the PM-QKD in Reference [38]. Therein, Reference [38] uses a different security poof method with Reference [8], and there is no in-depth formula derivation in the decoy state PM-QKD with discrete phase randomization. In this paper, we focus on these discrete global phase randomization issues in the PM-QKD protocol [39], study a concrete attack against PM-QKD with imperfect phase randomization, apply the decoy-state method to derive the single photon yield formula to exhibit performance of the key rate and compare the yield difference of continuous phase randomization with discrete phase randomization.

The paper is arranged as follows: in Section 2, we review the PM-QKD protocol in detail, based on the security analysis of symmetric-encoding PM-QKD, we estimate the overall phase error rate. In Section 3, we show a concrete attack against PM-QKD with imperfect phase randomization. In Section 4, we show how to apply the decoy-state method to obtain the upper bound of the phase-flip error rate with discrete phase randomization; moreover, the yield difference between continuous and discrete phase randomization is also studied in this section. The numerical simulation results are shown in Section 5, and then we conclude in Section 6.

2. The Protocol of PM-QKD

We employ the attenuated laser as a single photon source, which is regarded as the coherent state. When the coherent state is randomized by continuous phase, it is equivalent to the Fock state, with the photon number distribution as

$$P_{j|\alpha} = e^{-\alpha}\frac{\alpha^j}{j!} \quad (1)$$

In this section, we review the PM-QKD protocol, and without considering the security effects of discrete phase randomization, Equation (1) is used for formula derivation.

2.1. Protocol Description

The implementation process of the PM-QKD is similar to Reference [39].

- State preparation. In each round, the coherent state $\left|\sqrt{\alpha_A}e^{i(\pi\kappa_A+\frac{2\pi}{D}d_A)}\right\rangle$ is prepared by Alice, the intensity $\alpha_A \in \{\mu_A, \nu_A, \omega_A\}$, where μ_A is she signal state, ν_A is the decoy state, ω_A is the vacuum state, the random key bit $\kappa_A \in \{0,1\}$, the discrete phase randomization number d_A is randomly chosen from $\{0, 1, \cdots, D-1\}$, D is the number of maximum discrete phase that is modulated by Alice, for simplicity, assume

D is an even number. Similarly, Bob prepares the coherent state $\left|\sqrt{\alpha_B}e^{i(\pi\kappa_B+\frac{2\pi}{D}d_B)}\right\rangle$, therein, $\alpha_A = \alpha_B = \frac{\alpha}{2} \in \{\frac{\mu}{2}, \frac{\nu}{2}, \frac{\omega}{2}\}$.

- Measurement. Alice and Bob send their quantum states to Charlie with transmittances η_A and η_B, Charlie performs an interference measurement with a beam splitter and records which detector (L or R) clicks.
- Announcement. The detection result is announced by Charlie for each round; the intensity settings α_A, α_B and phase numbers d_A, d_B are also announced by Alice and Bob.
- Sifting. After that, the phase post-compensation method is used by Charlie to calculate and then Charlie announces the phase match pairs. Assume the phase compensation $d_\delta \in \{0, 1, \cdots D/2 - 1\}$, only one of the two detectors clicks is the successful detection. If the left detector clicks and $|d_A - d_B - d_\delta|$ mod $D = 0$, Alice and Bob keep κ_A and κ_B as the raw key. If the right detector clicks and $|d_A - d_B - d_\delta|$ mod $D = D/2$, Bob flips his key bit κ_B. If $|d_A - d_B - d_\delta|$ mod $D \neq 0, D/2$, for simplicity, we discard the phase mismatch pairs.
- Parameter estimation. Alice and Bob estimate the information leakage from the raw data that they have kept.
- Key generation. After reconciling the corresponding key string to perform error correction, Alice and Bob use privacy amplification to produce the final keys.

2.2. Phase Error Estimation

The security analysis of asymptotic case is considered, so there are no statistical fluctuations. The analysis method of the phase error rate that we use comes from [39], which is an important new viewpoint of QKD security, establishing the relationship between the symmetric encoding and privacy with the standard phase-error-correction approach [40], and we summarize briefly as follows.

If the joint state ρ_{AB} is a pure of even or odd state, the symmetric encoding PM-QKD protocol is perfectly private, the phase error rate $E_{ph} = 0$, if the joint state ρ_{AB} is a mixture of even and odd state, $\rho_{AB} = P_{odd}\rho_{odd} + P_{even}\rho_{even}$, the phase error rate $E_{ph} \neq 0$, the effective detection ratios of odd and even components of signal state are estimated by [39]

$$q_{odd|\mu} = P_{odd|\mu}\frac{Y_{odd|\mu}}{Q_\mu}$$
$$q_{even|\mu} = P_{even|\mu}\frac{Y_{even|\mu}}{Q_\mu} \tag{2}$$

where $Q_\mu = P_{odd|\mu}Y_{odd|\mu} + P_{even|\mu}Y_{even|\mu}$ is the total gain of mixture signal state ρ_{AB}. $Y_{odd|\mu}$ and $Y_{even|\mu}$ are the yield of odd signal state ρ_{odd} and even signal state ρ_{even}, respectively. $P_{odd|\mu}$ and $P_{odd|\mu}$ are the signal state probability of odd and even photon numbers.

The overall phase error rate comes from the even components, which is estimated by [39]

$$E_{ph} = P_{even|\mu}\frac{Y_{even|\mu}}{Q_\mu} \tag{3}$$

where $P_{even|\mu}$ is given by the above section, Q_μ is given by the experiment results, the important task is to estimate the parameter $Y_{even|\mu}$.

For simplicity, we use phase match pairs and discard phase mismatch pairs, so the upper bound of phase error rate comes from the signal state bounded by

$$E_{ph} \leq 1 - q_{1|\mu} \tag{4}$$

where $q_{1|\mu} = P_{1|\mu}\frac{Y_{1|\mu}}{Q_\mu}$.

According to the above discussion, we get the final secure key rate by

$$R_f = \frac{2}{D} Q_\mu [1 - H_2(E_{ph}) - f H_2(E_\mu)] \tag{5}$$

where Q_μ is the total gain of the signal state, E_{ph} is the phase error rate of the signal state, E_μ is the bit error rate of the signal state, f is the error correction efficiency, $H_2(x) = -x\log_2(x) - (1-x)\log_2(1-x)$ is the binary entropy function.

3. Attack PM-QKD with Imperfect Phase Randomization

Considering the extreme case that Eve knows, the exact phases of the signal and decoy states without phase randomization, the PM-QKD protocol will have a serious security loophole. Due to the signal state and the decoy state not being orthogonal, Eve can use USD measurement to distinguish the signal state and the decoy state with the probability $q < 1$. The optimal success probability [41] of USD measurement on each side is $q_{opt} = 1 - e^{-|\sqrt{\mu} - \sqrt{v}|^2/4}$, which is obtained by performing positive operator valued measurement. After performing USD measurement, Eve measures the number of photons in the pulse and performs a PNS attack.

For the sake of simplicity, we neglect the dark count and the misalignment error, and only consider the channel loss. Without attacking, the gains of the signal state and decoy state are

$$Q_\mu = 1 - e^{-\eta\mu}$$
$$Q_v = 1 - e^{-\eta v} \tag{6}$$

where η is the channel loss.

Under the PNS attack, the gains of the signal state and decoy state are

$$Q_\mu^{attack} = \sum_{j=1}^{\infty} q_{opt}^2 Z_j^\mu e^{-\mu} \frac{\mu^j}{j!}$$
$$Q_v^{attack} = \sum_{j=1}^{\infty} q_{opt}^2 Z_j^v e^{-v} \frac{v^j}{j!} \tag{7}$$

where Z_j^μ and Z_j^v represent the probability that Eve forwards j photons to the signal state and the decoy state, with j as the sum of the photons on both sides.

The simplified upper key rate under the PNS attack is bounded by

$$R^u = R_{PNS} = \sum_{j=1}^{\infty} q_{opt}^2 Z_j^\mu e^{-\mu} \frac{\mu^j}{j!} [1 - H_2(E_{ph})] \tag{8}$$

The lower key rate of the simplified Equation (5) is bounded by

$$R_{PM}^l = R_{PM} = Q_\mu [1 - H_2(E_{ph})] \tag{9}$$

Combining the USD measurement with PNS attack, the security of final key rate without the phase randomized system is vulnerable. We can optimize Z_j^μ to let $R_{PM}^l > R^u$, especially for long distance communication, due to channel loss is large enough, we can block single photon and release multiple photons. Then, the key rate will be higher than the secure key rate, and information will leak out. Hence, Eve's goal is to minimize R^u.

It is worth noting that the attack scheme of USD measurement and PNS attack, which requires the quantum non-demolition measurement [42] about the photon numbers, the lossless channel and the ability of controlling detector efficiency, all of these are beyond the current technology. Ma adopts the beam splitting (BS) attack [43] in Reference [8]. We briefly present his results as follows.

Ma [8] points out, under the BS attack, that the probability of successfully distinguishing the states is $P_{\text{suc}} = 1 - e^{-(1-\eta)\mu}$. The simplified key rate of PM-QKD is lower bounded by

$$R_{\text{BS}}^l = Q_\mu e^{-2(1-\eta)\mu} \tag{10}$$

Ma [8] supposes that the photon number channel model exists in PM-QKD, then Gottesman–Lo–Lutkenhaus–Preskill (GLLP) [26] analysis can be used to obtain the formula

$$R_{\text{GLLP}} = Q_{1|\mu}[1 - H_2(E_{1|\mu}^{ph})] - Q_\mu f H_2(E_\mu) \tag{11}$$

where $Q_{1|\mu}$ is the gain of the single photon signal state, $E_{1|\mu}^{ph}$ is the phase error rate.

Due to the yield being $Y_j = 1 - (1-\eta)^j$, the simplified GLLP key rate is lower bounded by

$$R_{\text{GLLP}}^l = R_{\text{GLLP}} = Q_{1|\mu} = \eta\mu e^{-\mu} \tag{12}$$

Final results show that, when η is smaller than a certain value, the GLLP formula cannot hold under the BS attack, so the photon number channel model is invalid. Fortunately, the PM formula can defend against BS attack; the precondition is that the intensity must be weaker.

4. The PM-QKD with Discrete Phase Modulation of Coherent State Sources

In this section, we introduce the security analysis of discrete phase randomized PM-QKD. Then, we apply the decoy-state method to derive the single photon yield formula. Finally, we compare the yield difference between continuous phase randomization and discrete phase randomization.

4.1. Coherent State with Discrete Phase Randomization

For the coherent state with discrete phase randomization, the joint state of Alice and Bob of PM-QKD is as follows

$$|\psi\rangle_{AB} = \sum_{d_A=0}^{D-1} \left|\sqrt{\alpha_A}e^{i(\pi\kappa_A + \frac{2\pi}{D}d_A)}\right\rangle_A \left|\sqrt{\alpha_B}e^{i(\pi\kappa_B + \frac{2\pi}{D}d_B)}\right\rangle_B \tag{13}$$

where $\kappa_A, \kappa_B \in \{0,1\}$, $|d_A - d_B - d_\delta| \mod D = 0$ or $|d_A - d_B - d_\delta| \mod D = D/2$.

Considering the simple case, $d_\delta = 0$, then $|d_A - d_B| = 0$ or $|d_A - d_B| = D/2$. Now, the density matrix can be written as

$$\begin{aligned}\rho_{AB}^D &= \frac{1}{D}\sum_{d_A=0}^{D-1} \left|\sqrt{\alpha_A}e^{i(\pi\kappa_A + \frac{2\pi}{D}d_A)}\right\rangle_A \left\langle\sqrt{\alpha_A}e^{-i(\pi\kappa_A + \frac{2\pi}{D}d_A)}\right| \\ &\otimes \left|\sqrt{\alpha_B}e^{i(\pi\kappa_B + \frac{2\pi}{D}d_B)}\right\rangle_B \left\langle\sqrt{\alpha_B}e^{-i(\pi\kappa_B + \frac{2\pi}{D}d_B)}\right| \\ &= \sum_{j=0}^{D-1} P_{j|\alpha}^D \left|\lambda_{j|\alpha}^D\right\rangle_{AB}\left\langle\lambda_{j|\alpha}^D\right|\end{aligned} \tag{14}$$

where $P_{j|\alpha}^D = \sum_{l=0}^{\infty} \frac{e^{-\alpha}\alpha^{lD+j}}{(lD+j)!}$, $\left|\lambda_{j|\alpha}^D\right\rangle_{AB} = \frac{e^{-\alpha/2}}{\sqrt{P_{j|\alpha}^D}}\sum_{l=0}^{\infty}\frac{(\sqrt{\alpha})^{lD+j}}{\sqrt{(lD+j)!}}|lD+j\rangle_{AB}$, with $|lD+j\rangle_{AB} = \frac{1}{\sqrt{2^{lD+j}(lD+j)}}(a^\dagger \pm b^\dagger)^{lD+j}|00\rangle_{AB}$.

In our security analysis with discrete phase randomization, we modify the final secure key rate Equation (5) to

$$R_f = \frac{2}{D} Q_\mu [1 - H_2(E_{ph}^D) - f H_2(E_\mu)] \tag{15}$$

where the upper bound of phase error rate E_{ph}^D comes from the signal state bounded by $E_{ph}^D \leq 1 - q_{1|\mu}^D$, with $q_{1|\mu}^D = P_{1|\mu}^D \frac{Y_{1|\mu}^D}{Q_\mu}$. The bit error rate E_μ and the gain Q_μ remain the same.

4.2. The Decoy-State Method

In discrete phase randomized PM-QKD, we estimate the yield $Y_{1|\mu}^D$ of the single-photon signal state. We use the vacuum and one decoy state, which is similar to the BB84 decoy state analysis [24].

We know that, in the security proof of the decoy state method with continuous phase randomization, there is an important assumption

$$Y_{j|signal} = Y_{j|decoy} \tag{16}$$

However, it is not strict in the condition of discrete phase randomization, $Y_{j|signal}^D \neq Y_{j|decoy}^D$; the reason lies in

$$\left| \lambda_{j|\mu}^D \right\rangle \neq \left| \lambda_{j|v}^D \right\rangle \tag{17}$$

Consider the properties of trace distance; we need to estimate the difference of yields for different intensities as [33]

$$\left| Y_{j|\mu}^D - Y_{j|v}^D \right| = \sqrt{1 - (F_{j|\mu v}^D)^2} \tag{18}$$

where $F_{j|\mu v}^D = \sum_{l=0}^{\infty} \frac{(\mu v)^{(lD+j)/2}}{(lD+j)!} / \sqrt{\sum_{l=0}^{\infty} \frac{\mu^{lD+j}}{(lD+j)!} \sum_{l=0}^{\infty} \frac{v^{lD+j}}{(lD+j)!}}$, that is the fidelity of $\left| \lambda_{j|\mu}^D \right\rangle$ and $\left| \lambda_{j|v}^D \right\rangle$.

The estimation of the yield $Y_{1|\mu}^D$ is similar to continuous phase randomization. The equation can be written as

$$\begin{aligned} Q_\mu &= \sum_{j=0}^{D-1} P_{j|\mu}^D Y_{j|\mu}^D \\ Q_v &= \sum_{j=0}^{D-1} P_{j|v}^D Y_{j|v}^D = \sum_{j=0}^{N-1} P_{j|v}^D Y_{j|\mu}^D + \sum_{j=0}^{D-1} P_{j|v}^D (Y_{j|v}^D - Y_{j|\mu}^D) \end{aligned} \tag{19}$$

We have

$$\begin{aligned} Y_{1|\mu}^D = &[P_{2|\mu}^D Q_v - P_{2|v}^D Q_\mu - (P_{2|\mu}^D P_{0|v}^D - P_{0|\mu}^D P_{2|v}^D) Y_{0|\mu}^D \\ &- P_{2|\mu}^D \sum_{j=0}^{D-1} P_{j|v}^D (Y_{j|v}^D - Y_{j|\mu}^D) - \sum_{j \geq 3}^{\infty} (P_{2|\mu}^D P_{j|v}^D - P_{j|\mu}^D P_{2|v}^D) Y_{j|\mu}^D] \\ &/ (P_{2|\mu}^D P_{1|v}^D - P_{1|\mu}^D P_{2|v}^D) \end{aligned} \tag{20}$$

with $\sum_{j \geq 3}^{\infty} (P_{2|\mu}^D P_{j|v}^D - P_{j|\mu}^D P_{2|v}^D) Y_{j|\mu}^D \leq 0$, $Y_{0|\mu}^D \leq Q_\omega / P_{0|\omega}^D + \sqrt{1 - (F_{0|\mu\omega}^D)^2}$ and $\sum_{j=0}^{D-1} P_{j|v}^D (Y_{j|v}^D - Y_{j|\mu}^D) = \sum_{j=0}^{D-1} P_{j|\mu}^D \sqrt{1 - F_{j|\mu v}^D{}^2}$.

Then

$$Y_{1|\mu}^D \geq \frac{P_{2|\mu}^D Q_v - P_{2|v}^D Q_\mu - (P_{2|\mu}^D P_{0|v}^D - P_{0|\mu}^D P_{2|v}^D)Y_{0|\mu}^D - P_{2|\mu}^D \sum_{j=0}^{D-1} P_{j|\mu}^D \sqrt{1 - F_{j|\mu v}^D{}^2}}{P_{2|\mu}^D P_{1|v}^D - P_{1|\mu}^D P_{2|v}^D} \quad (21)$$

4.3. The Yield Difference between Continuous and Discrete Phase Randomization

To compare the yield difference of continuous phase randomization and discrete phase randomization, the density matrix of the continuous phase randomization can be written as

$$\rho_{AB} = \frac{1}{2\pi} \int_0^{2\pi} \left|\sqrt{\alpha_A} e^{i(\pi \kappa_A + \varphi_A)}\right\rangle_A \left\langle\sqrt{\alpha_A} e^{-i(\pi \kappa_A + \varphi_A)}\right|$$
$$\otimes \left|\sqrt{\alpha_B} e^{i(\pi \kappa_B + \varphi_B)}\right\rangle_B \left\langle\sqrt{\alpha_B} e^{-i(\pi \kappa_B + \varphi_B)}\right| \quad (22)$$
$$= \sum_{j=0}^{\infty} P_{j|\alpha} |j\rangle_{AB}\langle j|$$

where the general Poisson distribution $P_{j|\alpha}$ is given by Equation (1), with $|j\rangle_{AB} = \frac{1}{\sqrt{2^j j!}} (a^\dagger \pm b^\dagger)^j |00\rangle_{AB}$.

In the ideal case, $D \to \infty$, the fidelity $F_{j|\alpha}^{C,D}$ between $|j\rangle_{AB}$ and $\left|\lambda_{j|\alpha}^D\right\rangle_{AB}$ should be the same. In the security analysis, the fidelity $F_{j|\alpha}^{C,D}$ between $|j\rangle_{AB}$ and $\left|\lambda_{j|\alpha}^D\right\rangle_{AB}$ is bounded by

$$F_{j|\alpha}^{C,D} = F\left(|j\rangle_{AB}, \left|\lambda_{j|\alpha}^D\right\rangle_{AB}\right) = \frac{\left|\langle j | \lambda_{j|\alpha}^D\rangle_{AB}\right|}{\sqrt{\langle j | j\rangle_{AB} \langle \lambda_{j|\alpha}^D | \lambda_{j|\alpha}^D\rangle_{AB}}}$$
$$= 1 / \frac{e^{-\alpha/2}}{\sqrt{P_{j|\alpha}^D}} \sum_{l=0}^{\infty} \frac{(\sqrt{\alpha})^{lD+j}}{\sqrt{(lD+j)!}} \quad (23)$$

which is related to the intensity α, photon number j and discrete phase numbers D. Therefore, the yield difference is bounded by

$$\left|Y_{j|\alpha} - Y_{j|\alpha}^D\right| \leq \sqrt{1 - F_{j|\alpha}^{C,D}} = \sqrt{1 - 1 / \frac{e^{-\alpha/2}}{\sqrt{P_{j|\alpha}^D}} \sum_{l=0}^{\infty} \frac{(\sqrt{\alpha})^{lD+j}}{\sqrt{(lD+j)!}}} \quad (24)$$

5. Numerical Results

Let's suppose the transmittances between Alice/Bob and Charlie are $\eta_A = \eta_B = \eta_f$, the detection efficiency of detectors is η_d, after the channel and detection losses, $\eta = \eta_f \eta_d$, the detection click probabilities are given by

$$P_\alpha(\bar{L}) = (1 - p_d) e^{-\eta \alpha \cos^2 \frac{\phi_{AB}}{2}}$$
$$P_\alpha(L) = 1 - P_\alpha(\bar{L})$$
$$P_\alpha(\bar{R}) = (1 - p_d) e^{-\eta \alpha \sin^2 \frac{\phi_{AB}}{2}} \quad (25)$$
$$P_\alpha(R) = 1 - P_\alpha(\bar{R})$$

where $P_\alpha(L)/P_\alpha(R)$ and $P_\alpha(\bar{L})/P_\alpha(\bar{R})$ are the detection click probabilities of the L/R click and no L/R click, ϕ_{AB} is the phase mismatch between Alice and Bob.

Due to the discrete phase randomization, we can obtain D phase slices. Although we keep the phase match pairs and discard all of the others, there is still an intrinsic bit error rate [4], $E_D = \frac{D}{2\pi} \int_0^{2\pi/D} \sin^2 \frac{\phi_{AB}}{2} d\phi_{AB}$. Significantly, this is very different from BB84 protocol with the global phase mismatch value $\phi_{AB} = 0$. When we use discrete phase randomization, we must consider the intrinsic bit error rate, which will deeply affect the bit error rate and phase error rate.

The error gain can be given by

$$Q_\alpha^E = \frac{D}{2\pi} \int_0^{\frac{2\pi}{D}} P_\alpha(R) P_\alpha(\bar{L}) d\phi_{AB}$$
$$= \frac{D}{2\pi} \int_0^{\frac{2\pi}{D}} (1-p_d) e^{-\eta\alpha \cos^2 \frac{\phi_{AB}}{2}} d\phi_{AB} - (1-p_d)^2 e^{-\eta\alpha} \qquad (26)$$

We can derive the total gain Q_α as

$$Q_\alpha = \frac{D}{2\pi} \int_0^{\frac{2\pi}{D}} [P_\alpha(L) P_\alpha(\bar{R}) + P_\alpha(R) P_\alpha(\bar{L})] d\phi_{AB}$$
$$= \frac{D}{2\pi} \int_0^{\frac{2\pi}{D}} (1-p_d) e^{-\eta\alpha \sin^2 \frac{\phi_{AB}}{2}} d\phi_{AB} - (1-p_d)^2 e^{-\eta\alpha} + Q_\alpha^E \qquad (27)$$

The bit error rate of signal states is given by

$$E_\mu = \frac{Q_\mu^E (1 - 2e_{opt}) + e_{opt} Q_\mu}{Q_\mu} \qquad (28)$$

The simulate parameters are listed in Table 1.

Table 1. List of parameters used in numerical simulations. Here p_d is the dark counts rate; e_{opt} is the misalignment error probability of the system; η_d is the detection efficiency; f is the error correction efficiency; η_f is the transmission fiber loss coefficient (dB/km).

p_d	e_{opt}	η_d	f	η_f
1×10^{-8}	1.5%	0.2	1.1	0.2

In the key rate versus the transmission distance of the finite decoy states PM protocol with a different number of phase values, as shown in Figure 1, the PLOB bound is plotted for comparison. The smaller D, the lower the key rate; the reason is that the smaller the D, the larger the intrinsic bit error rate. $D = 8$ can break the PLOB bound, and meanwhile, we can find that there is an optimal $D = 10$, which can guarantee better performance. With the increase of D, the key rate will become lower due to the sifting factor $2/D$. Hence, in an actual experiment of PM-QKD, we must find the suitable discrete phases value to guarantee security and performance. When $D \to \infty$, the key rate will tend to 0; we do not present it here.

Moreover, we compare the performance of PM-QKD with discrete phase randomization between infinite decoy states and vacuum and one decoy state. As depicted in Figure 2, when we adopt vacuum and one decoy state and small D, the key rate exhibits poor performance. As D increases, the key rate of adopting vacuum and one decoy state approaches infinite decoy states. Combining the conclusion of Figure 1, we find that the discrete phase $D = 10$ still maintains good security and performance when the finite decoy states are implemented.

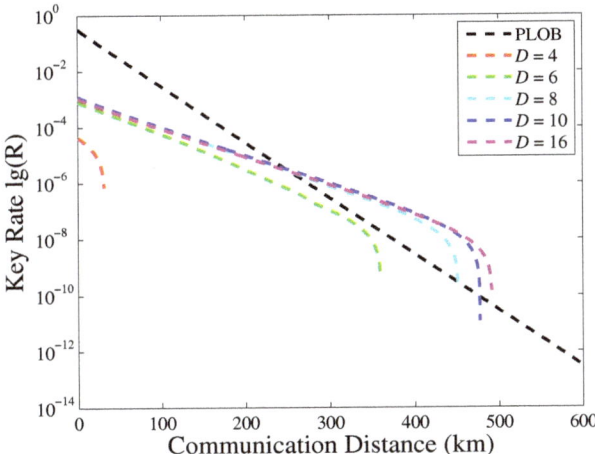

Figure 1. The key rate versus the transmission distance of the PM-QKD with different number of discrete phase values; the PLOB linear bound is plotted for comparison.

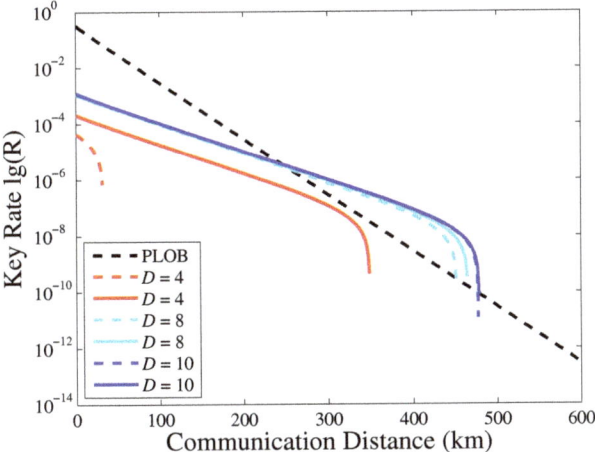

Figure 2. The key rate versus the transmission distance of the PM-QKD with different number of discrete phase values, infinite decoy states and vacuum and one decoy state are plotted for comparison. The dash line represents the case of vacuum and one decoy state; the solid line represents the case of infinite decoy states.

Due to there being a sifting factor $2/D$, we know that when $D \to \infty$, the key rate will tend to 0. In order to compare the key rate between continuous phase randomization and discrete phase randomization, we first compare the fidelity between $|j\rangle_{AB}$ and $\left|\lambda_{j|\alpha}^{D}\right\rangle_{AB}$, as shown in Figure 3a. The fidelity varies slightly with the intensity. With the increase of D, the fidelity gradually approaches 1. Therefore, when D is too small, the method of continuous phase randomization is not suitable; we cannot ignore the safety effect of discrete phase randomization.

Then, considering finite decoy states, the key rate between continuous phase randomization and discrete phase randomization has been studied in Figure 3b. As D increases, the performance of a key rate between discrete phase randomization and continuous phase randomization is almost the same. This is consistent with the conclusion in Figure 3a.

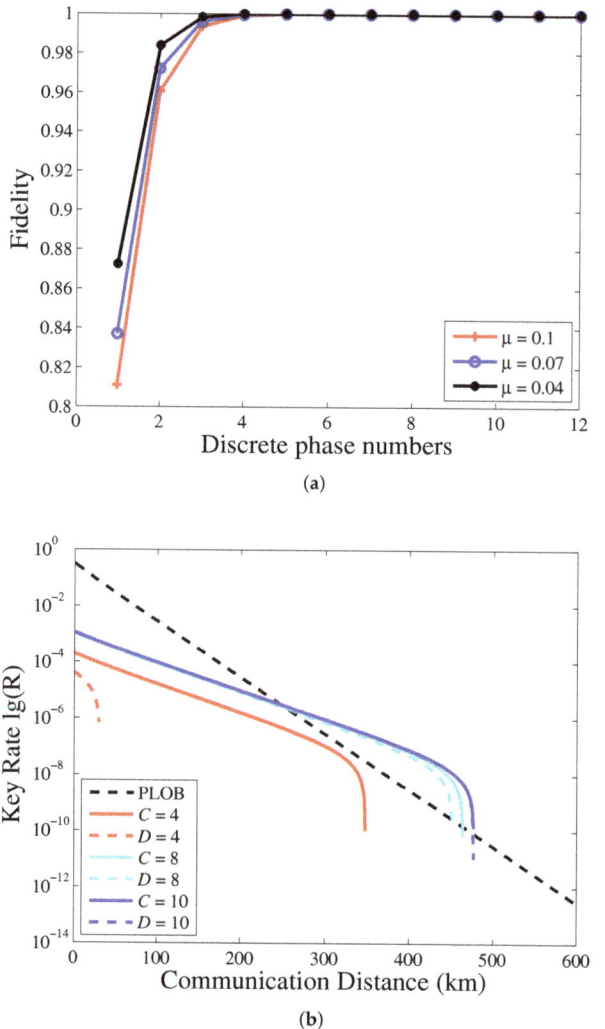

Figure 3. (a) The fidelity of different mean photon numbers. The fidelity refers to Equation (23), which we take $j = 1$. (b) The key rate versus the transmission distance of the PM-QKD with a different number of discrete phase values. The solid line represents the coherent state with continuous phase randomization; the dash line represents the coherent state with discrete phase randomization.

6. Conclusions

In this paper, we introduce the USD measurement and PNS attack against PM-QKD with imperfect phase randomization, and simultaneously, we deeply study the security of discrete phase randomization PM-QKD protocol with a decoy state in the asymptotic case. Our simulation results show that, as D increases, the key rate of adopting vacuum and one decoy state approaches infinite decoy states, and furthermore, the performance of key rate between discrete phase randomization and continuous phase randomization is almost the same. We also find that due to the intrinsic bit error rate and sifting factor, there is an optimal discrete phase randomization value to guarantee security and performance. Therefore, for the actual PM-QKD system, we should better adopt the suitable discrete phase randomization value to apply.

Author Contributions: X.Z. carried out numerical simulation and wrote the paper; Y.W. and W.B. assisted in discussing the research topic; M.J. contributed to attack; X.Z. and Y.L. derived the formulas; H.L. and C.Z. discussed the PM-QKD protocol. All authors participated in revising and all authors have read and agreed to the published version of the manuscript.

Funding: This work is sponsored by National Key Research and Development Program of China (Grant No. 2020YFA0309702), National Natural Science Foundation of China (Grants No. 61605248, No. 61675235 and No. 61505261) and Natural Science Foundation of Henan (Grant No. 202300410534 and No. 202300410532).

Institutional Review Board Statement: Not applicable.

Informed Consent Statement: Not applicable.

Data Availability Statement: The data presented in this study are available within the article.

Conflicts of Interest: The authors declare no conflict of interest.

References

1. Bennett, C.H.; Brassard, G. Quantum Cryptography: Public Key Distribution and Coin Tossing. In Proceedings of the IEEE International Conference on Computers, Systems and Signal Processing, Bangalore, India, 10–12 December 1984; pp. 175–179.
2. Pirandola, S.; Laurenza, R.; Ottaviani, C.; Banchi, L. Fundamental limits of repeaterless quantum communications. *Nat. Commun.* **2017**, *8*, 15043. [CrossRef]
3. Takeoka, M.; Guha, S.; Wilde, M.M. Fundamental rate-loss tradeoff for optical quantum key distribution. *Nat. Commun.* **2014**, *5*, 5235. [CrossRef] [PubMed]
4. Lucamarini, M.; Yuan, Z.L.; Dynes, J.F.; Shields, A.J. Overcoming the rate–distance limit of quantum key distribution without quantum repeaters. *Nature* **2018**, *557*, 400–403. [CrossRef] [PubMed]
5. Cui, C.; Yin, Z.Q.; Wang, R.; Chen, W.; Wang, S.; Guo, G.C.; Han, Z.F. Twin-Field Quantum Key Distribution without Phase Postselection. *Phys. Rev. Appl.* **2019**, *11*, 034053. [CrossRef]
6. Curty, M.; Azuma, K.; Lo, H.K. Simple security proof of twin-field type quantum key distribution protocol. *NPJ Quantum Inf.* **2019**, *5*, 64. [CrossRef]
7. Lin, J.; Lütkenhaus, N. Simple security analysis of phase-matching measurement-device-independent quantum key distribution. *Phys. Rev. A* **2018**, *98*, 042332. [CrossRef]
8. Ma, X.; Zeng, P.; Zhou, H. Phase-Matching Quantum Key Distribution. *Phys. Rev. X* **2018**, *8*, 031043. [CrossRef]
9. Tamaki, K.; Lo, H.K.; Wang, W.; Lucamarini, M. Information theoretic security of quantum key distribution overcoming the repeaterless secret key capacity bound. *arXiv* **2018**, arXiv:1805.05511v3.
10. Wang, X.B.; Yu, Z.W.; Hu, X.L. Twin-field quantum key distribution with large misalignment error. *Phys. Rev. A* **2018**, *98*, 062323. [CrossRef]
11. Clivati, C.; Meda, A.; Donadello, S.; Virzì, S.; Genovese, M.; Levi, F.; Mura, A.; Pittaluga, M.; Yuan, Z.L.; Shields, A.J.; et al. Coherent phase transfer for real-world twin-field quantum key distribution. *arXiv* **2020**, arXiv:2012.15199v1.
12. Chen, J.P.; Zhang, C.; Liu, Y.; Jiang, C.; Zhang, W.; Hu, X.L.; Guan, J.Y.; Yu, Z.W.; Xu, H.; Lin, J.; et al. Sending-or-Not-Sending with Independent Lasers: Secure Twin-Field Quantum Key Distribution over 509 km. *Phys. Rev. Lett.* **2020**, *124*, 070501. [CrossRef] [PubMed]
13. Fang, X.T.; Zeng, P.; Liu, H.; Zou, M.; Wu, W.; Tang, Y.L.; Sheng, Y.J.; Xiang, Y.; Zhang, W.; Li, H.; et al. Implementation of quantum key distribution surpassing the linear rate-transmittance bound. *Nat. Photonics* **2020**, *14*, 422–425. [CrossRef]
14. Liu, H.; Jiang, C.; Zhu, H.T.; Zou, M.; Yu, Z.W.; Hu, X.L.; Xu, H.; Ma, S.; Han, Z.; Chen, J.P.; et al. Field Test of Twin-Field Quantum Key Distribution through Sending-or-Not-Sending over 428 km. *arXiv* **2021**, arXiv:2101.00276v1.
15. Chen, J.P.; Zhang, C.; Liu, Y.; Jiang, C.; Zhang, W.; Han, Z.Y.; Ma, S.Z.; Hu, X.L.; Li, Y.H.; Liu, H.; et al. Twin-Field Quantum Key Distribution over 511 km Optical Fiber Linking two Distant Metropolitans. *Res. Sq.* **2021**. [CrossRef]
16. Liu, Y.; Yu, Z.W.; Zhang, W.; Guan, J.Y.; Chen, J.P.; Zhang, C.; Hu, X.L.; Li, H.; Jiang, C.; Lin, J.; et al. Experimental Twin-Field Quantum Key Distribution through Sending or Not Sending. *Phys. Rev. Lett.* **2019**, *123*, 100505. [CrossRef]
17. Minder, M.; Pittaluga, M.; Roberts, G.L.; Lucamarini, M.; Dynes, J.F.; Yuan, Z.L.; Shields, A.J. Experimental quantum key distribution beyond the repeaterless secret key capacity. *Nat. Photonics* **2019**, *13*, 334–338. [CrossRef]
18. Wang, S.; He, D.Y.; Yin, Z.Q.; Lu, F.Y.; Cui, C.H.; Chen, W.; Zhou, Z.; Guo, G.C.; Han, Z.F. Beating the Fundamental Rate-Distance Limit in a Proof-of-Principle Quantum Key Distribution System. *Phys. Rev. X* **2019**, *9*, 021046. [CrossRef]
19. Zhong, X.; Hu, J.; Curty, M.; Qian, L.; Lo, H.K. Proof-of-Principle Experimental Demonstration of Twin-Field Type Quantum Key Distribution. *Phys. Rev. Lett.* **2019**, *123*, 100506. [CrossRef]

20. Zhong, X.; Wang, W.; Qian, L.; Lo, H.K. Proof-of-principle experimental demonstration of twin-field quantum key distribution over optical channels with asymmetric losses. *NPJ Quantum Inf.* **2021**, *7*, 8. [CrossRef]
21. Mao, Y.; Zeng, P.; Chen, T. Recent Advances on Quantum Key Distribution Overcoming the Linear Secret Key Capacity Bound. *Adv. Quantum Technol.* **2021**, *4*, 2000084. [CrossRef]
22. Hwang, W.Y. Quantum key distribution with high loss: Toward global secure communication. *Phys. Rev. Lett.* **2003**, *91*, 057901. [CrossRef] [PubMed]
23. Lo, H.K.; Ma, X.; Chen, K. Decoy state quantum key distribution. *Phys. Rev. Lett.* **2005**, *94*, 230504. [CrossRef] [PubMed]
24. Ma, X.; Qi, B.; Zhao, Y.; Lo, H.K. Practical decoy state for quantum key distribution. *Phys. Rev. A* **2005**, *72*, 1–127. [CrossRef]
25. Wang, X.B. Beating the photon-number-splitting attack in practical quantum cryptography. *Phys. Rev. Lett.* **2005**, *94*, 230503. [CrossRef] [PubMed]
26. Gottesman, D.; Hoi-Kwong, L.; Lutkenhaus, N.; Preskill, J. Security of quantum key distribution with imperfect devices. *Quantum Inf. Comput.* **2004**, *4*, 325–360. [CrossRef]
27. van Enk, S.J.; Fuchs, C.A. Quantum State of an Ideal Propagating Laser Field. *Phys. Rev. Lett.* **2001**, *88*, 027902. [CrossRef] [PubMed]
28. Lo, H.K.; Preskill, J. Security of quantum key distribution using weak coherent states with nonrandom phases. *Quantum Inf. Comput.* **2006**, *7*, 431–458.
29. Xu, F.; Qi, B.; Ma, X.; Xu, H.; Zheng, H.; Lo, H.K. Ultrafast quantum random number generation based on quantum phase fluctuations. *Opt. Express* **2012**, *20*, 12366–12377. [CrossRef]
30. Inamori, H.; Lütkenhaus, N.; Mayers, D. Unconditional security of practical quantum key distribution. *Eur. Phys. J. D* **2007**, *41*, 599–627. [CrossRef]
31. Dušek, M.; Jahma, M.; Lütkenhaus, N. Unambiguous state discrimination in quantum cryptography with weak coherent states. *Phys. Rev. A* **2000**, *62*, 022306. [CrossRef]
32. Brassard, G.; Lütkenhaus, N.; Mor, T.; Sanders, B.C. Limitations on Practical Quantum Cryptography. *Phys. Rev. Lett.* **2000**, *85*, 1330–1333. [CrossRef]
33. Cao, Z.; Zhang, Z.; Lo, H.K.; Ma, X. Discrete-phase-randomized coherent state source and its application in quantum key distribution. *New J. Phys.* **2015**, *17*, 053014. [CrossRef]
34. Cao, Z. Discrete-phase-randomized measurement-device-independent quantum key distribution. *Phys. Rev. A* **2020**, *101*, 062325. [CrossRef]
35. Currás-Lorenzo, G.; Wooltorton, L.; Razavi, M. Twin-Field Quantum Key Distribution with Fully Discrete Phase Randomization. *Phys. Rev. Appl.* **2021**, *15*, 014016. [CrossRef]
36. Wang, R.; Yin, Z.Q.; Lu, F.Y.; Wang, S.; Chen, W.; Zhang, C.M.; Huang, W.; Xu, B.J.; Guo, G.C.; Han, Z.F. Optimized protocol for twin-field quantum key distribution. *Commun. Phys.* **2020**, *3*, 149. [CrossRef]
37. Jiang, C.; Yu, Z.W.; Hu, X.L.; Wang, X.B. Sending-or-not-sending twin-field quantum key distribution with discrete-phase-randomized weak coherent states. *Phys. Rev. Res.* **2020**, *2*, 043304. [CrossRef]
38. Zhang, C.M.; Xu, Y.W.; Wang, R.; Wang, Q. Twin-Field Quantum Key Distribution with Discrete-Phase-Randomized Sources. *Phys. Rev. Appl.* **2020**, *14*, 064070. [CrossRef]
39. Zeng, P.; Wu, W.; Ma, X. Symmetry-Protected Privacy: Beating the Rate-Distance Linear Bound Over a Noisy Channel. *Phys. Rev. Appl.* **2020**, *13*, 064013. [CrossRef]
40. Koashi, M. Simple security proof of quantum key distribution based on complementarity. *New J. Phys.* **2009**, *11*, 045018. [CrossRef]
41. Tang, Y.L.; Yin, H.L.; Ma, X.; Fung, C.H.F.; Liu, Y.; Yong, H.L.; Chen, T.Y.; Peng, C.Z.; Chen, Z.B.; Pan, J.W. Source attack of decoy-state quantum key distribution using phase information. *Phys. Rev. A* **2013**, *88*, 022308. [CrossRef]
42. Grangier, P.; Levenson, J.A.; Poizat, J.P. Quantum non-demolition measurements in optics. *Nature* **1998**, *396*, 537–542. [CrossRef]
43. Scarani, V.; Bechmann-Pasquinucci, H.; Cerf, N.J.; Dušek, M.; Lütkenhaus, N.; Peev, M. The security of practical quantum key distribution. *Rev. Mod. Phys.* **2009**, *81*, 1301–1350. [CrossRef]

Article

Nonclassical Attack on a Quantum Key Distribution System

Anton Pljonkin [1,*], Dmitry Petrov [1], Lilia Sabantina [2] and Kamila Dakhkilgova [3]

[1] Institute of Computer Technology and Information Security, Southern Federal University, 347900 Taganrog, Russia; dapetrov@sfedu.ru
[2] Junior Research Group Nanomaterials, Faculty of Engineering and Mathematics, Bielefeld University of Applied Sciences, 33619 Bielefeld, Germany; lilia.sabantina@fh-bielefeld.de
[3] Faculty of Information Technology, Chechen State University, 364024 Grozny, Chechen Republic, Russia; puma-i@mail.ru
* Correspondence: pljonkin@mail.ru; Tel.: +7-905-459-2158

Abstract: The article is focused on research of an attack on the quantum key distribution system and proposes a countermeasure method. Particularly noteworthy is that this is not a classic attack on a quantum protocol. We describe an attack on the process of calibration. Results of the research show that quantum key distribution systems have vulnerabilities not only in the protocols, but also in other vital system components. The described type of attack does not affect the cryptographic strength of the received keys and does not point to the vulnerability of the quantum key distribution protocol. We also propose a method for autocompensating optical communication system development, which protects synchronization from unauthorized access. The proposed method is based on the use of sync pulses attenuated to a photon level in the process of detecting a time interval with a signal. The paper presents the results of experimental studies that show the discrepancies between the theoretical and real parameters of the system. The obtained data allow the length of the quantum channel to be calculated with high accuracy.

Keywords: quantum key distribution; single-photon mode; synchronization; algorithm; detection probability; vulnerability

1. Introduction

This research was inspired by the works "Quantum man-in-the-middle attack on the calibration process of quantum key distribution" [1] and "Device calibration impacts security of quantum key distribution" [2], which describe attacks on the calibration system. In the beginning, it is necessary to clarify several important nuances about our research: the experiments were carried out with a two-pass quantum key distribution system (QKDS) Clavis[2]; we do not examine the security of the quantum BB84 protocol and do not claim that our attack is an attack on the BB84 protocol; and we do not test the strength of quantum keys and do not claim that the described attack affects the strength of the keys. These are important notes for understanding the aims of the paper. The quantum key distribution process and the synchronization process are different. There are many articles in the literature that describe these processes in detail. There are attacks on both quantum protocols and the synchronization process, but there is practically no literature describing attacks on the synchronization process. Our experiment was carried on the real Clavis[2] quantum key distribution system. These are two stations connected by a quantum channel-optical fiber. In real operating conditions, QKDS have many loopholes for an attacker. This is not about quantum cryptography protocols that are reasonably secure. We are referring to the technical imperfection of systems. The authors [1,2] discuss such imperfections and show that an attacker can use them for attacks. It is important to understand that the purpose of an attack on the QKDS may not only be the acquisition of a secret key. Implementation of a controlled interference can also be a target of an attacker. From the user's point of view, this looks like a technical failure of the system, and there are two options: the user understands that the failure was caused by an attacker, or the user does not detect the attacker. In this work, we will show experimentally how it is possible to interfere with the normal operation of the QKDS without revealing itself.

The basic principles of quantum cryptography are absolute theoretical secrecy of the transmitted data and the impossibility of unauthorized access to it. For cryptographic systems, the security issue is formulated as the problem of distributing the encryption key between legitimate users. Quantum cryptography systems solve the problem of generating and distributing the encryption key using methods that are based on the laws of quantum physics and are implemented in quantum key distribution systems. In the description of quantum key distribution systems, much attention is paid to the operation of quantum protocols. The main problem is the insufficient study of the synchronization process of quantum key distribution systems. This paper contains a general description of quantum cryptography principles. A two-way plug and play fiber-optic quantum key distribution system with phase coding of photon states in synchronization mode was examined. A quantum key distribution system was built on the basis of the scheme with automatic compensation of polarization mode distortions. Single-photon avalanche diodes were used as optical radiation detecting devices. The operation of such systems is impossible without the process of station coordination, i.e., synchronization of the transmitter and receiver separated in space. In the QKDS, synchronization consists of a high-precision determination of the length of the optical pulse propagation path and is based on the registration of the moment when the synchronizing pulse is received by photodetectors.

2. Experiment and Simulation

2.1. Signal Level in the QKD System

The most appropriate form of synchronization signal for the QKDS is a periodic sequence of optical pulses [3]. In this case, the time markers are the pulses themselves, and the measurement process consists of dividing the entire follow-up period into time intervals. The conversion of a photon to a primary electron is registered in each time interval. The results of live tests of a quantum cryptographic network based on the IDQuantique Clavis^2 3110 QKD system are described in [4–7], and it is shown that the synchronization process generates multiphoton pulses, and the photodetectors operate in linear mode. Using the constructed energy model of the current Clavis^2 3110 QKD system, we show that the synchronization mode does not involve algorithms for controlling the emission power. Figure 1 shows the dependence of the number of photons in the pulse on the length of the quantum channel. The quantum channel is a fiber-optic communication line connecting two stations of the QKD system. Dependencies demonstrate three synchronization modes and take into account the following complex losses: in the optical fiber at the junction points, and total losses in the encoding station (-47.7 dBm). The energy model of the QKD system describes the characteristics of the detection equipment. In the process of high-precision determination of the length of a quantum channel, pulses are sent from the transmitting station to the encoding station, where they are reflected from the Faraday mirror and follow back along the same optical path. The process is divided into three stages, for each of which the pulse power values correspond to $P1 = -48.3$ dBm, $P2 = -55.8$ dBm, and $P3 = -24.2$ dBm. The values of P1, P2, and P3 were obtained experimentally using Yokogawa AQ2202 equipment. The photon energy with the refraction index for the Corning®SMF-28e+ fiber is equal to

$$E(p) = \frac{h\frac{c}{n}}{\gamma} = \frac{6.62 \cdot 10^{-34} \cdot 2.01 \cdot 10^8}{1550 \cdot 10^{-9}} = 0.0085 \cdot 10^{-17} \tag{1}$$

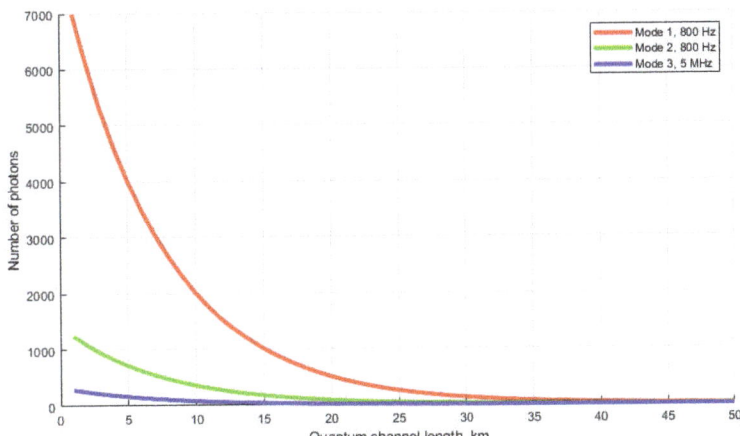

Figure 1. Dependence of the number of photons in a pulse on the length of the quantum channel.

Repetition rate f1 = 800 Hz, f2 = 800 Hz, f3 = 5 MHz, and pulse duration τ = 1 ns. The pulse duration is the same for the three modes. We performed the simulation based on the equation. The graphs were plotted using the classical formula for expressing the number of photons in terms of the pulse energy at a known repetition rate, taking into account the refraction index of the emission in the fiber.

The dependences clearly demonstrate that only when the quantum channel is L = 50 km long (taking into account the resulting losses and the double path of movement of the pulses), the average number of photons in the pulse approximates to unity (the average value of the three synchronization stages). The ordinate axis shows the resulting value, i.e., the pulse with this number of photons passed the distance L × 2 and entered the photodetector. It is apparent that the first stage had the most powerful energy characteristics. The latter was related to the need to ensure the highest probability of detecting the reflected signal at the first stage, since an erroneous detection or omission of the signal at the first stage will cause a complex detection error at subsequent stages. Note that the power of optical synchronizing pulses is constant for all values of the length of the quantum channel, i.e., the system does not adjust the laser power depending on the length of the quantum channel. A pulse with the number of photons m >> 10 is called a multiphoton pulse, 1 < m < 10 is a photon pulse, and m < 1 is a single-photon pulse. Therein, a single-photon should not be perceived as a division of a photon, but as the presence of a signal in each j-th pulse.

We showed experimentally that the multiphoton mode of calibration in the quantum key distribution system is a vulnerability. Note that the purpose of unauthorized access may be not only to intercept and read information, but also to synchronize the attacker's equipment in order to interfere with the work of the QKDS [8–10].

2.2. Experimental Attack on a Quantum Channel and Analysis

We configured the experimental design (Figure 2), where the quantum communication system stations were located in adjoining rooms. A quantum channel of variable length was organized between them. Corning®SMF-28e+ optical fiber coils with lengths (L) of 1, 2, 4, and 25 km were used for this. At the junction points of the optical coils, two fiber-optic couplers with division coefficients were connected in series: kC1 (70%, 30%) and kC2 (90%, 10%). The output of the transmitting station was connected to the input of the divider kC1, and the output of the divider kC1 (70%) was connected to the output of the divider kC2 (90%). The input of the kC2 divider was connected to the quantum channel in the direction of the receiver station. Outputs kC2 (10%) and kC1 (30%) were connected to an optical power meter (Yokogawa AQ2202) to capture signals.

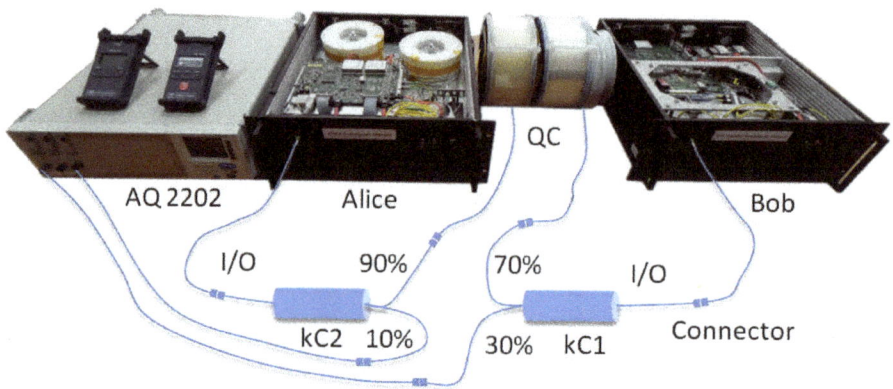

Figure 2. Experiment scheme. Clavis² 3110 QKD system with optical power couplers (kC1, kC2). I/O is input/output.

Note that the implementation of couplers in the optical communication channel was not technically difficult. The latter was provided by two welded joints in the fiber-optic communication line. The presence of two couplers allows one to calculate the time of re-reflection, since the moment of interception of an optical pulse in only one direction does not give complete information to the attacker about the operation of the system. It is crucial to intercept the optical pulse during the reverse propagation of the reflected signal. With information about the re-reflection time, an attacker can calculate the exact distance to the recipient's station and back [11–16]. This data allows one to perform some attacks on quantum communication protocols, for example, an attack in which the operation of the coding station is simulated. The attacker inserts their equipment instead of the encoding station and sends substitution signals to the transmitting station's photodetectors at the right time. The aim of our experiment was to prove the possibility of successful implementation of an attack on a quantum communication system by interference with the calibration stage.

In the described design, the QKD system is put into operation mode. The synchronization process and the operation of the quantum protocol BB84 function normally without critical errors, i.e., the presence of two power couplers in the optical communication channel is not detected by the system and does not affect its operation. Keys are formed in cycles, and the synchronization processes successfully. In this mode, the experiment lasted 24 h, and the system functioned without failures. After the signals at outputs kC1 (30%) and kC2 (10%) were repeatedly recorded, we connected the optical emission source (Yokogawa AQ2202) to the output kC2 (10%). The connection of the emission source also did not affect the operation of the QKDS. Further, at random times, we provided a signal-interference (τ = 1 ns, f = 270 Hz) to the output of the coupler kC2 (10%). The duration of interference activation varied from 5 s to 10 min. In interference mode, the system did not stop operating and did not issue errors but initiated the synchronization process again. After synchronization, the quantum protocol operation was restored, and the key distribution process resumed. We performed a simulation. We clearly demonstrated the effect of interference on the operation of the quantum key distribution protocol. Figure 3 shows the dynamics of the measured quantum error (QBER).

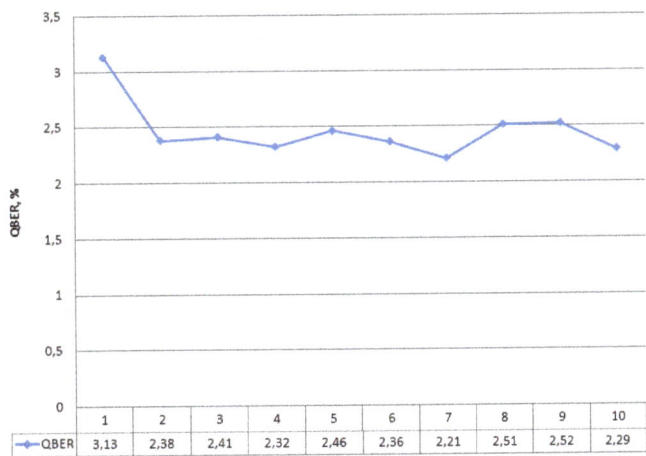

Figure 3. Dynamics measured by QKDS QBER software; 1–10 refer to iterations.

We can see that the graph does not contain any critical changes. Analysis of the dynamics of quantum error does not allow for the detection of unauthorized interference in the operation of the system. The latter is also confirmed by the graph in Figure 4, which shows the dynamics of generated quantum keys.

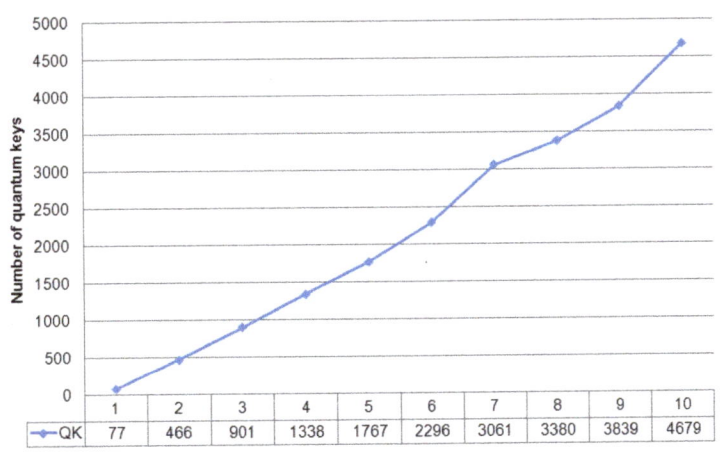

Figure 4. Dynamics of accumulated quantum keys. The length of each key is 512 bits; 1–10 refer to iterations.

Figure 4 shows the number of keys that are cyclically accumulated in the buffer. Note that the length of a single key is 512 bits. The dependencies in Figures 3 and 4 are presented for the length of the quantum channel L = 25,732 m. The graph in Figure 4 also does not indicate when the system was affected by the interference. If we consider the approximation of this dependence on the time axis, the time delay with an error of about 10% of the average key generation cycle will be visible in the intervals with interference enabled. This delay occurs periodically during the operation of the QKD system and may be due to the presence of in homogeneities in the quantum channel or physical changes in the optical fiber due to temperature influences. Thus, the time dependence analysis also does not allow for the detection of the presence of couplers in the communication channel or indicate unauthorized interference. Let us turn to Figures 5 and 6. Figure 5 shows statistics of accumulated quantum keys and QBER at different optical link lengths without using couplers (i.e., without introducing interference).

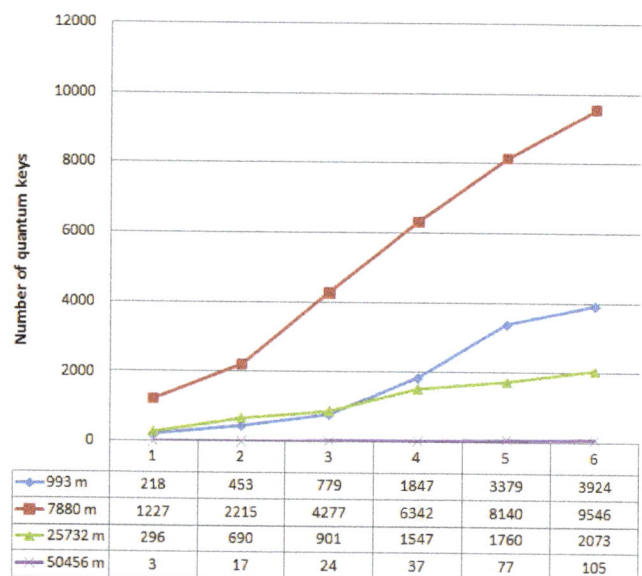

Figure 5. Statistical data of the BB84 quantum protocol, quantum keys; 1–6 refer to iterations.

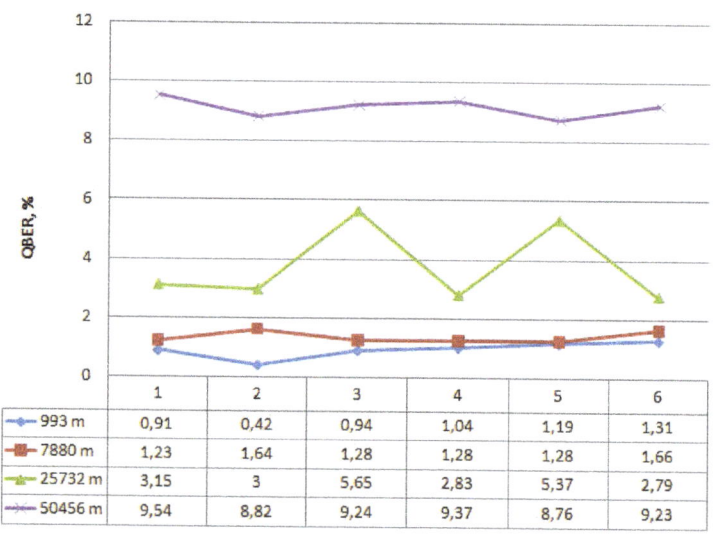

Figure 6. Statistical data on the operation of the quantum protocol BB84, QBER; 1–6 refer to iterations.

The graphs show that the maximum number of accumulated keys for 6 iterations is 9546, with a quantum channel length (L) of 7880 m. The graph shows a significant difference when the length of the fiber optic cable is 50,456 m. Here, the number of keys generated in one iteration differs significantly from the same value for a shorter length of the fiber optic link, while the growth dynamics is preserved. This dependence behavior is due to the fact that the limit length of the quantum channel introduces significant attenuation in the signal. The values 8.76 < QBER < 9.54 for a quantum channel length of 50,456 m are also high, but these values are not critical, because they do not exceed the calculated value QBER = 11%. Comparing the dynamics of changes in the number of accumulated keys and QBER in the presence of couplers and without them, let us turn to the dependencies in Figures 3–6 that are plotted for the length of the quantum channel in 25,732 m. The QBER value is within 2.3 < QBER < 3.1 if there are couplers, and within 2.8 < QBER < 5.7 if there are no couplers. These values are valid and do not indicate the presence of an attacker in the communication channel. Moreover, in the experiment, the values in the absence of couplers exceeded the values in the presence of couplers. The latter indicates that external destabilizing factors have a more significant impact on QBER than the presence of additional prepared connections in the communication channel.

When looking at graphs that reflect the accumulated keys, it is clear that for six iterations, the values do not differ significantly on the two curves (the average number of 512-bit keys per iteration is about 300). Analysis of the results confirms the conclusion that the presence of couplers in the communication channel and the impact of interference do not affect the statistical data of the quantum protocol. A similar conclusion can be drawn when considering the approximated curve on a time chart.

3. Single-Photon Synchronization Method

The results of the experiment show the vulnerability of the synchronization process QKDS and prove the possibility of interfering with the system, while remaining unnoticed. Note that the classical method of controlling the emission power in a quantum communication channel does not allow for detection of the presence of couplers. Under ideal experimental conditions, when the quantum channel consists of a continuous fiber (coil), the couplers can be detected using a reflectometer. In this case, it was possible to see attenuation of 0.2–0.4 dB at the places of split joints. If only welded joints are used, the presence of losses is almost impossible to detect. In real conditions, the completed length of the quantum channel does not exceed 1 km, and the presence of fiber optic splice closure is an integral part of the communication system. Fiber optic splice closure and inhomogeneities of optical fiber introduce additional attenuation and hide the possible presence of unauthorized connection to the communication channel. The reflectometric detection method does not allow one to distinguish legitimate inhomogeneities (of different types) from illegitimate ones.

We should also mention the quantum effects of the environment [17,18]. Note that the quantum fluctuations are not described by classical functions and cannot be compensated. Moreover, such quantum effects could be influencing the system, but it is expected that their effects would be small. Of course, such effects must be taken into account, and their influence on the quantum system should be investigated. There are environmental effects that can affect the physical properties of the fiber. For example, temperature tends to change the physical length of a fiber under certain conditions, but it is compensated for by checking the length in the program.

We propose a method that provides protection against an attack on the QKDS during the synchronization process. A distinctive feature of the method is the use of synchronization pulses weakened to a single-photon level. In this case, the optical signal is attenuated at the encoding station by a controlled attenuator, and the value of the insertion loss is calculated so that after reflection from the Faraday mirror, the average number of photons (m) in the synchronizing pulse is 0.1–0.5. Registration of single-photon pulses is performed by avalanche photodiodes in Geiger mode.

The maximum length of the fiber optic link in QKDS is $L = 100$ km. Taking into account the back propagation of emission to avoid overlapping of back transmitted pulses at $L = 100$ km, the repetition period is $T_s = 2 \times L/v_{fiber} \approx 1$ ms. Therefore, the maximum repetition rate of optical pulses should not exceed $f_{s.max} = 1/T_s \approx 1$ kHz. The repetition period T_s is divided into N_w time intervals with duration τ_w in such a way that $T_s = N_w \times \tau_w$. All intervals are analyzed sequentially. Each interval is analyzed N times, where N is the selection size. The pulse duration $\tau_s = 1$ ns and $\tau_w = (2 \ldots 4) \times \tau_s$. Absolute stability of the repetition period ΔT_s and the duration $\Delta \tau_s$ is assumed. In each interval, the number of accepted photoelectrons and/or dark current pulses (DCP) are recorded. After polling all N_w time intervals, an array of values is generated as follows:

$$\{n_{w.N}(j), j = \overline{1, N_w}\} = \{n_{w.N}(1), n_{w.N}(2), \ldots, n_{w.N}(j), \ldots, n_{w.N}(N_w)\}$$

At the values of τ_s and τ_w, the synchronizing pulse can lie entirely within one time interval or lie on the border of two neighboring ones. In the first case, the values $n_{w.N}(2), \ldots, n_{w.N}(j), \ldots, n_{w.N}(N_w)$ in $N_w - 1$ intervals are described by Poisson's law with the parameter $\overline{n}_{d.N} = N \times \xi_d \times \tau_w$. At the same time, in the interval with a synchronizing pulse, the number $n_{w.N}(1)$, with the parameter $\overline{n}_{w.N} = N \times \xi_d \times \tau_w + N \times \overline{n}_s$. Here ξ_d is the rate of occurrence of DCP, $\overline{n}_s$ is the average number of the photoelectrons registered for the duration of the pulse.

If the pulse lies in two neighboring intervals, then random values $n_{w.N}(3), \ldots, n_{w.N}(j), \ldots, n_{w.N}(N_w)$ in $N_w - 2$ noise intervals are described by Poisson's law with the parameter $\overline{n}_{d.N} = N \times \xi_d \times \tau_w$, and in neighboring intervals are the numbers $n_{w.N}(1)$ and $n_{w.N}(2)$, respectively, with parameters $\overline{n}_{w1.N} = N \times \xi_d \times \tau_w + N \times \overline{n}_{s1}$ and $\overline{n}_{w2.N} = N \times \xi_d \times \tau_w + N \times \overline{n}_{s2}$. Here $\overline{n}_{s1} = \overline{n}_s \times (1 - \tau_w/t_1)$ and $\overline{n}_{s2} = \overline{n}_s - \overline{n}_{s1}$ are, respectively, the average number of photons registered in neighboring intervals with the condition that the moment of occurrence of single-photon pulse (t_1) belongs to the first interval. Noise intervals should be understood as analyzed intervals in which the signal is not recorded. In such intervals, noise values can be recorded—the DCP of the photodetector [12,13]. To analyze the process of detecting a synchronizing signal using single-photon pulses, the laws of probability of the distribution density are applied [14].

The analytical expression (2) is used for calculating the probability of correct detection of the signaling interval (P_D).

$$P_D = \sum_{n_{w.N}=1}^{\infty} \frac{(\overline{n}_{w.N})^{n_{w.N}}}{n_{w.N}!} \cdot exp[-\overline{n}_{w.N}] \cdot P_{d.N}\{n_{w.N}\} \qquad (2)$$

Here

$$P_{d.N}\{n_{w.N}\} = \left(\sum_{n_{d.N}=0}^{n_{w.N}-1} \frac{\overline{n}_{d.N}^{n_{d.N}}}{n_{d.N}!} \cdot exp(-\overline{n}_{d.N}) \right)^{N_w - 1} \qquad (3)$$

represents the probability of registering no more than $(n_{w.N} - 1)$ DCP in all $(N_w - 1)$ noise time intervals during the analysis, provided that $n_{w.N}$ photoelectrons and DCP are registered in the signal time interval for a selection of size N. Taking into account the value N_w, the average number of DCP per sample in the noise interval tends to zero. This allows summation in the formula only for 2 values of $n_{d.N}$ equal to 0 and 1. Simplifying expression (2), we get

$$P_D = exp(-N_w \cdot \overline{n}_{d.N} + \overline{n}_{d.N})\overline{n}_{w.N} \cdot exp(-\overline{n}_{w.N}) \\ + [1 - exp(-\overline{n}_{w.N}) - \overline{n}_{w.N} \cdot exp(-\overline{n}_{w.N})] \cdot (1 + \overline{n}_{d.N})^{N_w - 1}. \qquad (4)$$

The simulation results show that the divergence of the calculation results for Equations (2)–(4) do not exceed 0.02% over the entire variation range in the number of time intervals. The registration validity condition for no more than one photoelectron and/or DCP is typical for a single-photon avalanche photodiode. This proves that it is possible to use expression (4) to calculate the probability of correctly detecting the time interval during the synchronization of the QKDS, provided that $\overline{n}_{w.N} \ll 1$. An important parameter of the avalanche photodiode is the recovery time of the operating mode (τ_{dead}). In the proposed method, the time interval poll is performed sequentially in each frame, i.e., one-time interval is analyzed for the repetition period (T); here $T \gg \tau_{dead}$. This approach allows the recovery time of the working mode of the photodetector to be ignored when calculating. Another distinctive feature of the single-photon mode of operation of the photodetector is the quantum efficiency coefficient of the photocathode (k), which must be taken into account when simulating. Let us look at the graphs in Figure 7, which demonstrate the dependence of the probability of correctly detecting the time interval with signal on the selection size. Dependencies are plotted using Equation (4). The developed method involves the use of a weakened optical synchronizing pulse with an average number of photons 0.1 < m < 1. Thus, given the critical values of the average number of photons per pulse, the frequency of DCP and the quantum efficiency of the photocathode, the variable value is only the selection size in each time interval. Let us explain that the DCP of the photodetector are its shot-noise, which can cause an avalanche effect [15–17].

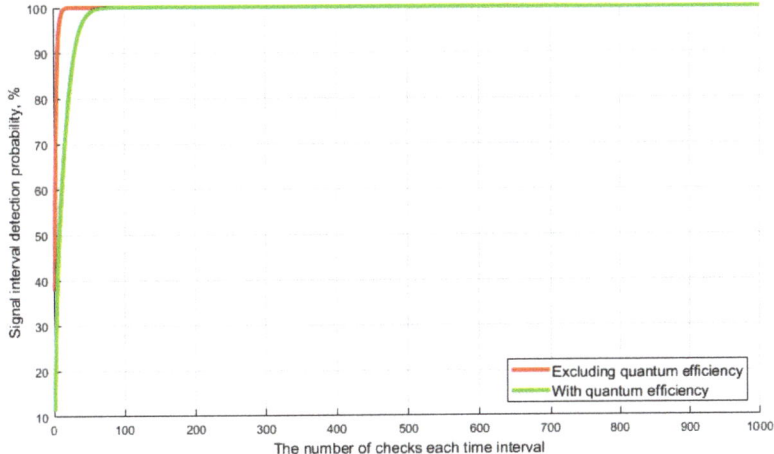

Figure 7. Dependence of the probability of correct detection on the selection size.

The graphs show that the probability of correct detection reaches maximum values ($P_D > 99.3\%$) already at the selection size N = 30 (without taking into account quantum efficiency) and at N = 150 with taking into account quantum efficiency. Note that the typical selection size of the current Clavis^2 3110 system is 800. Next, let us consider the simulation results that show the influence of the frequency of DCP and the selection size on the probabilistic characteristics of detecting the signaling time interval. The task of simulation is to find the optimal values of N and DCP, at which the maximum probability of detection is achieved. Calculations were made taking into account the above average quantum efficiency of the photocathode (k = 25%). Figure 8 shows the results of simulation of the algorithm for detecting a single-photon signal. The graphs show the dependence of the probability of correct detection of the signaling interval on selection size for different values of DCP.

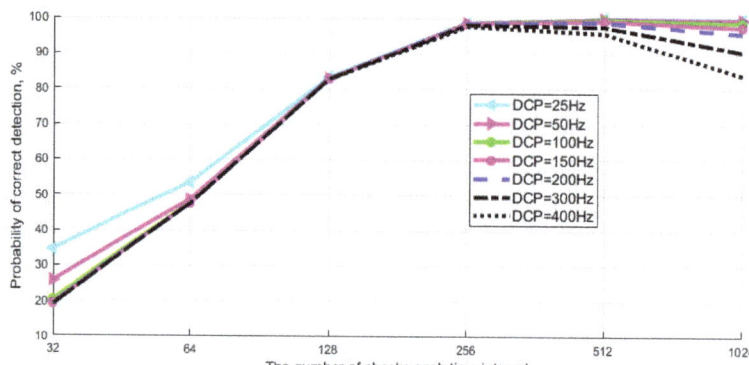

Figure 8. Probability of correct detection of a single-photon signal.

The average amount of photoelectrons (m) in a pulse is 0.1. The graph shows that at the minimum values of the selection size (128 < N < 32), the probability of detection (P_D) is no more than 80%, and the number of DCP does not matter. This behavior of the curves is explained by a small difference in the number of DCP and photoelectrons in time intervals. The divergence is leveled when the selection size increases. On the other hand, if the value of DCP > 200, the selection size does not matter, since the probability of detection (P_D) over the entire range of values does not exceed 98%. The optimal values of DCP and N for achieving high probability values ($P_D > 99.3\%$) are the limits of N > 256 for DCP < 150. Consider Figure 9, where calculations of the probability of erroneous detection of a signaling time interval with a single-photon pulse are presented.

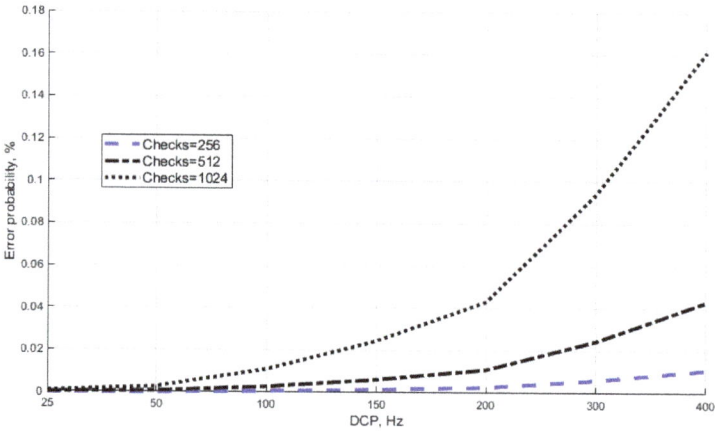

Figure 9. Probability of erroneous detection of a single-photon signal.

The figure is made for three values of the selection size (N = 256, 512, 1024) and the range of values of DCP $\in \{25 : 400\}$. It is apparent that the selection size N = 1024 has a significant impact on the probability at the maximum values of DCP. Thus, in the single-photon mode, the probability of erroneous detection increases sharply at DCP > 200. This is due to the fact that with the statistical accumulation of summands in Equation (4), an increase in the direct dependence of the number of DCP and the selection size causes an increase in noise signals, which are interpreted as "false positives" of single-photon avalanche photodiode. Note that the average value of DCP for the photodiodes used in QKD systems is within the range of 25 < DCP < 100. For example, the typical DCP value for id210 and id230 photodetectors is 40 and 50 Hz, respectively [18,19]. Such photodetectors are used in the Clavis[2] and Clavis[3] QKDS [20–24]. We applied the real characteristics of the id230 photodetector to our calculations (see Figure 10). The average number of photoelectrons m = 0.1 was achieved by attenuating the signal in the receiver station. The quantum efficiency of the photocathode k = 25%.

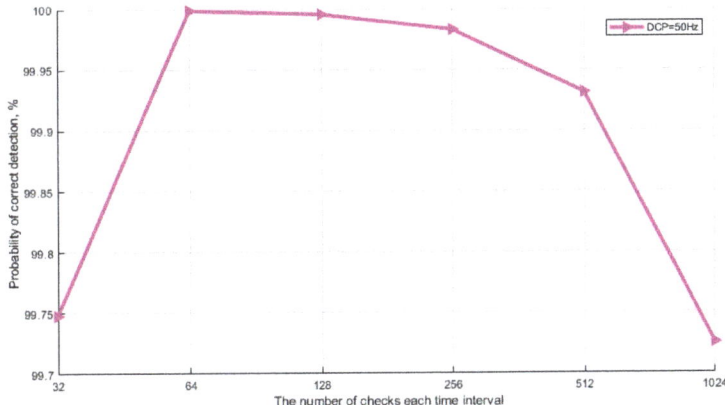

Figure 10. Calculating the detection probability for id230.

4. Discussion

The experimental part was strongly considered in this work. Due to the lack of a QKD system, most research groups are concerned with theoretical research. Our research team conducted theoretical research based on real experiences and found weak points by exploring real systems. By conducting experiments, we can demonstrate that this weakness can be very critical for practical application. Then, we proposed a new theoretical method to reduce the possibility of this vulnerability. The synchronization process is not part of the quantum protocol, but as shown in practice, the attacker can also access the hardware if they can access the synchronization. This can have serious consequences in real situations.

In addition, during the experiment, it was found that a new synchronization method can protect the system from quantum channel attacks. This does not represent an attack on quantum protocols but means an attack on optical communication circuits. The purpose of this attack is to destroy the key distribution.

5. Conclusions

Results of research show that an attack on the QKDS synchronization system can be successfully implemented. A method to counter this type of attack is presented. An important feature is that this is not a classic attack on a quantum protocol. We show that quantum key distribution systems have vulnerabilities not only in the operation of protocols. The described type of attack does not affect the cryptographic strength of the received keys, but it allows disrupting the operation of the QKDS. We are disrupting the quantum channel, but we are not interfering with the quantum protocol. Here is a simple example: if an attacker simply damages the optical cable (cuts it), the system will easily detect it; if we use our method, then the system does not detect an intruder in the quantum channel. We also propose a method that protects synchronization data from unauthorized access. The method is based on the use of sync pulses attenuated to a photon level in the process of detecting a time interval with a signal. Note that the classical attack by a compressed powerful light pulse cannot be realized, since we use an avalanche photodiode in the Geiger mode.

Synchronizing pulses are registered by single-photon avalanche photodiodes in Geiger mode. The algorithm for detecting an optical signal is described, and analytical expressions are presented for calculating probabilistic characteristics that show the undiminished dynamics of correct detection of an optical synchronizing signal. The method is simulated for optical communication systems that operate according to a two-pass scheme. The paper presents the results of experimental studies that show the vulnerability of the synchronization process in autocompensation quantum key distribution systems with phase encoding of states. An additional measure of control against unauthorized interference is the use of variable power synchronizing pulse at varying lengths of the quantum channel. Together with controlled signal attenuation, this measure will increase the security of the QKD system from unauthorized access. The results of the experiment show that the system uses pulses of the same power regardless of the length of the quantum channel. Simple calculations of sufficient synchronizing pulse power will allow the intensity of the emission source to be adjusted and pulses of calculated power to be generated depending on the length of the quantum channel.

Author Contributions: A.P. supervision, developed the algorithm, analyzed data, and performed the experiments; D.P. analyzed the experimental data; L.S. and K.D. checked the data and wrote the paper; Writing—review and editing, all authors. All authors have read and agreed to the published version of the manuscript.

Funding: The publication was carried out as part of the support of the publication activity of the Southern Federal University.

Institutional Review Board Statement: The study was conducted according to the guidelines of the Declaration of Helsinki, and approved by the Institutional Review Board of Southern federal university (12/05-2015).

Data Availability Statement: All results and data obtained can be found in open access publications.

Acknowledgments: The authors express their gratitude to Pljonkins Inc. for the support.

Conflicts of Interest: The authors declare no conflict of interest.

References

1. Fei, Y.-Y.; Meng, X.-D.; Gao, M.; Wang, H.; Ma, Z. Quantum man-in-the-middle attack on the calibration process of quantum key distribution. *Sci. Rep.* **2018**, *8*, 4283. [CrossRef]
2. Jain, N.; Wittmann, C.; Lydersen, L.; Wiechers, C.; Elser, D.; Marquardt, C.; Makarov, V.; Leuchs, G. Device calibration impacts security of quantum key distribution. *Phys. Rev. Lett.* **2011**, *107*. [CrossRef] [PubMed]
3. Gisin, N.; Ribordy, G.; Tittel, W.; Zbinden, H. Quantum cryptography. *Rev. Mod. Phys.* **2002**, *74*, 145–195. [CrossRef]
4. Kurochkin, V.; Zverev, A.; Kurochkin, J.; Riabtzev, I.; Neizvestnyi, I. Quantum cryptography experimental investigations. *Photonics* **2012**, *5*, 54–66.
5. Stucki, D.; Gisin, N.; Guinnard, O.; Ribordy, G.; Zbinden, H. Quantum key distribution over 67 km with a plug&play system. *New J. Phys.* **2002**, *4*, 41.1–41.8.
6. Pljonkin, A.P. Vulnerability of the synchronization process in the quantum key distribution system. *Int. J. Cloud Appl. Comput.* **2019**, *9*, 50–58. [CrossRef]
7. Lydersen, L.; Wiechers, C.; Wittmann, C.; Elser, D.; Skaar, J.; Makarov, V. Hacking commercial quantum cryptography systems by tailored bright illumination. *Nat. Photonics.* **2010**, *4*, 686. [CrossRef]
8. Bennet, C.H.; Bessette, F.; Brassard, G.; Salvail, L.; Smolin, J. Experimental quantum cryptography. *J. Cryptol.* **1992**, *5*, 3–28. [CrossRef]
9. Bennett, C.H.; Brassard, G. Quantum Cryptography: Public key distribution and coin tossing. In Proceeding of the IEEE International Conference on Computer, Systems and Signal Processing, Bangalore, India, 9–12 December 1984; pp. 175–179.
10. Scarani, V.; Bechmann-Pasquinucci, H.; Cerf, N.J.; Dušek, M.; Lütkenhaus, N.; Peev, M. The security of practical quantum key distribution. *Rev. Mod. Phys.* **2009**, *81*, 1301–1350. [CrossRef]
11. Sajeed, S.; Huang, A.; Sun, S.; Xu, F.; Makarov, V.; Curty, M. Insecurity of detector-device-independent quantum key distribution. *Phys. Rev. Lett.* **2016**, *117*, 250505. [CrossRef]
12. Fujiwara, M.; Honjo, T.; Shimizu, K.; Tamaki, K.; Sasaki, M. Characteristics of superconducting single photon detector in DPS-QKD system under bright illumination blinding attack. *Optics Express* **2013**, *21*, 6304–6312. [CrossRef] [PubMed]
13. Pljonkin, A.; Singh, P.K. The review of the commercial quantum key distribution system. In Proceedings of the 5th International Conference on Parallel, Distributed and Grid Computing, Solan, India, 20–22 December 2018. [CrossRef]
14. Gagliardi, R.M.; Karp, S. *Optical Communications*; John Wiley & Son: New York, NY, USA, 1976.

15. Peloso, M.P.; Gerhardt, I. Statistical tests of randomness on quantum keys distributed through a free-space channel coupled to daylight noise. *J. Lightwave Technol.* **2013**, *31*, 3794–3805. [CrossRef]
16. Eleuch, H.; Rotter, I. Nearby states in non-Hermitian quantum systems I: Two states. *Eur. Phys. J. D* **2015**, *69*, 229. [CrossRef]
17. Eleuch, H.; Rotter, I. Clustering of exceptional points and dynamical phase transitions. *Phys. Rev. A* **2016**, *93*, 042116. [CrossRef]
18. Huang, D.; Huang, P.; Lin, D.; Wang, C.; Zeng, G. High-speed continuous-variable quantum key distribution without sending a local oscillator. *Optics Lett.* **2015**, *40*, 3695–3698. [CrossRef] [PubMed]
19. Pljonkin, A.; Rumyantsev, K.; Singh, P.K. Synchronization in quantum key distribution systems. *Cryptography* **2017**, *1*, 18. [CrossRef]
20. Chistiakov, V.; Huang, A.; Egorov, V.; Makarov, V. Controlling single-photon detector ID210 with bright light. *Optics Express* **2019**, *27*, 32253–32262. [CrossRef] [PubMed]
21. Wu, Z.; Huang, A.; Chen, H.; Sun, S.-H.; Ding, J.; Qiang, X.; Fu, X.; Xu, P.; Wu, J. Hacking single-photon avalanche detectors in quantum key distribution via pulse illumination. *Optics Express* **2020**, *28*, 25574–25590. [CrossRef]
22. Daneshgaran, F.; Mondin, M.; Kupferman, J.; Arnon, S.; Genovese, M.; Degiovanni, I.; Meda, A.; Di Stasio, F.; Bari, I. Realistic QKD system hacking and security. *Quantum Commun. Quantum Imaging* **2018**, *XVI*, 107710T.
23. Eriksson, T.A.; Hirano, T.; Puttnam, B.J.; Rademacher, G.; Luís, R.S.; Fujiwara, M.; Namiki, R.; Awaji, Y.; Takeoka, M.; Wada, N.; et al. Wavelength division multiplexing of continuous variable quantum key distribution and 18.3 Tbit/s data channels. *Commun. Physics.* **2019**, *2*, 1–8. [CrossRef]
24. Calderaro, L.; Stanco, A.; Agnesi, C.; Avesani, M.; Dequal, D.; Villoresi, P.; Vallone, G. Fast and simple qubit-based synchronization for quantum key distribution. *Phys. Rev. Appl.* **2020**, *13*, 054041. [CrossRef]

Article

QKD Based on Symmetric Entangled Bernstein-Vazirani

Michael Ampatzis [†] and Theodore Andronikos [*,†]

Department of Informatics, Ionian University, 7 Tsirigoti Square, 49100 Corfu, Greece; p16abat@ionio.gr
* Correspondence: andronikos@ionio.gr
† These authors contributed equally to this work.

Abstract: This paper introduces a novel entanglement-based QKD protocol, that makes use of a modified symmetric version of the Bernstein-Vazirani algorithm, in order to achieve secure and efficient key distribution. Two variants of the protocol, one fully symmetric and one semi-symmetric, are presented. In both cases, the spatially separated Alice and Bob share multiple EPR pairs, each one qubit of the pair. The fully symmetric version allows both parties to input their tentative secret key from their respective location and acquire in the end a totally new and original key, an idea which was inspired by the Diffie-Hellman key exchange protocol. In the semi-symmetric version, Alice sends her chosen secret key to Bob (or vice versa). The performance of both protocols against an eavesdroppers attack is analyzed. Finally, in order to illustrate the operation of the protocols in practice, two small scale but detailed examples are given.

Keywords: quantum cryptography; quantum key distribution; the Bernstein-Vazirani algorithm; EPR pairs; quantum entanglement; quantum information theory

1. Introduction

In the course of the last century, the scientific community experimented with different ideas and forms of computation, trying to harness the power of nature and create machines that allowed us to process immeasurable amounts of information in mere seconds, thus radically changing the world around us in the span of a few decades. However, in the present era classical computers are reaching a point where it will be infeasible to substantially enhance their efficiency due to the physical limitations of transistors. This has started a new incentive to resurrect previous attempts concerning research of new types of computation. Out of all the different proposals for a viable substitute to classical computing, undoubtedly the most promising of them all is quantum computation, mainly due to the fact that it allows the exploitation of the most fundamental properties of physics.

1.1. Related Work

As technology comes closer to the realization of this goal, it appears that certain profound adaptations regarding different branches of computer science need to take place in order to achieve a smoother transition from the classical to the quantum era. One of the most important such branches is the field of cryptography, due to the vulnerability of the current security algorithms against quantum computers [1,2]. This inherent weakness in the modern security protocols and the race for building a resilient security infrastructure against quantum computers [3] before they become a reality, were the two catalysts that resulted in a schism of the field into two sub-fields, which are based on two different philosophies and ideologies. The first sub-field, known as post-quantum cryptography or quantum-resistant cryptography, relies on the complexity of mathematics as its security basis. It is an attempt to develop cryptographic systems that are secure against both quantum and classical computers and can also be interpreted within the already existing communications protocols and networks. The second sub-field, which is called quantum cryptography,

Citation: Ampatzis, M.; Andronikos, T. QKD Based on Symmetric Entangled Bernstein-Vazirani. *Entropy* **2021**, *23*, 870. https://doi.org/10.3390/e23070870

Academic Editor: Ivan B. Djordjevic

Received: 9 June 2021
Accepted: 5 July 2021
Published: 7 July 2021

Publisher's Note: MDPI stays neutral with regard to jurisdictional claims in published maps and institutional affiliations.

Copyright: © 2021 by the authors. Licensee MDPI, Basel, Switzerland. This article is an open access article distributed under the terms and conditions of the Creative Commons Attribution (CC BY) license (https://creativecommons.org/licenses/by/4.0/).

is being built upon the implementation of the properties of quantum mechanics and, thus, takes advantage of nature's own fundamental laws in order to achieve security.

The sub-field of quantum cryptography, on which the primary interest of the current paper lies upon, has seen enormous growth of both theoretical and practical nature. Two landmark papers, the BB84 protocol [4] and the E91 protocol [5], were the first papers that proved that key distribution between two parties relying on the properties of quantum mechanics was possible. These two protocols have established the two schemes that all quantum key distribution (QKD) protocols are based on, the *prepare-and-measure-based scheme* and the *entanglement-based scheme*. After the publications of these two protocols, a plethora of interesting proposals for different QKD protocols based on these two schemes were suggested, further expanding the field on a theoretical level. At the same time, some truly remarkable real life implementations of some protocols were demonstrated as in [6–11]. These implementations have demonstrated that quantum cryptography is not just a mere theoretical experiment, but a possible reality in the near future.

Over the last few years, there was a noticeable increase in the effort to find new viable applications for well-known quantum algorithms, such as the Deutsch-Jozsa algorithm [12], the Bernstein-Vazirani algorithm [13] and Simon's periodicity algorithm [14]. Many of these proposals have been made in the field of quantum cryptography, using these algorithms as viable QKD protocols [15–17]. Motivated from these attempts, this paper proposes two novel variants of an entanglement-based QKD protocol that makes use of the Bernstein-Vazirani algorithm. The novelty of this work lies on the fact that it uniquely combines some key ingredients. Starting with entanglement, which is an integral part of the protocol, the corresponding qubits in Alice and Bob's input registers are maximally entangled. Thus, the proposed protocols exhibit all the inherent advantages that an entanglement-based QKD protocol provides in terms of security against an eavesdropper, as first demonstrated in the E91 protocol [5]. Additionally, the Bernstein–Vazirani algorithm [13], a fast and useful quantum algorithm that guarantees the creation of the key using just one application of the appropriate function, is used in a critical manner. Furthermore, the fully symmetric variant is inspired by the Diffie-Hellman idea [18] of deriving the final key from a random combination of two separate keys. This idea is not just cosmetic, as the ability to obtain a key that neither Alice or Bob know from the start, adds an additional layer of security, further improving the strength of the protocol. Finally, the proposed protocol can be implemented in two versions: the fully symmetric version and the semi-symmetric one. In the fully symmetric variant, both Alice and Bob can input their tentative secret keys from their respective locations and acquire in the end a totally new and original key. In the semi-symmetric one, Alice (alternatively Bob) constructs the secret key that she (or he) communicates securely to the other party.

The protocol is described as a quantum game, which despite the rather playful name, it is another noteworthy field that has emerged due to the transition to the quantum era and is used to address difficult and interesting problems within the quantum realm. This approach was chosen in an effort to make the presentation more mnemonic and easier to follow, due to the close connection that both fields share and the fact that any cryptographic situation can be conceived as a game between the two fictional heroes Alice and Bob, who play the roles of two remote parties that are trying to communicate, and the enemy Eve who tries to eavesdrop the conversation, a case which becomes apparent with the quantum game of coin tossing and the BB84 protocol [4,19] and references therein. This situation has been generalized in [20] to quantum dice rolling. For the reader striving for a more rounded understanding of the connection of the two fields, one can start with the two important works in the field of quantum game theory dating back to 1999, which were instrumental for the creation of the field: Meyer's PQ penny flip game [21], which can be regarded as the quantum analogue of the classical penny flip game, and the introduction of the Eisert-Wilkens-Lewenstein scheme [22] that is widely used in the field. Regarding the PQ penny flip game, some recent results can be found in [23,24], were its connection to the dihedral groups was established. As for the Eisert-Wilkens-Lewenstein scheme, it proved fruitful in providing many interesting results. For example, it led to quantum adaptations of the famous prisoners' dilemma in which the quantum strategies are better than any classical strategy ([22]), as well as extensions of the classical repeated prisoners' dilemma conditional strategies to a quantum setting ([25]).

1.2. Organization

The paper is structured as follows. Section 1 provides a brief introduction to the subject and gives the most relevant references. Section 2 introduces and explains the tools used for the formulation of the protocols in this article. Section 3 presents and thoroughly analyzes the fSEBV and sSEBV protocols, so that their functionality can be completely understood. Section 4 contains two detailed examples, one for each protocol, to demonstrate their operation. Finally, Section 5 summarizes the proposed protocols and discusses their potential applications in various situations.

2. Preliminaries

2.1. Quantum Entanglement and Bell States

Quantum entanglement is one of the fundamental principles of quantum mechanics and can be described mathematically as the linear combination of two or more product states. The Bell states are specific quantum states of two qubits, sometimes called an EPR pair, that represent the simplest examples of quantum entanglement. From the perspective of quantum computation, an EPR pair can be produced by a circuit with two qubits, in which a Hadamard gate is applied to the first qubit and subsequently a CNOT gate is applied to both qubits. These states can be elegantly described by the following equation taken from [26].

$$|\beta_{x,y}\rangle = \frac{|0\rangle|y\rangle + (-1)^x|1\rangle|\bar{y}\rangle}{\sqrt{2}}, \qquad (1)$$

where $|\bar{y}\rangle$ is the negation of $|y\rangle$.

In a more detailed manner, the Bell states can be described as follows.

$$|\Phi^+\rangle = |\beta_{00}\rangle = \frac{|0\rangle|0\rangle + |1\rangle|1\rangle}{\sqrt{2}} \qquad (2)$$

$$|\Phi^-\rangle = |\beta_{10}\rangle = \frac{|0\rangle|0\rangle - |1\rangle|1\rangle}{\sqrt{2}} \qquad (3)$$

$$|\Psi^+\rangle = |\beta_{01}\rangle = \frac{|0\rangle|1\rangle + |1\rangle|0\rangle}{\sqrt{2}} \qquad (4)$$

$$|\Psi^-\rangle = |\beta_{11}\rangle = \frac{|0\rangle|1\rangle - |1\rangle|0\rangle}{\sqrt{2}} \qquad (5)$$

The main advantage of quantum entanglement is that if one qubit of the pair is measured, then the other will collapse immediately despite the distance between the two. This unique characteristic of quantum entanglement can be used on quantum key distribution as first described by Ekert in the E91 protocol. Therefore, in order to achieve quantum key distribution, multiple EPR pairs will be needed. For this reason, the mathematical representation of multiple EPR pairs will be expedient. If one starts with the entangled Bell state $|\Phi^+\rangle$, which can be cast as

$$|\Phi^+\rangle = \frac{1}{\sqrt{2}}(|0\rangle_A|0\rangle_B + |1\rangle_A|1\rangle_B), \qquad (6)$$

some easy computations show that

$$|\Phi^+\rangle^{\otimes n} = \frac{1}{\sqrt{2^n}} \sum_{x \in \{0,1\}^n} |x\rangle_A |x\rangle_B,\qquad(7)$$

which will be required in the presentation of Section 3.

2.2. A Brief Description of the Bernstein-Vazirani Algorithm

Regarded as one of the earliest quantum algorithms, along with the Deutsch-Josza algorithm and Simon's periodicity algorithm, the Bernstein-Vazirani algorithm, first introduced by Ethan Bernstein and Umesh Vazirani, can be considered to be a useful extension of the Deutsch-Josza algorithm, due to the fact that it was directly inspired by it and shared multiple common characteristics on both structure and implementation. Yet, despite the similarities, it has proved its value by demonstrating that the superiority of a quantum computer can be successfully used for more complex problems than the Deutsch-Josza problem.

The Bernstein-Vazirani problem can be described as the ensuing game between two players, namely Alice and Bob, who are spatially separated. Alice in Athens is corresponding with Bob in Corfu using letters. Alice starts the game by selecting a number x from 0 to $2^n - 1$ and mails its binary n-bit representation $\mathbf{x}$ to Bob. After Bob receives this message, he calculates the value of some function

$$f : \{0, 1, \ldots, 2^n - 1\} \rightarrow \{0, 1\},\qquad(8)$$

and replies with the result, which is either 0 or 1. The rules of the game dictate that Bob must use a function $f_\mathbf{s}(\mathbf{x})$, where $\mathbf{s} = s_{n-1} \ldots s_1 s_0$ and $\mathbf{x} = x_{n-1} \ldots x_1 x_0$ are n-bit binary numbers representing integers in the range $0, 1, \ldots, 2^n - 1$, such that

$$f_\mathbf{s}(\mathbf{x}) = \mathbf{s} \cdot \mathbf{x} \bmod 2.\qquad(9)$$

The inner product modulo 2 is defined as

$$\mathbf{s} \cdot \mathbf{x} \bmod 2 = s_{n-1} x_{n-1} \oplus \cdots \oplus s_0 x_0,\qquad(10)$$

where $\oplus$ is the exclusive-or operator. Therefore, the function is guaranteed to return the bitwise product of Alice's input $\mathbf{x}$ with a secret key $\mathbf{s}$ that Bob has chosen. Alice's goal in this game is to determine with certainty the secret key $\mathbf{s}$ that Bob has picked, corresponding with him as little as possible. How fast can she succeed?

In the *classical* version of this problem, Alice can find the secret key $\mathbf{s}$ by taking advantage of the nature of the function $f_\mathbf{s}(\mathbf{x})$ and, in particular, by sending Bob the inputs shown in Table 1.

Table 1. Alice must communicate with Bob n times in order find the secret key $\mathbf{s}$.

The Evolution of the Bernstein-Vazirani Game	
Alice's Input x	Bob's Response
$\mathbf{x} = 10 \ldots 00$	s_{n-1}
$\vdots$	$\vdots$
$\mathbf{x} = 00 \ldots 10$	s_1
$\mathbf{x} = 00 \ldots 01$	s_0

In that way, Alice will discover a bit of the string $\mathbf{s}$ (the bit s_i) with each query she sends. For example, with $\mathbf{x} = 10 \ldots 0$ she can obtain the most significant bit of $\mathbf{s}$, with $\mathbf{x} = 01 \ldots 0$ she will find the next most significant bit of $\mathbf{s}$, and by following the same procedure, when she reaches $\mathbf{x} = 00 \ldots 1$, she will have finally managed to reveal the entire string **s**. Despite, the efficiency of this method, Alice is still limited by sending to Bob only one query at a time. Therefore, the best possible classical scenario requires from her to correspond with Bob at least n times, in order for her to succeed in her goal.

By observing the core attributes of the aforementioned game, we can divide it into the following three big steps, which are:

- Alice provides an input,
- Bob applies the function $f_\mathbf{s}(\mathbf{x})$, and
- after multiple repetitions of the previous two steps, Alice is finally able to reveal the secret key **s**.

It can be seen from the above steps that the game can easily become more efficient by implementing certain tools from quantum mechanics. If Alice and Bob were able to exchange information with the use of qubits instead of classical bits, then Alice could send the superposition of these qubits to Bob with only one message. Furthermore, if Bob was using a unitary transformation U_f instead of a function $f_\mathbf{s}(x)$, then Alice would be able to achieve her goal with only one communication.

The *quantum* version of the Bernstein-Vazirani algorithm, can be described by the following quantum game. The game initially starts with Alice preparing two quantum registers, one of size n to store her query in and one of size 1, in which Bob will store his answer in. We will refer to these registers as Alice's input and output registers, respectively. Next, she applies the Hadamard gate to every qubit, in order to acquire the even superposition state of each register and then she sends both registers to Bob. Right after Bob receives the contents of the registers, he applies the unitary transform U_f and sends them back to Alice. In the final stage of the game, Alice concludes the algorithm by measuring her input register and obtaining the secret key **s**. The whole process of the game, is summarized in Figure 1 below.

The Bernstein-Vazirani algorithm

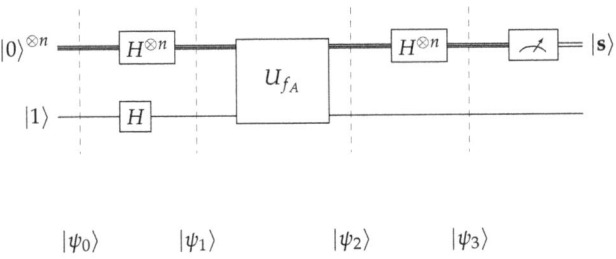

Figure 1. This figures gives a schematic representation of the Bernstein-Vazirani algorithm.

Now, in order to obtain a better understanding of the nature of the algorithm, let us examine the evolution of the quantum states more closely. First, Alice starts with the initial state

$$|\psi_0\rangle = |0\rangle^{\otimes n} |1\rangle. \qquad (11)$$

The n qubits of her input register are all prepared at state $|0\rangle$ and the qubit of the output register is prepared at state $|1\rangle$. Next, Alice applies the Hadamard transform to both registers and the state becomes

$$|\psi_1\rangle = \frac{1}{\sqrt{2^n}} \sum_{\mathbf{x}\in\{0,1\}^n} |\mathbf{x}\rangle \left(\frac{|0\rangle - |1\rangle}{\sqrt{2}}\right). \qquad (12)$$

The derivation of the previous equation is based on the fact that

$$H^{\otimes n} |0\rangle^{\otimes n} = \frac{1}{\sqrt{2^n}} \sum_{\mathbf{x} \in \{0,1\}^n} |\mathbf{x}\rangle , \qquad (13)$$

a standard result in the literature (for its derivation see [26,27]). At this point the input register is in an even superposition of all possible states and the output register is in an evenly weighted superposition of $|0\rangle$ and $|1\rangle$. Thus, Alice is now ready to send both registers to Bob so he may apply the function $f_\mathbf{s}(x)$ using

$$U_f : |\mathbf{x}, y\rangle \rightarrow |\mathbf{x}, y \oplus f(\mathbf{x})\rangle , \qquad (14)$$

which results in the next state

$$|\psi_2\rangle = \frac{1}{\sqrt{2^n}} \sum_{\mathbf{x} \in \{0,1\}^n} (-1)^{f(\mathbf{x})} |\mathbf{x}\rangle \left(\frac{|0\rangle - |1\rangle}{\sqrt{2}} \right) . \qquad (15)$$

The appearance of $(-1)^{f(\mathbf{x})}$ in Equation (15) is due to the fact that if $|y\rangle = \frac{|0\rangle - |1\rangle}{\sqrt{2}}$, then

$$|y \oplus f(\mathbf{x})\rangle = \begin{cases} \frac{|0\rangle - |1\rangle}{\sqrt{2}} & \text{if } f(\mathbf{x}) = 0 \\ \frac{|1\rangle - |0\rangle}{\sqrt{2}} & \text{if } f(\mathbf{x}) = 1 \end{cases} \Rightarrow |y \oplus f(\mathbf{x})\rangle = (-1)^{f(\mathbf{x})} \left(\frac{|0\rangle - |1\rangle}{\sqrt{2}} \right) . \qquad (16)$$

In view of (9) and (15) becomes

$$|\psi_2\rangle = \frac{1}{\sqrt{2^n}} \sum_{\mathbf{x} \in \{0,1\}^n} (-1)^{\mathbf{s} \cdot \mathbf{x}} |\mathbf{x}\rangle \left(\frac{|0\rangle - |1\rangle}{\sqrt{2}} \right) , \qquad (17)$$

which is the state returned back to Alice.

Let us now recall the following well-known equation that gives in a succinct form the result of the application of the Hadamard transformation to an arbitrary n-qubit basis ket $|\mathbf{x}\rangle$ (see [26,27]).

$$H^{\otimes n} |\mathbf{x}\rangle = \frac{1}{\sqrt{2^n}} \sum_{\mathbf{z} \in \{0,1\}^n} (-1)^{\mathbf{z} \cdot \mathbf{x}} |\mathbf{z}\rangle . \qquad (18)$$

Thus, after Alice receives the registers back, she applies the Hadamard transform to the input register for a second time. Via the use of Equation (18), the resulting state can be written as

$$\begin{aligned}
|\psi_3\rangle &= \frac{1}{\sqrt{2^n}} \sum_{\mathbf{x} \in \{0,1\}^n} (-1)^{\mathbf{s} \cdot \mathbf{x}} H^{\otimes n} |\mathbf{x}\rangle \left(\frac{|0\rangle - |1\rangle}{\sqrt{2}} \right) \\
&= \frac{1}{\sqrt{2^n}} \sum_{\mathbf{x} \in \{0,1\}^n} (-1)^{\mathbf{s} \cdot \mathbf{x}} \left(\frac{1}{\sqrt{2^n}} \sum_{\mathbf{z} \in \{0,1\}^n} (-1)^{\mathbf{z} \cdot \mathbf{x}} |\mathbf{z}\rangle \right) \left(\frac{|0\rangle - |1\rangle}{\sqrt{2}} \right) \\
&= \frac{1}{2^n} \sum_{\mathbf{x} \in \{0,1\}^n} \sum_{\mathbf{z} \in \{0,1\}^n} (-1)^{\mathbf{s} \cdot \mathbf{x} \oplus \mathbf{z} \cdot \mathbf{x}} |\mathbf{z}\rangle \left(\frac{|0\rangle - |1\rangle}{\sqrt{2}} \right) \\
&= \frac{1}{2^n} \sum_{\mathbf{z} \in \{0,1\}^n} \sum_{\mathbf{x} \in \{0,1\}^n} (-1)^{(\mathbf{s} \oplus \mathbf{z}) \cdot \mathbf{x}} |\mathbf{z}\rangle \left(\frac{|0\rangle - |1\rangle}{\sqrt{2}} \right) = |\mathbf{s}\rangle \left(\frac{|0\rangle - |1\rangle}{\sqrt{2}} \right)
\end{aligned} \qquad (19)$$

The last equation is due to the following fact: if $\mathbf{s} = \mathbf{z}$, then $\forall \mathbf{x} \in \{0,1\}^n$ $(\mathbf{s} \oplus \mathbf{z}) \cdot \mathbf{x} = 0$, otherwise for exactly half of the inputs $\mathbf{x}$ the exponent will be 0 and for the remaining half the exponent will be 1. This is typically written in a more concise manner as follows:

$$\sum_{\mathbf{x} \in \{0,1\}^n} (-1)^{(\mathbf{s} \oplus \mathbf{z}) \cdot \mathbf{x}} = 2^n \delta_{\mathbf{s},\mathbf{z}} . \qquad (20)$$

The algorithm terminates with the final measurement of the input register by Alice whereby she obtains the secret key **s** and concludes the whole process.

3. QKD Based on Symmetric Entangled B-V

In this section, the two versions of the proposed symmetric entangled QKD protocol based on the Bernstein-Vazirani algorithm are presented and described in great detail. These are the *fully symmetric* version of the protocol, or **fSEBV** for short, and the *semi-symmetric* version of the protocol, or **sSEBV** for short.

3.1. The fSEBV Protocol

Starting with the fSEBV protocol we consider a slight alteration of the aforementioned Bernstein-Vazirani game. As before, the game starts with the two players Alice and Bob who are spatially separated. This time, instead of using normal qubits in a separable state, they use maximally entangled EPR pairs, and they both share a qubit from each pair. An important rule of the game is that there are no limitations on which entity will actually create the EPR pairs in the first place. The pairs can be created and distributed accordingly by Alice or Bob, or they can be acquired from a third party source. This last situation is depicted in Figure 2. Exactly as in the previous game, the goal of the current game is to acquire a secret key **s**. However, in this specific protocol symmetry plays a crucial role, as Alice and Bod behave in a perfectly symmetrical way by both having their own secret keys, which they will attempt to input into the system, exactly as in the original algorithm. Alice's key is denoted by $\mathbf{s}_A$, Bob's key by $\mathbf{s}_B$ and they both take identical actions. Please note that neither Alice nor Bob need apply the Hadamard transform onto their input registers because they are already in the desired even superposition of all basis states, as they are populated by n pairs in the $|\Phi^+\rangle$ Bell state. In this respect the fSEBV protocol differs from the vanilla Bernstein-Vazirani algorithm.

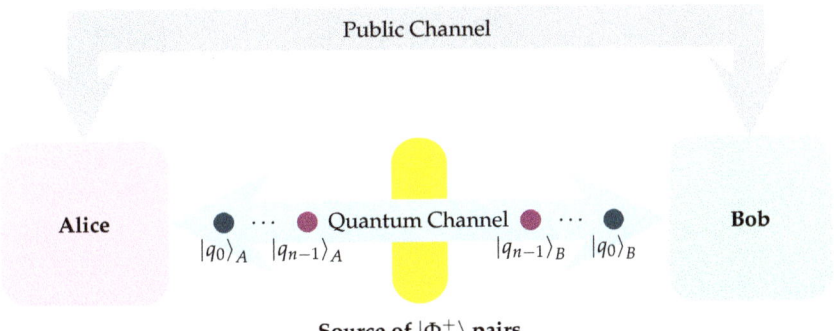

Figure 2. Alice and Bob are spatially separated. A third party, the source, creates n pairs of $|\Phi^+\rangle$ entangled photons and sends one qubit from every pair to Alice and the other qubit to Bob.

Following the aforementioned steps of the fSEBV protocol, a valid question may arise regarding what will Alice and Bob acquire after they both apply their starting secret keys $\mathbf{s}_A$ and $\mathbf{s}_B$ into their own pieces of the EPR pairs? To provide the answer, let us examine the algorithm more closely. With the help of Equation (7), the initial state of the protocol can be written as

$$|\psi_0\rangle = |\Phi^+\rangle^{\otimes n} |1\rangle_A |1\rangle_B = \frac{1}{\sqrt{2^n}} \sum_{\mathbf{x} \in \{0,1\}^n} |\mathbf{x}\rangle_A |\mathbf{x}\rangle_B |1\rangle_A |1\rangle_B \ . \tag{21}$$

Subscripts A and B are consistently used to designate Alice's and Bob's registers respectively. Alice and Bob initiate the protocol by applying the Hadamard transform to their output registers, which produces the ensuing state

$$|\psi_1\rangle = \frac{1}{\sqrt{2^n}} \sum_{\mathbf{x} \in \{0,1\}^n} |\mathbf{x}\rangle_A |\mathbf{x}\rangle_B \left(\frac{|0\rangle - |1\rangle}{\sqrt{2}}\right)_A \left(\frac{|0\rangle - |1\rangle}{\sqrt{2}}\right)_B. \quad (22)$$

Now, both Alice and Bob can apply their functions on their registers using the standard scheme

$$U_f : |\mathbf{x}, y\rangle \to |\mathbf{x}, y \oplus f(\mathbf{x})\rangle. \quad (23)$$

Consequently, the next state becomes

$$|\psi_2\rangle = \frac{1}{\sqrt{2^n}} \sum_{\mathbf{x} \in \{0,1\}^n} (-1)^{f_A(\mathbf{x})} |\mathbf{x}\rangle_A (-1)^{f_B(\mathbf{x})} |\mathbf{x}\rangle_B \left(\frac{|0\rangle - |1\rangle}{\sqrt{2}}\right)_A \left(\frac{|0\rangle - |1\rangle}{\sqrt{2}}\right)_B. \quad (24)$$

At this stage, let us recall that Alice's and Bob's functions are

$$f_A(\mathbf{x}) = \mathbf{s}_A \cdot \mathbf{x} \bmod 2 \quad (25)$$

$$f_B(\mathbf{x}) = \mathbf{s}_B \cdot \mathbf{x} \bmod 2, \quad (26)$$

where $\mathbf{s}_A$ and $\mathbf{s}_B$ are the keys chosen by Alice and Bob, respectively. Based on (24)–(26) can be written as

$$|\psi_2\rangle = \frac{1}{\sqrt{2^n}} \sum_{\mathbf{x} \in \{0,1\}^n} (-1)^{\mathbf{s}_A \cdot \mathbf{x}} |\mathbf{x}\rangle_A (-1)^{\mathbf{s}_B \cdot \mathbf{x}} |\mathbf{x}\rangle_B \left(\frac{|0\rangle - |1\rangle}{\sqrt{2}}\right)_A \left(\frac{|0\rangle - |1\rangle}{\sqrt{2}}\right)_B$$

$$= \frac{1}{\sqrt{2^n}} \sum_{\mathbf{x} \in \{0,1\}^n} (-1)^{\mathbf{s}_A \cdot \mathbf{x} \oplus \mathbf{s}_B \cdot \mathbf{x}} |\mathbf{x}\rangle_A |\mathbf{x}\rangle_B \left(\frac{|0\rangle - |1\rangle}{\sqrt{2}}\right)_A \left(\frac{|0\rangle - |1\rangle}{\sqrt{2}}\right)_B \quad (27)$$

$$= \frac{1}{\sqrt{2^n}} \sum_{\mathbf{x} \in \{0,1\}^n} (-1)^{(\mathbf{s}_A \oplus \mathbf{s}_B) \cdot \mathbf{x}} |\mathbf{x}\rangle_A |\mathbf{x}\rangle_B \left(\frac{|0\rangle - |1\rangle}{\sqrt{2}}\right)_A \left(\frac{|0\rangle - |1\rangle}{\sqrt{2}}\right)_B.$$

Subsequently, both Alice and Bob apply the Hadamard transformation to their input registers. This drives the system into the next state, which, by utilizing Equation (18) twice, can be written as

$$|\psi_3\rangle = \frac{1}{\sqrt{2^n}} \sum_{\mathbf{x} \in \{0,1\}^n} (-1)^{(\mathbf{s}_A \oplus \mathbf{s}_B) \cdot \mathbf{x}} H^{\otimes n} |\mathbf{x}\rangle_A H^{\otimes n} |\mathbf{x}\rangle_B \left(\frac{|0\rangle - |1\rangle}{\sqrt{2}}\right)_A \left(\frac{|0\rangle - |1\rangle}{\sqrt{2}}\right)_B$$

$$= \frac{1}{\sqrt{2^n}} \sum_{\mathbf{x} \in \{0,1\}^n} (-1)^{(\mathbf{s}_A \oplus \mathbf{s}_B) \cdot \mathbf{x}} \left(\frac{1}{\sqrt{2^n}} \sum_{\mathbf{z} \in \{0,1\}^n} (-1)^{\mathbf{z} \cdot \mathbf{x}} |\mathbf{z}\rangle_A\right) \left(\frac{1}{\sqrt{2^n}} \sum_{\mathbf{w} \in \{0,1\}^n} (-1)^{\mathbf{w} \cdot \mathbf{x}} |\mathbf{w}\rangle_B\right)$$

$$\left(\frac{|0\rangle - |1\rangle}{\sqrt{2}}\right)_A \left(\frac{|0\rangle - |1\rangle}{\sqrt{2}}\right)_B \quad (28)$$

$$= \frac{1}{(\sqrt{2^n})^3} \sum_{\mathbf{x} \in \{0,1\}^n} \sum_{\mathbf{z} \in \{0,1\}^n} \sum_{\mathbf{w} \in \{0,1\}^n} (-1)^{(\mathbf{s}_A \oplus \mathbf{s}_B \oplus \mathbf{z} \oplus \mathbf{w}) \cdot \mathbf{x}} |\mathbf{z}\rangle_A |\mathbf{w}\rangle_B \left(\frac{|0\rangle - |1\rangle}{\sqrt{2}}\right)_A \left(\frac{|0\rangle - |1\rangle}{\sqrt{2}}\right)_B$$

$$= \frac{1}{(\sqrt{2^n})^3} \sum_{\mathbf{z} \in \{0,1\}^n} \sum_{\mathbf{w} \in \{0,1\}^n} \sum_{\mathbf{x} \in \{0,1\}^n} (-1)^{(\mathbf{s}_A \oplus \mathbf{s}_B \oplus \mathbf{z} \oplus \mathbf{w}) \cdot \mathbf{x}} |\mathbf{z}\rangle_A |\mathbf{w}\rangle_B \left(\frac{|0\rangle - |1\rangle}{\sqrt{2}}\right)_A \left(\frac{|0\rangle - |1\rangle}{\sqrt{2}}\right)_B.$$

When $\mathbf{z} \oplus \mathbf{w} = \mathbf{s}_A \oplus \mathbf{s}_B$, then $\forall \mathbf{x} \in \{0,1\}^n$, the expression $(-1)^{(\mathbf{s}_A \oplus \mathbf{s}_B \oplus \mathbf{z} \oplus \mathbf{w}) \cdot \mathbf{x}}$ becomes $(-1)^0 = 1$ and the sum $\sum_{\mathbf{x} \in \{0,1\}^n} (-1)^{(\mathbf{s}_A \oplus \mathbf{s}_B \oplus \mathbf{z} \oplus \mathbf{w}) \cdot \mathbf{x}} = 2^n$.

Whenever $\mathbf{z} \oplus \mathbf{w} \neq \mathbf{s}_A \oplus \mathbf{s}_B$, the sum is just 0 because for exactly half of the inputs $\mathbf{x}$ the exponent will be 0 and for the remaining half the exponent will be 1. Hence, one may write that

$$\sum_{\mathbf{x} \in \{0,1\}^n} (-1)^{(\mathbf{s}_A \oplus \mathbf{s}_B \oplus \mathbf{z} \oplus \mathbf{w}) \cdot \mathbf{x}} = 2^n \delta_{\mathbf{s}_A \oplus \mathbf{s}_B, \mathbf{z} \oplus \mathbf{w}} . \qquad (29)$$

Using Equation (29), and ignoring for the moment the two factors $\left(\frac{|0\rangle - |1\rangle}{\sqrt{2}} \right)_A$ and $\left(\frac{|0\rangle - |1\rangle}{\sqrt{2}} \right)_B$, the following two equivalent and symmetric forms can be derived

$$\sum_{\mathbf{z} \in \{0,1\}^n} \sum_{\mathbf{w} \in \{0,1\}^n} \sum_{\mathbf{x} \in \{0,1\}^n} (-1)^{(\mathbf{s}_A \oplus \mathbf{s}_B \oplus \mathbf{z} \oplus \mathbf{w}) \cdot \mathbf{x}} |\mathbf{z}\rangle_A |\mathbf{w}\rangle_B = 2^n \sum_{\mathbf{z} \in \{0,1\}^n} |\mathbf{z}\rangle_A |\mathbf{s}_A \oplus \mathbf{s}_B \oplus \mathbf{z}\rangle_B , \qquad (30)$$

and

$$\sum_{\mathbf{w} \in \{0,1\}^n} \sum_{\mathbf{z} \in \{0,1\}^n} \sum_{\mathbf{x} \in \{0,1\}^n} (-1)^{(\mathbf{s}_A \oplus \mathbf{s}_B \oplus \mathbf{z} \oplus \mathbf{w}) \cdot \mathbf{x}} |\mathbf{z}\rangle_A |\mathbf{w}\rangle_B = 2^n \sum_{\mathbf{w} \in \{0,1\}^n} |\mathbf{s}_A \oplus \mathbf{s}_B \oplus \mathbf{w}\rangle_A |\mathbf{w}\rangle_B . \qquad (31)$$

By combining (28) with (30) and (31), state $|\psi_3\rangle$ can be written in two different ways:

$$
\begin{aligned}
|\psi_3\rangle &= \frac{1}{\sqrt{2^n}} \sum_{\mathbf{z} \in \{0,1\}^n} |\mathbf{z}\rangle_A |\mathbf{s}_A \oplus \mathbf{s}_B \oplus \mathbf{z}\rangle_B \left(\frac{|0\rangle - |1\rangle}{\sqrt{2}} \right)_A \left(\frac{|0\rangle - |1\rangle}{\sqrt{2}} \right)_B \\
&= \frac{1}{\sqrt{2^n}} \sum_{\mathbf{w} \in \{0,1\}^n} |\mathbf{s}_A \oplus \mathbf{s}_B \oplus \mathbf{w}\rangle_A |\mathbf{w}\rangle_B \left(\frac{|0\rangle - |1\rangle}{\sqrt{2}} \right)_A \left(\frac{|0\rangle - |1\rangle}{\sqrt{2}} \right)_B .
\end{aligned} \qquad (32)
$$

Finally, Alice and Bob measure their EPR pairs in the input registers, obtaining

$$|\psi_4\rangle = |\mathbf{z}_0\rangle_A |\mathbf{s}_A \oplus \mathbf{s}_B \oplus \mathbf{z}_0\rangle_B = |\mathbf{s}_A \oplus \mathbf{s}_B \oplus \mathbf{w}_0\rangle_A |\mathbf{w}_0\rangle_B , \quad \text{for some} \quad \mathbf{z}_0, \mathbf{w}_0 \in \{0,1\}^n . \qquad (33)$$

Please note that in general $\mathbf{z}_0 \neq \mathbf{w}_0$. The quantum part of the protocol is now complete. The final secret key is the string $\mathbf{s}_A \oplus \mathbf{s}_B \oplus \mathbf{z}_0$ that Bob measured in his input register. In the highly unlikely event that $|\mathbf{s}_A \oplus \mathbf{s}_B \oplus \mathbf{z}_0\rangle = |0\rangle^{\otimes n}$, Bob should inform Alice through the use of the public channel that the whole procedure must be repeated once again, since such a key is clearly unacceptable. However, for a n-bit key the probability of this happening is negligible, specifically $\frac{1}{2^n}$, which rapidly tends to 0 as $n \to \infty$. Hence, it may be safely assumed that Bob possesses a viable secret key, namely $\mathbf{s}_A \oplus \mathbf{s}_B \oplus \mathbf{z}_0$. Now the final step is for Alice to obtain the secret key too. This is easily achieved by simply having Bob publicly announce his tentative secret key $\mathbf{s}_B$ to Alice via the use of the public channel. Alice, who has measured the binary string $\mathbf{z}_0$ and she is already aware of her initial secret key $\mathbf{s}_A$, can easily obtain the final key, by simply calculating the XOR of $\mathbf{s}_A$, her measurement $\mathbf{z}_0$ and Bob's initial key $\mathbf{s}_B$, which she learns from the public channel. This concludes the fSEBV protocol.

The symmetry inherent in this protocol, enables the seamless reversal of roles. The protocol, as stated above, grants the initiative to Bob: it is his measurement $\mathbf{s}_A \oplus \mathbf{s}_B \oplus \mathbf{z}_0$ that produces the secret key and it is his task to send his initial key $\mathbf{s}_B$ to Alice, in order to successfully complete the procedure. It is equally feasible to have Alice instead of Bob drive the whole process by taking her measurement $\mathbf{s}_A \oplus \mathbf{s}_B \oplus \mathbf{w}_0$ to be the secret key, as shown in (33). In such an implementation of the fSEBV protocol, Alice must reveal her initial key $\mathbf{s}_A$ to Bob via the public channel.

During the transmission of Bob's key $\mathbf{s}_B$ using a public channel, any potential eavesdropper, namely Eve, does not gain any advantage by listening to the public channel. Due to the fact that she is oblivious of $\mathbf{z}_0$ and $\mathbf{s}_A$, she has no way of knowing or computing the final secret key. Hence, the fSEBV protocol ensures that if Alice and Bob can create their keys using a random number generator, in order to avoid possible patterns in the keys, Eve will be left with 2^n different combinations to test in order to find the secret key.

The steps of the protocol from Alice's and Bob's side are shown below in an algorithmic manner. Figure 3 depicts the protocol graphically in the form of a quantum circuit.

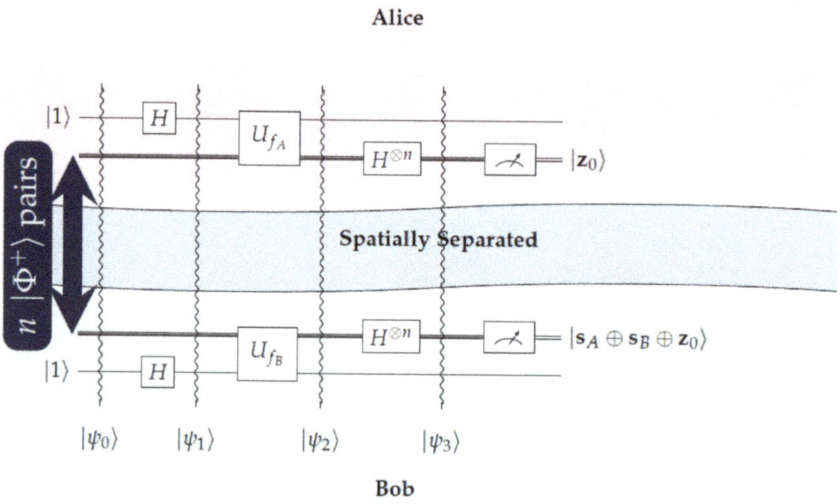

Figure 3. This figures gives a schematic representation of the proposed protocol.

Protocol fSEBV: Alice's actions

Alice's input register is populated with entangled qubits
- Alice's output register is set to $|1\rangle$
- Alice applies the Hadamard transform to her output register
- Alice applies her tentative key $\mathbf{s}_A$
- Alice applies the Hadamard transform to her input register
- Alice measures her input register to find the random binary string $\mathbf{z}_0$
- Alice receives information from Bob whether the process was a success or must be repeated
- If the procedure was successful, Alice receives from Bob his key $\mathbf{s}_B$ and, by already knowing $\mathbf{s}_A$ and $\mathbf{z}_0$, she computes the final key $\mathbf{s}_A \oplus \mathbf{s}_B \oplus \mathbf{z}_0$

Protocol fSEBV: Bob's actions

- Bob's input register is populated with entangled qubits
- Bob's output register is set to $|1\rangle$
- Bob applies the Hadamard transform to his output register
- Bob applies his tentative key $\mathbf{s}_B$
- Bob applies the Hadamard transform to his input register
- Bob measures his input register to find the final secret key $\mathbf{s}_A \oplus \mathbf{s}_B \oplus \mathbf{z}_0$
- In the unlikely event that $|\mathbf{s}_A \oplus \mathbf{s}_B \oplus \mathbf{z}_0\rangle = |0\rangle^{\otimes n}$, Bob informs Alice that the process must be repeated from the start
- Otherwise Bob communicates his tentative key $\mathbf{s}_B$ to Alice via the public channel

---

3.2. The sSEBV Protocol

The sSEBV protocol explores a special but important case of the fSEBV protocol, which differs from the latter in one important aspect. Alice possesses her random initial key $\mathbf{s}_A$, but Bob's key $\mathbf{s}_B$ is not a random binary string anymore; it is specifically taken to be $\mathbf{0} = 0\ldots0$. Essentially, sSEBV protocol answers the question of what will happen, if one of the players, either Alice or Bob, decides not to send a key. As before Alice and Bob are spatially separated and they both share n EPR pairs. In this variant, Alice and Bod behave in a semi-symmetrical way. Alice still uses her random initial key s_A, but Bob is obliged to use $\mathbf{0}$ as his initial key.

In this case, by using Equation (7), it can seen that the initial state of the system is the following

$$|\psi_0\rangle = |\Phi^+\rangle^{\otimes n} |1\rangle_A |1\rangle_B = \frac{1}{\sqrt{2^n}} \sum_{\mathbf{x} \in \{0,1\}^n} |\mathbf{x}\rangle_A |\mathbf{x}\rangle_B |1\rangle_A |1\rangle_B . \qquad (34)$$

Similarly, Alice and Bob initiate the protocol by applying the Hadamard transform to their output registers, which produces the ensuing state

$$|\psi_1\rangle = \frac{1}{\sqrt{2^n}} \sum_{\mathbf{x} \in \{0,1\}^n} |\mathbf{x}\rangle_A |\mathbf{x}\rangle_B \left(\frac{|0\rangle - |1\rangle}{\sqrt{2}} \right)_A \left(\frac{|0\rangle - |1\rangle}{\sqrt{2}} \right)_B . \qquad (35)$$

Next Alice and Bob apply their corresponding functions on their registers via the standard scheme

$$U_f : |\mathbf{x}, y\rangle \to |\mathbf{x}, y \oplus f(\mathbf{x})\rangle , \qquad (36)$$

only now the situation is quite different because Bob must necessarily use $\mathbf{0}$:

$$f_A(\mathbf{x}) = \mathbf{s}_A \cdot \mathbf{x} \bmod 2 \qquad (37)$$

$$f_B(\mathbf{x}) = \mathbf{0} \cdot \mathbf{x} \bmod 2 = 0 . \qquad (38)$$

In view of Equations (37) and (38), the next state becomes

$$|\psi_2\rangle = \frac{1}{\sqrt{2^n}} \sum_{\mathbf{x} \in \{0,1\}^n} (-1)^{f_A(\mathbf{x})} |\mathbf{x}\rangle_A (-1)^0 |\mathbf{x}\rangle_B \left(\frac{|0\rangle - |1\rangle}{\sqrt{2}} \right)_A \left(\frac{|0\rangle - |1\rangle}{\sqrt{2}} \right)_B$$

$$= \frac{1}{\sqrt{2^n}} \sum_{\mathbf{x} \in \{0,1\}^n} (-1)^{\mathbf{s}_A \cdot \mathbf{x}} |\mathbf{x}\rangle_A |\mathbf{x}\rangle_B \left(\frac{|0\rangle - |1\rangle}{\sqrt{2}} \right)_A \left(\frac{|0\rangle - |1\rangle}{\sqrt{2}} \right)_B . \qquad (39)$$

Subsequently, both Alice and Bob apply the Hadamard transformation to their input registers. Taking into account Equation (18), one can see that their combined actions drive the system into the next state

$$|\psi_3\rangle = \frac{1}{\sqrt{2^n}} \sum_{\mathbf{x} \in \{0,1\}^n} (-1)^{\mathbf{s}_A \cdot \mathbf{x}} H^{\otimes n} |\mathbf{x}\rangle_A H^{\otimes n} |\mathbf{x}\rangle_B \left(\frac{|0\rangle - |1\rangle}{\sqrt{2}} \right)_A \left(\frac{|0\rangle - |1\rangle}{\sqrt{2}} \right)_B$$

$$= \frac{1}{\sqrt{2^n}} \sum_{\mathbf{x} \in \{0,1\}^n} (-1)^{\mathbf{s}_A \cdot \mathbf{x}} \left(\frac{1}{\sqrt{2^n}} \sum_{\mathbf{z} \in \{0,1\}^n} (-1)^{\mathbf{z} \cdot \mathbf{x}} |\mathbf{z}\rangle_A \right) \left(\frac{1}{\sqrt{2^n}} \sum_{\mathbf{w} \in \{0,1\}^n} (-1)^{\mathbf{w} \cdot \mathbf{x}} |\mathbf{w}\rangle_B \right)$$

$$\left(\frac{|0\rangle - |1\rangle}{\sqrt{2}} \right)_A \left(\frac{|0\rangle - |1\rangle}{\sqrt{2}} \right)_B \qquad (40)$$

$$= \frac{1}{(\sqrt{2^n})^3} \sum_{\mathbf{x} \in \{0,1\}^n} \sum_{\mathbf{z} \in \{0,1\}^n} \sum_{\mathbf{w} \in \{0,1\}^n} (-1)^{(\mathbf{s}_A \oplus \mathbf{z} \oplus \mathbf{w}) \cdot \mathbf{x}} |\mathbf{z}\rangle_A |\mathbf{w}\rangle_B \left(\frac{|0\rangle - |1\rangle}{\sqrt{2}} \right)_A \left(\frac{|0\rangle - |1\rangle}{\sqrt{2}} \right)_B$$

$$= \frac{1}{(\sqrt{2^n})^3} \sum_{\mathbf{z} \in \{0,1\}^n} \sum_{\mathbf{w} \in \{0,1\}^n} \sum_{\mathbf{x} \in \{0,1\}^n} (-1)^{(\mathbf{s}_A \oplus \mathbf{z} \oplus \mathbf{w}) \cdot \mathbf{x}} |\mathbf{z}\rangle_A |\mathbf{w}\rangle_B \left(\frac{|0\rangle - |1\rangle}{\sqrt{2}} \right)_A \left(\frac{|0\rangle - |1\rangle}{\sqrt{2}} \right)_B .$$

When $\mathbf{z} \oplus \mathbf{w} = \mathbf{s}_A$, then $\forall \mathbf{x} \in \{0,1\}^n$, the expression $(-1)^{(\mathbf{s}_A \oplus \mathbf{z} \oplus \mathbf{w}) \cdot \mathbf{x}}$ becomes $(-1)^0 = 1$ and the sum $\sum_{\mathbf{x} \in \{0,1\}^n} (-1)^{(\mathbf{s}_A \oplus \mathbf{z} \oplus \mathbf{w}) \cdot \mathbf{x}} = 2^n$. Whenever $\mathbf{z} \oplus \mathbf{w} \neq \mathbf{s}_A$, the sum is just 0 because for exactly half of the inputs $\mathbf{x}$ the exponent will be 0 and for the remaining half the exponent will be 1. Therefore, again one may write that

$$\sum_{\mathbf{x}\in\{0,1\}^n} (-1)^{(\mathbf{s}_A\oplus\mathbf{z}\oplus\mathbf{w})\cdot\mathbf{x}} = 2^n \delta_{\mathbf{s}_A,\mathbf{z}\oplus\mathbf{w}} . \quad (41)$$

Using Equation (41), and ignoring for the moment the two factors $\left(\frac{|0\rangle-|1\rangle}{\sqrt{2}}\right)_A$ and $\left(\frac{|0\rangle-|1\rangle}{\sqrt{2}}\right)_{B'}$ the following two equivalent and symmetric forms can be derived

$$\sum_{\mathbf{z}\in\{0,1\}^n} \sum_{\mathbf{w}\in\{0,1\}^n} \sum_{\mathbf{x}\in\{0,1\}^n} (-1)^{(\mathbf{s}_A\oplus\mathbf{s}_B\oplus\mathbf{z}\oplus\mathbf{w})\cdot\mathbf{x}} |\mathbf{z}\rangle_A |\mathbf{w}\rangle_B = 2^n \sum_{\mathbf{z}\in\{0,1\}^n} |\mathbf{z}\rangle_A |\mathbf{s}_A\oplus\mathbf{z}\rangle_B , \quad (42)$$

and

$$\sum_{\mathbf{w}\in\{0,1\}^n} \sum_{\mathbf{z}\in\{0,1\}^n} \sum_{\mathbf{x}\in\{0,1\}^n} (-1)^{(\mathbf{s}_A\oplus\mathbf{z}\oplus\mathbf{w})\cdot\mathbf{x}} |\mathbf{z}\rangle_A |\mathbf{w}\rangle_B = 2^n \sum_{\mathbf{w}\in\{0,1\}^n} |\mathbf{s}_A\oplus\mathbf{w}\rangle_A |\mathbf{w}\rangle_B . \quad (43)$$

By combining (40) with (42) and (43), state $|\psi_3\rangle$ can be written in two different ways:

$$\begin{aligned}|\psi_3\rangle &= \frac{1}{\sqrt{2^n}} \sum_{\mathbf{z}\in\{0,1\}^n} |\mathbf{z}\rangle_A |\mathbf{s}_A\oplus\mathbf{z}\rangle_B \left(\frac{|0\rangle-|1\rangle}{\sqrt{2}}\right)_A \left(\frac{|0\rangle-|1\rangle}{\sqrt{2}}\right)_B \\ &= \frac{1}{\sqrt{2^n}} \sum_{\mathbf{w}\in\{0,1\}^n} |\mathbf{s}_A\oplus\mathbf{w}\rangle_A |\mathbf{w}\rangle_B \left(\frac{|0\rangle-|1\rangle}{\sqrt{2}}\right)_A \left(\frac{|0\rangle-|1\rangle}{\sqrt{2}}\right)_B .\end{aligned} \quad (44)$$

Now, when Alice and Bob measure their input registers, they will obtain

$$|\psi_4\rangle = |\mathbf{z}_0\rangle_A |\mathbf{s}_A\oplus\mathbf{z}_0\rangle_B = |\mathbf{s}_A\oplus\mathbf{w}_0\rangle_A |\mathbf{w}_0\rangle_B , \quad \text{for some} \quad \mathbf{z}_0,\mathbf{w}_0\in\{0,1\}^n . \quad (45)$$

As in the fSEBV protocol, here also holds that $\mathbf{z}_0 \neq \mathbf{w}_0$ in general. This time, there are two ways in which the final part of the protocol can unfold. One way, exactly like before, is to take Bob's measurement as the new secret key. The other, equally viable choice, is to take Alice's initial key $\mathbf{s}_A$ as the final secret key. In that case Alice must publicly announce $\mathbf{z}_0$ to Bob via a public channel, so that he can compute $\mathbf{s}_A$. This is a suitable choice in cases where, for whatever reason, Alice must set the secret key herself, not wanting to leave anything to chance. In that way she may securely communicate her chosen key to Bob. As before, during the transmission of Alice's measurement $\mathbf{z}_0$ using a public channel, Eve does not gain any advantage by eavesdropping on their communication. Due to the fact that she is oblivious to $\mathbf{s}_A$, she has no way of knowing or computing the final secret key. Hence, the sSEBV protocol also ensures that if Alice devises her key using a random number generator, in order to avoid possible patterns in the keys, Eve will be left with 2^n different combinations to test in order to find the secret key.

The detailed actions for the implementation of the sSEBV protocol from Alice's and Bob's side are given below. Although the sSEBV protocol is not perfectly symmetric, reversal of Alice's and Bob's roles is still trivially easy. As can be seen from the following description, not only is Alice the one to choose the secret key, but it is also she that sends the final measurement $\mathbf{z}_0$ to Bob so that he can successfully derive the secret key. It is equally feasible to have Bob instead of Alice choose the secret key and have Alice use **0** in the first stage. In such a realization of the sSEBV protocol, Bob must also reveal his final measurement $\mathbf{w}_0$ to Alice via the public channel.

4. Examples Illustrating the Operation of the Protocols

This section presents and analyzes two small scale but detailed examples in order to illustrate the operation of the fSEBV and sSEBV protocols in practice. The fSEBV and sSEBV protocols were simulated using IBM's *Qiskit* open source SDK ([28]). Specifically, the Aer provider using the high performance *qasm* simulator for simulating quantum circuits [29] in its default settings was used. Please note that during our tests it was not possible to simulate in Qiskit Alice and Bob being spatially separated or a third party source providing the entangled EPR pairs. So these important assumptions cannot be accurately reflected in the simulation and for that reason the examples do not represent a real life environment. As a result Alice and Bob appear in the same circuit. Specifically, Alice's input register consists of the qubits $|q_2 q_1 q_0\rangle$ and her output register is $|q_3\rangle$. Symmetrically, Bob's input register consists of the qubits $|q_6 q_5 q_4\rangle$ and his output register is $|q_7\rangle$. Moreover, the entangled EPR pairs are created by the circuit itself. This is depicted in Figures 4, where in the initial stage of the corresponding circuits Hadamard and CNOT gates are used to populate Alice's and Bob's input registers with entangled EPR pairs, exactly as explained in Section 2.

Protocol sSEBV: Alice's actions
- Alice's input register is populated with entangled qubits
- Alice's output register is set to $|1\rangle$
- Alice applies the Hadamard transform to her output register
- Alice applies her chosen key s_A
- Alice applies the Hadamard transform to her input register
- Alice measures her input register to find the random binary string z_0
- Alice announces the binary string z_0 to Bob via the public channel

---
Protocol sSEBV: Bob's actions
- Bob's input register is populated with entangled qubits
- Bob's output register is set to $|1\rangle$
- Bob applies the Hadamard transform to his output register
- Bob applies his key **0**
- Bob applies the Hadamard transform to his input register
- Bob measures his input register to find the binary string $s_A \oplus z_0$
- Bob receives z_0 and computes the key s_A

4.1. Example for the fSEBV Protocol

In this example it is assumed that $s_A = 101$ and $s_B = 110$. The resulting circuit in displayed in Figure 4.

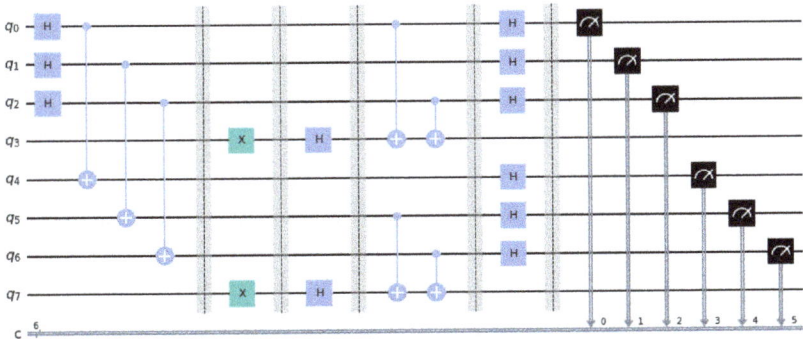

Figure 4. The circuit for the fSEBV protocol.

The final measurement by Alice and Bob will produce one of the 8 outcomes shown in Figure 5 along with their corresponding probabilities as given by running the qasm simulator for 2048 shots. A simple inspection of the possible outcomes confirms Equation (33). This is because every possible outcome can be written either as $|z_0\rangle_A |s_A \oplus s_B \oplus z_0\rangle_B$ or as $|s_A \oplus s_B \oplus w_0\rangle_A |w_0\rangle_B$, for some, generally different, $z_0, w_0 \in \{0,1\}^n$. Hence, Bob, after measuring (and accepting) the secret key $\mathbf{s}_A \oplus \mathbf{s}_B \oplus \mathbf{z}_0$, just needs to send his secret key $\mathbf{s}_B = 110$ to Alice so that she too can derive the secret key.

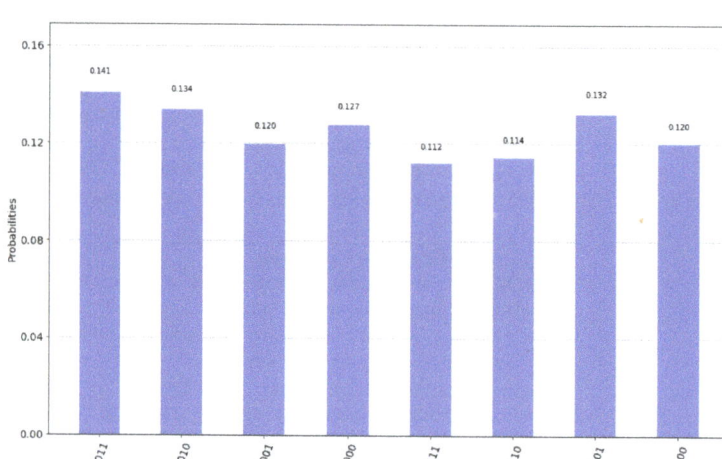

Figure 5. The possible outcomes of the measurement and their corresponding probabilities for the circuit in Figure 4.

To avoid any confusion, we clarify that the measurements shown in Figure 5 depict both Alice's and Bob's input registers as $|q_6 q_5 q_4 q_2 q_1 q_0\rangle$. In particular, every one of the eight possible outcomes is shown along with the probability of measuring this outcome, as computed by the qasm simulator. The three most significant bits represent Bob's measurement or $|\mathbf{s}_A \oplus \mathbf{s}_B \oplus \mathbf{z}_0\rangle_B$ and the three least significant bits represent Alice's measurement or $|\mathbf{z}_0\rangle_A$. Thus, for this specific example, if Bob announces his initial key $\mathbf{s}_B = 110$ to Alice, and Alice performs a XOR operation upon her measurement with Bob's initial key and her own initial key $\mathbf{s}_A = 101$, then Alice will obtain Bob's final measurement, which is the secret key.

4.2. Example for the sSEBV Protocol

In this example too, the entangled EPR pairs are created by the circuit itself. In the initial stage of the corresponding circuits Hadamard and CNOT gates are used to populate Alice's and Bob's input registers with entangled EPR pairs, as explained in Section 2. Moreover, it is assumed that $\mathbf{s}_A = 101$ and $\mathbf{s}_B = 000$. The resulting circuit in displayed in Figure 6.

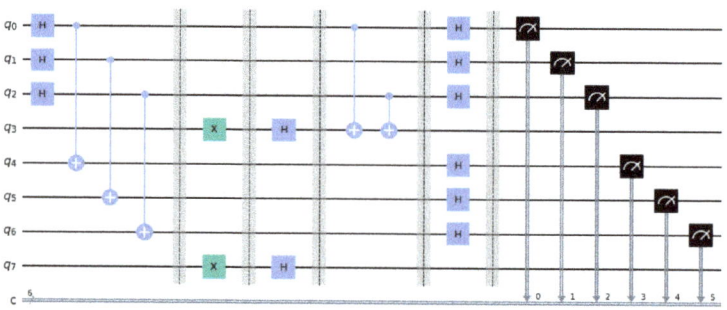

Figure 6. The circuit for the sSEBV protocol.

This time the final measurement by Alice and Bob will produce one of the 8 outcomes shown in Figure 7 along with their corresponding probabilities as given by running the qasm simulator for 2048 shots. As noted in the previous case, it suffices to inspect the possible outcomes in order to confirm Equation (45). Now the correct interpretation of the outcomes means viewing them either as $|z_0\rangle_A |s_A \oplus z_0\rangle_B$ or as $|s_A \oplus w_0\rangle_A |w_0\rangle_B$, for some, generally different, $z_0, w_0 \in \{0,1\}^n$. Hence, Alice, after making her final measurement and finding a random binary string z_0, she just needs to send z_0 to Bob. Then Bob will be able to derive Alice's chosen secret key $s_A = 101$.

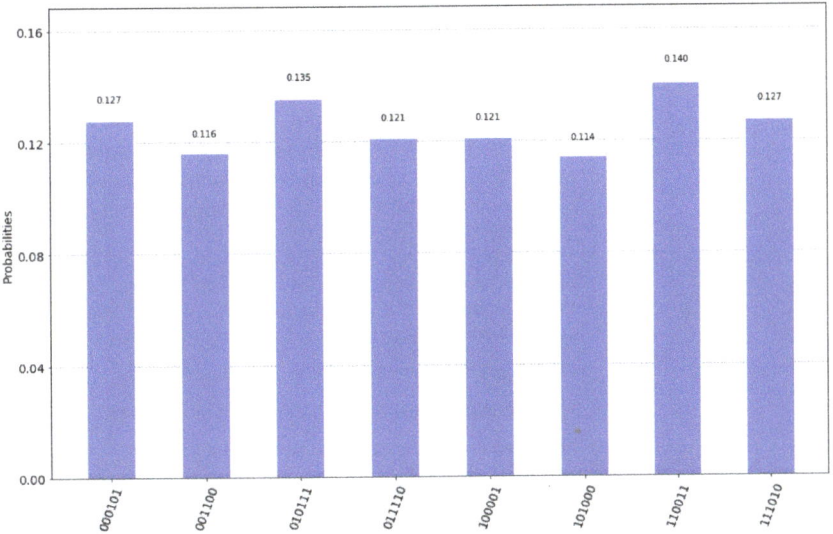

Figure 7. The possible outcomes of the measurement and their corresponding probabilities for the circuit in Figure 6.

Again, all of the eight possible outcomes are shown along with the probability of measuring each one of them, as computed by the qasm simulator. The measurements shown in Figure 7 depict both Alice's and Bob's input registers as $|q_6 q_5 q_4 q_2 q_1 q_0\rangle$, that is the three most significant bits represent Bob's measurement or $|s_A \oplus z_0\rangle_B$ and the three least significant bits represent Alice's measurement or $|z_0\rangle_A$. In this specific example, if Alice announces her measurement $|z_0\rangle_A$ to Bob, and Bob performs a XOR operation upon his measurement, with Alice's measurement, then Bob will obtain the secret key $s_A = 101$ chosen by Alice.

5. Discussion and Conclusions

QKD protocols have surely proved by now that they are the future of key distribution. Their advantage stems from the fact that they allow us to harness the power of quantum-mechanics and nature's own laws, without having to rely on the complexity of certain mathematical problems. In this paper, we tried to further expand the field of quantum cryptography, by proposing a novel use for the Bernstein-Vazirani algorithm as a symmetrical entanglement-based QKD protocol, coming in two flavors.

These two flavors differ on the degree of symmetry employed by the protocol. In the fully symmetric variant, Alice and Bob take completely identical actions. This variant has the ability to create a totally new and original key, a key that both Alice and Bob were initially oblivious of. This can be useful in many situations as it ensures an additional advantage security wise. Furthermore, it provides a degree of fairness, by putting both parties on an equal footing, in the sense that neither Alice nor Bob can solely determine the secret key.

On the other hand, the semi-symmetric variant, which can technically be viewed as a special case of the first protocol, deviates from this symmetry. In effect, the semi-symmetric protocol answers the question of what will happen if one of the two players wants to specify the secret key. In the presentation given in Section 3 it was Alice that chose the secret key, but it is trivial to adjust the protocol so that Bob can be the party to decide the secret key. This protocol can be useful in situations where a specific key must be chosen by either Alice or Bob, and this key must be securely transmitted to the other party.

Additionally, we demonstrated two small scale but comprehensive examples, illustrating the operation of the two protocols in practice. Finally, we explained the protocols strength against an eavesdropping attack by Eve. Both variants exhibit the inherent robustness of entanglement-based protocols against Eve's attacks, as originally described by Ekert. Moreover, the use of extra inputs in order to acquire the final secret key, adds another layer of security.

In closing, we remark that we also believe that the rest of the old quantum algorithms, such as the Deutsch-Jozsa algorithm and Simon's periodicity algorithm, can all be implemented as a symmetrical entanglement-based QKD protocols, posing a viable suggestion for future work, along with the performance of these proposals against different quantum attacks.

Author Contributions: Conceptualization, T.A. and M.A.; methodology, T.A.; validation, M.A.; formal analysis, T.A.; investigation, M.A.; writing original draft preparation, M.A. and T.A. All authors have read and agreed to the published version of the manuscript.

Funding: This research received no external funding.

Institutional Review Board Statement: Not applicable.

Informed Consent Statement: Not applicable.

Data Availability Statement: Data sharing not applicable.

Conflicts of Interest: The authors declare no conflict of interest.

References

1. Shor, P.W. Polynomial-time algorithms for prime factorization and discrete logarithms on a quantum computer. *SIAM Rev.* **1999**, *41*, 303–332. [CrossRef]
2. Grover, L. A fast quantum mechanical algorithm for database search. In Proceedings of the Twenty-Eighth Annual ACM Symposium on the Theory of Computing, Philadelphia, PA, USA, 22–24 May 1996; [CrossRef]
3. Chen, L.; Chen, L.; Jordan, S.; Liu, Y.K.; Moody, D.; Peralta, R.; Perlner, R.; Smith-Tone, D. *Report on POST-Quantum Cryptography*; US Department of Commerce, National Institute of Standards and Technology: Gaithersburg, MD, USA, 2016; Volume 12.
4. Bennett, C.H.; Brassard, G. Quantum Cryptography: Public Key Distribution and Coin Tossing. In Proceedings of the IEEE International Conference on Computers, Systems, and Signal Processing, Bangalore, India, 10–12 December 1984; pp. 175–179.
5. Ekert, A.K. Quantum cryptography based on Bell's theorem. *Phys. Rev. Lett.* **1991**, *67*, 661–663. [CrossRef] [PubMed]
6. Bennett, C.H.; Brassard, G. Experimental quantum cryptography: The dawn of a new era for quantum cryptography: the experimental prototype is working. *ACM Sigact News* **1989**, *20*, 78–80. [CrossRef]
7. Elliott, C.; Colvin, A.; Pearson, D.; Pikalo, O.; Schlafer, J.; Yeh, H. Current status of the DARPA quantum network. In *Quantum Information and Computation III*; International Society for Optics and Photonics: Bellingham, Washington, USA, 2005; Volume 5815, pp. 138–149.
8. Elliott, C. The DARPA quantum network. In *Quantum Communications and Cryptography*; CRC Press: Boca Raton, FL, USA, 2018; pp. 91–110.
9. Peev, M.; Pacher, C.; Alléaume, R.; Barreiro, C.; Bouda, J.; Boxleitner, W.; Debuisschert, T.; Diamanti, E.; Dianati, M.; Dynes, J.; et al. The SECOQC quantum key distribution network in Vienna. *New J. Phys.* **2009**, *11*, 075001. [CrossRef]
10. Sasaki, M.; Fujiwara, M.; Ishizuka, H.; Klaus, W.; Wakui, K.; Takeoka, M.; Miki, S.; Yamashita, T.; Wang, Z.; Tanaka, A.; et al. Field test of quantum key distribution in the Tokyo QKD Network. *Opt. Express* **2011**, *19*, 10387–10409. [CrossRef] [PubMed]
11. Liao, S.K.; Cai, W.Q.; Liu, W.Y.; Zhang, L.; Li, Y.; Ren, J.G.; Yin, J.; Shen, Q.; Cao, Y.; Li, Z.P.; et al. Satellite-to-ground quantum key distribution. *Nature* **2017**, *549*, 43–47. [CrossRef] [PubMed]
12. Deutsch, D.; Jozsa, R. Rapid solution of problems by quantum computation. *Proc. R. Soc. Lond. Ser. A Math. Phys. Sci.* **1992**, *439*, 553–558. [CrossRef]
13. Bernstein, E.; Vazirani, U. Quantum Complexity Theory. *SIAM J. Comput.* **1997**, *26*, 1411–1473. [CrossRef]
14. Simon, D.R. On the Power of Quantum Computation. *SIAM J. Comput.* **1997**, *26*, 1474–1483. [CrossRef]

15. Nagata, K.; Nakamura, T.; Farouk, A. Quantum Cryptography Based on the Deutsch-Jozsa Algorithm. *Int. J. Theor. Phys.* **2017**, *56*, 2887–2897. [CrossRef]
16. Nagata, K.; Nakamura, T. Quantum Cryptography, Quantum Communication, and Quantum Computer in a Noisy Environment. *Int. J. Theor. Phys.* **2017**, *56*, 2086–2100. [CrossRef]
17. Nagata, K.; Nakamura, T.; Geurdes, H.; Batle, J.; Abdalla, S.; Farouk, A. Secure quantum key distribution based on a special Deutsch-Jozsa algorithm. *Asian J. Math. Phys.* **2017**, *2*, 6–13.
18. Diffie, W.; Hellman, M. New directions in cryptography. *IEEE Trans. Inf. Theory* **1976**, *22*, 644–654. [CrossRef]
19. Bennett, C.H.; Brassard, G. Quantum cryptography: Public key distribution and coin tossing. *Theor. Comput. Sci.* **2014**, *560*, 7–11. [CrossRef]
20. Aharon, N.; Silman, J. Quantum dice rolling: A multi-outcome generalization of quantum coin flipping. *New J. Phys.* **2010**, *12*, 033027. [CrossRef]
21. Meyer, D.A. Quantum strategies. *Phys. Rev. Lett.* **1999**, *82*, 1052. [CrossRef]
22. Eisert, J.; Wilkens, M.; Lewenstein, M. Quantum games and quantum strategies. *Phys. Rev. Lett.* **1999**, *83*, 3077. [CrossRef]
23. Andronikos, T.; Sirokofskich, A.; Kastampolidou, K.; Varvouzou, M.; Giannakis, K.; Singh, A. Finite Automata Capturing Winning Sequences for All Possible Variants of the PQ Penny Flip Game. *Mathematics* **2018**, *6*, 20. [CrossRef]
24. Andronikos, T.; Sirokofskich, A. The Connection between the PQ Penny Flip Game and the Dihedral Groups. *Mathematics* **2021**, *9*, 1115. [CrossRef]
25. Giannakis, K.; Theocharopoulou, G.; Papalitsas, C.; Fanarioti, S.; Andronikos, T. Quantum Conditional Strategies and Automata for Prisoners' Dilemmata under the EWL Scheme. *Appl. Sci.* **2019**, *9*, 2635. [CrossRef]
26. Nielsen, M.A.; Chuang, I.L. *Quantum Computation and Quantum Information*; Cambridge University Press: Cambridge, UK, 2010.
27. Mermin, N. *Quantum Computer Science: An Introduction*; Cambridge University Press: Cambridge, UK, 2007.10.1017/cbo9780511813870. [CrossRef]
28. Qiskit. Qiskit Open-Source Quantum Development. Available online: https://qiskit.org (accessed on 5 June 2021).
29. Qasm. The Qasm Simulator. Available online: https://qiskit.org/documentation/stubs/qiskit.providers.aer.QasmSimulator.html (accessed on 3 July 2021).

Article

Protecting Physical Layer Secret Key Generation from Active Attacks

Miroslav Mitev [1,*], Arsenia Chorti [2], E. Veronica Belmega [2] and H. Vincent Poor [3]

- [1] Barkhausen Institut gGmbH, Würzburger Str. 46, 01187 Dresden, Germany
- [2] ETIS, UMR 8051 CY Cergy Paris Université, ENSEA, CNRS, 95000 Cergy, France; arsenia.chorti@ensea.fr (A.C.); veronica.belmega@ensea.fr (E.V.B.)
- [3] School of Engineering and Applied Science, Princeton University, Princeton, NJ 08544, USA; poor@princeton.edu
- * Correspondence: Miroslav.Mitev@barkhauseninstitut.org

Citation: Mitev, M.; Chorti, A.; Belmega, E.V.; Poor, H.V. Protecting Physical Layer Secret Key Generation from Active Attacks. *Entropy* **2021**, *23*, 960. https://doi.org/10.3390/e23080960

Academic Editor: Ivan B. Djordjevic

Received: 15 June 2021
Accepted: 23 July 2021
Published: 27 July 2021

Publisher's Note: MDPI stays neutral with regard to jurisdictional claims in published maps and institutional affiliations.

Copyright: © 2021 by the authors. Licensee MDPI, Basel, Switzerland. This article is an open access article distributed under the terms and conditions of the Creative Commons Attribution (CC BY) license (https://creativecommons.org/licenses/by/4.0/).

Abstract: Lightweight session key agreement schemes are expected to play a central role in building Internet of things (IoT) security in sixth-generation (6G) networks. A well-established approach deriving from the physical layer is a secret key generation (SKG) from shared randomness (in the form of wireless fading coefficients). However, although practical, SKG schemes have been shown to be vulnerable to active attacks over the initial "advantage distillation" phase, throughout which estimates of the fading coefficients are obtained at the legitimate users. In fact, by injecting carefully designed signals during this phase, a man-in-the-middle (MiM) attack could manipulate and control part of the reconciled bits and thus render SKG vulnerable to brute force attacks. Alternatively, a denial of service attack can be mounted by a reactive jammer. In this paper, we investigate the impact of injection and jamming attacks during the advantage distillation in a multiple-input–multiple-output (MIMO) system. First, we show that a MiM attack can be mounted as long as the attacker has one extra antenna with respect to the legitimate users, and we propose a pilot randomization scheme that allows the legitimate users to successfully reduce the injection attack to a less harmful jamming attack. Secondly, by taking a game-theoretic approach we evaluate the optimal strategies available to the legitimate users in the presence of reactive jammers.

Keywords: physical layer security; secret key generation; injection attacks; jamming attacks; pilot randomization

1. Introduction

The increasing interest in physical layer security (PLS) has been stimulated by many practical needs, particularly in the context of Internet of things (IoT) applications [1]. For example, in [2,3], secret key generation (SKG) from wireless fading coefficients was analyzed, showing its potential as a lightweight alternative to standard security schemes. In fact, the SKG scheme allows two legitimate parties (Alice and Bob) to extract on-the-fly secret keys, without the need for significant infrastructure. Furthermore, it has been information-theoretically proven that by following the SKG process, Alice and Bob can extract a shared secret over unauthenticated channels [4–6]. Building on that, numerous practical experiments have demonstrated the feasibility of the scheme [7,8]. Moreover, it has been shown that SKG can be combined with authenticated encryption (AE) schemes [9,10] in order to overcome trivial man-in-the-middle (MiM) attacks, similarly to known MiM attacks on unauthenticated Diffie–Hellman schemes.

The success of the SKG scheme relies on the reciprocity and variability of wireless channels. On the one hand, the reciprocity property allows both Alice and Bob to measure an identical channel impulse response during the coherence time of the channel [11–13], while on the other hand, the variability property of the wireless channel directly affects the key generation rates [14–17].

However, the exchange of pilots during the channel estimation phase between Alice and Bob could allow an adversary (Mallory) to estimate the channels Alice–Mallory and Bob–Mallory. Having this information, Mallory could inject suitably precoded signals during the SKG process and could potentially control a significant part of the reconciled sequence while remaining undetected. To overcome this, instead of transmitting publicly known pilot signals, we propose a two-way randomized pilot transmission between Alice and Bob. An earlier work studied this problem for an orthogonal frequency-division multiplexing (OFDM) system [18]. Here, we investigate the scenario of a multiple-input–multiple-output (MIMO) system. We prove that if Mallory has one extra antenna with respect to Alice and Bob, she could always launch an injection attack. Next, through theoretical analysis, we show that the proposed pilot randomization scheme successfully reduces an injection attack to a less harmful uncorrelated jamming attack, ensuring that the extracted key bits are secret from both active and passive adversaries.

In the second part of this paper, we delve deeper into jamming attacks over MIMO systems. In particular, we focus on denial of service (DoS) in the form of reactive jamming. We derive the optimal strategies for both the attacker and the legitimate users. Through numerical evaluation, we demonstrate that, depending on their capabilities, reactive jammers could provoke legitimate users to transmit at full power in order to achieve a positive SKG rate.

2. System Model

In this work, we consider a time-division duplex MIMO (TDD–MIMO) system consisting of two legitimate nodes and an active adversary, namely, Alice, Bob, and Mallory, respectively. On the one hand, Alice and Bob are generating secret keys using the wireless SKG procedure, while on the other hand, Mallory performs an injection attack on the MIMO links Mallory–Alice and Mallory–Bob. The number of antennas at Alice N_A and Bob N_B are assumed to be equal, i.e., $N_A = N_B = N$. To better illustrate the considered scenario, we give a brief overview of the SKG procedure, and show how an injection attack could affect the process.

2.1. Secret Key Generation from Fading Coefficients

As illustrated in Figure 1, the standard SKG procedure consists of three phases [19]: (1) advantage distillation: the legitimate nodes exchange pilot signals, each using N transmit and N receive antenna elements, in order to estimate their reciprocal channel state information (CSI).

$$\mathbf{z}_A = \mathbf{H}\mathbf{x} + \mathbf{n}_A \tag{1}$$

$$\mathbf{z}_B = \mathbf{H}^T\mathbf{x} + \mathbf{n}_B, \tag{2}$$

where $\mathbf{H}$ represents the channel matrix of size $N_r \times N_t = N \times N$ such that its (i,j) entry represents the channel linking the i-th receive antenna, and the j-th transmit antenna, $\mathbf{z}$ represents the received vector of length N_r, $\mathbf{x}$ denotes the transmitted vector consisting of $N_t = N_r = N$ elements, $\mathbf{n}_A$ and $\mathbf{n}_B$ are the received noise vectors at Alice and Bob, each of length N_r, respectively. Note that, due to the reciprocity of the wireless channel, Alice and Bob observe $\mathbf{H}$ and $\mathbf{H}^T$, respectively. To conclude this step, $\mathbf{z}_A$ and $\mathbf{z}_B$ are passed through suitable quantizers [20], generating binary vectors $\mathbf{r}_A$ and $\mathbf{r}_B$, respectively; (2) information reconciliation: discrepancies, due to imperfect channel estimation in the quantizer local outputs, are reconciled through a public exchange of helper data $\mathbf{s}_A$ (see Figure 1), e.g., by using Slepian–Wolf reconciliation techniques [10,21]; (3) privacy amplification: the legitimate nodes apply universal hash functions to the reconciled information $\mathbf{r}_A$ and obtain key $\mathbf{k}$. This step ensures that the generated key $\mathbf{k}$ is uniformly distributed and completely unpredictable by an adversary.

During the process above, an eavesdropping adversary could obtain channel observations, given as follows:

$$z_{AM} = H_{AM}x + n_{AM}, \quad (3)$$
$$z_{BM} = H_{BM}x + n_{BM}, \quad (4)$$

where the channel matrices in the links Alice–Mallory and Bob–Mallory are denoted by H_{AM} and by H_{BM}, respectively, while the received noise vectors are demoted by n_{AM} and n_{BM}. Afterward, the SKG capacity between Alice and Bob is expressed as the conditional mutual information between the observations of Alice, Bob, and Mallory.

$$I(z_A; z_B | z_{AM}, z_{BM}). \quad (5)$$

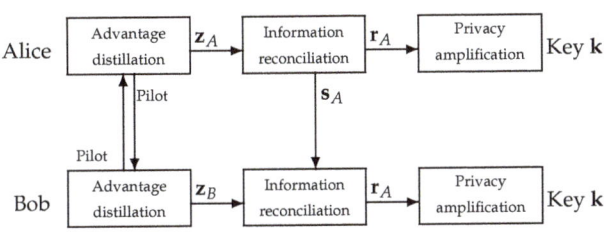

Figure 1. Secret key generation process between Alice and Bob.

2.2. Injection Attacks during SKG

One of the most critical threats to the SKG model, given in Figure 1, is MiM in the form of an injection attack [11,22,23]. The main components of the injection attack are captured in Figure 2. While, the legitimate nodes Alice and Bob exchange pilot signals during the advantage distillation phase, Mallory injects signals p. Based on the results in [22], we assume that Mallory has perfect knowledge of the channel vectors in the MIMO links Mallory–Alice, $H_{MA} = H_{AM}^T$ and Mallory–Bob, $H_{MB} = H_{BM}^T$. This is a reasonable assumption since Mallory can estimate the channel vectors while Alice and Bob exchange pilot signals, as long as the channel's coherence time is respected (a plausible scenario in slow-fading, low-mobility environments). Finally, Mallory chooses the vector p such that the same signal is "injected" at both Alice and Bob, i.e., $H_{MA}p = H_{MB}p$.

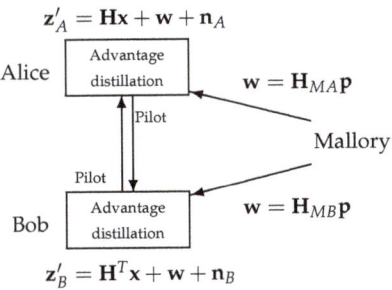

Figure 2. Injection attack performed by Mallory: While Alice and Bob exchange pilot signals x over a Rayleigh fading channel with realization H, Mallory injects a signal p such that the received signals at both Alice and Bob coincide $w = H_{MA}p = H_{MB}p$.

3. Analysis of Injection Attacks in MIMO SKG

In this section, we first prove that if Mallory has one extra antenna, with respect to Alice and Bob, she could always launch an injection attack. Next, we propose a pilot randomization scheme and show that when employed, legitimate users could successfully reduce the attack to a jamming attack.

Lemma 1. *While Alice and Bob perform advantage distillation using N antennas, Mallory could always launch an injection attack, as long as she has at least $N + 1$ antennas.*

Proof. The precoding vector of Mallory $\mathbf{p}$ of size $(N + 1) \times 1$ is represented as

$$\mathbf{p} = \begin{bmatrix} p_1 \\ \vdots \\ p_{N+1} \end{bmatrix}. \tag{6}$$

The channel matrices $\mathbf{H}_{MA}$ and $\mathbf{H}_{MB}$ have size $N \times (N + 1)$, such that

$$\mathbf{H}_{MA} = \begin{bmatrix} H_{MA_{1,1}} & \cdots & H_{MA_{1,N+1}} \\ \vdots & \cdots & \vdots \\ H_{MA_{N,1}} & \cdots & H_{MA_{N,N+1}} \end{bmatrix}, \tag{7}$$

and

$$\mathbf{H}_{MB} = \begin{bmatrix} H_{MB_{1,1}} & \cdots & H_{MB_{1,N+1}} \\ \vdots & \cdots & \vdots \\ H_{MB_{N,1}} & \cdots & H_{MB_{N,N+1}} \end{bmatrix}. \tag{8}$$

Next, we can represent the equation

$$\mathbf{H}_{MA}\mathbf{p} = \mathbf{H}_{MB}\mathbf{p}, \tag{9}$$

as

$$(\mathbf{H}_{MA} - \mathbf{H}_{MB})\mathbf{p} = 0, \tag{10}$$

where $\mathbf{H}_M = \mathbf{H}_{MA} - \mathbf{H}_{MB}$ is equal to:

$$\mathbf{H}_M = \begin{bmatrix} H_{MA_{1,1}} - H_{MB_{1,1}} & \cdots & H_{MA_{1,N+1}} - H_{MB_{1,N+1}} \\ \vdots & \cdots & \vdots \\ H_{MA_{N,1}} - H_{MB_{N,1}} & \cdots & H_{MA_{N,N+1}} - H_{MB_{N,N+1}} \end{bmatrix}. \tag{11}$$

Given the above, Equation (10) can be rewritten as $\mathbf{H_M p} = 0$, where $\mathbf{H_M}$ is given in Equation (11). The equality $\mathbf{H_M p} = 0$ is equivalent to solving the following linear system of equations:

$$\begin{cases} H_{M_{1,1}} p_1 + H_{M_{1,2}} p_2 + \cdots + H_{M_{1,N+1}} p_{N+1} &= 0 \\ \qquad \vdots \\ H_{M_{N,1}} p_1 + H_{M_{N,2}} p_2 + \cdots + H_{M_{N,N+1}} p_{N+1} &= 0. \end{cases} \tag{12}$$

Due to the fact that Mallory has an additional degree of freedom (one extra antenna), as compared to Alice and Bob, she can treat one of the elements in $\mathbf{p}$ as a constant and solve for the others in terms of it. Based on this, we let p_{N+1} be a constant and rewrite the system in (12) as

$$\begin{cases} H_{M_{1,1}} p_1 + H_{M_{1,2}} p_2 + \cdots + H_{M_{1,N}} p_N &= -H_{M_{1,N+1}} p_{N+1} \\ \qquad \vdots \\ H_{M_{N,1}} p_1 + H_{M_{N,2}} p_2 + \cdots + H_{M_{N,N}} p_N &= -H_{M_{N,N+1}} p_{N+1}. \end{cases} \tag{13}$$

The system of equations in (13) can be represented as $\mathbf{Ax} = \mathbf{b}$, where the $N \times N$ matrix $\mathbf{A}$ is the $N \times N$ matrix containing the first N lines and N columns of $\mathbf{H}_M$, $\mathbf{x} = (p_1, p_2, \ldots, p_N)^T$, and $\mathbf{b}$ contains the right-hand side of the system, i.e., $\mathbf{b} = (-H_{M_{1,N+1}} p_{N+1}, \ldots, -H_{M_{N,N+1}} p_{N+1})^T$.

Finally, since $\det(\mathbf{A}) \neq 0$ almost surely, (i.e., under the assumptions in Section 2, $\det(\mathbf{A})$ is a continuous random variable, hence $\det(\mathbf{A}) \neq 0$ with probability 1) and therefore the system's solution is unique and given by

$$(p_1, p_2, \ldots, p_N)^T = \mathbf{A}^{-1}\mathbf{b}. \tag{14}$$

Note that if Mallory has the same number of antennas as Alice and Bob, she will not have one extra degree of freedom and the transition from the system in Equation (12) to the system in Equation (13) would not be possible. However, as shown here, if Mallory has one extra antenna, with respect to Alice and Bob, she can treat one of the elements in $\mathbf{p}$ as constant, which allows her to find the rest of the elements as in Equation (14). This concludes the proof of Lemma 1. □

Based on Lemma 1, the observations of Alice and Bob are now given by

$$\mathbf{z}_A = \mathbf{H}\mathbf{x} + \mathbf{w} + \mathbf{n}_A \tag{15}$$

$$\mathbf{z}_B = \mathbf{H}^T\mathbf{x} + \mathbf{w} + \mathbf{n}_B, \tag{16}$$

where $\mathbf{w} = \mathbf{H}_{MA}\mathbf{p} = \mathbf{H}_{MB}\mathbf{p}$ denotes the observed injected signals at Alice and Bob, which are identical due to the precoding vector $\mathbf{p}$. By injecting $\mathbf{w}$, Mallory controls the secret key rate, which is now upper bounded by [18,24]

$$L \leq I(\mathbf{z}_A, \mathbf{z}_B; \mathbf{w}). \tag{17}$$

Pilot Randomization as a Countermeasure to Injection Attacks

It has been shown that a countermeasure to injection attacks can be built by randomizing the pilot sequence exchanged between Alice and Bob [18,23,24]. In this work, we propose a MIMO pilot randomization scheme in which pilots are drawn from a (scaled) QPSK modulation. Specifically, Alice and Bob do not transmit the same pilot signal $\mathbf{x}$; instead, they transmit independent, random pilot signals $\mathbf{x}$ and $\mathbf{y}$ drawn from i.i.d. zero-mean discrete uniform distributions in which the individual elements of the vectors have probability mass functions as $\mathcal{U}(\{\pm r \pm jr\}, \ldots, \{\pm r \pm jr\})$, where $j = \sqrt{-1}, r = \sqrt{P/2}$, so that $\mathbb{E}[\mathbf{x}] = \mathbb{E}[\mathbf{y}] = (0, \ldots, 0)^T$, $(\mathbb{E}[|x_1|^2], \ldots, \mathbb{E}[|x_N|^2])^T = (\mathbb{E}[|y_1|^2], \ldots, \mathbb{E}[|y_N|^2])^T = (P, \ldots, P)^T$ and $(\mathbb{E}[x_1 y_1], \ldots, \mathbb{E}[x_N y_N])^T = (0, \ldots, 0)^T$, i.e., the pilots are randomly chosen QPSK signals. Given that Alice's and Bob's observation $\mathbf{z}_A$ and $\mathbf{z}_B$ are modified as

$$\mathbf{z}_A = \mathbf{H}\mathbf{y} + \mathbf{w} + \mathbf{n}_A, \tag{18}$$

$$\mathbf{z}_B = \mathbf{H}^T\mathbf{x} + \mathbf{w} + \mathbf{n}_B. \tag{19}$$

Finally, to generate shared randomness, Alice and Bob post-multiply $\mathbf{z}_A$ and $\mathbf{z}_B$ by their own randomized pilot signals, such as $\tilde{\mathbf{z}}_A = \mathbf{x}^T \mathbf{z}_A$ and $\tilde{\mathbf{z}}_B = \mathbf{y}^T \mathbf{z}_B$ (unobservable by Mallory). Given this, the modified observations are expressed as

$$\tilde{\mathbf{z}}_A = \mathbf{x}^T \mathbf{H} \mathbf{y} + \mathbf{x}^T \mathbf{w} + \mathbf{x}^T \mathbf{n}_A, \tag{20}$$

$$\tilde{\mathbf{z}}_B = \mathbf{y}^T \mathbf{H}^T \mathbf{x} + \mathbf{y}^T \mathbf{w} + \mathbf{y}^T \mathbf{n}_B, \tag{21}$$

where the shared randomness between Alice and Bob is now represented by $\mathbf{x}^T \mathbf{H} \mathbf{y} = \mathbf{x} \mathbf{H}^T \mathbf{y}^T$. Furthermore, the independence of $\mathbf{x}$ and $\mathbf{y}$ ensures the following:

$$L \leq I(\tilde{\mathbf{z}}_A, \tilde{\mathbf{z}}_B; \mathbf{w}) = 0. \tag{22}$$

4. Jamming Attacks on SKG

In this section, we focus on reactive jamming attacks in SKG systems and examine the scenario in which Mallory reactively jams Alice (note that the scenario in which Mallory jams Bob is identical). A reactive jamming attack is an intelligent approach in which the jammer initially senses the spectrum and jams only if a transmission is detected. Due to the difficulty to be detected, reactive jamming attacks are considered to be a great threat to legitimate transmission [25,26]. Next, we assume that Alice and Bob perform SKG in a TDD–MIMO system with a spatially uncorrelated channel. It has been proven that the optimal power strategy for Alice and Bob in this scenario is to employ equal power distribution [27], which is also assumed for this study, i.e.,

$$\left(\mathbb{E}\left[|x_1|^2\right], \ldots, \mathbb{E}\left[|x_N|^2\right]\right)^T = (p, \ldots, p)^T \text{ with } p \in [0, P]. \tag{23}$$

In the following, we assume that Mallory has N antennas, and as a reactive jammer, she senses the spectrum and jams in the link Mallory–Alice only if she detects a power greater than a certain threshold p_{th}. Thus, instead of considering Mallory's power allocation matrix, we work with the sum jamming power for all antennas, which can be represented as a power allocation vector $\underline{\gamma} = (\gamma_1, \ldots, \gamma_N)$. By denoting the available jamming power by $N\Gamma$, the following short-term power constraint is considered:

$$\underline{\gamma} \in \mathbb{R}_+^N, \quad \sum_{i=1}^N \gamma_i \leq N\Gamma. \tag{24}$$

Assuming that $\mathbf{H}$ is uncorrelated with $\mathbf{H}_{AM}, \mathbf{H}_{BM}$ and that all channel matrices have independent and identically distributed elements that are drawn from circularly symmetric zero-mean Gaussian distributions of variances σ^2 and σ_J^2, respectively, then the SKG capacity can be expressed as [27]

$$C_K(p, \underline{\gamma}) = N \sum_{i=1}^N \log\left(1 + \frac{p\sigma^2}{2(1 + \gamma_i \sigma_J^2) + \frac{(1+\gamma_i \sigma_J^2)^2}{p\sigma^2}}\right). \tag{25}$$

4.1. Optimal Power Allocation Strategies

In the following, we take a game-theoretic approach in order to evaluate the optimal strategies of Alice, Bob and Mallory. Throughout the following Alice and Bob's common objective is to maximize $C_K(p, \underline{\gamma})$ with respect to (w.r.t.) p, while Mallory wants to minimize $C_K(p, \underline{\gamma})$ w.r.t. $\underline{\gamma}$. Due to the reversed objectives, we formulated a noncooperative zero-sum game, which studies the strategic interaction between the legitimate users and the jammer: $\mathcal{G} = (\{L, J\}, \{\mathcal{A}_L, \mathcal{A}_J(p)\}, C_K(p, \underline{\gamma}))$. The game $\mathcal{G}$ has three components: (i) there are two players, namely, L, denoting the legitimate users (Alice and Bob act as a single player), and J being the jammer (Mallory); (ii) player L has a set of possible actions $\mathcal{A}_L = [0, P]$, while player J's set of actions is

$$\mathcal{A}_J(p) = \begin{cases} \{(0, \ldots, 0)\}, & \text{if } p \leq p_{\text{th}}, \\ \{\underline{\gamma} \in \mathbb{R}_+^N | \sum_{i=1}^N \gamma_i \leq N\Gamma\}, & \text{if } p > p_{\text{th}}. \end{cases} \tag{26}$$

Lastly, $C_K(p, \underline{\gamma})$ denotes the payoff function of player L.

Given the fact that player J is a reactive jammer, i.e, first observes the transmit power of player L and subsequently chooses a strategy, we study a hierarchical game in which player L is the leader, and player J is the follower. In this game, the solution is the Stackelberg equilibrium (SE)—rather than Nash—and it is defined as a strategy profile $(p^{\text{SE}}, \underline{\gamma}^{\text{SE}})$ where player L chooses their optimal strategy first, by anticipating the strategic reaction of player J (i.e., its best response). This is expressed as:

$$p^{\text{SE}} \triangleq \arg\max_{p \in \mathcal{A}_L} C_K(p, \underline{\gamma}^*(p)), \text{ and } \underline{\gamma}^{\text{SE}} \triangleq \underline{\gamma}^*(p^{\text{SE}}), \tag{27}$$

where $\underline{\gamma}^*(p)$ defines the best response (BR) of player J to any strategy $p \in \mathcal{A}_L$ chosen by player L, and it is defined as follows:

$$\underline{\gamma}^*(p) \triangleq \arg\min_{\underline{\gamma}\in\mathcal{A}_J(p)} C_K(p,\underline{\gamma}). \tag{28}$$

Finally, based on the detection capabilities at player L, two scenarios are considered: (i) when the detection threshold p_{th} is fixed (defined by the sensing capability of Mallory's receiver); (ii) when p_{th} is part of player L's strategy and could vary.

4.2. Stackelberg Equilibrium with Fixed Detection Threshold

In this section, we evaluate SE, when player J's detection threshold p_{th} is predefined and constant. Note that the case $P \leq p_{th}$ is trivial as $\underline{\gamma}^{SE} = (0,\ldots,0)$, and the legitimate users will optimally use their maximum available power, i.e., ($p^{SE} = P$). Indeed, due to the poorly chosen threshold p_{th} or low sensing capabilities of Mallory, the legitimate transmission will not be detected and therefore will not be jammed. In the following, we assume that $P > p_{th}$.

Lemma 2. *The BR of player J for any $p \in \mathcal{A}_L$ chosen by player L defined in (28) is the uniform power allocation, given as*

$$\underline{\gamma}^*(p) \triangleq \begin{cases} (\Gamma,\ldots,\Gamma), & \text{if } p > p_{th}, \\ (0,\ldots,0), & \text{if } p \leq p_{th}. \end{cases} \tag{29}$$

Proof. Note that $C_K(p,\gamma_i)$ is a monotonically decreasing convex function w.r.t γ_i, $i = 1,\ldots,N$ for any $p > 0$. Based on the principles of convexity in order to minimize C_K, Mallory has to transmit with full power from all antennas. The detailed proof can be found in [18]. □

Based on the result from Lemma 1, the SKG rate can have the following two forms:

$$C_K(p,\underline{\gamma}^*(p)) = \begin{cases} C_K(p,(0,\ldots,0)), & \text{if } p \leq p_{th}, \\ C_K(p,(\Gamma,\ldots,\Gamma)), & \text{if } p > p_{th}, \end{cases} \tag{30}$$

which simplifies the players' options.

Theorem 1. *Depending on their available power P for SKG, Alice and Bob will either transmit at P or p_{th}. The SE point of the game is unique when $P \neq p_{th}(\Gamma\sigma_J^2+1)$ and is given by*

$$(p^{SE},\underline{\gamma}^{SE}) = \begin{cases} \{(p_{th},(0,\ldots,0))\}, & \text{if } P < p_{th}(\sigma_J^2\Gamma+1), \\ \{(P,(\Gamma,\ldots,\Gamma))\}, & \text{if } P > p_{th}(\sigma_J^2\Gamma+1). \end{cases} \tag{31}$$

When $P = p_{th}(\sigma_J^2\Gamma+1)$, the game $\mathcal{G}$ has two SEs: $(p^{SE},\underline{\gamma}^{SE}) \in \{(p_{th},(0,\ldots,0)),(P,(\Gamma,\ldots,\Gamma))\}$.

Proof. Given the BR of player J defined in (29), the legitimate users want to identify their optimal $p \in \mathcal{A}_L$ that maximizes

$$C_K(p,\underline{\gamma}^*(p)) = \begin{cases} C_K(p,(0,\ldots,0)), & \text{if } p \leq p_{th}, \\ C_K(p,(\Gamma,\ldots,\Gamma)), & \text{if } p > p_{th}. \end{cases} \tag{32}$$

Given the fact that $C_K(p,\underline{\gamma})$ is monotonically increasing with p for fixed $\underline{\gamma}$, two cases are distinguished: (a) $p \in [0,p_{th}]$, (b) $p \in (p_{th},P]$. The optimal p in each case is given by
(a) $\arg\max\limits_{p\in[0,p_{th}]} C_K(p,\underline{\gamma}^*(p)) = \arg\max\limits_{p\in[0,p_{th}]} C_K(p,(0,\ldots,0)) = p_{th}$,
(b) $\arg\max\limits_{p\in(p_{th},P]} C_K(p,\underline{\gamma}^*(p)) = \arg\max\limits_{p\in(p_{th},P]} C_K(p,(\Gamma,\ldots,\Gamma)) = P$.

From (a) and (b), it can be concluded that the overall solution is $p^{SE} =$

$$\arg\max_{p \in \mathcal{A}_L} C_K(p, \underline{\gamma}^*(p)) = \begin{cases} p_{\text{th}}, & \text{if } C_K(P, \Gamma) < C_K(p_{\text{th}}, 0), \\ P, & \text{if } C_K(P, \Gamma) > C_K(p_{\text{th}}, 0), \\ \{p_{\text{th}}, P\}, & \text{if } C_K(P, \Gamma) = C_K(p_{\text{th}}, 0). \end{cases}$$

To simplify the above possibilities, we focus on the case when the utility function $C_K(P, \Gamma)$, i.e., being detected and jammed, equals the utility function when player L is transmitting at threshold p_{th} (player J is silent), i.e., $C_K(P, \Gamma) = C_K(p_{\text{th}}, 0)$. Using this equality, by substituting appropriately into (25), we obtain a quadratic equation in P.

$$P^2(2\sigma^2 p_{\text{th}} + 1) - P(2p_{\text{th}}^2\sigma^2 + 2\sigma_J^2\Gamma p_{\text{th}}^2\sigma^2) - (1 + \sigma_J^2\Gamma)^2 p_{\text{th}}^2 = 0.$$

Note that Equation (33) has a unique positive root equal to $p_{\text{th}}(\sigma_J^2\Gamma + 1)$. Furthermore, due to the fact that the leading coefficient of (33): $(2\sigma^2 p_{\text{th}} + 1) \geq 0$ and $P > 0$, we can state that the inequalities $C_K(P, \Gamma) > C_K(p_{\text{th}}, 0)$ and $C_K(P, \Gamma) < C_K(p_{\text{th}}, 0)$ are equivalent to $P > p_{\text{th}}(\sigma_J^2\Gamma + 1)$ and $P < p_{\text{th}}(\sigma_J^2\Gamma + 1)$, respectively. □

A numerical evaluation of the SKG rate is presented in Figure 3. The parameters used are $N = 10$, $p_{\text{th}} = 2$, $\Gamma = 3$, and $\sigma^2 = \sigma_J^2 = 1$. Figure 3 compares the achievable SKG rates of the SE strategy, i.e., $p = p^{SE}$ with the two alternative strategies, i.e., $p = P$ or $p = p_{\text{th}}$. It can be seen that if player L deviates from the SE point the achievable SKG rate can decrease by up to 40%.

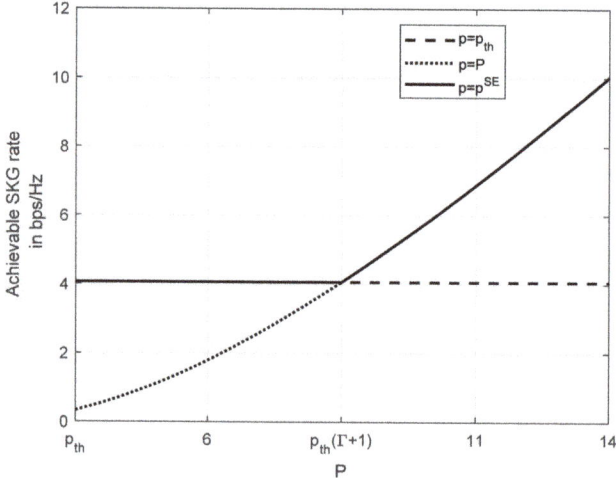

Figure 3. SE policy, compared to always transmitting with either full power or with p_{th}. Used parameters $p_{\text{th}} = 2, \Gamma = 3, N = 10, \sigma^2 = \sigma_J^2 = 1$.

4.3. Stackelberg Equilibrium with Strategic p_{th}

Finally, we investigate the case when Mallory could optimally adjust p_{th} and show how her choice impacts Alice's and Bob's strategies. Allowing p_{th} to vary modifies the game under study as follows $\hat{\mathcal{G}} = (\{L, J\}, \{\mathcal{A}_L, \hat{\mathcal{A}}_J(p)\}, C_K(p, \underline{\gamma}, p_{\text{th}}))$, where

$$\hat{\mathcal{A}}_J(p) \triangleq \begin{cases} \{((0, \ldots, 0), p_{\text{th}}), \ p_{\text{th}} \geq 0\}, & \text{if } p_{\text{th}} \geq p, \\ \{(\underline{\gamma}, p_{\text{th}}) \in \mathbb{R}_+^N \mid \sum_{i=1}^N \gamma_i \leq N\Gamma\}, & \text{if } p_{\text{th}} < p. \end{cases} \quad (33)$$

The BR of the jammer can then be defined as

$$(\widehat{\underline{\gamma}}^*(p), \widehat{p_{\text{th}}}^*(p)) \triangleq \underset{(\underline{\gamma}, p_{\text{th}}) \in \hat{\mathcal{A}}_J(p)}{\arg\min} C_K(p, \underline{\gamma}, p_{\text{th}}). \tag{34}$$

Lemma 3. *Mallory's BR in this scenario is a set of strategies as follows:*

$$(\widehat{\underline{\gamma}}^*(p), \widehat{p_{\text{th}}}^*(p)) \in \{ ((\Gamma, \ldots, \Gamma)\epsilon),\ \epsilon \in [0, p)\}. \tag{35}$$

Proof. The problem that the jammer wants to solve is $\underset{(\underline{\gamma}, p_{\text{th}}) \in \hat{\mathcal{A}}_J(p)}{\min} C_K(p, \underline{\gamma}, p_{\text{th}})$, which can be split as follows:

$$\underset{p_{\text{th}} \geq 0}{\min}\ \underset{\underline{\gamma} \in \hat{\mathcal{A}}_J(p)}{\min} C_K(p, \underline{\gamma}(p), p_{\text{th}}). \tag{36}$$

The solution of the inner minimization is known from (29). For the outer problem, we have to find the optimal $p_{\text{th}} \geq 0$ that minimizes $C_K(p, \widehat{\underline{\gamma}}^*(p), p_{\text{th}})$. Given that

$$\underset{p_{\text{th}} \geq 0}{\min} C_K(p, \widehat{\underline{\gamma}}^*(p), p_{\text{th}}) = \begin{cases} C_K(p, \Gamma, p_{\text{th}}), & \text{if } p_{\text{th}} < p, \\ C_K(p, 0, p_{\text{th}}), & \text{if } p_{\text{th}} \geq p, \end{cases} \tag{37}$$

and that $C_K(p, \Gamma, p_{\text{th}}) < C_K(p, 0, p_{\text{th}})$, player J can optimally choose any p_{th} such that $p_{\text{th}} = \epsilon$, $\forall \epsilon < p$. This allows the jammer to detect any ongoing transmission and to perform a jamming attack. □

Theorem 2. *The game $\hat{\mathcal{G}}$ has an infinite number of SEs as follows:*

$$(\widehat{p}^{SE}, \widehat{\underline{\gamma}}^{SE}, \widehat{p_{\text{th}}}^{SE}) \in \{ (P, (\Gamma, \ldots, \Gamma)\epsilon),\ \forall \epsilon < P\}. \tag{38}$$

Proof. Given Mallory's BR, we evaluate the SE of the game $\hat{\mathcal{G}}$. The definition for $\widehat{p}^{SE}$ is given as follows:

$$\widehat{p}^{SE} \triangleq \underset{p \in \mathcal{A}_L}{\arg\max}\, C_K(p, \widehat{\underline{\gamma}}^*(p), \widehat{p_{\text{th}}}(p)^*). \tag{39}$$

Since Mallory will act as in (35), we have

$$C_K(p, \widehat{\underline{\gamma}}^*(p), \widehat{p_{\text{th}}}(p)^*) = C_K(p, \Gamma, \epsilon),\ \forall \epsilon < p, \tag{40}$$

and the fact that $C_K(p, \Gamma, \epsilon)$ is monotonically increasing with p results in $\widehat{p}^{SE} = P$. □

Figure 4 illustrates the achievable SKG rate when p_{th} is part of player J's strategy. As in Figure 3, the parameters are chosen as $\Gamma = 3$, $N = 10$ and $\sigma_J^2 = 1$. It can be seen that due to a strategically chosen threshold from player J the legitimate users have no other choice but to transmit at full power $p = P = p^{SE}$. In fact, if the legitimate users deviate from the SE strategy and transmit with low power $p = p_{\text{th}}$, player J could successfully disrupt their SKG process and decrease their achievable SKG rate by up to 97%.

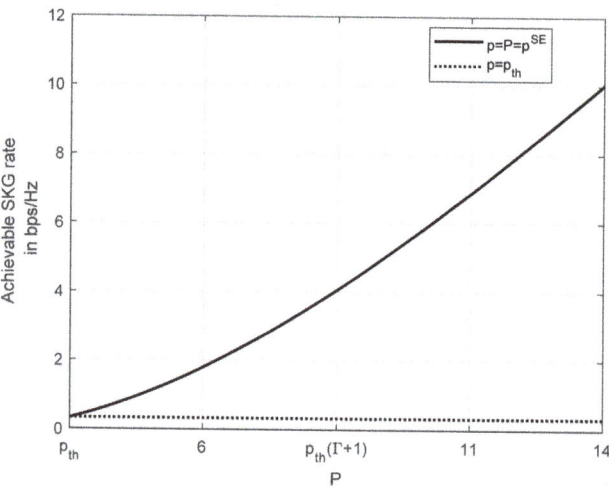

Figure 4. The effect to the SE policy when p_{th} is part of player J strategy. Comparison of the achievable SKG rate when player L chooses $p = p^{SE}$ with the case when transmitting with power p_{th}. Used parameters $\Gamma = 3, N = 10, \sigma^2 = \sigma_J^2 = 1$.

5. Conclusions

In this study, injection and reactive jamming attacks were analyzed in MIMO SKG systems. With respect to injection attacks, the study demonstrated that a trivial advantage in the form of one extra antenna allows a MiM to mount such an attack. As a countermeasure, we showed that a pilot randomization scheme can successfully reduce injection attacks to jamming attacks. With respect to jamming attacks, using a game-theoretic approach, we showed that an intelligent reactive jammer should optimally jam with full power when a transmission is sensed. Finally, by strategically choosing her jamming threshold, i.e., just below the power level used by the legitimate users, Mallory could perform a much more effective attack. In fact, our theoretical analysis suggests that in this case, Alice and Bob have no choice but to use their full power available for SKG. An important topic for further research in this area is an examination of these initial findings in practical scenarios.

Author Contributions: Conceptualization, M.M., A.C., E.V.B. and H.V.P.; Methodology, M.M., A.C., E.V.B. and H.V.P.; Software, M.M.; Validation, M.M., A.C., E.V.B. and H.V.P.; Supervision, A.C., E.V.B. and H.V.P.; Writing—review and editing, M.M., A.C., E.V.B. and H.V.P. All authors have read and agreed to the published version of the manuscript.

Funding: H.V. Poor was supported in part by the U.S. National Science Foundation under Grant CCF-1908308. E.V. Belmega and A. Chorti were supported by the ELIOT ANR-18-CE40-0030 and FAPESP 2018/12579-7 project. A. Chorti was also supported by CYU Initiative of Excellence (INEX) funding.

Institutional Review Board Statement: Not applicable.

Informed Consent Statement: Not applicable.

Conflicts of Interest: The authors declare no conflict of interest.

References

1. Xu, W.; Jha, S.; Hu, W. LoRa-key: Secure Key Generation System for LoRa-based Network. *IEEE Internet Things J.* **2019**, *6*. [CrossRef]
2. Mitev, M.; Chorti, A.; Reed, M. Subcarrier Scheduling for Joint Data Transfer and Key Generation Schemes in Multicarrier Systems. In Proceedings of the IEEE Global Communications Conference (GLOBECOM , Waikoloa, HI, USA, 9–13 December 2019; pp. 1–6.

3. Mitev, M.; Chorti, A.; Reed, M. Optimal Resource Allocation in Joint Secret Key Generation and Data Transfer Schemes. In Proceedings of the 15th International Wireless Communications Mobile Computing Conference (IWCMC), Tangier, Morocco, 24–28 June 2019; pp. 360–365.
4. Maurer, U.; Wolf, S. Secret-key Agreement Over Unauthenticated Public Channels-Part I: Definitions and a Completeness Result. *IEEE Trans. Inf. Theory* **2003**, *49*, 822–831. [CrossRef]
5. Maurer, U.; Wolf, S. Secret-key Agreement Over Unauthenticated Public Channels-Part II: The Simulatability Condition. *IEEE Trans. Inf. Theory* **2003**, *49*, 832–838. [CrossRef]
6. Maurer, U.; Wolf, S. Secret-key Agreement Over Unauthenticated Public Channels-Part III: Privacy Amplification. *IEEE Trans. Inf. Theory* **2003**, *49*, 839–851. [CrossRef]
7. Premnath, S.N.; Jana, S.; Croft, J.; Gowda, P.L.; Clark, M.; Kasera, S.K.; Patwari, N.; Krishnamurthy, S. Secret Key Extraction from Wireless Signal Strength in Real Environments. *IEEE Trans. Mob. Comput.* **2013**, *12*, 917–930. [CrossRef]
8. Pierrot, A.J.; Chou, R.A.; Bloch, M.R. Experimental Aspects of Secret Key Generation in Indoor Wireless Environments. In Proceedings of the IEEE 14th Workshop Signal Processing Advances in Wireless Communications (SPAWC), Darmstadt, Germany, 16–19 June 2013; pp. 669–673.
9. Mitev, M.; Chorti, A.; Reed, M.; Musavian, L. Authenticated Secret Key Generation in Delay-Constrained Wireless Systems. *EURASIP J. Wirel. Commun. Netw.* **2020**, *122*. [CrossRef]
10. Saiki, C.; Chorti, A. A Novel Physical Layer Authenticated Encryption Protocol Exploiting Shared Randomness. In Proceedings of the IEEE Conference on Communications and Network Security (CNS), Florence, Italy, 28–30 September 2015.
11. Jana, S.; Premnath, S.N.; Clark, M.; Kasera, S.K.; Patwari, N.; Krishnamurthy, S. On the Effectiveness of Secret Key Extraction from Wireless Signal Strength in Real Environments. In Proceedings of the 15th Annual International Conference on Mobile Computing and Networking ACM, Beijing, China, 20–25 September 2009; pp. 321–332.
12. Rappaport, T. *Wireless Communications: Principles and Practice*, 2nd ed.; Prentice Hall PTR: Upper Saddle River, NJ, USA, 2001.
13. Wan, J.; Lopez, A.B.; Al Faruque, M.A. Exploiting Wireless Channel Randomness to Generate Keys for Automotive Cyber-Physical System Security. In Proceedings of the IEEE 7th nternational Conference on Cyber-Physical Systems (ICCPS), Vienna, Austria, 11–14 April 2016; pp. 1–10.
14. Zoli, M.; Barreto, A.N.; Köpsell, S.; Sen, P.; Fettweis, G. Physical-Layer-Security Box: A Concept for Time-Frequency Channel-Reciprocity Key Generation. *EURASIP J. Wirel. Commun. Netw.* **2020**, *114*. [CrossRef]
15. Xiao, L.; Greenstein, L.J.; Mandayam, N.B.; Trappe, W. Using the Physical Layer for Wireless Authentication in Time-Variant Channels. *IEEE Trans. Wirel. Commun.* **2008**, *7*, 2571–2579. [CrossRef]
16. Chorti, A.; Hollanti, C.; Belfiore, J.-C.; Poor, H.V. *Physical Layer Security: A Paradigm Shift in Data Confidentiality*; Springer, Lect. Notes Electr. Eng.: Cham, Switzerland, 2015; pp. 1–15
17. Shakiba, M.; Chorti, A.; Poor, V. Physical Layer Security: Authentication, Integrity, and Confidentiality. In *Physical Layer Security*; Le, K., Ed.; Springer: Cham, Switzerland, 2021.
18. Mitev, M.; Chorti, A.; Belmega, E.V.; Reed, M. Man-in-the-Middle and Denial of Service Attacks in Wireless Secret Key Generation. In Proceedings of the IEEE Global Communication Conference (GLOBECOM), Waikoloa, HI, USA, 9–13 December 2019; pp. 1–6.
19. Maurer, U. Secret Key Agreement by Public Discussion from Common Information. *IEEE Trans. Inf. Theory* **1993**, *39*, 733–742. [CrossRef]
20. Wang, Q.; Su, H.; Ren, K.; Kim, K. Fast and Scalable Secret Key Generation Exploiting Channel Phase Randomness in Wireless Networks. In Proceedings of the IEEE International Conference on Computer Communication (INFOCOM), Shanghai, China, 10–15 April, 2011.
21. Ye, C.; Reznik, A.; Shah, Y. Extracting Secrecy from Jointly Gaussian Random Variables. In Proceedings of the IEEE International Symposium on Information Theory (ISIT), Seattle, WA, USA, 9–14 July 2006.
22. Eberz, S.; Strohmeier, M.; Wilhelm, M.; Martinovic, I. *A Practical Man-in-the-Middle Attack on Signal-Based Key Generation Protocols*; Springer, Lect. Notes Comput. Sci.: Berlin/Heidelberg, Germany, 2012; pp. 235–252.
23. Rong, J.; Kai, Z. Physical Layer Key Agreement Under Signal Injection Attacks. In Proceedings of the IEEE Conference on Communications and Network Security (CNS), Florence, Italy, 28–30 September 2015; pp. 254–262.
24. Chorti, A. *A Study of Injection and Jamming Attacks in Wireless Secret Sharing Systems*; Springer, Lect. Notes in Electr. Eng.: Cham, Switzerland, 2018; pp. 1–14.
25. Fang, S.; Liu, Y.; Ning, P. Wireless Communications Under Broadband Reactive Jamming Attacks. *IEEE Trans. Dependable Secur. Comput.* **2016**, *13*, 394–408. [CrossRef]
26. Spuhler, M.; Giustiniano, D.; Lenders, V.; Wilhelm, M.; Schmitt, J.B. Detection of Reactive Jamming in DSSS-based Wireless Communications. *IEEE Trans. Wirel. Commun.* **2014**, *13*, 1593–1603. [CrossRef]
27. Jorswieck, E.; Wolf, A.; Engelmann, S. Secret Key Generation from Reciprocal Spatially Correlated MIMO Channels. In Proceedings of the IEEE Global Communication Workshops, (GLOBECOM Workshops), Atlanta, GA, USA, 9–13 December 2013; pp. 1245–1250.

Article

Qubit-Based Clock Synchronization for QKD Systems Using a Bayesian Approach

Roderick D. Cochran * and Daniel J. Gauthier

Department of Physics, The Ohio State University, 191 West Woodruff Ave., Columbus, OH 43210, USA; gauthier.51@osu.edu
* Correspondence: cochran.467@osu.edu

Abstract: Quantum key distribution (QKD) systems provide a method for two users to exchange a provably secure key. Synchronizing the users' clocks is an essential step before a secure key can be distilled. Qubit-based synchronization protocols directly use the transmitted quantum states to achieve synchronization and thus avoid the need for additional classical synchronization hardware. Previous qubit-based synchronization protocols sacrifice secure key either directly or indirectly, and all known qubit-based synchronization protocols do not efficiently use all publicly available information published by the users. Here, we introduce a Bayesian probabilistic algorithm that incorporates all published information to efficiently find the clock offset without sacrificing any secure key. Additionally, the output of the algorithm is a probability, which allows us to quantify our confidence in the synchronization. For demonstration purposes, we present a model system with accompanying simulations of an efficient three-state BB84 prepare-and-measure protocol with decoy states. We use our algorithm to exploit the correlations between Alice's published basis and mean photon number choices and Bob's measurement outcomes to probabilistically determine the most likely clock offset. We find that we can achieve a 95 percent synchronization confidence in only 4140 communication bin widths, meaning we can tolerate clock drift approaching 1 part in 4140 in this example when simulating this system with a dark count probability per communication bin width of 8×10^{-4} and a received mean photon number of 0.01.

Keywords: quantum key distribution (QKD); clock synchronization; Bayesian statistics

1. Introduction

Introduced in 1984 [1], quantum key distribution (QKD) is a symmetric encryption protocol that promises unconditional information security founded on the fundamental laws of physics, rather than on the difficulty of computational problems. Bennett and Brassard established the first QKD protocol (BB84), which used the polarization degree of freedom of single photons to transmit information. Subsequently developed protocols have extended QKD to different types of systems [2] and relaxed the requirement for a true single-photon source [3], paving the way for practical implementations of quantum cryptography.

For the sake of concreteness, we consider a polarization-based prepare-and-measure protocol. Here, one user (Alice) prepares and transmits a periodic sequence of quantum states with period τ_A encoded in at least two mutually unbiased orthonormal bases. In our example system, we use two bases: horizontal/vertical (H/V) polarization and left circular/right (L/R) circular polarization. We also use the decoy-state protocol where Alice occasionally sends the vacuum quantum state. A second user (Bob), measures each quantum state randomly in one of the two bases and records the result. After the measurement phase is complete, Alice and Bob publish their basis choices for each measurement and keep only the measurements where Bob registers a click with his single-photon counting detectors and they use the same basis. This process, called sifting, allows distilling a raw key, which, after error correction and privacy amplification [4], becomes the secret classical key securely shared between Alice and Bob. Because qubits are lost to the environment via transmission loss and environmental radiation is detected due to stray light and thermal effects, our system is formally considered open. However, the security of the system is still guaranteed using privacy amplification based on the quantum bit error rate (QBER). Our example system uses a pulsed stochastic photonic source with decoy states [3], where the decoys are photonic wavepackets with a lower mean photon number. To simplify the example system and make it more efficient, we only transmit one state in the monitoring basis, which gives an equivalent secure key rate in comparison to transmitting both states in this basis [5,6].

A practical issue in quantum communication protocols is synchronizing Alice and Bob's two data streams. If Bob does not know precisely when Alice begins data transmission, he must begin recording measurements early or else risk missing some of Alice's transmission. In either case, because some signals do not arrive at Bob due to channel loss, and extraneous events are caused by stray light and detector dark counts, the first event Bob records is unlikely to be the first event Alice sends, resulting in some timing offset that must be determined. Correcting this offset is an essential precursor to sifting: If Alice and Bob do not agree on the timing of the events, they will compare basis choices from different events, resulting in a high QBER and likely share no information. In addition, determining which time bins correspond to Alice's wavepacket arrival and which do not allows timing-based noise filtering.

Further complicating the communication protocol is that the relative clock offset may not be a constant due to drift in the relative phase and frequency between the transmitter and receiver clocks. Alice has a communication protocol temporal bin width τ_A that may be different from Bob's bin width τ_B. The timing offset between their clocks Δ at the nth communication time bin since the most recent clock synchronization is given by

$$\Delta = t_0 + (\tau_A - \tau_B)n + \varepsilon \tag{1}$$

for an initial timing offset t_0 and higher-order timing error ε. In this way, small differences in clock frequencies can gradually change the clock offset so that a previously calculated synchronization is no longer valid. Other timing errors, such as clock jitter and frequency drift, also contribute to the need for a more robust synchronization solution. We denote the time over which synchronization is maintained as T_b, i.e., the time over which the error in $\Delta \ll \tau_A$.

Clock synchronization is sometimes achieved by directly sending Alice's clock signal to Bob over a separate channel via an optical link or using a radio-frequency signal [7–16]. However, this introduces additional hardware requirements and increases the cost and complexity of the setup. One way to avoid these additional resource requirements is to use the quantum channel itself to transmit the information necessary to perform the synchronization [17–20]. One such qubit-based synchronization protocol was introduced and demonstrated by Calderaro et al. [17]. Their protocol uses a dedicated clock-synchronization phase followed by a key distribution phase. In the synchronization phase, a pre-agreed synchronization string is transmitted to Bob and the clocks are aligned during post-processing.

The pre-agreed synchronization string is used to find the initial offset between Alice and Bob's clocks. Because it must be public knowledge, it cannot be used to generate a secure key. If the clock frequencies are not consistent, simple clock offset recovery only temporarily aligns until the clock drift becomes of-the-order-of the communication protocol temporal bin width τ_A. Correcting for this clock frequency drift using only clock offset recovery requires repeated synchronization/key distribution phases with a regularity that depends on the stability of the clocks used in the experiment. This reduces the overall secure key rate because no QKD states can be sent while the synchronization states are being sent, which may result in zero key rate due to finite-key effects [21,22]. However, to account for this drift without needing to send regular synchronization strings, Calderaro et al. performs clock frequency recovery using the periodic arrival times of Alice's qubits. Unlike the clock offset recovery, this does not require a pre-agreed synchronization string and thus does not decrease the amount of key that can be sent.

While our method only uses clock offset recovery at this time, it avoids these potential impacts on secure key rate by synchronizing the clocks using only information that is already publicly sent over the insecure classical channel by Alice and Bob for sifting and security analysis: The basis choices and the mean photon number of the transmitted signal. Because we are transmitting only one state in the monitoring basis, the basis choices provide information about which of Bob's measurement outcomes are more likely. The decoy state choices, which determine Alice's mean photon number for each wavepacket, also contain information about Bob's measurement outcomes. For example, Bob is unlikely to record any detections if Alice sends the vacuum decoy state.

By comparing this information to his measurement outcomes, Bob can probabilistically determine the timing offset. To account for potential clock drift, Bob can perform this synchronization in subsets of length T_b. Thus, Bob can find the up-to-date timing offset and ensure that the basis choices he publishes are properly lined up with the ones sent to him by Alice, but this requires an efficient analysis method to reduce the data requirements. Of course, our approach as well as Calderaro's requires low enough channel loss so that there are enough events received by Bob over a drift interval as discussed below.

Another example of a qubit-based synchronization protocol for continuously-pumped entanglement-based QKD systems was introduced by Ho et al. [20]. Here, they correlate Alice and Bob's detection events without considering basis information. Their synchronization method relies on Alice's knowledge that some communication time bins are empty (assuming essentially unit detection efficiency for Alice's setup) and hence Bob's corresponding time bin should also be empty. There is a single dominant peak in the correlation function that identifies Δ assuming a large enough number of Bob's detection events. Because the detection timing information must already be shared publicly, this strategy does not sacrifice any secure key. This method fails when the probability of Alice generating a photon per communication time bin approaches unity because every time bin is likely to be filled and hence the correlation function will have multiple high-value peaks that create timing ambiguity.

In the next section, we outline our synchronization algorithm and its advantages, and derive a formula for the synchronization probability using Bayesian analysis. In Section 3 we introduce a model system, and in Section 4 we simulate data in this model system to demonstrate the effectiveness of our method. In Section 5 we present our conclusions and the potential applicability of this work to other QKD systems.

2. Qubit-Based Synchronization Algorithm

Similar to previous approaches, our algorithm uses a cross-correlation of Alice's periodically transmitted data and Bob's received data to find the number of each type of event pairing, where the cross-correlation is computed efficiently using a Fast Fourier Transform (FFT). One complication of a prepare-and-measure scheme is that Alice attempts to send a quantum state every communication time bin, corresponding to the high-photon-probability limit of the Ho et al. [20] method discussed above. This problem is addressed here using the decoy-state protocol [3], which must be used anyway to prevent a photon-number-splitting attack.

Decoy states are sent by Alice randomly and correspond to wavepackets with a mean photon number smaller than the signal state and often includes sending the vacuum state. The vacuum state is particularly effective in the synchronization process because Alice has high certainty that she sent no photons, limited by her ability to completely block the source. Bob should then also see no photons, limited by the source of detection clicks from non-ideal effects such as detector dark counts, detector afterpulsing, stray light, and the bleed through of light from Alice's source.

Beyond the decoy states, there are additional sources of correlation that can be exploited to help improve the synchronization process. For example, Alice's use of the efficient three-state protocol, where she only sends one state in the monitoring basis, gives useful information if Alice and Bob also share basis-state information, which is already required for sifting. We use a Bayesian statistical method, described below, that uses all prior knowledge of the system characteristics, such as the state fidelities, the mean photon numbers, the channel loss, the fractional sorting of Bob's device for the two bases, and the detector efficiency, to generate a lookup table of Bob's detection probabilities for Alice's different inputs. With these, we can easily compute the synchronization probabilities of different possible offsets using Bayesian statistics. Alice and Bob's data is most correlated when they are synchronized.

A significant advantage of our approach is that it does not sacrifice any secure key: We only use the information that is already sent publicly over the insecure classical channel. This is an improvement over synchronization protocols that share some fraction of the raw data for synchronization purposes, as well as protocols that have a dedicated clock-synchronization phase [17] during which no QKD states can be sent.

Bayesian analysis is a logical choice for synthesizing all available information and using it to make accurate predictions about Δ. It also has the advantage that it predicts the probability that $\hat{\Delta}$ is the best estimate of synchronization offset. This allows us to quantitatively express our level of confidence in the synchronization estimate. Furthermore, the additional information we incorporate in the protocol allows us to make a decision with fewer received qubits, which makes the system more robust to clock drift.

Our algorithm uses FFTs to compute cross-correlations between Alice's inputs and Bob's outputs, allowing us to count the number of each type of input-output pairing for the different time offsets. The computational complexity of our algorithm is dominated by these FFTs, which go as $\mathcal{O}(N \log N)$ where N is the number of sampling bins. Each cross-correlation requires three FFT computations, so the number of FFTs that must be performed is $3 \times n_{in} \times n_{out}$ for a number of distinct inputs n_{in} and distinct outputs n_{out}. In this example, $n_{in} = 5$ (H/V signal, H/V decoy, L/R signal, L/R decoy, and vacuum) and $n_{out} = 4$ (H,V,L, and R), thus maintaining the computational complexity of $\mathcal{O}(N \log_2 N)$.

Synchronization Probability

Here we will use the strings of Alice and Bob's data. A string of Bob's data consists of the results of each of his detectors at each sampling bin. Typically, Bob's strings are very sparse because there are many sampling bins in which he registers no detections. A string of Alice's data consists of her published information at each sampling bin. If the communication time bin width is greater than the sampling time bin width, Alice will have multiple string entries for each state she sends, each corresponding to what she is sending at that part of her duty cycle. Determining the synchronization probability consists of comparing different strings of Bob's data (starting at different temporal offsets) to strings of Alice's data and calculating which of Bob's strings D is most likely to be the one generated by Alice's corresponding string. We determine, for a particular string of Bob's, the probability that it could have been generated by Alice's published string.

Mathematically, we phrase this as the likelihood $p(D|S)$ of generating Bob's string D given the assumption that its generating string is the one Alice has published, denoted by S. The uninformed assumption, which we will denote as $\bar{S}$, is that Bob's string D has been generated by a random string other than Alice's published string (from some other portion of Alice's sent data), with the stipulation that the other string is also periodic. This mathematical framework will consider a subset of Alice's data of N sampling bin widths compared against a subset of Bob's data of $N + M$ sampling bin widths, meaning there will be M possible offsets to consider.

To begin in our protocol formalism, we note that D is a string of length $M + N$ of Bob's measurements at each sampling bin (including sampling bins where no detections were received). Each measurement B_i in Bob's string consists of the click or no-click results at all of Bob's detectors. Bob's string D can be written as

$$D = \{B_1, ..., B_{M+N}\}, \tag{2}$$

which we can rewrite as

$$D = \{B_1, D'\}, \tag{3}$$

where

$$D' = \{B_2, ..., B_{M+N}\}. \tag{4}$$

We prefer to write the likelihood $p(D|S)$ in terms of known quantities such as the $p(B_1|S)$, the conditional probability of a time bin measurement B_1 given S. Using this notation, $p(D|S)$ is given by

$$p(D|S) = p(B_1, D'|S) = p(B_1|D', S)p(D'|S), \tag{5}$$

where the final equality is a result of the product rule. Because we have assumed that B_1 is generated from Alice's string, knowing D' gives us no additional information about B_1. At best, it informs us whether S is true, which is already assumed; the bits are otherwise independent because Alice's sequence is random. Using these observations, we obtain

$$p(B_1|D', S) = p(B_1|S), \tag{6}$$

and, by extension,

$$p(D|S) = \prod_{i=1}^{N+M} p(B_i|S), \tag{7}$$

allowing us to write the likelihood as the product of the measurement probabilities at each sampling bin. We note that even in the example where Alice only sends one state in the monitoring basis, Bob must still measure both states in each basis to detect potential eavesdropper attacks [5,6]. For computational ease, we also determine each sampling bin measurement probability as the product of the probabilities of the outcomes at the four different detectors b_ℓ, which are given by

$$p(B_i|S) = \prod_{\ell=1}^{4} p(b_\ell|S). \tag{8}$$

Again, because the detectors' events are assumed to be generated by independent random processes, these probabilities can be considered independent when the generating string is known.

When the generating string is not known (under the uninformed assumption $\bar{S}$), the detection probabilities can be approximated as independent when the received mean photon number is low. Because the synchronization task is most difficult in low-signal regimes, we use this approximation going forward. Thus,

$$p(D|\bar{S}) = \prod_{i=1}^{N+M} p(B_i|\bar{S}) \tag{9}$$

and

$$p(B_i|\bar{S}) = \prod_{\ell=1}^{4} p(b_\ell|\bar{S}). \tag{10}$$

For a given input from Alice, each of Bob's four detectors has an opportunity to detect a photon above the detection clicks arising from non-ideal behaviors. Naturally, we will use our knowledge of the system (the state fidelities, the quality of the polarization sorting, the dark count rates, the detector efficiencies, and the signal and decoy received mean photon number) to estimate the detection probabilities as accurately and efficiently as possible. Using a lookup table of the detection probabilities for the different inputs from Alice, these likelihoods can be calculated using standard statistical methods.

However, the likelihood of generating D from Alice's published string is not the same as the probability that Alice's published string is the one that generated D, which is given by $p(S|D)$ and is the most relevant quantity to determine synchronization. Bayes' theorem allows us to rewrite this quantity, called the posterior, as

$$p(S|D) = \frac{p(D|S)p(S)}{p(D)}. \qquad (11)$$

In addition, we must also include the information that we expect exactly one correct synchronization offset (not just one on average).

To formulate the problem as an exclusive synchronization, we must find the probability that some discreet timing offset, given by the time-bin index j, is the correct synchronization offset, and that all the other offsets are incorrect. In other words, the probability that, for a given string of length N published by Alice, all the measurements before the jth bin are generated randomly, the measurements from j to $j + N$ are generated from Alice's published string, and the measurements after $j + N$ are generated randomly. Under these assumptions, we can write $p(B_1, ..., B_{M+N}|S_j)$ as a product of the likelihoods of these three sections as

$$p(B_1, ..., B_{M+N}|S_j) = p(B_1, ..., B_{j-1}|\bar{S}_j) p(B_j, ..., B_{j+N}|S_j) p(B_{j+N+1}, ..., B_{M+N}|\bar{S}_j). \qquad (12)$$

Here we introduce $\bar{S}_j$, the assumption that the data is produced by a random string other than the synchronization string in question, but one with the same phase (i.e., the signal arrives at the same time bin in each period as it does for S_j).

We can find the conditional probability for matching Alice's string to Bob's string at a potential synchronization index j in this framework using Equation (11), which gives

$$p(S_j|B_1, ..., B_{M+N}) = \frac{p(B_1, ..., B_{M+N}|S_j)p(S_j)}{p(B_1, ..., B_{M+N})}. \qquad (13)$$

Equation (13) is our main result and is the quantity of interest to identify clock synchronization between Alice and Bob. We determine the optimum synchronization index based on the value of j that maximizes this quantity, and the quantity itself gives us our confidence in that choice.

The denominator in Equation (13) can be written in terms of known quantities using marginalization. Marginalization consists of rewriting a probability as a sum of the comprehensive conditional probabilities; in this case, the different possible synchronization indices written as

$$p(S_j|B_1, ..., B_{M+N}) = \frac{p(B_1, ..., B_{M+N}|S_j)p(S_j)}{\sum_{i=1}^{M} p(B_1, ..., B_{M+N}|S_i)p(S_i)}, \qquad (14)$$

where the i denotes the other potential synchronization indices.

To evaluate Equation (13), the likelihoods $p(B_1, ..., B_{M+N}|S_j)$ and $p(B_1, ..., B_{M+N}|S_i)$ can be determined using Equations (7), (9) and (12). The quantity $p(S_j)$, called the prior, is the ad hoc probability that D corresponds to Alice's published string. That is, $p(S_j)$ is the probability that we are at the correct synchronization index. We use a uniform prior, which assumes each candidate has a naïve $1/M$ probability of being the correct one given that we have M candidate indices, which means that

$$p(S_i) = p(S_j) = \frac{1}{M} \qquad (15)$$

so that the prior terms cancel, giving us

$$p(S_j|B_1,...,B_{M+N}) = \frac{p(B_1,...,B_{M+N}|S_j)}{\sum_{i=1}^{M} p(B_1,...,B_{M+N}|S_i)}. \tag{16}$$

Next, we apply Equation (12) to obtain

$$p(S_j|B_1,...,B_{M+N}) = \tag{17}$$
$$\frac{p(B_1,...,B_{j-1}|\bar{S}_j)p(B_j,...,B_{j+N}|S_j)p(B_{j+N+1},...,B_{M+N}|\bar{S}_j)}{\sum_{i=1}^{M} p(B_1,...,B_{i-1}|\bar{S}_i)p(B_i,...,B_{i+N}|S_i)p(B_{i+N+1},...,B_{M+N}|\bar{S}_i)}$$

and use Equations (7) and (9) (of which the latter uses a low received mean photon number approximation) to write everything in terms of known quantities as

$$p(S_j|B_1,...,B_{M+N}) \approx \frac{\prod_{k=1}^{j-1} p(B_k|\bar{S}_j) \prod_{k=j}^{j+N} p(B_k|S_j) \prod_{k=j+N+1}^{M+N} p(B_k|\bar{S}_j)}{\sum_{i=1}^{M} \left(\prod_{k=1}^{i-1} p(B_k|\bar{S}_i) \prod_{k=i}^{i+N} p(B_k|S_i) \prod_{k=i+N+1}^{M+N} p(B_k|\bar{S}_i) \right)} \tag{18}$$

Equation (18) is our master equation for the synchronization probability of an index j. The numerator consists of the probability of an N-length string of Bob's data starting at j being produced by Alice's published string, along with the probability that the remaining data was produced by an unknown string of Alice's data. The denominator sums this same quantity over all possible synchronization indices, ensuring normalization. We take the value of j that maximizes this quantity to be the optimum synchronization index, and the value of $p(S_j|B_1,...,B_{M+N})$ gives us the probability that we are correct. We can compute this conditional probability using FFTs to count the number of each unique bin measurement along with a lookup table of the probabilities of the events.

3. Model System

To illustrate our protocol, we simulate a model QKD system using a polarization-based prepare-and-measure protocol with decoy states and only sending one state in the monitoring basis. We set Alice's repetition rate to be $f_A = 1/\tau_A$ and a wavepacket duration of $\Delta t = \tau_A/m$ with $m = 8$ for a duty cycle of 12.5 percent. We set Bob's sampling rate to nf_A with $n = 8$ so that his sample period is matched to the wavepacket duration. These conditions are illustrated in Figure 1. Alice generates a pseudorandom sequence such that four quantum states L/R/H and a vacuum decoy state (a decoy state with mean photon number equal to zero) are sent in equal parts on average.

For our numerical experiments, we simulate a QKD session by generating data that emulates the state preparation and measurement, including aspects such as the *received* mean photon number μ, probability of a detector dark count d over one communication bin width τ_A, and variation in Δ due to clock drift, assumed to be constant over T_b. This allows us to test how these factors impact the synchronization performance. We assume a transmitted mean photon number $\mu_A = 1$ where the received mean photon number $\mu = \eta\mu_A$ for a channel transmission η. While this μ_A is on the upper end of values used in typical experiments, it allows us to explore the performance and limitations of our algorithm at or beyond the greatest received mean photon number one would realistically use: $\mu_A = 1$ with zero loss.

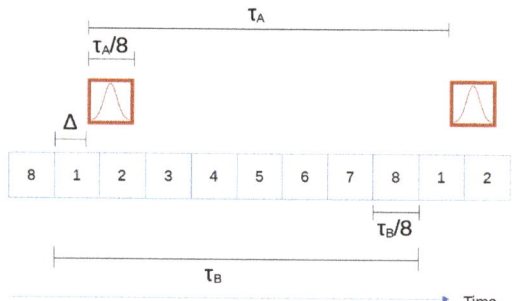

Figure 1. Illustration of the relative times used in the QKD protocol. Here, the signal (red) straddles bins 1–2 due to an offset of Δ, and we do not consider bins 3–8. We take $\tau_A = \tau_B$, which is approximately correct for a short enough data subset.

Assuming a Poisson distribution for Alice's source, the probability of Bob registering a click $p(click, \ell)$ over a period τ_A at a particular detector ℓ is given by

$$p(click, \ell) = 1 - (1-d)e^{-\mu_\ell} \qquad (19)$$

where μ_ℓ is the mean photon number received by detector ℓ. The portion of the total mean photon number μ that goes to the different detectors depends on which polarization state is sent. We use ideal BB84 sorting in our model system so that all states have an equal chance of being measured in either basis. States measured in the same basis as they are prepared are detected accurately, while states measured in the opposite basis have an equal chance of being measured in either opposite-basis state. For example, if Alice prepared an H-state that Bob receives $\mu = 0.8$, Bob's measures $\mu_H = 0.4$, $\mu_v = 0$, and $\mu_L = \mu_R = 0.2$.

We assume that the observation window is long enough so that the p's and μ's can be estimated accurately from the finite number of observations. This means the average click probability can be extracted from the Bob's raw data and we rewrite Equation (19) as a function of $p(click, \ell)$ so that

$$\mu_\ell = \ln\left(\frac{1-d}{1-p(click, \ell)}\right) \qquad (20)$$

The mean photon numbers of the constituent pulses incident at the four detectors sum to the average mean photon number of the main pulse just before it enters Bob's detection apparatus, so we can estimate the received mean photon number of a signal state as

$$\mu = \frac{4}{3}\sum_{\ell=1}^{4} \ln\left(\frac{1-d}{1-p(click, \ell)}\right), \qquad (21)$$

where the factor of 4/3 accounts for the fact that we are sending vacuum states 25% of the time.

We divide the data set into subsets duration T_b and perform synchronization and sifting on each subset. Bob can record up to eight events (each of which may or may not include a detection event or dark count) assuming that the detector deadtime is less than Bob's sampling time. However, because the clocks can only be synchronized to a resolution of Bob's sampling bin width, we expect Alice's wavepacket to straddle 2 bins as illustrated in Figure 1, with the end bins only having a partial wavepacket. The remaining six bins only contain dark counts, which can be discarded after we determine Δ to reduce noise. This amounts to detector time-gating in the post-analysis.

We assume that Bob begins recording before Alice begins transmitting, and continues to record after she stops sending, so our received data is bookended by low signal regions.

We find a best-fit step function to identify where the transmission begins and ends, which gives us a coarse approximation of the synchronization index. For a range of different string lengths N that determine the number of sampling bin widths in each synchronization subset, we examine a window of $M = 4000$ nearby potential synchronization indices. This value is chosen based on the typical precision of the coarse approximation of the synchronization given by the best-fit step function.

4. Synchronization Simulations

To verify that our algorithm returns an accurate probability of synchronization, we run 1000 simulated trials with a known synchronization index and compare the average calculated probability of synchronization $p(S_j|B_1,...,B_{M+N})$ to the average rate of finding the correct index, which we denote by $f(S_j|B_1,...,B_{M+N})$, in Figure 2. If our model is accurate, then $p(S_j|B_1,...,B_{M+N}) \sim f(S_j|B_1,...,B_{M+N})$, in which case we can take $p(S_j|B_1,...,B_{M+N})$ to be a reliable metric for quantifying our confidence in obtaining the correct Δ.

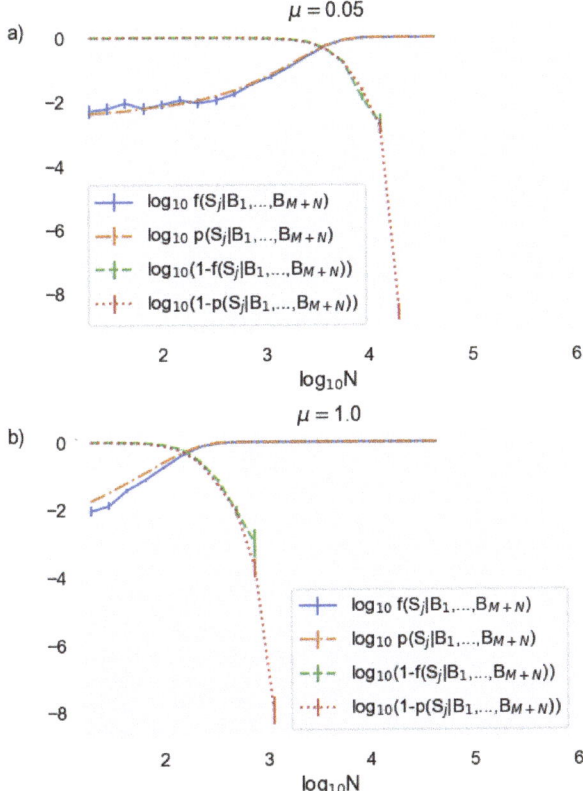

Figure 2. Bob's required data record length needed to determine synchronization for two different channel transmissions of (**a**) $\eta = 0.05$, corresponding to $\mu = 0.05$ and (**b**) $\eta = 1$, corresponding to $\mu = 1$. We also show the probability of not obtaining synchronization, which better highlights transition to high-certainty synchronization.

We see that $p(S_j|B_1,...,B_{M+N}) \sim f(S_j|B_1,...,B_{M+N})$ to within our errorbars for moderate channel loss (Figure 2a). However, $p(S_j|B_1,...,B_{M+N})$ is consistently larger than $f(S_j|B_1,...,B_{M+N})$ for the case of zero channel loss (Figure 2b), a condition that is unlikely to be encountered in an experiment but highlights the limitation of our algorithm. This result is not surprising given that our derivation given in Section 2 assumes low μ to arrive at Equation (9). Assuming a transmitted mean photon number of 1, Figure 2b corresponds to a zero channel loss system. This represents an upper limit on μ encountered in a typical decoy state protocol where $\mu_A \lesssim 1$ and thus, also serves as a lower bound on the accuracy of our calculated synchronization probability.

A lower received mean photon number means a lower density of detected events. Because detected events provide more information than no-detection events, a lower μ requires us to consider a larger set of sampling bin widths N to achieve the same synchronization confidence. Despite the fact that $p(S_j|B_1,...,B_{M+N})$ does not match $f(S_j|B_1,...,B_{M+N})$ as well at higher values of μ, we can still achieve equivalent average values of $f(S_j|B_1,...,B_{M+N})$ at lower values of N. This fact is also illustrated in Figure 3, where we see a direct correlation between μ and the N at which the synchronization probabilities converge to one. The higher values of μ converge at lower values of N.

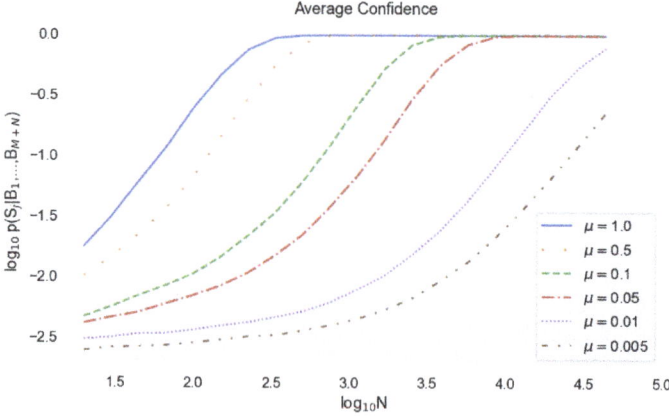

Figure 3. Average calculated synchronization probability as a function of string length on a logarithmic scale for different received mean photon numbers. The probability of registering a dark count during one communication bin width is $d = 8 \times 10^{-4}$.

Another way to view this relation between μ, N, and $p(S_j|B_1,...,B_{M+N})$ is to consider the string length N required to achieve a particular synchronization confidence as a function of μ as shown in Figure 4. For high μ and low N, we observe an approximately linear relation between $log_{10}\mu$ and $log_{10}N$ with a slope of ~ -1, which means that $N \sim 1/\mu$. For lower μ, where there are fewer events and dark counts play a larger role, the probability curves exhibit steeper slopes, demonstrating that synchronization becomes increasingly difficult. This data can be used to estimate whether it is possible to synchronize over an experimentally measured temporal block length T_b and, if it is possible, how low a value of μ can be tolerated while still synchronizing reliably. As a concrete example, Bob needs 33,110 sampling bin widths, or about 4140 communication bin widths, to achieve a 95% confidence for clock synchronization for $\mu = 0.01$ and $d = 8 \times 10^{-4}$. This means we can tolerate clock drifts approaching 1 part in 4140, or 242 µs of drift per second, because our method assumes that the clock drift is much less than one communication bin width. For context, we measure the rate of clock drift between two phase lock loops driven by crystal oscillator clocks on DE10 Standard field programmable gate arrays (FPGAs), and find the average clock drift rate to be 13.5 µs per second. Thus, our algorithm can tolerate realistic clock drift rates in this example.

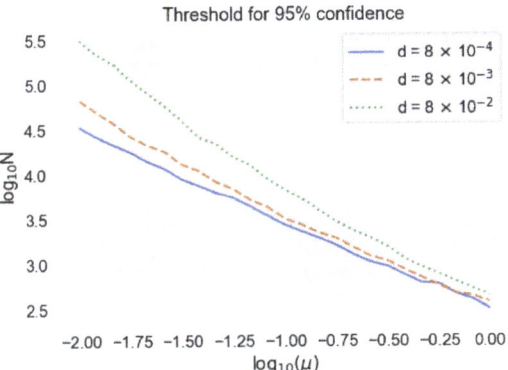

Figure 4. Dependence of string length threshold to achieve 95 percent synchronization confidence on received mean photon number on a logarithmic scale, parameterized by different dark count probabilities.

5. Conclusions

In conclusion, we develop a novel probabilistic approach to qubit-based clock synchronization using Bayesian analysis. By exploiting correlations between information Alice shares publicly, such as basis and decoy state choices, and Bob's detection events, we can find the correct synchronization clock offset without sacrificing any secret key. Additionally, our algorithm is more robust to noise, loss, and clock drift in comparison to other protocols by incorporating all publicly available information using the Bayesian framework. Finally, we demonstrate that our algorithm is successful and robust using a simulated BB84 communication scheme, which confirms that our synchronization metric corresponds to the probability of synchronization, especially in the low-μ limit. Our algorithm is applicable to other QKD systems that use other degrees-of-freedom of the photon for which it is possible to divulge some timing information.

Author Contributions: Conceptualization, R.D.C.; methodology, R.D.C.; software, R.D.C.; validation, R.D.C.; formal analysis, R.D.C.; investigation, R.D.C.; resources, R.D.C.; data curation, R.D.C.; writing—original draft preparation, R.D.C.; writing—review and editing, R.D.C. and D.J.G.; visualization, R.D.C. and D.J.G.; supervision, D.J.G.; project administration, D.J.G.; funding acquisition, R.D.C. and D.J.G. All authors have read and agreed to the published version of the manuscript.

Funding: This material is based on research sponsored by NASA under grant 80NSSC20K0629 and the Air Force Research Laboratory and the Southwestern Council for Higher Education under agreement FA8650-19-2-9300. The U.S. Government is authorized to reproduce and distribute reprints for Governmental purposes notwithstanding any copyright notation thereon. The views and conclusions contained herein are those of the authors and should not be interpreted as necessarily representing the official policies or endorsements, either expressed or implied, of NASA, the Southwestern Council for Higher Education and the Air Force Research Laboratory (AFRL), or the U.S. Government.

Data Availability Statement: All code and data used in simulations is publicly available on GitHub: https://github.com/roderickdcochran/qubit_based_synchronization (accessed on 29 July 2021).

Acknowledgments: We thank Daniel Sanchez-Rosales for help in collecting the data on FPGA clock drift. R.D.C. acknowledge discussions of the Bayesian analysis with Richard Furnstahl.

Conflicts of Interest: The authors declare no conflict of interest. The funders had no role in the design of the study; in the collection, analyses, or interpretation of data; in the writing of the manuscript, or in the decision to publish the results.

References

1. Bennett, C.H.; Brassard, G. Quantum cryptography: Public key distribution and coin tossing. *Theor. Comput. Sci.* **2014**, *560*, 7–11. [CrossRef]
2. Ekert, A. Quantum cryptography based on bell theorem. *Phys. Rev. Lett.* **1991**, *67*, 661–663.10.1103/PhysRevLett.67.661. [CrossRef] [PubMed]
3. Lo, H.K.; Ma, X.; Chen, K. Decoy State Quantum Key Distribution. *Phys. Rev. Lett.* **2005**, *94*, 230504. 230504. [CrossRef] [PubMed]
4. Bennett, C.H.; Bessette, F.; Brassard, G.; Salvail, L.; Smolin, J. Experimental quantum cryptography. *J. Cryptol.* **1992**, *5*, 3–28. [CrossRef]
5. Islam, N.T.; Lim, C.C.W.; Cahall, C.; Kim, J.; Gauthier, D.J. Securing quantum key distribution systems using fewer states. *Phys. Rev. A* **2018**, *97*, 042347. [CrossRef]
6. Tamaki, K.; Curty, M.; Kato, G.; Lo, H.K.; Azuma, K. Loss-tolerant quantum cryptography with imperfect sources. *Phys. Rev. A* **2014**, *90*, 052314. [CrossRef]
7. D'Auria, V.; Fedrici, B.; Ngah, L.A.; Kaiser, F.; Labonté, L.; Alibart, O.; Tanzilli, S. A Universal, Plug- Synchronisation Scheme Pract. Networks. *Npj Quantum. Inf.* **2020**, *6*, 21. [CrossRef]
8. Korzh, B.; Lim, C.C.W.; Houlmann, R.; Gisin, N.; Li, M.J.; Nolan, D.; Sanguinetti, B.; Thew, R.; Zbinden, H. Provably secure and practical quantum key distribution over 307 km of optical fibre. *Nat. Photonics* **2015**, *9*, 163–168. [CrossRef]
9. Liu, Y.; Chen, T.Y.; Wang, J.; Cai, W.Q.; Wan, X.; Chen, L.K.; Wang, J.H.; Liu, S.B.; Liang, H.; Yang, L.; et al. Decoy-state quantum key distribution with polarized photons over 200 km. *Opt. Express* **2010**, *18*, 8587–8594. [CrossRef]
10. Liu, P.; Yin, H.L. Secure and efficient synchronization scheme for quantum key distribution. *OSA Contin.* **2019**, *2*, 2883–2890. [CrossRef]
11. Walenta, N.; Burg, A.; Caselunghe, D.; Constantin, J.; Gisin, N.; Guinnard, O.; Houlmann, R.; Junod, P.; Korzh, B.; Kulesza, N.; et al. A fast and versatile quantum key distribution system with hardware key distillation and wavelength multiplexing. *New J. Phys.* **2014**, *16*, 013047. [CrossRef]
12. Dynes, J.; Tam, W.; Plews, A.; Fröhlich, B.; Sharpe, A.W.; Lucamarini, M.; Yuan, Z.; Radig, C.; Straw, A.; Edwards, T.; et al. Ultra-High Bandwidth Quantum Secur. Data Transm. *Sci. Rep.* **2016**, *6*, 35149. [CrossRef] [PubMed]
13. Sasaki, M.; Fujiwara, M.; Ishizuka, H.; Klaus, W.; Wakui, K.; Takeoka, M.; Miki, S.; Yamashita, T.; Wang, Z.; Tanaka, A.; et al. Field test of quantum key distribution in the Tokyo QKD Network. *Opt. Express* **2011**, *19*, 10387–10409. [CrossRef]
14. Wang, S.; Chen, W.; Yin, Z.Q.; Li, H.W.; He, D.Y.; Li, Y.H.; Zhou, Z.; Song, X.T.; Li, F.Y.; Wang, D.; et al. Field and long-term demonstration of a wide area quantum key distribution network. *Opt. Express* **2014**, *22*, 21739–21756. [CrossRef] [PubMed]
15. Vallone, G.; Marangon, D.G.; Canale, M.; Savorgnan, I.; Bacco, D.; Barbieri, M.; Calimani, S.; Barbieri, C.; Laurenti, N.; Villoresi, P. Adaptive real time selection for quantum key distribution in lossy and turbulent free-space channels. *Phys. Rev. A* **2015**, *91*, 042320. [CrossRef]
16. Bourgoin, J.P.; Gigov, N.; Higgins, B.L.; Yan, Z.; Meyer-Scott, E.; Khandani, A.K.; Lütkenhaus, N.; Jennewein, T. Experimental quantum key distribution with simulated ground-to-satellite photon losses and processing limitations. *Phys. Rev. A* **2015**, *92*, 052339. [CrossRef]
17. Calderaro, L.; Stanco, A.; Agnesi, C.; Avesani, M.; Dequal, D.; Villoresi, P.; Vallone, G. Fast and Simple Qubit-Based Synchronization for Quantum Key Distribution. *Phys. Rev. Appl.* **2020**, *13*, 054041. [CrossRef]
18. Agnesi, C.; Avesani, M.; Calderaro, L.; Stanco, A.; Foletto, G.; Zahidy, M.; Scriminich, A.; Vedovato, F.; Vallone, G.; Villoresi, P. Simple quantum key distribution with qubit-based synchronization and a self-compensating polarization encoder. *Optica* **2020**, *7*, 284–290. [CrossRef]
19. Avesani, M.; Calderaro, L.; Foletto, G.; Agnesi, C.; Picciariello, F.; Santagiustina, F.B.L.; Scriminich, A.; Stanco, A.; Vedovato, F.; Zahidy, M.; et al. Resource-effective quantum key distribution: A field trial in Padua city center. *Opt. Lett.* **2021**, *46*, 2848–2851. [CrossRef]
20. Ho, C.; Lamas-Linares, A.; Kurtsiefer, C. Clock synchronization by remote detection of correlated photon pairs. *New J. Phys.* **2009**, *11*, 045011. [CrossRef]
21. Hayashi, M. Upper bounds of eavesdropper's performances in finite-length code with the decoy method. *Phys. Rev. A* **2007**, *76*, 012329. [CrossRef]
22. Lim, C.C.W.; Curty, M.; Walenta, N.; Xu, F.; Zbinden, H. Concise security bounds for practical decoy-state quantum key distribution. *Phys. Rev. A* **2014**, *89*, 022307. [CrossRef]

Article

Randomized Oblivious Transfer for Secure Multiparty Computation in the Quantum Setting

Bruno Costa [1,2], Pedro Branco [1,3], Manuel Goulão [1,3], Mariano Lemus [1] and Paulo Mateus [1,3,*]

1. Departamento de Matemática, Instituto Superior Técnico, Av. Rovisco Pais, 1049-001 Lisbon, Portugal; brunofilipe.antunescosta@capgemini.com (B.C.); pedrodemelobranco@gmail.com (P.B.); manuel.goulao@tecnico.ulisboa.pt (M.G.); marianojlemush@gmail.com (M.L.)
2. Capgemini Engineering, Av. D. João II, Lote 1.07.2.1, Piso 2, 1990-096 Lisbon, Portugal
3. Instituto de Telecomunicações, IST Av. Rovisco Pais, 1049-001 Lisbon, Portugal
* Correspondence: pmat@math.tecnico.ulisboa.pt

Abstract: Secure computation is a powerful cryptographic tool that encompasses the evaluation of any multivariate function with arbitrary inputs from mutually distrusting parties. The oblivious transfer primitive serves is a basic building block for the general task of secure multi-party computation. Therefore, analyzing the security in the universal composability framework becomes mandatory when dealing with multi-party computation protocols composed of oblivious transfer subroutines. Furthermore, since the required number of oblivious transfer instances scales with the size of the circuits, oblivious transfer remains as a bottleneck for large-scale multi-party computation implementations. Techniques that allow one to extend a small number of oblivious transfers into a larger one in an efficient way make use of the oblivious transfer variant called randomized oblivious transfer. In this work, we present randomized versions of two known oblivious transfer protocols, one quantum and another post-quantum with ring learning with an error assumption. We then prove their security in the quantum universal composability framework, in a common reference string model.

Keywords: oblivious transfer; quantum cryptography; post-quantum cryptography; universal composability

1. Introduction

Oblivious transfer (OT), first introduced by Rabin in 1981 [1], is an important primitive in modern cryptography. The OT primitive is known to be a basic building block for other cryptographic tasks, including secure Multi-Party Computation (MPC), Bit Commitment (BC), Coin-Tossing, and Zero-Knowledge Proofs [2–7].

A 1-out-of-2 OT protocol [8] consists of two parties, a sender with two input messages (m_0, m_1) and a receiver with a choice bit $b \in \{0,1\}$. The goal of the protocol is to output only the message m_b to the receiver, with no information about m_{1-b}, and the sender remains oblivious to the receiver's input bit b. Note that, in the original work by Rabin, called all-or-nothing OT [1], the sender has a single input message, while the receiver has none. The protocol outputs the message to the receiver with probability $\frac{1}{2}$, such that the receiver has no information whether or not the receiver obtained the message. It was shown that one can construct 1-out-of-2 OT from all-or-nothing OT [9]. Another OT variant is that of Randomized Oblivious Transfer (ROT), where neither of the parties have any inputs. The ROT protocol, instead, outputs the messages (m_0, m_1) to the sender and (b, m_b) to the receiver, with (m_0, m_1, b) chosen uniformly at random from their domains.

MPC [10,11], which is an extremely useful cryptographic tool to compute arbitrary functionalities, can be reduced to the OT primitive; i.e., having access to a secure OT is sufficient [2]. MPC implementations based on oblivious-circuit evaluation techniques require a large number of OT (one per input wire for Yao [10], and one per AND gate for

GMW [11]). Since classical OT schemes (being based on asymmetric-key cryptography) are relatively slow, the development of large-scale MPC implementations has been severely hindered by the required OT rates. In order to deal with this issue of OT efficiency, the concept of OT extension was introduced by Ishai et al. in 2003 [12]. This technique refers to extending a small number of computationally expensive *base* OTs into a larger number of OTs, using only cheap symmetric cryptography primitives. For proving the security of these OT extension techniques in the malicious-adversary setting [13], it turns out that one is required to use ROT instances as the base OTs. Additionally, ROT finds direct application in designing efficient Private Set Intersection (PSI) protocols [14], one of the most popular MPC techniques.

Moreover, even though the efficiency issue can be solved by the use of OT extensions for MPC applications, there is the underlying threat that asymmetric-key based schemes (e.g., integer-factorization or discrete-logarithm problems) will be faced with the arrival of quantum computers [15]. The research initiatives for developing quantum-resistant solutions have been following two paths. The first being on the development of more hard-to-break classical cryptography algorithms that will remain secure even against a quantum adversary. These solutions include the approximate Shortest Vector Problem (SVP) on ideal lattices [16], the Learning with Errors (LWE) problem [17] and its ring version, Ring Learning with Errors (RLWE) [16], constituting a new area of research, called post-quantum cryptography. The second approach is that of quantum cryptography, where solutions for Quantum Key Distribution (QKD), BC, and OT already exist [18]. While unconditional security for QKD has been proven [19], there are impossibility results to achieve for the case of BC and OT [20–22]. Nevertheless, practical solutions for BC and OT were proposed under the assumption of physical limitations on the devices, such as noisy storage and bounded quantum memories [23–27].

Our Contribution

In this work, we explore the construction of two ROT protocols in the quantum Universal Composability (UC) framework, in the Common Reference String (CRS) model:

- A quantum protocol based on the UC construction by Unruh [28] and augmented with an additional subroutine to enforce randomized outputs.
- A classical protocol based on a variant of the RLWE assumption that adapts the one presented in [29,30] but does not require a random oracle model and, instead, uses a composable commitment scheme and a composable non-interactive zero knowledge (NIZK) protocol.

In both cases, the basic idea is to build upon existing non-randomized OT protocols in such a way as to force the values of all of the protocol's outputs to be influenced by both parties. This allows us to randomize both the messages m_0, m_1 and the choice bit b as long as at least one party is honest, leading to a ROT protocol. Furthermore, we prove that the resulting protocols are secure in the quantum UC framework.

This paper is organized in five sections. In Section 2, we briefly review some definitions and functionalities relevant for the description and analysis of the protocols. In Section 3, we present the generic construction of ROT from OT and afterwards present the commitment scheme and OT protocols that we will be using to achieve the quantum security we need. The security of the protocols are then shown in Section 4. Finally, in Section 5, we present the main results of this work.

2. Background

The problems regarding Ring Learning with Errors are conjectured to be hard on both classical and quantum computers. Before defining the RLWE distribution and its decision problem, we first present the notation used. Let $R_q = \mathbb{Z}_q[X]/f(X)$ be a ring, where $q > 2$ is a prime, and $f(X)$ is a cyclotomic polynomial of degree n. Let $\beta \in \mathbb{N}$ and χ be the error distribution that outputs elements of R_q with a norm greater than β with negligible probability.

Definition 1 (RLWE distribution). *Let q, R_q and χ be as above. The RLWE distribution $A_{s,\chi}$ is obtained by sampling $a \in R_q$ uniformly, choosing $e \leftarrow_s \chi$ and outputting $(a, b = as + e \mod q)$ for a secret $s \in R_q$.*

Definition 2 (decision-RLWE). *Let q, R_q, χ and $A_{s,\chi}$ be as above. For $s \leftarrow_s R_q$, given many polynomial samples, the goal is to distinguish between $A_{s,\chi}$ and a uniform distribution over $R_q \times R_q$.*

By using the the RLWE variant of the LWE problem we are able to not only work with smaller keys but also increase the speed of the operations by using the Number Theoretic Transform (NTT). The protocol we will be analyzing uses a variant of the RLWE problem, the Hermite Normal Form of the RLWE problem (HNF-RLWE), in which the secret s is sampled from the error distribution χ instead of being chosen uniformly at random from the ring R_q. This version of the problem is assumed to be hard as well, since RLWE reduces to it [31].

Often times studying the standalone security of protocols is not enough, since they will be frequently used as subroutines in more complex tasks, as is the case of OT, as well as Coin Tossing, Commitment schemes, Zero-Knowledge proofs, etc. In order to ensure that protocols are secure in any computational environment, Canetti [32] introduced the Universal Composability (UC) framework, which we define next.

Let π be an n-party protocol and $\mathcal{F}$ be an ideal functionality. We denote as IDEAL$_{\mathcal{F},\mathcal{S},\mathcal{Z}}$ the output of the environment $\mathcal{Z}$ at the end of the ideal-world execution of functionality $\mathcal{F}$ with adversary $\mathcal{S}$, and as EXEC$_{\pi,\mathcal{A},\mathcal{Z}}$ the output of the environment $\mathcal{Z}$ at the end of the real-world execution of π with adversary $\mathcal{A}$. The notion of a protocol securely emulating some ideal functionality is as follows:

Definition 3 (UC-secure). *We say that π UC-emulates $\mathcal{F}$ if for any adversary $\mathcal{A}$ there exists a simulator $\mathcal{S}$, such that, for all environment $\mathcal{Z}$,*

$$\text{IDEAL}_{\mathcal{F},\mathcal{S},\mathcal{Z}} \approx \text{EXEC}_{\pi,\mathcal{A},\mathcal{Z}}.$$

When discussing UC security, we can consider either a bounded (computational) or unbounded (statistical) approach. In computational UC security, we restrict the adversary, simulator, and environment to polynomial-time machines, and this approach is used when showing security based on computational assumptions. On the other hand, in statistical UC security, we quantify over all adversaries, simulators, and environments; as such, we can model statistical security.

In this work, we consider *malicious* adversaries, that is, adversaries that can deviate in any way from the protocol. However, we assume that the corruption of a party happens before the start of the protocol, and both the sender or the receiver may be corrupted.

In Figures 1–5 we present the functionalities that will be relevant in this work.

Functionality $\mathcal{F}_{OT}$

Parameters: String size ℓ.
Parties: The sender S and the receiver R.

1. Upon receiving inputs $(m_0, m_1) \in \{0,1\}^\ell \times \{0,1\}^\ell$ from S and $b \in \{0,1\}$ from R, $\mathcal{F}_{OT}$ sends m_b to R.

Figure 1. OT functionality.

Functionality $\mathcal{F}_{ROT}$

Parameters: String size ℓ.
Parties: The sender S and the receiver R.

1. Upon receiving message START from both S and R, $\mathcal{F}_{ROT}$ samples $m_0, m_1 \xleftarrow{\$} \{0,1\}^\ell$ and $b \xleftarrow{\$} \{0,1\}$. It then sends (m_0, m_1) to S and (b, m_b) to R.

Figure 2. ROT functionality.

Functionality $\mathcal{F}_{COM}$

Parameters: Commitment size ℓ (for bit commitment, $\ell = 1$).
Parties: The sender S and the recipient R.

1. Upon input (COMMIT, x) with $x \in \{0,1\}^\ell$ from S, $\mathcal{F}_{COM}$ records x and sends a receipt to R.
2. Upon input OPEN from S, send (OPEN, x) to R.

Figure 3. Commitment functionality.

Functionality $\mathcal{F}_{CRS}$

Parameters: Distribution $\mathcal{D}$.

1. When activated for the first time on input VALUE, $\mathcal{F}_{CRS}^{\mathcal{D}}$ chooses a value $d \xleftarrow{\$} \mathcal{D}$ and sends d back to the activating party. Every other activation will return the same d to the activating party.

Figure 4. Common Reference String functionality.

Functionality $\mathcal{F}_{NIZK}$

Parameters: Common statement x.
Parties: The verifier V and the prover P.

- **Proof:** On input (x, w) from P, if $\mathcal{R}(x, w) = 1$, then send $p(w)$ to P.
- **Verification:** On input $(x, p(w))$ from V, send $\mathcal{R}(x, w)$ to V.

Figure 5. Non-Interactive Zero-Knowledge functionality.

We stress that the definition of $\mathcal{F}_{ROT}$ presented here is stronger than the one presented in Unruh's original paper [28], in which the outputs are only random if the parties are both honest. In the same paper, the UC framework is extended to the quantum setting by allowing the protocol π, the adversary $\mathcal{A}$, the simulator $\mathcal{S}$, and the environment $\mathcal{Z}$ to be quantum.

Unruh [28] also showed that, when π is a classical protocol and π statistically UC-emulates $\mathcal{F}$, then π statistically quantum-UC-emulates $\mathcal{F}$, providing a lift from statistical classical-UC to statistical quantum-UC. A similar result exists for the computational case [28], but it is required that the adversary in the classical case is given the same computational power as in the quantum setting; in other words, we need to guarantee that the classical machines present in the proof of UC security are as powerful as quantum-polynomial-time machines.

Consider protocols π and σ, we denote the protocol where σ invokes instances of π by σ^π. A usual situation would be $\sigma^\mathcal{F}$, being a protocol that uses some ideal functionality $\mathcal{F}$, and σ^π would then be the protocol that results from implementing that functionality with some protocol π. Composition has been shown to be secure, both in the classical [32] and quantum settings [28].

Theorem 1 (Universal Composition Theorem [28]). *Let $\mathcal{F}, \mathcal{G}$ be ideal functionalities. Let π be an n-party protocol that UC-emulates $\mathcal{G}$ in the $\mathcal{F}$-hybrid model, and let η be an n-party protocol that UC-emulates $\mathcal{F}$. Protocol π^η then UC-emulates $\mathcal{G}$.*

3. Protocols

In this section, we start by presenting the generic construction of ROT from OT, using a commitment scheme, and afterwards describe the commitment scheme and the quantum OT protocol that will allow our ROT protocol to computationally quantum-UC-emulate $\mathcal{F}_{ROT}$. Finally, we describe a post-quantum approach, a ROT protocol based on the RLWE assumption, inspired by the recent work of [30], with a small tweak to avoid using random oracles, which misbehave against quantum adversaries.

3.1. Generating an UC-Secure Random OT

The protocol $\pi_{OT \to ROT}$ is presented in Figure 6. We consider the two parties: the sender S and the receiver R. It begins with R sampling two strings $r_0, r_1 \in \{0,1\}^\ell$ and committing them to S. R then chooses a random bit c, and S chooses two random strings, $w_0, w_1 \in \{0,1\}^\ell$. With these, the parties invoke the $\mathcal{F}_{OT}$ functionality. Following that, S chooses a random bit d and sends it over to R. Finally, R opens his commitment, and S checks if it matches the initial commit. If it does not, it aborts; otherwise, it outputs $(M_0 = w_d \oplus r_d, M_1 = w_{d\oplus 1} \oplus r_{d\oplus 1})$. R outputs $(b = c \oplus d, M_b = w_c \oplus r_c)$.

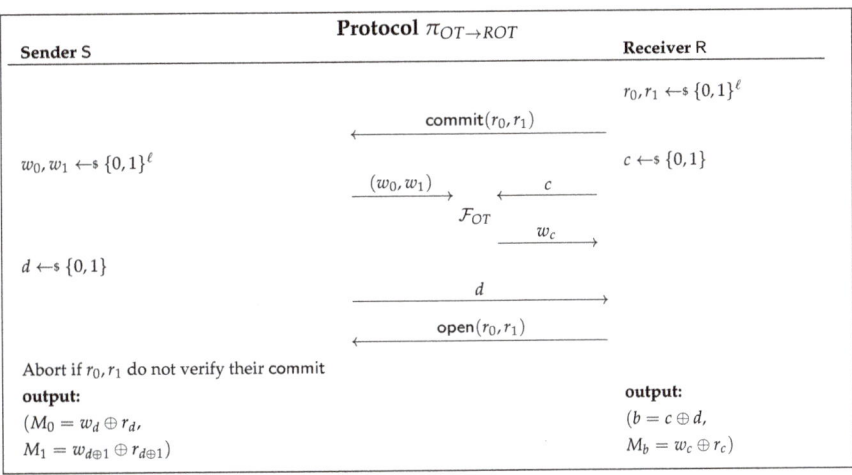

Figure 6. ROT protocol based on secure commitments.

3.2. UC-Secure Commitment Scheme

Canetti [33] showed that UC-secure commitment schemes are impossible in the plain model, and the same result was later proven for the quantum setting as well [22]. With that in mind, we will be working on the Common Reference String (CRS) model defined in Figure 4.

The protocol π_{COM} in Figure 7 has been shown to be computationally UC-secure in the CRS model [33]. The key to this protocol's composability is the use of a trapdoor pseudorandom generator (PRNG) G_{pk}, which is described by its public key pk. This generator G_{pk} stretches n-bit inputs to $4n$-bit outputs, and has a trapdoor td. Having access to both pk and td, we can easily check if a given string $y \in \{0,1\}^{4n}$ is in the range of G_{pk}.

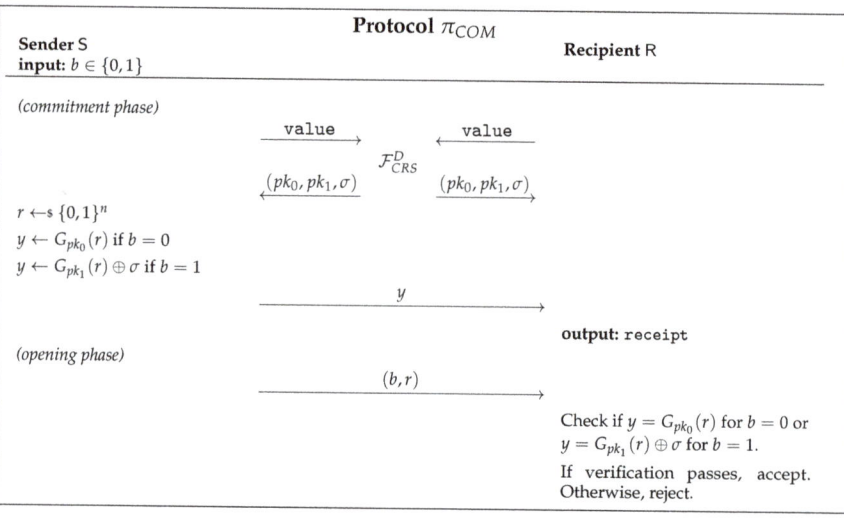

Figure 7. UC-secure BC scheme in the One-Time CRS Model [32].

Note that the protocol π_{COM} is a bit commitment protocol, and for string commitment, an instance of π_{COM} is needed to run for each bit of the string.

3.3. UC-Secure Quantum OT Protocol

The protocol in Figure 8 was proposed by Yao and has been shown to be statistically quantum-UC-secure with ideal commitments [28].

We describe the logical qubit states $|0\rangle$ and $|1\rangle$ (representing the computational basis), and the states $|+\rangle = (|0\rangle + |1\rangle)/\sqrt{2}$, $|-\rangle = (|0\rangle - |1\rangle)/\sqrt{2}$ (representing the Hadamard basis). We use the following notation to define the states $|(s_i, a_i)\rangle$ for $s_i, a_i \in \{0,1\}$:

$$|(0,0)\rangle = |0\rangle \quad |(0,1)\rangle = |+\rangle,$$
$$|(1,0)\rangle = |1\rangle \quad |(1,1)\rangle = |-\rangle.$$

The protocol begins with the sender S preparing qubit states and sending them to the receiver R, which then samples a random string $\tilde{a}$. For every qubit received, R measures the i-th state on a computational basis if $\tilde{a}_i = 0$ or, on the Hadamard basis, if $\tilde{a}_i = 1$. Therefore, approximately half of R's measurement results will be correlated with the prepared states by S, while the rest will be uncorrelated. To ensure security against a dishonest R, it is required to commit information on all of his measurement bases and outcomes to S, which then picks a random subset of them and tests for correlations. The passing of this test (statistically) ensures that R measured its qubits honestly. Next, S shares with R the bases it used for her state-preparation and, with this information, R knows which of its results are correlated with the sender's. The receiver, then, creates two sets: I_0, with indices where it is measured on the same basis as S, and I_1, where their measuring bases differ. Following that, R uses its choice bit b to select the order in which it sends the two sets to S. The sender samples two hash functions f_0, f_1 at random, from a *2-universal* family of hash functions **F**, in order to generate uniform keys of appropriate size, as that of the messages m_0, m_1. S sends the encrypted messages w_0, w_1 to R, which can only decrypt the message corresponding to the set I_0.

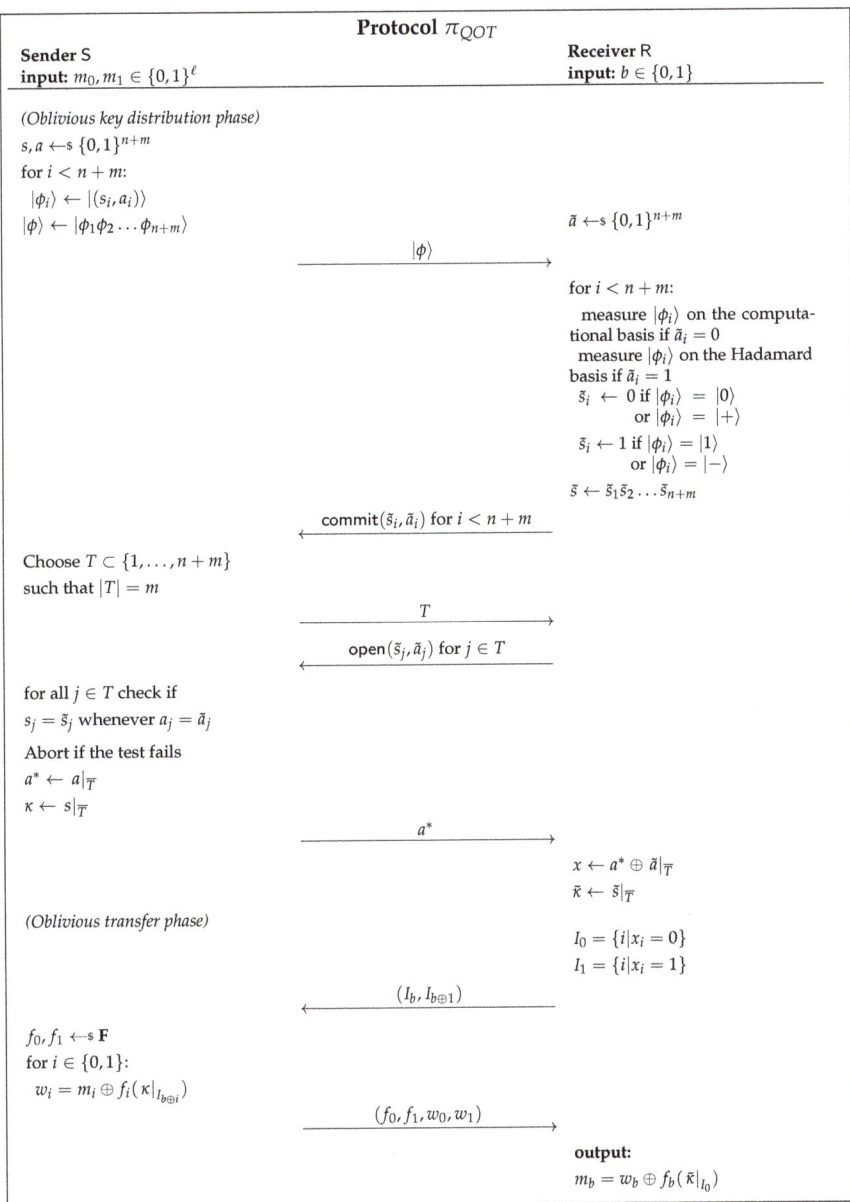

Figure 8. Quantum UC-secure Quantum OT Protocol based on secure commitments [28].

3.4. Post-Quantum UC-Secure ROT Protocol

The protocol in Figure 9 is based on the recently proposed protocol by [30] (which was based on [29]), which has been shown to be UC-secure under the RLWE assumption in the Random Oracle Model (ROM). However, UC security using ROM does not directly lift to UC security against quantum adversaries. Taking that into consideration, our idea is to replace the random oracle calls, which are used to either commit to a string or to generate a random string.

In order to understand the protocol π_{ROT}, we need to provide some preliminary definitions. A signal function Sig and an extraction function Ext are described as in the key exchange protocol using RLWE of [34], to be used by the involved parties to reconcile a shared key.

Let $\sigma_0, \sigma_1 : \mathbb{Z}_q \to \{0,1\}$. We define σ_0, σ_1 as follows:

$$\sigma_0(a) = \begin{cases} 0, & a \in [-\lfloor \frac{q}{4} \rfloor, \lfloor \frac{q}{4} \rfloor] \\ 1, & \text{otherwise} \end{cases} \quad \text{and} \quad \sigma_1(a) = \begin{cases} 0, & a \in [-\lfloor \frac{q}{4} + 1 \rfloor, \lfloor \frac{q}{4} + 1 \rfloor] \\ 1, & \text{otherwise} \end{cases}$$

Next, we need to extend σ_0, σ_1 to the ring case. For any $a = \sum_{i=0}^{n-1} a_i X^i \in R_q$, we define $\sigma_0, \sigma_1 : R_q \to R_2$ as follows:

$$\sigma_0(a) = \sum_{i=0}^{n-1} \sigma_0(a_i) X^i \quad \text{and} \quad \sigma_1(a) = \sum_{i=0}^{n-1} \sigma_1(a_i) X^i$$

The signal function $\text{Sig} : R_q \to R_2$ can now be defined as $\text{Sig}(a) = \sigma_b(a)$, where $b \leftarrow^s \{0,1\}$, while the extraction function $\text{Ext} : R_q \times R_2 \to R_2$ is

$$\text{Ext}(a, \sigma) = \left(a + \sigma \frac{q-1}{2} \mod q \right) \mod 2.$$

We can now describe the ROT protocol based on the RLWE assumption, Figure 9, which can be seen as a tweaked version of the protocol of [30], where we replace the random oracles by a commitment scheme and a NIZK protocol, modeled as functionalities.

Let χ and q be as in Definition 2 and ℓ be the security parameter. Let (m, h) be the common string, where $m, h \in R_q$, and let Ext and Sig be the algorithms defined above.

The protocol starts with both parties generating an RLWE sample. The sender S generates $p_S = m s_S + 2 e_S \mod q$, and the receiver R generates $p_R^c = m s_R + 2 e_R \mod q$, where c is a bit randomly chosen by R. If the sampled bit $c = 1$, then R computes $p_R^0 = p_R^1 - h \mod q$. The receiver then samples two strings $t_0, t_1 \leftarrow^s \{0,1\}^\ell$, commits both strings, and sends p_R^0 to S. The sender uses the common string h and p_R^0 to compute $p_R^1 = p_R^0 + h \mod q$ and uses both values p_R^0, p_R^1 to generate two RLWE samples. $k_S^i = s_S p_R^i + 2 e_S'$ mod q for $i \in \{0,1\}$. S now computes $\sigma_i = \text{Sig}(k_S^i)$ and $\text{sk}_S^i = \text{Ext}(k_S^i, \sigma_i)$, for $i \in \{0,1\}$, and sends p_S, σ_0, σ_1 to R. The receiver then generates an RLWE sample $k_R = s_R p_S + 2 e_R'$ mod q from p_S and computes $\text{sk}_R = \text{Ext}(k_R, \sigma_c)$. The key exchange protocol guarantees that $\text{sk}_S^c = \text{sk}_R$ with overwhelming probability, so as to guarantee that R did not cheat (and indeed the computed sk_R). Both parties engage in a NIZK protocol. If the proof fails, S aborts; otherwise, he samples a bit a and two strings $r_0, r_1 \leftarrow^s \{0,1\}^\ell$ and sends a, r_0, r_1 to R. The receiver opens his initial commitment to S, and if the test passes, both parties output their messages: S outputs $(M_0 = \text{sk}_S^a \oplus r_a \oplus t_a, M_1 = \text{sk}_S^{a \oplus 1} \oplus r_{a \oplus 1} \oplus t_{a \oplus 1})$, and R outputs $(b = a \oplus c, M_b = \text{sk}_R \oplus r_c \oplus t_c)$.

To simplify the description of π_{ROT} in Figure 9, we represent $\mathcal{F}_{NIZK}$ with a single input from the prover R (the witness w) and a single output to the verifier S, where this output is 1 if w satisfies $\mathcal{R}$ or 0 otherwise. Let the binary relation $\mathcal{R}$ be such that

$$\mathcal{R}(x, w) = 1 \iff w = \text{sk}_S^0 \vee w = \text{sk}_S^1,$$

where $x = \text{Enc}(\text{sk}_S^0, \text{sk}_S^1)$ for a given public key encryption scheme.

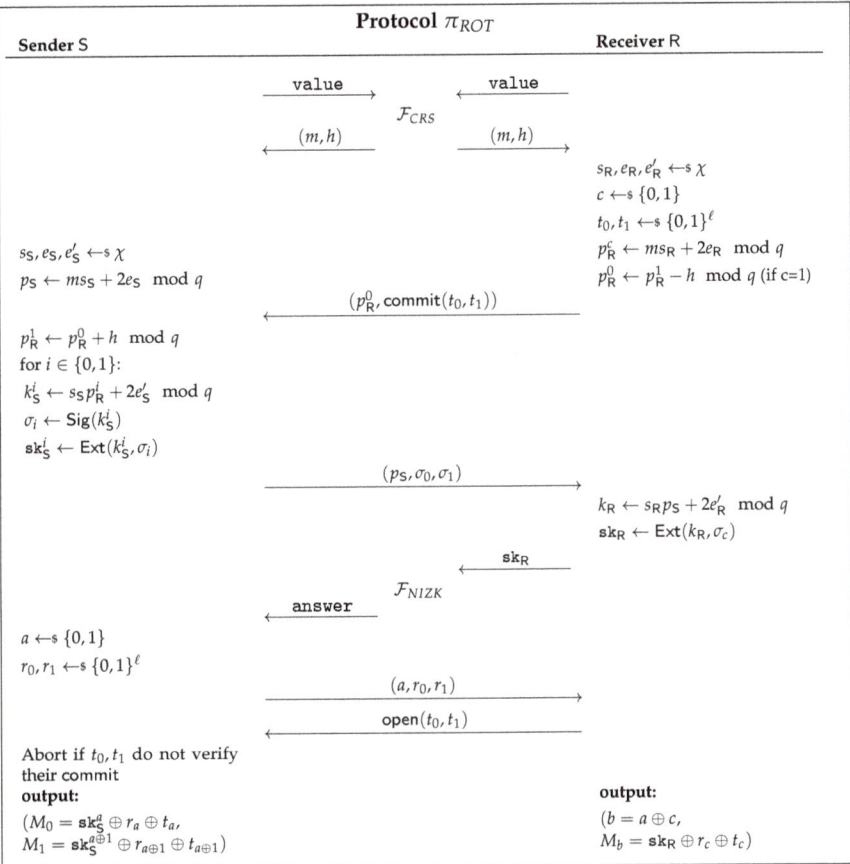

Figure 9. UC ROT protocol in the CRS model based on the RLWE assumption.

The $\mathcal{F}_{NIZK}$ functionality can, for instance, be instantiated using the protocol described in [35]. This protocol is shown to be quantum-composable in the CRS model, based on the LWE assumption.

4. Security

In this section, we establish the quantum-UC security of the proposed protocols in the CRS model. We begin by analyzing the quantum protocol first and proving that $\pi_{OT \to ROT}$ is quantum-UC-secure when instantiated with π_{COM} and $\pi_{QOT}^{\pi_{COM}}$. We then prove the quantum-UC security of the π_{ROT}.

4.1. Quantum-UC Security of the Quantum ROT Protocol

Theorem 2. *Protocol $\pi_{OT \to ROT}$ quantum-UC-emulates $\mathcal{F}_{ROT}$ in the $\langle \mathcal{F}_{OT}, \mathcal{F}_{COM} \rangle$-hybrid model.*

Proof. We start by describing how the simulator $\mathcal{S}$ behaves in each of the possible cases for the execution of the protocol when an adversary $\mathcal{A}$ is present.

Corrupted Sender. In this case, $\mathcal{S}$ simulates the view of the sender, effectively controlling the inputs to $\mathcal{F}_{COM}$ and the input bit to $\mathcal{F}_{OT}$. In order to do so, we start by replacing $\mathcal{F}_{COM}$ by a commitment functionality $\mathcal{F}_{FakeCOM}$, which allows the receiver to cheat. In the commit phase, $\mathcal{F}_{FakeCOM}$ expects a message COMMIT instead of (COMMIT, x); in the open phase, $\mathcal{F}_{FakeCOM}$ expects a message (OPEN, x) instead of OPEN, which is then sent to the sender. We now change the receiver's implementation to match with the new functionality; that is, when committing to message m, the receiver stores that message and later gives it to $\mathcal{F}_{FakeCOM}$ when opening the commitment.

We can now describe how the simulator works. $\mathcal{S}$ starts by receiving (M_0, M_1) from $\mathcal{F}_{ROT}$; afterwards, it sends COMMIT to $\mathcal{F}_{FakeCOM}$, samples $c \leftarrow_s \{0,1\}$, and sends c to $\mathcal{F}_{OT}$. Upon receiving d, the simulator extracts w_0, w_1 from observing the sender's call to $\mathcal{F}_{OT}$ and computes $r_d = M_0 \oplus w_d$ and $r_{d\oplus 1} = M_1 \oplus w_{d\oplus 1}$. Finally, it sends (OPEN,(r_0, r_1)) to $\mathcal{F}_{FakeCOM}$.

Corrupted Receiver. Now, $\mathcal{S}$ simulates the view of the receiver, controlling the input messages to $\mathcal{F}_{OT}$. The simulator starts by receiving (b, M) from $\mathcal{F}_{ROT}$. After receiving the commitment message, $\mathcal{S}$ extracts the strings r_0, r_1 and the bit c from observing the receiver's call to $\mathcal{F}_{COM}$ and $\mathcal{F}_{OT}$, respectively. It then computes $w_c = r_c \oplus M$ and $d = b \oplus c$ and samples $w_{c\oplus 1} \leftarrow_s \{0,1\}^\ell$; afterwards, send (w_0, w_1) to $\mathcal{F}_{OT}$ and d to $\mathcal{A}$. When $\mathcal{F}_{COM}$ replies with open(r_0, r_1), it checks if the values received match the original commitments and aborts if they do not.

Both/None parties corrupted. When both parties are corrupted, $\mathcal{S}$ internally runs $\mathcal{A}$, which generates the messages for both parties.

When the adversary does not corrupt any party, the simulator does not have an input from the ideal functionality $\mathcal{F}_{ROT}$. As such, $\mathcal{S}$ runs the honest receiver and the honest sender, executing the needed algorithms when a dummy party is called in the ideal execution. The simulator forwards the messages of the honestly simulated protocol to $\mathcal{A}$.

To finish the proof, it remains to show that the simulated executions of the protocol are indistinguishable from the real one.

Claim 1. *If the adversary $\mathcal{A}$ corrupts the sender, then the real execution of the protocol $\pi_{OT \to ROT}$ is indistinguishable from the simulated one.*

Proof. The real world execution can be viewed as a game that proceeds as follows:
1. Sample values $r_0, r_1 \leftarrow_s \{0,1\}^\ell$ and commit to values r_0, r_1.
2. Sample bit $c \leftarrow_s \{0,1\}$ and run the OT protocol with the choice bit c.
3. Open the commitment to values r_0, r_1.

The ideal world execution can be viewed as a game that proceeds as follows:
1. Send COMMIT to $\mathcal{F}_{FakeCOM}$.
2. Sample bit $c \leftarrow_s \{0,1\}$ and send c to $\mathcal{F}_{OT}$.
3. Send (OPEN, (r_0, r_1)) to $\mathcal{F}_{FakeCOM}$, where $r_d = M_0 \oplus w_d$ and $r_{d\oplus 1} = M_1 \oplus w_{d\oplus 1}$.

The differences between the two traces are the commitment functionality and how the values r_0, r_1 are generated. However, since the commitments are opened in the same way, replacing $\mathcal{F}_{COM}$ by $\mathcal{F}_{FakeCOM}$ leads to a perfectly indistinguishable network. Regarding r_0, r_1, since M_0, M_1 are uniform random values, which come from $\mathcal{F}_{ROT}$, the values r_0, r_1 are also statistically indistinguishable from uniform random values. Therefore, the two executions are statistically indistinguishable. □

Claim 2. *If the adversary $\mathcal{A}$ corrupts the receiver, then the real execution of the protocol $\pi_{OT \to ROT}$ is indistinguishable from the simulated one.*

Proof. The real world execution can be viewed as a game that proceeds as follows:
1. Sample strings $w_0, w_1 \leftarrow_s \{0,1\}^\ell$ and run the OT protocol with w_0, w_1.
2. Sample bit d and send it to R.
3. Check if the received values verify their commitment.

The ideal world execution can be viewed as a game that proceeds as follows:

1. Sample string $w_{c\oplus 1} \leftarrow^\$ \{0,1\}^\ell$ and compute $w_c = r_c \oplus M$; afterwards, send (w_0, w_1) to $\mathcal{F}_{OT}$.
2. Compute $d = b \oplus c$ and send it to R.
3. Check if the received values verify their commit.

In this case, the difference between both traces is in how w_c and d are generated. Since M and b are uniform random values, which come from $\mathcal{F}_{ROT}$, both the string w_c and the bit d are statistically indistinguishable from a uniform random string and a uniform random bit, respectively. Thus, the above two executions are statistically indistinguishable. □

Finally, it is trivial to conclude that, when both parties are corrupted and when neither parties are corrupted, the simulated executions of the protocol are indistinguishable from the real execution. This concludes the proof. □

We have shown that, with $\pi_{OT \to ROT}$, we can transform π_{QOT} into a ROT. We now need to prove that π_{COM} remains UC-secure when working in a quantum setting.

Theorem 3. *Let G_{pk} be a quantum robust PRNG. π_{COM} then (computationally) quantum UC-emulates $\mathcal{F}_{COM}$ in the CRS model.*

Proof. We start by briefly describing the UC security proof of π_{COM} by Canneti in [33].

The simulation starts with the simulator $\mathcal{S}$ by generating pk_0, pk_1, sampling random $r_0, r_1 \in \{0,1\}^n$, and setting $\sigma = G_{pk_0}(r_0) \oplus G_{pk_1}(r_1)$. With this fake string, $\mathcal{S}$ tells the adversary $\mathcal{A}$ that the sender is committed to $y = G_{pk_0}(r_0)$. By later sending r_0 or r_1, the simulator is able to open the commitment to either $b = 0$ or to $b = 1$, respectively. If it were possible to distinguish the fake string from the real one, it would contradict the pseudo-randomness of the generator.

When working in a quantum setting, the indistinguishability of the fake string reduces to the pseudo-randomness of the generator; that is, the environment can only distinguish between the real world and ideal world executions if it is possible to distinguish the fake string σ from the real one. As such, if the generators are quantum robust, the environment will not be able to distinguish between both strings. Therefore, the arguments used in the classical UC security proof follow for quantum UC security as well. □

Finally, we analyze the security of the proposed composition of protocols. Let π_{QROT} denote $\pi_{OT \to ROT}$ instantiated with π_{COM} and $\pi_{QOT}^{\pi_{COM}}$.

Theorem 4. *Protocol π_{QROT} quantum-UC-emulates $\mathcal{F}_{ROT}$.*

Proof. First, we analyze the UC security of $\pi_{QOT}^{\pi_{COM}}$. Protocol π_{QOT} with ideal commitments is known to be universally composable [28]; as such, since π_{COM} is a composable commitment scheme, we have that $\pi_{QOT}^{\pi_{COM}}$ quantum-UC-emulates $\mathcal{F}_{OT}$.

Finally, as was shown in Theorem 2, $\pi_{OT \to ROT}$ with ideal commitments and an ideal OT is universally composable. Since both π_{COM} and $\pi_{QOT}^{\pi_{COM}}$ are universally composable, the result follows directly. □

A downside of using π_{COM} as the commitment scheme is that we require a call to π_{COM} for each bit of the string we intend to commit, which will affect the protocol's efficiency. However, since a composable commitment is required, this is our best suggestion in the CRS model.

4.2. Quantum-UC Security of the Post-Quantum ROT Protocol

We now analyze the security of π_{ROT}. The simulator will use its ability to program the CRS and extract the NIZK witness in order to obtain the desired UC security.

Theorem 5. *Protocol π_{ROT} (computationally) quantum-UC-emulates $\mathcal{F}_{ROT}$ in the CRS model, given that the HNF-RLWE assumption holds.*

Proof. Once again, we describe the behavior of the simulator $\mathcal{S}$ in each of the possible cases for the execution of the protocol when an adversary $\mathcal{A}$ is present.

Corrupted Sender. The simulator $\mathcal{S}$ simulates the view of the sender, meaning that it controls the communication with R as well as the inputs of $\mathcal{F}_{COM}$ and $\mathcal{F}_{NIZK}$. As in the proof of security for π_{QROT}, we will be replacing $\mathcal{F}_{COM}$ by the functionality $\mathcal{F}_{FakeCOM}$ and changing the receiver's implementation to match $\mathcal{F}_{FakeCOM}$.

$\mathcal{S}$ starts by receiving (M_0, M_1) from $\mathcal{F}_{ROT}$. It then samples $c \leftarrow^s \{0,1\}$ and $t_0, t_1 \leftarrow^s \{0,1\}^\ell$, as an honest receiver would. Next, it computes two RLWE samples, $p_R^0 = ms_R^0 + 2e_R^0 \mod q$ and $p_R^1 = ms_R^0 + 2e_R^0 \mod q$, sets $h = p_R^1 - p_R^0$, and programs $\mathcal{F}_{CRS}$ to return (m, h) when queried. Following that, it sends p_R^0 to $\mathcal{A}$ and sends COMMIT to $\mathcal{F}_{FakeCOM}$.

After receiving $(p_S, \sigma_0, \sigma_1)$, $\mathcal{S}$ computes $\mathsf{sk}_R^i = \mathsf{Ext}(s_R^i p_S + 2{e'_R}^i, \sigma_i)$, for $i \in \{0,1\}$, and sends sk_R^c to $\mathcal{F}_{NIZK}$. Finally, upon receiving a, r_0, r_1, S computes $t_a = M_0 \oplus \mathsf{sk}_S^a \oplus r_a$ and $t_{a \oplus 1} = M_1 \oplus \mathsf{sk}_S^{a \oplus 1} \oplus r_{a \oplus 1}$ and sends (OPEN, (t_0, t_1)) to $\mathcal{F}_{FakeCOM}$.

Corrupted Receiver. In this case, $\mathcal{S}$ simulates the view of the receiver, controlling the communication with S. The simulator starts by receiving (b, M) from $\mathcal{F}_{ROT}$. It computes p_S as an honest sender; after receiving p_R^0 as well as the receipt of the commitment, it computes $\mathsf{sk}_S^i, \sigma_i$ honestly, for $i \in \{0,1\}$, and sends p_S, σ_0, σ_1 to $\mathcal{A}$. After receiving the reply from $\mathcal{F}_{NIZK}$, if the test passed, $\mathcal{S}$ extracts c from observing the call made to $\mathcal{F}_{NIZK}$ and comparing sk_R to sk_S^0 and sk_S^1. Finally, it computes $a = b \oplus c$ and $r_c = M \oplus \mathsf{sk}_S^c \oplus t_c$, samples $r_{c \oplus 1} \leftarrow^s \{0,1\}^\ell$ and sends a, r_0, r_1 to $\mathcal{A}$. At the end, it checks if t_0, t_1 match the initial commitment, aborting if they do not.

Both/None parties corrupted. Here, both cases work as in the previous UC security proof. When both parties are corrupted, the adversary is ran internally by $\mathcal{S}$. When neither of the parties are corrupted, $\mathcal{S}$ runs the honest receiver and sender, sending all the messages between them to $\mathcal{A}$.

Again, we now need to show that the real execution of the protocol is indistinguishable from the simulated ones.

Claim 3. *If the adversary $\mathcal{A}$ corrupts the sender, then the real execution of the protocol π_{ROT} is indistinguishable from the simulated one.*

Proof. The real world execution can be viewed as a game that proceeds as follows:

1. Sample bit $c \leftarrow^s \{0,1\}$ and strings $t_0, t_1 \leftarrow^s \{0,1\}^\ell$.
   Generate RLWE sample p_R and, if $c = 1$, compute $p_R^0 = p_R^1 - h$.
   Send p_R^0 and commit to values t_0, t_1.
2. Compute $\mathsf{sk}_R = \mathsf{Ext}(s_R p_S + 2e'_R, \sigma_c)$ and run the NIZK protocol with sk_R.
3. Open the commitment to values t_0, t_1.

The ideal world execution can be viewed as a game that proceeds as follows:

1. Sample bit $c \leftarrow^s \{0,1\}$.
   Generate RLWE samples p_R^0, p_R^1 and program $\mathcal{F}_{CRS}$ to return $(m, p_R^1 - p_R^0)$.
   Send p_R^0 to $\mathcal{A}$ and send COMMIT to $\mathcal{F}_{FakeCOM}$.
2. Compute $\mathsf{sk}_R^i = \mathsf{Ext}(s_R^i p_S + 2{e'_R}^i, \sigma_i)$, for $i \in \{0,1\}$, and send sk_R^c to $\mathcal{F}_{NIZK}$.
3. Send (OPEN,(t_0, t_1)) to $\mathcal{F}_{FakeCOM}$, where $t_a = M_0 \oplus \mathsf{sk}_S^a \oplus r_a$ and $t_{a \oplus 1} = M_1 \oplus \mathsf{sk}_S^{a \oplus 1} \oplus r_{a \oplus 1}$.

The first difference between both games is in p_R^0 and p_R^1. In the real world game, only p_R^c is an RLWE sample ($p_R^{c \oplus 1}$ is a uniform random sample), while in the ideal world game, both p_R^0 and p_R^1 are RLWE samples. Given that the RLWE assumption holds, both situations are indistinguishable.

Once again, replacing $\mathcal{F}_{COM}$ by $\mathcal{F}_{FakeCOM}$ leads to an indistinguishable network, since the commitments are opened in the same way. Finally, in the real world, t_0, t_1 are uniform random values, while in the ideal world, they are not. However, since M_0, M_1 are uniform random values that come from $\mathcal{F}_{ROT}$, the values in the ideal world are statistically indistinguishable from uniform random values.

Thus, the two executions are indistinguishable, assuming the RLWE assumption holds. □

Claim 4. *If the adversary $\mathcal{A}$ corrupts the receiver, then the real execution of the protocol π_{ROT} is indistinguishable from the simulated one.*

Proof. The real world execution can be viewed as a game that proceeds as follows:
1. Generate RLWE sample p_S.
2. Compute $p_R^1 = p_R^0 + h \mod q$. Compute σ_i and sk_S^i, for $i \in \{0,1\}$. Send $(p_S, \sigma_0, \sigma_1)$.
3. Run the NIZK protocol and check if the test passes; abort if it does not. Sample $a \leftarrow_s \{0,1\}$ and $r_0, r_1 \leftarrow_s \{0,1\}^\ell$. Send (a, r_0, r_1).
4. Check if the received values verify their commitment; abort if they do not.

The ideal world execution can be viewed as a game that proceeds as follows:
1. Generate RLWE sample p_S.
2. Compute $p_R^1 = p_R^0 + h \mod q$. Compute σ_i and sk_S^i, for $i \in \{0,1\}$. Send $(p_S, \sigma_0, \sigma_1)$.
3. Check if the received answer from $\mathcal{F}_{NIZK}$ is 1; abort if it is not. Send (a, r_0, r_1), where $a = b \oplus c$, $r_c = M \oplus \text{sk}_S^c \oplus t_c$, and $r_{1-c} \leftarrow_s \{0,1\}^\ell$.
4. Check if the received values verify their commitment; abort if they do not.

The games differ in how a and r_c are generated; however, since b and M are uniform random values that come from $\mathcal{F}_{ROT}$, both r_c and a are statistically indistinguishable from a uniform random string and a uniform random bit, respectively. Hence, the real world execution and the ideal world execution are indistinguishable, assuming that the RLWE assumption holds. □

It remains to be seen whether the simulated executions where both parties are corrupted and when no party is corrupted are also indistinguishable. As in the previous proof, both are trivial, which concludes the proof. □

5. Conclusions

In view of the usefulness of MPC and the steady evolution of both quantum technology and post-quantum cryptography techniques, as well as recognizing the potential threat quantum computers can present in the landscape of information security, we have proposed two potential solutions for quantum secure implementations of ROT.

Both of these protocols have in common that they use a commitment scheme based on quantum-secure pseudo-random generators, which is universally composable in the CRS model. The CRS assumption has the advantage of being weaker and better understood than the quantum random oracle, and it is independent of technological limitations as opposed to the noisy storage assumptions, which are two of the most common models in which the security of OT protocols is studied.

The first construction is based on a quantum OT protocol composed with a quantum secure bit commitment, which is then transformed into a ROT protocol. The usage of a PRNG, which is secure against any poly-time quantum distinguisher, is the key to the commitment scheme's quantum composability. The second construction is based on a highly efficient UC-secure ROT protocol from the RLWE assumption, initially proposed in the ROM. Our protocol differs in that we remove the random oracle's requirement, replacing it by a commitment scheme and non-interactive zero knowledge protocol, which allows us to make a quantum-secure UC protocol, but in the CRS model instead.

Potential future work directions include the following:

- Further optimization of the commitment scheme to reduce the number of CRS calls and PRNG computations per committed bit in the context of a string commitment scheme.
- The implementation of both protocols and a comparison of their performance, taking available (quantum) technologies into account. This poses a challenge, as the limitations of quantum technologies are much less known than traditional computational power and communication.

Author Contributions: Conceptualization, P.M.; investigation and formal analysis B.C., P.B., M.G., M.L. and P.M.; writing—original draft preparation, B.C.; writing—review and editing, M.G.; validation, M.G. and M.L.; supervision, P.M. All authors have read and agreed to the published version of the manuscript.

Funding: This research was funded by Fundação para a Ciência e a Tecnologia (FCT) with reference UIDB/50008/2020 (Instituto de Telecomunicações via actions QuRUNNER, QUESTS) and Projects QuantumMining POCI-01-0145-FEDER-031826, PREDICT PTDC/CCI-CIF/29877/2017, and QuantumPrime PTDC/EEI-TEL/8017/2020. BC thanks Capgemini Engineering. PB gratefully acknowledges the support from DP-PMI and FCT (Portugal) through the grant PD/BD/135181/2017. MG gratefully acknowledges the support from DP-PMI and FCT (Portugal) through the grant PD/BD/135182/2017.

Data Availability Statement: Not applicable.

Acknowledgments: The authors thank Preeti Yadav for editorial improvements.

Conflicts of Interest: The authors declare no conflict of interest.

References

1. Rabin, M.O. How To Exchange Secrets with Oblivious Transfer. *IACR Cryptol. ePrint Arch.* **2005**, *2005*, 187. Originally published as: Technical Report TR-81, Aiken Computation Lab, Harvard University, Cambridge, MA, USA, 1981.
2. Ishai, Y.; Prabhakaran, M.; Sahai, A. Founding Cryptography on Oblivious Transfer—Efficiently. In Proceedings of the Advances in Cryptology—CRYPTO 2008, Santa Barbara, CA, USA, 17–21 August 2008; Wagner, D., Ed.; Springer: Berlin/Heidelberg, Germany, 2008; pp. 572–591.
3. Kilian, J. Founding Cryptography on Oblivious Transfer. In Proceedings of the Twentieth Annual ACM Symposium on Theory of Computing, Chicago, IL, USA, 4–6 May 1988; Association for Computing Machinery: New York, NY, USA, 1988; pp. 20–31. [CrossRef]
4. Goldreich, O.; Micali, S.; Wigderson, A. How to play any mental game, or a completeness theorem for protocols with honest majority. In *Providing Sound Foundations for Cryptography: On the Work of Shafi Goldwasser and Silvio Micali*; Association for Computing Machinery: New York, NY, USA, 2019; pp. 307–328.
5. Blum, M. Coin flipping by telephone a protocol for solving impossible problems. *ACM SIGACT News* **1983**, *15*, 23–27. [CrossRef]
6. Cramer, R.; Damgård, I.; Maurer, U. General secure multi-party computation from any linear secret-sharing scheme. In Proceedings of the Advances in Cryptology—EUROCRYPT 2000, Bruges, Belgium, 14–18 May 2000; Springer: Berlin/Heidelberg, Germany, 2000; pp. 316–334.
7. Lindell, Y.; Pinkas, B. Secure two-party computation via cut-and-choose oblivious transfer. *J. Cryptol.* **2012**, *25*, 680–722. [CrossRef]
8. Even, S.; Goldreich, O.; Lempel, A. A randomized protocol for signing contracts. *Commun. ACM* **1985**, *28*, 637–647. [CrossRef]
9. Crépeau, C. Equivalence between two flavours of oblivious transfers. In Proceedings of the Advances in Cryptology—CRYPTO '87, Santa Barbara, CA, USA, 16–20 August 1987; Springer: Berlin/Heidelberg, Germany, 1987; pp. 350–354.
10. Yao, A.C. Protocols for secure computations. In Proceedings of the 23rd Annual Symposium on Foundations of Computer Science (SFCS 1982), Chicago, IL, USA, 3–5 November 1982; IEEE Computer Society: Washington, DC, USA, 1982; pp. 160–164. [CrossRef]
11. Goldreich, O.; Micali, S.; Wigderson, A. How to Play ANY Mental Game. In Proceedings of the Nineteenth Annual ACM Symposium on Theory of Computing, New York, NY, USA, 25–27 May 1987; Association for Computing Machinery: New York, NY, USA, 1987; pp. 218–229. [CrossRef]
12. Ishai, Y.; Kilian, J.; Nissim, K.; Petrank, E. Extending Oblivious Transfers Efficiently. In Proceedings of the Advances in Cryptology—CRYPTO 2003, Santa Barbara, CA, USA, 17–21 August 2003; Boneh, D., Ed.; Springer: Berlin/Heidelberg, Germany, 2003; pp. 145–161.
13. Orrù, M.; Orsini, E.; Scholl, P. Actively Secure 1-out-of-N OT Extension with Application to Private Set Intersection. In Proceedings of the Topics in Cryptology—CT-RSA 2017, San Francisco, CA, USA, 14–17 February 2017; Handschuh, H., Ed.; Springer International Publishing: Cham, Switzerland, 2017; pp. 381–396.

14. Pinkas, B.; Rosulek, M.; Trieu, N.; Yanai, A. Spot-light: Lightweight private set intersection from sparse ot extension. In Proceedings of the Advances in Cryptology—CRYPTO 2019, Santa Barbara, CA, USA, 18–22 August 2019; Springer International Publishing: Cham, Switzerland, 2019; pp. 401–431.
15. Shor, P.W. Algorithms for Quantum Computation: Discrete Logarithms and Factoring. In Proceedings of the 35th Annual Symposium on Foundations of Computer Science, Santa Fe, NM, USA, 20–22 November 1994; IEEE Computer Society: Washington, DC, USA, 1994; pp. 124–134. [CrossRef]
16. Lyubashevsky, V.; Peikert, C.; Regev, O. On Ideal Lattices and Learning with Errors over Rings. In Proceedings of the Advances in Cryptology—EUROCRYPT 2010, French Riviera, France, 30 May–3 June 2010; Gilbert, H., Ed.; Springer: Berlin/Heidelberg, Germany, 2010; pp. 1–23.
17. Regev, O. On Lattices, Learning with Errors, Random Linear Codes, and Cryptography. In Proceedings of the Thirty-Seventh Annual ACM Symposium on Theory of Computing, Baltimore, MD, USA, 22–24 May 2005; Association for Computing Machinery: New York, NY, USA, 2005; pp. 84–93. [CrossRef]
18. Broadbent, A.; Schaffner, C. Quantum cryptography beyond quantum key distribution. *Des. Codes Cryptogr.* **2015**, *78*, 351–382. [CrossRef] [PubMed]
19. Renner, R.; Gisin, N.; Kraus, B. Information-theoretic security proof for quantum-key-distribution protocols. *Phys. Rev. A* **2005**, *72*, 012332. [CrossRef]
20. Shenoy-Hejamadi, A.; Pathak, A.; Radhakrishna, S. Quantum Cryptography: Key Distribution and Beyond. *Quanta* **2017**, *6*, 1. [CrossRef]
21. Lo, H.K.; Chau, H.F. Is Quantum Bit Commitment Really Possible? *Phys. Rev. Lett.* **1997**, *78*, 3410–3413. [CrossRef]
22. Mayers, D. Unconditionally Secure Quantum Bit Commitment is Impossible. *Phys. Rev. Lett.* **1997**, *78*, 3414–3417. [CrossRef]
23. Erven, C.; Ng, N.; Gigov, N.; Laflamme, R.; Wehner, S.; Weihs, G. An experimental implementation of oblivious transfer in the noisy storage model. *Nat. Commun.* **2014**, *5*. [CrossRef] [PubMed]
24. Furrer, F.; Gehring, T.; Schaffner, C.; Pacher, C.; Schnabel, R.; Wehner, S. Continuous-Variable Protocol for Oblivious Transfer in the Noisy-Storage Model. *Nat. Commun.* **2018**, *9*. [CrossRef] [PubMed]
25. Ng, N.H.Y.; Joshi, S.K.; Chen Ming, C.; Kurtsiefer, C.; Wehner, S. Experimental implementation of bit commitment in the noisy-storage model. *Nat. Commun.* **2012**, *3*. [CrossRef] [PubMed]
26. Qiang, X.; Zhou, X.; Aungskunsiri, K.; Cable, H.; O'Brien, J.L. Quantum processing by remote quantum control. *Quantum Sci. Technol.* **2017**, *2*, 045002. [CrossRef]
27. Long, G.L.; Liu, X.S. Theoretically efficient high-capacity quantum-key-distribution scheme. *Phys. Rev. A* **2002**, *65*, 032302. [CrossRef]
28. Unruh, D. Universally Composable Quantum Multi-party Computation. In Proceedings of the Advances in Cryptology—EUROCRYPT 2010, French Riviera, France, 30 May–3 June 2010; Gilbert, H., Ed.; Springer: Berlin/Heidelberg, Germany, 2010; pp. 486–505.
29. Branco, P.; Ding, J.; Goulão, M.; Mateus, P. A Framework for Universally Composable Oblivious Transfer from One-Round Key-Exchange. In Proceedings of the IMA International Conference on Cryptography and Coding, Oxford, UK, 15–17 December 2019; Albrecht, M., Ed.; Springer International Publishing: Cham, Switzerland, 2019; pp. 78–101.
30. Branco, P.; Fiolhais, L.; Goulão, M.; Martins, P.; Mateus, P.; Sousa, L. ROTed: Random Oblivious Transfer for Embedded Devices. IACR Transactions of Cryptographic Hardware and Embedded Systems. Available online: https://eprint.iacr.org/2021/935 (accessed on 7 June 2021).
31. Applebaum, B.; Cash, D.; Peikert, C.; Sahai, A. Fast Cryptographic Primitives and Circular-Secure Encryption Based on Hard Learning Problems. In Proceedings of the Advances in Cryptology—CRYPTO 2009, Santa Barbara, CA, USA, 16–20 August 2009; Halevi, S., Ed.; Springer: Berlin/Heidelberg, Germany, 2009; pp. 595–618.
32. Canetti, R. Universally Composable Security: A New Paradigm for Cryptographic Protocols. In Proceedings of the 42nd IEEE Symposium on Foundations of Computer Science, Las Vegas, NV, USA, 14–17 October 2001; IEEE Computer Society: Washington, DC, USA, 2001; p. 136.
33. Canetti, R.; Fischlin, M. Universally Composable Commitments. In Proceedings of the Advances in Cryptology—CRYPTO 2001, Santa Barbara, CA, USA, 19–23 August 2001; Kilian, J., Ed.; Springer: Berlin/Heidelberg, Germany, 2001; pp. 19–40.
34. Ding, J.; Xie, X.; Lin, X. A Simple Provably Secure Key Exchange Scheme Based on the Learning with Errors Problem. Cryptology ePrint Archive, Report 2012/688. 2012. Available online: https://eprint.iacr.org/2012/688 (accessed on 7 June 2021).
35. Canetti, R.; Sarkar, P.; Wang, X. Triply Adaptive UC NIZK. Cryptology ePrint Archive, Report 2020/1212. 2020. Available online: https://eprint.iacr.org/2020/1212 (accessed on 7 June 2021).

MDPI
St. Alban-Anlage 66
4052 Basel
Switzerland
Tel. +41 61 683 77 34
Fax +41 61 302 89 18
www.mdpi.com

Entropy Editorial Office
E-mail: entropy@mdpi.com
www.mdpi.com/journal/entropy

www.ingramcontent.com/pod-product-compliance
Lightning Source LLC
LaVergne TN
LVHW070738100526
838202LV00013B/1264